MW01039394

Imaginative Conservatism

Imaginative Conservatism

The Letters of Russell Kirk

Edited by James E. Person Jr.

UNIVERSITY PRESS OF KENTUCKY

The University Press of Kentucky

Scholarly publisher for the Commonwealth,
serving Bellarmine University, Berea College, Centre
College of Kentucky, Eastern Kentucky University,
The Filson Historical Society, Georgetown College,
Kentucky Historical Society, Kentucky State University,
Morehead State University, Murray State University,
Northern Kentucky University, Transylvania University,
University of Kentucky, University of Louisville,
and Western Kentucky University.
All rights reserved.

Editorial and Sales Offices: The University Press of Kentucky
663 South Limestone Street, Lexington, Kentucky 40508-4008
www.kentuckypress.com

Frontispiece courtesy of Annette Kirk.

Cataloging-in-Publication data is available from the Library of Congress

ISBN 978-0-8131-7546-1 (hardcover : alk. paper)
ISBN 978-0-8131-7548-5 (pdf)
ISBN 978-0-8131-7547-8 (epub)

This book is printed on acid-free paper meeting
the requirements of the American National Standard
for Permanence in Paper for Printed Library Materials.

Manufactured in the United States of America.

Member of the Association of University Presses

*Dedicated to the memory of
Russell Amos Kirk (1918–1994),
whose words endure.*

Contents

Introduction

"I receive a good many long and interesting letters—usually from people quite unknown to me—in my enormous volume of mail; but it is too true that the art of letter-writing is sadly decayed," wrote Russell Kirk in 1971 to his friend David Lindsay, Earl of Crawford. Kirk ventured, "Telephone and television have much to do with this degeneration. Telephones are tremendous wasters of time: people call me and ramble on in desultory fashion, and I can't make head or tail of what they desire. If only they were capable of writing ordinary notes, I might be able to handle their business with dispatch."

A man noted for the clarity and wisdom of his prose, Russell Kirk (1918–1994) is today renowned worldwide as one of the founders of modern cultural conservatism. He was a historian of ideas, a biographer, a novelist and writer of ghostly tales in the tradition of M. R. James, a literary scholar, a book reviewer, the editor of two serious periodicals, a newspaper and magazine columnist, a social critic, and a memoirist who is best known today for two books, *The Conservative Mind* (1953) and *The Roots of American Order* (1974). He is less known for his body of personal letters, which is as voluminous as it is varied in subject matter and marked by the seriousness and care he invested in everything he wrote. Anybody who received a letter from Russell Kirk could see he was a writer of far more than mere "ordinary notes."

During his life, he corresponded with thousands of his readers, adversaries, friends, and curious readers from the worlds of literature, history, politics, academia, and the arts. The list of Kirk's correspondents included T. S. Eliot, William F. Buckley Jr., Ray Bradbury,

Cleanth Brooks, Charlton Heston, Nikolai Tolstoy, Wendell Berry, Richard Nixon, Eric Voegelin, Jacques Barzun, Henry Kissinger, Ronald Reagan, Elliot Richardson, and Arthur Schlesinger Jr., among hundreds of others.

It is entirely due to the thoughtfulness of Kirk's relatives and a few other early correspondents that we have the relatively few pre-1966 letters available in the Kirk Archives today. Until the mid-1960s, Kirk failed to make carbons or photocopies of his outgoing letters; and this unfortunate practice led to disappointing gaps in the correspondence he exchanged with Wyndham Lewis, Albert Jay Nock, Willmoore Kendall, and Roy Campbell, among others. But his wife, Annette, intuited that someday her husband's letters would be of interest to the wider world; and through her efforts it was arranged that all his correspondence was to be photocopied. Thus, there exists a nearly complete archive of Kirk's outgoing letters from roughly 1966 through 1994.

The letters included in this volume span from 1940, when Kirk was a graduate student at Duke University, until shortly before his death. They trace his development from a shy, precocious young man unsure of his direction in life into a gentleman firm in his beliefs and generous with his time and resources when called on to provide for refugees, the homeless, and the outcasts of life—all while maintaining an active schedule of writing and speaking engagements throughout the world. The letters written later in life also reveal a thoughtful man critical of America's drift toward social atomism, materialism, and utilitarianism and away from true community and adherence to wise tradition.

"The Art of Letter-Writing Is Sadly Decayed"

Kirk's lament to Lindsay—the words of a busy middle-aged man of letters at the height of his powers—shines ambient light on his upbringing during the 1920s and '30s in the slow-moving small town of Plymouth, Michigan. For that period, before the era of junk mail, e-mail, and text messaging, was a time when "the art of letter writing" was an important aspect of American society, taught in the nation's schools and homes and practiced throughout one's life.

Introduction

None of Kirk's letters from his boyhood and teens have survived. But during his undergraduate years at Michigan State College (today Michigan State University) he met a handful of men whose names figure recurrently in his earliest extant letters to one of their number, William C. "Bill" McCann, who seems to have saved every letter he received from Kirk, beginning in 1940. Several years older than Kirk, McCann was an insurance underwriter, sometime book reviewer, and founding member (along with Kirk) of the George Ade Society, a dining and literary discussion club in East Lansing. Although McCann leaned left, a liberal/progressive in nature, and young Kirk—having never embraced a religious faith—was a Stoical libertarian in his cultural demeanor, the two men were temperamentally alike. As the years passed, they grew apart in terms of philosophical outlook, but their friendship remained strong throughout their lives, with McCann publishing a glowing review of his friend's study *Eliot and His Age* in the *Progressive* in 1972.

Reading the extant letters written during his twenties to McCann and to his close relatives, it is apparent that the young Russell Kirk is a man of superior learning—and he knows it. There is about these letters a faint but distinct sense of a young man who is somewhat full of himself and a bit disdainful of the less-well-read souls with whom he is forced to associate in college and, later, in the army, during World War II. Throughout his life, Kirk was afflicted by a painful shyness, and he compensated for this in his early correspondence by "talking to win," expressing opinions with bold confidence while speaking dismissively of opinions and viewpoints other than his own, which is to say that Kirk's early letters are typical of a young single man who "doesn't know what he doesn't know" and has no idea what life has in store.

Arguably, it took the hard blow he suffered at the death of his gentle mother in early 1943 to begin Kirk's journey toward the humility and generosity of spirit that characterized his later life. He was greatly aided in this journey by the examples of wise, goodhearted men and women in England and Scotland who befriended him and sometimes

3

took him in as a houseguest for extended periods during his years of doctoral study at St. Andrews University, notably author George Scott-Moncrieff; Ralph and Margret Christie, proprietors of Durie House; Hew and Mary Lorimer, owners of Kellie Castle; David and Mary Lindsay, Earl and Countess of Crawford and Balcarres; Canon Basil A. Smith, treasurer of York Minster; the great T. S. Eliot; and others. By their example, he developed far toward becoming a man of high character, confident in his beliefs; and his letters to them bespeak his gratitude to them.

In the Utah Desert

"Leisure is necessary for good letter-writing, of course, and I wrote my best and longest letters when I was a soldier in desert or jungle," wrote Kirk to Lindsay in 1971. In truth, he did write lengthy, descriptive letters to Bill McCann and others during the years 1942 through 1946, when he served in a U.S. Army chemical-warfare unit stationed at Camp Dugway, in a bleak, windblown corner of Utah. (Dugway is to-day part of the mysterious "Area 51," about which there has been much speculation.) There, with relatively little to do during the day, Kirk read books, edited the camp newsletter, and typed daily three-to-five-page single-spaced letters to his friends and family describing the landscape and everyday foibles of life in an army camp.

Kirk continued writing letters daily after his unit was transferred for a time to a swampy camp in Florida, where chemical-warfare tests were conducted on goats and even on men. These and other wartime letters sometimes reflect his uneasiness at being associated with a form of warfare he considered barbaric.

It is worth mentioning that during his years in the armed forces in Utah and Florida he entered into correspondence with libertarian legend Albert Jay Nock (after reading Nock's *Memoirs of a Superfluous Man*) and acerbic *New York Herald-Tribune* book critic Isabel M. Paterson. Unfortunately, all Kirk's letters to Nock and Paterson have been lost, though he tantalizingly mentions their correspondence in his letters to others.

Introduction

Taking Flight

After World War II ended and Kirk left the armed services, he returned to his hometown of Plymouth to find much had changed, through the death of loved ones and the scattering of his remaining family and friends. With no real reason to remain, Kirk shifted his home to the upstate village of his great-grandparents in Mecosta, Michigan: a former lumbering town where lived a small number of elderly relatives at their ancestral home, called Piety Hill. Mecosta was Kirk's home for the rest of his life; from here he ventured out to teach at Michigan State, to travel to Scotland for his doctoral studies, and, in time, to visit the wide world.

As noted, it was in Britain that Kirk met the gracious men and women who steadied and shaped him, who opened his eyes to the depth and breadth of tradition, community, faith, and what Eliot called "the permanent things." And it was while writing his magisterial doctoral thesis that he came to understand his own writing as something of a calling, an effort to shore up the fragments of Western culture against the coming chaos of rootlessness, lostness, hopelessness, and social atomism of the modern age. In a letter to conservative publisher Henry Regnery in 1952, Kirk wrote of his thick doctoral dissertation as part of this calling:

> It is my contribution to our endeavor to conserve the spiritual and intellectual and political tradition of our civilization; and if we are to rescue the modern mind, we must do it very soon. What Matthew Arnold called "an epoch of concentration" is impending, in any case. If we are to make that approaching era a time of enlightened conservatism, rather than an era of stagnant repression, we need to move with decision. The struggle will be decided in the minds of the rising generation—and within that generation, substantially by the minority who have the gift of reason. I do not think we need much fear the decaying "liberalism" of

5

the retiring generation; as Disraeli said, "Prevailing opinions generally are the opinions of the generation that is passing." But we need to state some certitudes for the benefit of the groping new masters of society.

Kirk added, "More than anyone else in America, Mr. Regnery, you have been doing just this in the books you publish." Regnery was honored to publish Kirk's dissertation under the title *The Conservative Mind,* which became a modern classic in the history of ideas.

Thus began a forty-year friendship that endured despite periodic arguments and fallings-out. Regnery published several of Kirk's earliest works and worked from his offices in Chicago to launch a conservative quarterly review he and Kirk had long envisioned, *Modern Age,* with Kirk editing the journal from his home in Mecosta. Their friendship survived even the icy relations that developed between the two men when Kirk resigned his editorship of *Modern Age* after a mere two years of operation, for reasons that appear in these pages; as editor of the periodical, Kirk was increasingly annoyed at being treated in a high-handed manner by editorial associate David Collier, who had Regnery's ear and about whom Kirk had little kind to say. The decisive offense occurred when Collier pulled a Kirk-approved article written by Hilaire du Berrier at the typesetting stage, shortly before an issue was due to be sent to the printer, and replaced it with an article of his own liking. This, Kirk could not abide. He left *Modern Age,* and for a time his correspondence with Regnery was little more than polite. But over time, relations thawed and the two remained friends. During the 1980s, Kirk resumed contributing essays and reviews to *Modern Age.*

Kirk's correspondence with Regnery and others demonstrates a mind that could compartmentalize fully, separating business disagreements from personal friendship. In letter after letter, Kirk speaks with pointed disagreement on one matter or another but concludes by inviting his correspondent to come spend the weekend at his home for conversation and canoeing in the nearby Little Muskegon River.

Conservatism in Theory and Practice

From the 1950s until his death, Kirk was associated in the public mind with the so-called conservative movement, which was no movement at all but rather (as Kirk preferred to call it) "the conservative impulse." Members of this loose amalgam of anti-Communists, libertarians, traditionalists, neoconservatives, members of the religious right, neo-Confederates, and others tended to quarrel among themselves and often had little in common save a concern that the progressive Leviathan state should be slowed or stopped. What Kirk says in his letters about his fellow "conservatives" is interesting and not always favorable. In 1954, he confided to automotive executive B. E. Hutchinson, "Mr. Frank Chodorov is a crotchety old anarchist, quite impractical, and can influence no one but a small coterie, *entre nous.*" And economist Friedrich A. Hayek, wrote Kirk to William F. Buckley Jr. in 1961, "is a vain and impractical person, rather doctrinaire, who thinks that he is the law and all the prophets, and that nothing is needed for the salvation of humanity but the obedient reading of Hayek's works." Kirk had hard words for certain of his adversaries, as well. Writing to Folke Leander in 1978, he declared logical positivist A. J. Ayer to be "a shallow, vain man, much like Bertrand Russell—and, unlike Russell, a total bore!"

But Kirk was also generous with his praise of others, telling fellow Michiganian Gloria Whelan, "You are undoubtedly the best writer of short stories ever to inhabit Michigan!"—high praise indeed, considering Whelan lives less than one hour from Petoskey and Horton Bay, towns Ernest Hemingway had frequented during the summers of his youth. Writing to Thomas Chaimowicz in 1972, he described Henry Kissinger as " a disciple of Metternich primarily, a well-read and clever man, sound on all counts, so far as I can tell; personally ambitious, but that ambition has been gratified; he has more influence upon Richard Nixon than do all others combined." And in 1975, in a letter to Swiss economist Albert Hunold, he described Irving Kristol as "a force for good"—which may surprise readers who are aware of the dim view Kirk held toward neoconservatives in general.

Kirk's own conservatism was not primarily political but moral and imaginative, focusing always on the relationship of the human soul in community with others and with the transcendent. All-or-nothing conservatives, he explained to Richard Nixon, "tend to forget, from time to time, that conservatism is not a strange set of immutable rules of policy, fixed as the laws of Lycurgus, but instead a way of looking at man and society: a cast of mind and character, governed indeed by certain sound general principles, but capable of prudential application in different ways in varying circumstances." For as he had stated in *The Conservative Mind,* the modern conservative should be "concerned, first of all, for the regeneration of the spirit and character—with the perennial problem of the inner order of the soul, the restoration of the ethical understanding, and the religious sanction upon which any life worth living is founded."

There is something vulnerable and approachable about this highly learned man expressing his appreciation of simple things during his outreach to others through his writings and lectures, and especially through his letters. In 1982, he confided to one correspondent:

By the way, I too have diabetes; and heart trouble also.
All I do about either is to reform my diet somewhat.
I am supposed to have had a coronary, as you did, but
I walked through it without knowing anything very serious was amiss. Apropos of finance, I never have owned a
share of stock or a bond; have no regular life insurance;
have no savings account in banks; never speculate (lacking
the money, even had I the will); have no regular income
from any source—that is, no salary or wage; and am content to lay up treasure in Heaven. Existence at Piety Hill is
hand to mouth, month upon month, but debt certainly is
a stimulant to literary production. My exertions are further stimulated by the presence at my long board of various
Ethiopians, Vietnamese, Poles, impecunious students, and

Lord knows who all, all of them desirous of being dined
and wined. In short, I live very much the sort of life that
Walter Scott did at Abbotsford. Both Annette and
I spend a large part of our times in unremunerated
charitable activities.

The Outer Order and the Inner Order

As he aged and his health began to decline during the 1980s and '90s,
Kirk maintained a prudent, levelheaded view of America's cultural and
political life. He was especially concerned by the slow decay of the nation's civil social order. To true crime author Robert A. Waters, he
wrote, "The question remains as to whether conservatively-inclined
people possess imagination and resolution sufficient to contend tolerably well with our present discontents and difficulties." This question
hangs in the air still.

In terms of accomplishment, Kirk came a long way from his upbringing beside the railroad tracks in Plymouth. In 1982, he wrote to
Italian businessman Mario Marcolla,

> But how brief our lives are, and how short all memories! In
> our childhood, we assume that we will live almost forever,
> and that civilizations are eternal; yet even the existence of
> great cultures is brief enough, for they commenced to decay
> at the hour of their splendor. "Dark, dark, dark: they all go
> into the dark."
>
> Yet be of good cheer! Annette and the four daughters
> join me in cordial best wishes to you and yours.

It was typical of Russell Kirk to end on a note of encouragement. The
reader of these letters may find within them much that is striking,
beautifully stated, thought-provoking, humorous, and encouraging in
this hour of "our present discontents and difficulties."

A Note on the Editing of Kirk's Letters

Almost all the letters that appear in this volume are courtesy of Annette Kirk. Of these, most were in holograph form, from which I made photocopies. Russell Kirk was a fast, expert typist, and he typed most of his letters. (He went so far as to carry a small portable typewriter with him on his travels throughout the United States and abroad.) I have silently corrected the few typos I encountered. On the rare occasions when Kirk's typewriter needed repair, he handwrote his letters; several missives to T. S. Eliot fall into this camp. While his handwriting was somewhat difficult to decipher, it could (with patience) be transcribed quite accurately. In a few cases in which Kirk's handwriting and/or meaning were unclear, I have indicated this as such within square brackets.

Beyond this, it is worth noting that because Kirk was a prolific writer of letters both personal and professional, he tended to repeat personal anecdotes and bits of family news to many correspondents during the course of weeks and months. (News of the Ash Wednesday Fire of 1975, when Kirk's family home was completely destroyed, is one example of a recurrent item that appeared in many letters during 1975.) To avoid repetition, I have omitted such sections from certain letters and indicated their omission with ellipses.

James E. Person Jr.
May 19, 2017

The 1940s

. . . time for reading, time for writing, time for wandering, with few distractions and no gnawing need for money.
from a letter to William C. McCann, October 18, 1948

Letter to William C. McCann

Kirk met William C. "Bill" McCann in East Lansing, Michigan, in the mid-1930s, during his undergraduate years at Michigan State College. Mc-Cann was ten years older than Kirk, married with a daughter, and working as an insurance actuary after majoring in journalism at Michigan State College. Bill and Isabelle McCann took the shy, bookish Kirk under their wings, resulting in a friendship that lasted nearly sixty years. Of the early years of their friendship, Kirk later wrote, "McCann's library . . . overflowed his house; and he was ready to talk at length about everything, but especially matters literary. Kirk spent many, many evenings with the McCanns, who were patient with him."

October 25, 1940
Box 4992
Duke Station
Durham
North Carolina

Dear Bill, Isabel [*sic*], and Jane,

Happy to get your letter. I'd asked several people in letters to them what your address is, but no one told me. My regards to Jane. Warren [Fleischauer] wrote me that there was a new McCann. Is she able yet to recite Demosthenes on the Crown?

Don't bother to send my books to me. I'll be around to see you Christmas vacation, if you're home then, and I'll get them at that time. Sorry I didn't get to see you during the summer, but I got to East Lansing only once, and then could find not one soul I knew, didn't know if you had moved, and there was no one home at your old apartment, anyway. . . .

The library here is splendid. Duke has some six hundred thousand volumes, and can get any book from North Carolina's library, seven miles away, on a few hours' notice; altogether, about 1,100,000 volumes. Six hundred thousand manuscripts at Duke also—papers of Calhoun, Robert E. Lee, Beauregard, etc., etc. The one book I need most, though, isn't here—*Proceedings of the Virginia Constitutional Convention of 1829–1830*. It contains Randolph's most important speeches in the field of constitutionalism, as well as the speeches of Marshall, Monroe, Madison, Barbour, Tazewell, and others. I'll have to buy a copy or go to Richmond to find one.

As it appears now, I'll be writing my thesis about "John Randolph of Roanoke and Southern Political Thought"—an analysis of his philosophy and its later influence, particularly on Calhoun. Immense amount of work to do, but am well advanced. You want to read Bouldin's *Home Reminiscences of John Randolph of Roanoke*, if you can find it. I've mentioned it already to John.[1] It's sometimes unreliable, but it's difficult to lay it down once you've begun reading it. The fear that Randolph inspired in his contemporaries was something amazing.

Typical minor anecdote: the founders of Randolph-Macon College asked Randolph for permission to name their institution after him; they told him it was designed to educate young Methodists. "Yes, sir," said Mr. Randolph, "you may use my name; for once they are educated, they will cease to be Methodists."

I hope to write a book of biographical sketches of the Old Republicans before too long; short biographies of Randolph, Macon, Tazewell, Spencer Roane, Nicholson, Beverly Tucker, R. G. Garnett, and the rest. Most never have had regular biographies.

Am having an easy enough time here; am assisting a professor who teaches freshman European history and advanced Russian history. He says he loves to correct freshman papers and wouldn't think of letting anyone else do it, and that he wouldn't think of having me do any work for him in Russian history, as he knows I'll need my time for my own field; therefore, I am paid without work. Am taking a very good course in Southern literature and culture from Professor Hubbell.[2] . . .

I went over to Hillsboro, ten miles west of here, last week. The town, of about 500 or 600 people, was the capital of North Carolina during the Revolution; here the Regulators were hanged after their defeat at the Alamance in 1771; here Tories captured Governor Burke and carried him off to Charleston in 1781; here Boone started his expedition for Kentucky. The town looks just as it did then, except for the main street, in part; the old houses, apparently unrepaired but generally in good condition, are still occupied; queer windows and double-slating roofs. The courthouse is only 130 years old, built on the site of the old State House. The courthouse clock was hidden in the river during Cornwallis' raid on this area. It's a typical sprawling, scattered old North Carolina town. There's a gigantic, ruinous inn here dating back to colonial times, still in use.[3]

Just outside the limits of Durham, to the west, is the site of Johnston's surrender to Sherman, marked by a small monument. The chimney of the house in which the surrender was negotiated still stands.

I find very few Confederates here. All these Southerners have been reading Boston and New York and Chicago history texts these many years, and think Lincoln was the great American political philosopher. The Willkie cause is strong here at Duke, however, I am happy to say. Remember to get out all your henchmen to vote next week—and not for the Country Squire. Willkie made a spirited defense of states' rights yesterday, I see. Glad to be able to cast my first vote for him. I think we'll win.[4] . . .

Write me as soon as you can; my chief delight here in splendid isolation is to open a full mailbox. See you Christmas.

Yours,

Russell

Letter to Marjorie Kirk

Kirk's gentle, kindly mother, Marjorie Rachel Kirk (1895–1943), continued to reside in Plymouth, Michigan, with her husband and mother during her son's college years at Michigan State College and, later, at Duke University. During the early 1940s, she began to experience painful physical ailments that were diagnosed as symptoms of intestinal cancer. She underwent several major surgeries, but to no effect, and she died of the disease in early 1943. For his part, stoical "Junior," as she addressed him, did not know how to respond to his mother's declining health, and his letters to her have about them an occasional awkward tone of denial.

Monday, February 3, 1941
Box 4992
Duke Station
Durham
North Carolina

Dear Mama,

Perhaps when you receive this you will have had your final operation and will no longer have to worry about that. If you recover from its effects as rapidly as you did from those of the first one, you'll be feeling fine when I come home in March. Are you in the same room in the hospital as you were before? You will have to tell me all about your new room-mates. When will you be going home again? Be sure not to move until you feel well enough. I wish I could have your operation for you; it probably would help me lose some of my fat (although I have reduced slightly, of late, I think).

Classes are progressing most satisfactorily now; I have a very interesting one in American literature, 1800–1870, from Dr. Hubbell, and am reading Claude Newlin's (English dept., East Lansing—the owner of that house which was on fire—you remember) biography of Hugh Henry Brackenridge, the early American novelist and satirist. How is your reading coming now?

A friend of mine here, Ralph Purcell, also has to do considerable work in the libraries in Richmond, and he and I are going to stop there when I am heading north for spring vacation. He is from Lakeland, Florida, and is going to spend all his vacation in Richmond.

I must work hard if I am to get my degree in June, and am reading two or three books a day. Saw *Escape* in the movies Sunday; good.

Write me when you can; I'll write again soon. Must leave for the library now.

Love,
Jr.

Letter to William C. McCann

Kirk wrote the following letter on the eve of receiving his master's degree from Duke University, having successfully defended his 204-page thesis, titled "The Political Thought of John Randolph." The thesis became Kirk's first book, published by the University of Chicago Press in 1951 as Randolph of Roanoke: A Study in Conservative Thought.

May 22, 1941
Box 4992
Duke Station
Durham
North Carolina

Dear Bill,

I now am a finished scholar, in more ways than two. All work is done, except for one easy examination due a week from today. I had my oral exam on my thesis, which turned into a fierce battle, although all members of my examining committee signed my thesis. The chief battle was with a political science man, whom the dean's office had put on my committee by mistake, instead of an English man, since I'm minoring in English. He was a scowling, burly, heavily-mustached creature who objected to everything from the title onward, most sincerely.[5] He was a great nationalist, and hardly agreed with Randolph and me. I should have written in jargon, he said. "Your title is deceptive and false. 'Political thought' has a special technical meaning. To be political thought, it has to be unique. What contribution did Randolph make that was unique?"

"None," said I. "Nothing has been unique since Aristotle."

"Well, in American political philosophy, I mean," he said.

17

"None," said I. "Thought doesn't have to be unique."

"It does," quoth he. "It's a special technical term."

"I'm not in favor of special technical terms," said I. "We're speaking different languages."

"Your thesis has nothing to do with political thought," he said.

"What else could I call my thesis?"

He ignored that. "It's a special technical term."

"Well, I'm no great philologist, but, . . ."

"It's not a matter of philology," he said. "It's a matter of definition and history and meaning."

"What is your special technical meaning of 'philology'?" I inquired.

Ad infinitum. He was no gentleman, but I had the history men, particularly Sydnor, on my side, since they hate all political science men, who reject almost every history man's thesis they examine, if there is any excuse for it; they're said to resent the fact that history men usually teach political science on the side. Afterward Sydnor told me he was surprised when he found they had put a political scientist on my committee, but he concluded it was just as well, so I "could see how those men's minds work" in case I should have something to do with them again. Gibson (the political scientist) signed my thesis without any demur, however. The day before, though, he had rejected a doctor's dissertation on "The American Party in the South" (a gigantic thing) because the author hadn't read any political science book on parties. From what Sydnor intimated, the thesis wasn't much good, anyway.

I'll get my degree here June 2, and expect to be in East Lansing Saturday evening, June 7, after making several stops on my way north. . . . This date may be changed, but I'll let you know. If you have something scheduled for that week-end, I can stay elsewhere in East Lansing without any trouble, you know, so don't hesitate to tell me. . . .

My only opinion on the Hess question is that he listened to "We're sailing for England" once too often, and decided to be the first to land. . . .[6]

I have almost finished the works of Cooper here. Haven't read his *Naval History* as yet, though. His *American Democrat* is fine.

Have shown John's *Essays* to Hubbell, who agreed that it was good.[7] Am now engaged in promoting its adoption in the College of the Ozarks. A friend of mine here, Ralph Purcell, a Floridian, has been offered a job in the English department there next year. He is to teach freshman English, freshman French, survey of English literature, expository writing, and contemporary literature! I am going to get some copies of John's reading lists, etc., if he has some, still, in the two latter courses, to help Ralph out. The president of the College of the Ozarks warned him that the Arkansan students out there are not brilliant. Ralph has no less than five brothers and sisters, as well as his mother, teaching English in colleges scattered throughout the country.

It is sorry indeed to hear of the spiritlessness of the faculty at M.S.C.[8] Stuart Chase, than whom I know of no man who has written more folly, still wasn't too bad in his "The Luxury of Integrity." It's all a part of this spineless popular craving for "security" (asserted), regardless of manhood. "Life is not so important as the duties of life," said Randolph. Although I've very little of the heroic in me, I know that if I were bullied as most teachers are bullied, I'd feel that there was more than one job and more than one kind of job in the world. One should save money more as a reserve to secure liberty than to secure prosperity. . . . There's a good article in the *Reader's Digest* (anomaly!) this month denouncing the draft, by a member of the House Military Affairs Committee.

I'll be working at Greenfield Village this summer, if I want to, I have been assured by the powers that be. If only the army gets the head research man, I can have a very nice job there. The place seems pretty artificial after wandering around real old American towns, without any sidewalks, down here, though. Hillsboro really would be the place to live. At Chapel Hill, all the walks are of a sort of sand-and-gravel; one of the benefactors of the University specified that if they ever put in concrete walks, they would lose his bequest. The students and faculty who pride themselves on belonging to the most "liberal" institution in the South, and think change means reform, are forever trying to have hot and hideous cement substituted, but as yet they've been able to find no loophole in the bequest. I am going to walk over to Chapel Hill (twelve miles) tomorrow to see *Romeo and Juliet* presented. I'm not very busy now, you may surmise. . . .

I am going out to drink some lemonade to abate this dreadful heat. Warren had better bring a big electric fan down here with him for the summer.

See you soon.

Yours,

Russell

Letter to William C. McCann

The remarks Kirk makes below, regarding his Jeffersonian skepticism in religious matters, stand in marked contrast to the Christian orthodoxy he came to embrace over time, eventually leading to his being baptized into the Roman Catholic Church, in 1964.

June 1 [, 1942]

873 Mill Street

Dear Bill,

I am much surprised and pleased to learn of the Civil War diary of my great-great uncle. As I mentioned, I'd hardly more than glanced at the papers in that box, and for that reason, among others, brought it along. It is most humiliating to have someone else make such a discovery; I'm anxious to read the journal. Mr. W. C. McCann has full permission to copy, print, and publish all memoirs found therein or in other of the papers. I have a huge framed roll of Frank Pierce's company, embellished with triumphant eagles, etc., in my possession. My grandfather was named after him. . . .

I think you would find the Jefferson Bible worth your money. It is simply a *Readers' Digest* Bible, of course, but it makes Christ's doctrines appear far clearer than they do when one reads the Gospels. I should warn you, however, that if you have any lingering remnants of Christian faith, it will dispel them. For years I've tried to convince myself that I should be a Christian, that there must be something in Christianity, that the great weight of authority behind the Christian faith, including all my chief authorities—Johnson, Randolph, etc.— excluding the ancients of course—all of them ardent Christians, must prove its truth. I have attempted to be a missionary, and renew the faith of all those silly young scoffers at religion who are indoctrinated in materialism by teachers of psychology and sociology. But I never had any conviction, and now I am the Gibbon of Michigan. . . . The Catholic Church sometimes approaches Christianity, and the closer it comes the further I draw away from it. I can admire Christ as a sort of pacifist Osawatomie Brown; but I abhor his doctrines. Christianity is truly a religion for the expropriated, and I don't want to be one of the expropriated; if the Communists had any real cleverness they'd make great use of Christianity instead of calling it an opiate. If ever there was a social-revolutionary creed, Christianity is it. And there is a ruinous moral laxity, a sort of indiscriminate sentimentalism, in the parables, particularly the one of the woman taken in adultery. Once you start thinking of that "let him throw the first stone who . . ." business, you begin to feel that the E. Lansing People's Church is more a real return to primitive Christianity than a degenerate survival.[9] To abandon Christianity need not be to abandon religion, of course. I am a stern Pharisee. Don't say I didn't warn you, now.

The World Publishing Company, which puts out Tower Books, has printed a lot of odd things in similar, though inferior, format for years—among them Ruxton's *In the Old West*—an unsuccessful attempt at a novel by an English adventurer in our West during the eighteen-thirties, with a lot of real color and historical material. I think it was an important source for Stewart Edward White's stories of the mountain trappers.

Reading Parkes' *Jonathan Edwards* has given me quite a taste for theology. Parkes disagrees violently with Edwards, and I disagree with them both. Yesterday I read Holmes' *The Professor at the Breakfast Table*, in which he has a great deal to say against Edwards and Puritanism. I disagree with him, too. Parkes takes a species of delight in thinking that the actual morality—particularly sexual—of the New Englanders was lax, and should have been more lax. He is all for Rousseauean freedom. I think he is wrong in his historical interpretation, particularly in his ardent account of bundling, and can quote my family history to prove it. There was a most deplorable case in which a great-great-great-great-great-great-great uncle was involved; I shall read it to you when next I appear at your fireside.

Judging by tonight's paper, the British have won a very considerable victory in Africa. Auchinleck apparently is a fighting general as well as a talking one.[10] He certainly can give interviews and write dispatches. His cheerful vigor contrasts most favorably with MacArthur's strutting platitudes. I thought What's-his-name—the former minister of aircraft in England—gave a good Wright Address on the war over Europe.[11] Did you read it? He says the British are wasting planes needed desperately in the East, and that they won't get any further with indiscriminate bombing than the Germans did. Matters certainly appear stalemated in Russia—let us hope they remain so. . . .

In keeping with my cheerful ancestral custom, let me inform you that all my relatives and friends are ailing, and especially that my grandmother is in the hospital with a ruptured appendix and a hospital bill that promises to empty my coffers for months to come; but we are a fierce and godless race, and she is recovering rapidly, and soon will be home, I trust. I wrote a masterly letter to the auto rationing board, and the very next day they wrote back, giving my father permission to buy a new car. He doesn't want a new car, but he has to have tires; they won't let him retread his present ones, but they'll let him have new ones, provided he pays a thousand or so for them.

Let me have a missive without delay.

Yours,
Julian the Apostate

Letter to William C. McCann

On August 14, 1942, Kirk reported to the U.S. Army induction center in Detroit, opposite the Fort Street train station. This marked the beginning of four critical years in his intellectual and spiritual development. Outwardly, Kirk's army experience seemed boring and inane, as he remained stateside for the duration of World War II. But those years of routine and inactivity afforded the young conscript much time to read, think through first principles, and correspond with the likes of Bill McCann and, in time, Albert Jay Nock.

Tuesday, August 18, 1942
873 Mill Street

Dear Bill,

I now am a private in our heroic army of the Republic, having been sworn in last Friday, after trials and tribulations. My services are to be "limited," however. It is just possible that I may escape via the physical exam at Camp Custer, August 28; I came close to failing the eye examination Friday.

Trusting that it will be all right with you, as you stated in your letter, I'll be in East Lansing next Friday night, arriving in the Union station about seven. If you aren't doing anything, you might be there with the car to help transport the two suitcases of books I'm bringing; if it would be any trouble, don't bother, because I can put a suitcase in the lockers and we can pick it up later. Some of my treasured volumes are coming up to stay with you for the duration, if you'd like them; you don't have any of them. I'm afraid you've lost out on the books I bought for you, though; I can't resist keeping most of them for myself. . . .

Thursday I leave the Ford Motor Company forever. After me, the deluge: they are bringing in several girl typists to replace me. All are unhappy in our Eveless Eden. We'd hope it would stay Eveless.

Multitudinous affairs cut this missive short, but I'll see you soon.

Yours,
Russell

Letter to Marjorie Kirk

In a lengthy letter to his mother, Kirk describes a walking trip into the waste-land near the army base in Dugway.

October 24, 1942
Dugway

Dear Mama,

Your letters of October 17, 19, and 20 came today; I was most pleased to receive my photographs and learn all about your wedding-anniversary celebration. Nine other letters came, as well, including one from Carolyn. I'm glad to have your pictures, and will be looking forward to another one of you, as well. If I get some film for my camera tomorrow, I'll send you a picture of me; in any case, I'm sending you a little package. . . .

This should be a long letter, for I've a great deal to describe to you, sleepy as I am now, at midnight. I thought of writing you last night concerning the sky I saw yesterday night, just after I'd sent off my daily letter to you, but decided to save my information until today.

You'd have been much pleased to see that desert night. The moon—no different from our Michigan one—was full, and lighted the winding white road from our camp up toward Johnson Pass—an incarnation of the road to adventure, and as deceptive. To the west, opposite the moon, the last redness from the sun died behind Granite Mountain. But the best part of the effect was contributed by the strange clouds that hung about the moon. Directly above it, and extending upward and westward at an angle of forty-five degrees, lay motionless a weird, serried cloud, layer on layer, like a rail fence. Just to the left of the moon, a cloud shaped like a perfect egg hung unmoving. And just below was a flat, thin, elongated ribbon of cloud, widening at each end, much like a scroll. All were perfectly black, except for having a regular gray edge outlined by the moon. It was like one of the abstractions of the execrable Dali. The sky appeared thus for a full hour; then the rail-fence cloud sank over the face of the moon, producing an effect like that of a light behind Venetian blinds. What happened later, I cannot say, for I slept. The portents of these phenomena I shall not divulge.

This has been a most arduous day for me; Robert Shaw and I have explored a part of the Dugway Range, north-west of us, and are tired and stiff enough. We set out on foot from camp about 1:30, and climbed over the stile which allows civilians from their ground outside our camp to enter; we crossed the little airfield, and disappeared into the brush.

Near camp the ground is broken into segments and parched, like new-dried mud; but it has been thus for thousands of years. A little further on, it is covered with "alkali flowers"—caked incrustations of alkali, a blossom of which I enclose in my little package. Later one comes to vast sand dunes, to volcanic ash and pebble patches, and to rock. Varieties of sage grow grimly from the soil; we found great ant houses covered with piles—sometimes two feet high—of empty sage and cedar needles, from which the ants seem to get their food. Great rabbits leaped out of our way; but we found not one rattlesnake, or snake of any kind, although I was equipped with a six-foot stick of timber to repulse their assaults. Little lizards darted out from bushes constantly; they're all head and tail, and leave strange markings in the sand, dragging their tails as they do. The sand, indeed, is covered with the impressions, undisturbed except by the wind, of the feet of all sorts of animals; many we could not guess. There are numerous coyote tracks; I'm sending Rosie a tooth from a coyote skull. One strange creature apparently had slid down a dune in zig-zag fashion, leaving an / mark connecting his paw-prints. Cattle sometimes wander here, far from their ranches; they have regular trails. But of man, there is no sign.

The plain looks flat enough at first; but we found it full of dips, sand banks, and knolls, which made walking far from easy. Half-dead sage brush is everywhere; we found strange vine-like roots, the identity of which we were at first unable to guess, but finally found to belong to tiny, ground-grasping cedar, which, as the slope increases, become good-sized trees, sometimes thirty feet high, immensely bushy, and with many trunks from one center. The sand forms circles around the larger trees, and hides them in bowls.

The skulls and bones of dead little creatures are everywhere; there are no leaves and weeds to conceal them, as there are in our forests. I'm sending a collection to Rosie. To you I'm sending some of the strange little plants that grow in the desert—a star-like, tiny thing that has its leaves flat with the ground, and its stem entirely beneath the sand; white, cottony berries from a fairly common shrub; cedar "berries" from one of the larger cedar tree; and a sort of tiny puff-ball. You'll find also a collection of obsidian chips, half-carved by Indians who came here fifty thousand years ago, perhaps, when there still was a lake in the valley; quite probable it is that they obtained their obsidian from the volcanoes of the Dugway Range, and came here to fashion them. . . . You'll find nothing of man's older than this in Utah.

We plodded on through this strange land, the mountains seeming distant as ever; and at last we came to a mighty loose sand ridge, stretching thousands of rods in each direction, perhaps seventy feet high, and looking precisely like pictures of the Sahara. We climbed it, and rested in the warm sun, atop the dune, drinking from our canteens. Then we marched on toward the little peak we had in view. As we came closer, we could see reddish-purple outcroppings of rock on its sides; and atop it, to our wonder, a mightier sand dune than ever before, perched at the tip of a mountain. We climbed over pitted and honeycombed little cliffs of limestone, which broke in our hands; something had seemed to move behind the rocks as we approached—something large, and very like a man—but there was nothing to be seen, once we arrived. The slope became steeper; we walked near the twisted, tormented larger cedars; we stumbled through little beds of scoria and volcanic ash and pebbles; a volcanic deposit had been here first, and then water covered it. In your package is one of the volcanic pebbles, smoothed by water. To our immediate left appeared a great ridge of stone, ten feet wide and thirty feet high, and hundreds of yards long, stretching up the mountain side; it was a rude, conglomerate lava flow, in which half-cooled lava had carried boulders. It ended abruptly, without an apparent source, and we were at the last steep slope of firm rock and soil; we went up it, and came to the foot of the mighty crowning dune, perhaps a hundred and

26

fifty or two hundred—no, three hundred—feet in height. We plunged in; sand almost to my knees in the loose sand; but up we struggled, in an agony of exhaustion, and reached the top. I flung myself backward on the wind-swept crest, and almost rolled down the other side of the mountain, for the northern side is one smooth sweep of sand, and the crest is cut to an edge as sharp as a knife. The blowing sand cut into our faces; the great dune is constantly moving east, and eventually will descend from its hill and roll toward Dugway. We could see in every direction for scores of miles. To the north, another part of the Dugway Valley lay, separating us from the major peaks of the Dugway Range; ours was merely a foot-mountain. Opposite, we saw the camp, eight miles distant, with a long line of dust marking the course of a truck driving toward the camp. To the west was Granite Mountain; close beside it the mirage of a mountain which was not there at all; and behind it the Gold Hill range, far away. To the northeast were the pointed Simpsons; to the north, the Cedar Mountains, with Johnson and Lookout passes showing clearly enough. All was silence and death. We rested, despite the blowing sand, for a half-hour; then we marked our names on the side of the dune, with my long stick, while the empty, malevolent land around us reminded me that all is vanity, and sand-writing is symbolic. We slid and ran down; but the trip back to camp seemed three times as long as the ascent, and I became separated from Bob among the hollows and the sage, and almost was lost, for the camp vanished from my sight; but I regained my way.

Almost immediately after reaching camp, we climbed into a jeep, and bounced out to the target area, drinking each a quart of milk from a paper container—all we could find in the mess hall, for we had not returned to camp from our climb until eight in the evening. (Lucky it was that we arrived just as the sun went down, for surely we'd never have found our way otherwise.) On our return from the target area, where we had taken wind velocity and temperature reading, we passed by the barracks being erected, presumably, for the WAAC; a sort of gully is the road there, and as we passed through, with a pile of lumber towering above us; I saw a crouching figure, in the dusk, peering over the lumber at us.[12] What it may have been, I know not; we went not back. It may have been Simon. This begins to be a Montague Rhodes James story.

In the last half-hour I've been consoled for my lack of supper by a vast bologna sandwich, made for me by Sergeant Walker of the Signal Corps, who crept into the kitchen and purloined food for himself and me. I look forward to a pleasant time tomorrow, writing and reading.

The weather is a bit warmer now, and no time could be nicer for walking. Does your autumn continue as pleasant as it has been? I hope you and daddy can go to the park often.

I must rest my stiff muscles now, and write more tomorrow. Receiving your letters has comforted me much. I'll have a great deal to tell you tomorrow, too, I trust.

Love,

Jr.

Letter to Marjorie Kirk

In one of his final letters to his dying mother before hurrying home to Plymouth on furlough, Kirk details news about everyday events in Dugway and the nearby city of Tooele, Utah.

November 22, 1942
Dugway

Dear Mama,

My Thanksgiving box from Mom came today, and I've devoured one pie already.[13] This day was spent in doing a variety of little things, in reading [George] Borrow's *The Zingali*), and in writing. I had a letter from Bill McCann, in which he states that East Lansing is experiencing a shortage of peanut butter. Are you? John [Abbot Clark]'s next review is to be of *London Calling*, an English anthology. There was no other mail. I anticipate much pleasure from my box, and shall present Robert Shaw with some goodies. He had to work today, and George Neff is on furlough, so I didn't go walking, although the weather was most pleasant, our cold in the valley having departed, although the mountains remain snow-covered.

Work continues on my furlough; don't be surprised to have me with you much sooner than you think. How have you felt the last few days? I hear you had a fall; I hope it didn't pain you much. Donald Blessing always used to be leaping out of bed in the morning and falling flat on the floor, his legs having gone to sleep. Is Daddy much better?[14]

I was offered the job of military policeman yesterday; Whitey Santercier, who behaved so violently in Tooele at the last dance and is too ashamed to show his face there again, was ordered to go to yesterday's dance as a military policeman; he begged me on his knees to take his place. I was tempted by the idea of swaggering about Tooele's streets with pistol and club, but was too busy. He's not come back as yet; perhaps the citizens of Tooele have wreaked their vengeance.

Within a few minutes I shall go to see the mysterious movie, *Now, Voyager*, with Bob and one of our Finns, Onnie Wiikus. . . .

I must go out to get an envelope for this; more tomorrow.

Love,

Jr.

Letter to William C. McCann

Kirk shares news of new literary discoveries with McCann, including his first encounter with a work that strongly influenced him during the 1940s, Albert Jay Nock's Memoirs of a Superfluous Man *(1943).*

October 9, 1943

Dear Bill,

I have read many good books since last I wrote to you. The first of them was Marquand's *So Little Time;* but perhaps—indeed, I am sure—I mentioned that to you in my last letter. I am very surprised to see it the best-seller in every city in the *Herald-Tribune*'s survey; such incidents almost revive one's hopes for popular intelligence.

Incidentally, Marquand, who is dead against the soldier's life in this novel, was himself an officer along the Mexican border for two years before our entry into the World War, I believe. In *Memoirs of a Super-fluous Man*, Albert Jay Nock writes, in a footnote referring to the State as the organized expression of economism: "For an illustration of this point I may again refer to Mr. Marquand's novel *passim;* and I might take this occasion to remark that *H. M. Pulham, Esquire* is in my judgement the nearest thing to adult fiction that has come from an American pen in many years."[15]

You may have surmised that the second good book I've gotten is Nock's *Memoirs of a Superfluous Man*. This, Bill, is a book you should buy. It is three dollars. If you desire, I'll send my copy off for you to read before deciding upon the purchase. I hope that Nock will be surprised at the large sale of a book like his, for he holds that no books of merit can be published today without ruin for the publishers. Nock is a livelier writer than Henry Adams, though not such a stylist; he is even more gloomy; and he is a bold and determined man. We'll have a good time reading aloud passages of this book to each other. The chapter on colleges is particularly fine. Here is a passage:

"As the process of general barbarisation goes on, as its speed accelerates, as its calamitous consequences recur with ever-increasing frequency and violence, the educable person can only take shelter against his insensate fellow-beings, as Plato says, like a man crouching behind a wall in a whirlwind."[16]

And there are few other men that have the courage to put such words as these into print:

"As for the present war, the Principality of Monaco, the Grand Duchy of Luxemburg, would have taken up arms against the United States on receipt of such a note as the State Department sent the Japanese Government on the eve of Pearl Harbour."[17]

Nock has his flaws, however. He accepts almost fatuously the ridiculous assertion of some psychologists that "the average American has the intelligence of a thirteen-year-old"; he lauds his "old friend Hendrik Willem Van Loon" (who, incidentally, writes the jacket blurb for the *Memoirs*); he praises Sue's *Wandering Jew* (a sillier and more boring novel I never read—not even Dumas' *Han of Iceland*); and although he confesses that he has been compelled to deny many of Jefferson's doctrines, he seems utterly unaware of the political thought of Randolph and of Calhoun. Of John Adams he knows much. . . .

My third treasure is a one-volume edition of Aubrey's *Miscellanies* and Browne's *Urn-Burial*. It was printed in 1890, and is excellently illustrated, with a revealing portrait of Aubrey. Miss Shepherd, an impressively tall and white-haired old woman, looked fondly at my find in her dusty and dim old store. "We always try to give soldier boys a special rate, if we possibly can," said she, "but I'm afraid this one will have to be sold at the original price—$1.50. It's a new book." The little volume was black with dust and faded by the sun. No doubt she remembers well the day when it was brought, literally new, into the store, then her father's. The pages were uncut, and I paid my dollar and a half. "We can't sell anything for less than we paid for it, of course," says Miss Shepherd. One admires such foolhardy obstinacy in these times. I think myself the only profitable customer of the sisters Shepherd; and yet they never remember me, and always want to know what sort of books I am interested in. "Everything," say I. They have a wonderful collection of Elizabethan and Jacobean folios, as I have mentioned—Francis' *Demosthenes*, Sidney, L'Estrange—everyone. "We always used to make catalogs of all our books," says the Miss Shepherd who is the dominant half of the partnership, "but lately we haven't kept them up, because—well, I don't know quite why." The answer is obvious, of course—poverty, inefficiency, and old age are manifest "It must be a great deal of bother," I say. One of their catalogs is enclosed.

W. Clausewitz McCann and R. Frederick Kirk have not been betrayed by their Russian proteges. It appears that already the Russians have burst across the Dnieper, and will have Kiev, and the Crimea, and perhaps everything else; let Hitler call this shortening the lines, if he can. With every foot the Germans give back, they become more uncertain of survival; and with every foot, the Russian spirit is heightened. Apparently the Germans are able to counter our ponderous and faltering armies in Italy with a few swift divisions. We are in Capua, and are lucky not to have met a Roman fate there. The British will have the Aegean, it appears; I am surprised that the Germans can offer any successful resistance there. Leros, Cos, Lemnos, Lesbos, Rhodes— those are magic and classic names. Lemnos had at least two important city-states in Periclean times; Samos had three or more; now these islands are taken and lost in a day.

The generally despicable *Saturday Evening Post* had a pretty good editorial attacking William Shirer and others for their denunciations of collaboration with Badoglio.[18] Henderson (Leon) wants "people's councils" to run affairs in Italy, it appears.[19] What folly! These very journalists and parlour-pinks have been boosting Badoglio for years as the staunch old liberal, the great threat to Fascism; and now that he is in the saddle, they think him a worse Fascist than Mussolini. Badoglio's course in Ethiopia showed him to be a stern and relentless man; but beyond all doubt he is a competent general, a foe of dictatorship, an able leader, and the possessor of actual power, and has done us great services. What any American of honest principles should be interested in is getting this war out of the way and preventing another one within a few years; and both these objectives would be terribly injured by sponsoring hot-house governments in nations nominally allied with us. I am in favor of De Gaulle because he represents the most able and energetic and stable element among our French allies; for the same reason I am in favor of the Italian monarch and Badoglio. Only they can provide a core of tradition and strength in post-war Italy. For once our State Department is right. Stalin, that reactionary old fogy, doesn't seem to worry about setting up people's councils in Italy.

I would give much to see the Irish Hills; and soon, I trust, I shall see that country.[20] I have not been there since I was a very small boy. . . .

We now have men at Dugway who have been conscripts for three years. How long, O Lord? If the scoundrels of selective service get you Bill, you will have the consolation that your term of service is likely to be short, at the present rate of Russian success. Assistant Secretary Patterson announces that we may need many, many more men, however. The

New Deal is accustomed to these tactics of asking for the moon and then pretending to compromise by accepting all the green cheese we have in the house. My espionage in the correspondence we receive at Dugway inclines me to believe that we already have more than twelve million men in arms. Ah, wouldn't I enjoy kicking Roosevelt and MacLeish out of bed every morning at four-thirty, let us say, to give them a taste of the privilege of fighting for the Brave New World, in post-war days![21]
Write.

Yours,
Russell

. . . .

Letter to Margaret, Jane, and Frank Pierce Jr.

During his years in the army, Kirk frequently corresponded with Frank and Marg Pierce, his uncle and aunt who lived in Plymouth with their young daughter, Jane. (Frank was the son and namesake of Kirk's beloved maternal grandfather, a major formative influence upon Kirk's life.)

October 31, 1943
Dugway

Dear Marg, Frank, and Jane,
        Hallowe'en brought violence and dismay to Dugway. Some wretch tossed a tear-gas bomb into the theatre during the evening dance, with catastrophic results; a wild unknown drove a car round and round the runways of the airport, while the guard fired at him, and escaped unscathed; two scoundrels already under sentence of court-martial cornered and beat one of their comrades, kicking him repeatedly in the head; they were interrupted by Sergeant Liebling, whom they cursed and struck; and now they repose in the guard-house. The WACs got thoroughly drunken for a free-for-all party in their dayroom, and one, adorned with purposely smearable lipstick, kissed soldiers by the hundred. I know all this by my spy Novak the bugler; he reports all such doings to me while I sit peacefully in headquarters, typing.

I have been somewhat ill, or I would have written sooner; perhaps too many candy-bars have been my undoing. I am in a reasonable state of health now, however, and am planning an arduous expedition to the ghost towns of Ophir and Mercur, where they still extract a little gold from the heart of the Oquirrhs—or did, at least, until the war came.

Of late I have been reading Arthur Smith's *Book of Canadian Poetry;* my friend of East Lansing has edited a very good anthology. Some of his own verse is included, perfectly mysterious and perfectly incomprehensible.[22]

The war in Russia begins to assume a European aspect once more, with the Crimea and the Bug coming back into the headlines. Time was when the Germans had the Russians backed into Asia, for all practical purposes; but now the disengagement will continue until the war in Europe ends—in May, perhaps. But our prospects in Italy are not bright; we talk ominously of preparing for the great counter-attack by Rommel, and the difficulties of supplying our troops in the Boot during the winter. All the British and Americans must be sitting tight in the Tight Little Isle, awaiting the opening of the vaunted second front—which will come about the time Stalin is in Cologne, Rommel is back in Syracuse, and the Fifth and Eighth Armies are in Davy Jones' locker.

I hear the present Hass house in Plymouth—the old Hough house—is to be converted into six apartments for war-workers. I love the look of that old house; I would give a good deal to save it from such a fate. We rapidly are approaching a Russian sort of existence, with the government quartering its serfs kennel-like in decayed old mansions.

How does Jane with her studies? What would she like for Christmas?

Write.

Yours,

RAK Jr.

Letter to Eva Pierce

In The Sword of Imagination: Memoirs of a Half-Century of Literary Conflict *(Grand Rapids, MI: Eerdmans, 1995), Kirk described his maternal grandmother, Eva Johnson Pierce (1871–1953), as "a strong-willed and indefatigable woman"(7). She corresponded regularly with Kirk during his years in the army.*

December 18, 1945
Dugway Proving Ground

Dear Mom,

I have been neglecting you and everyone else, these past three weeks; I did not sit down long enough in California, when alone, to write a single letter. A fine time I had, and of it you shall learn something in this letter—the first of fifteen I have to write to neglected correspondents—and more in later ones and when I come home. I hope to have definite word any day as to when I shall be discharged; it certainly will not be later than the first days of February. According to new regulations, men to be discharged will be sent to the separation-center nearest their home, for that purpose; this may delay matters a few days for me, as well as deprive me of my travel-money. I suppose I shall be sent to Fort Sheridan, near Chicago, for separation; I don't believe Fort Custer [in Michigan] is a full-fledged separation center. . . .

I hope your sight is better now. What doctor are you seeing? Having been talking with Robert Shaw, a student of optometry, for some weeks; I know a bit about eye-doctors.

On January 1, I'll send you the eighty dollars I owe you, or most of it, Mom. Don't forget to mark down the ten dollars paid to Ann in my debits. My post-discharge plans remain nebulous but numerous. Red Smith is negotiating for the purchase of the Wiest library—the thousands of books of the late Judge Wiest of Williamston (doubtless you've seen his country place, "Shagbark"); if he gets them, we shall be in business, right away. I may need several hundred dollars to finance my half of the transaction; I could get it without too much difficulty were I out of the army, but I have no cash on hand as matters stand. At any rate, the library has not yet been bought. It would be a tremendous bargain, could we get it for less than a thousand dollars. We would sell the books chiefly to dealers. Red suggests that if we can't find a site and capital for our bookshop immediately after my discharge, that I come to Lansing and get a job; we could begin setting up our business in our leisure time. There are other possibilities: President Ruthven invites me to visit him at the University of Michigan and see about employment, and Louis B. Wright of the Huntington Library, whom I visited in California, hinted that he would have something for me, should I be interested. I could get a good fellowship at Duke, too. If I want to arrange a loan to go into business, I might have to put a second mortgage on our house; but we need not discuss that yet. It would easily sustain a second mortgage in the eyes of a bank, what with the less than three thousand dollars I owe upon it.[23]

I know not what might have been lost from my insured box of Christmas presents; I trust nothing has been. There were no small articles loose inside, at any rate. Carolyn knows the contents, and can check for us. As for presents for me, socks or a shirt would be warmly received by yours truly—particularly a shirt. I wear a shirt with 32" sleeves and a 14½" or 15" neck—color is no question, although I prefer colored shirts to white. I wear size 10½ or 11 in socks.

I don't know where to begin my account of my furlough in California, spent everywhere from Catholic churches and missions to rowdy music-halls and saloons, from art galleries to the Coney Island of San Francisco, from the mansions of San Marino to the dens of old Main Street in Los Angeles. A great part of my time was spent in the company of Robert and Cathy Shaw and their infant Susan, and another great part in the company of Dorothy Belle Leston, the Rose of Deseret. I spent much less money than I had expected to get rid of. I could have stayed there another month very pleasantly; I didn't see half the places I wanted to. Foods of all sorts I ate, from swordfish on Fisherman's Wharf in San Francisco to strange Chinese delicacies in Jerry's Joynt on the Plaza of Los Angeles. I got me a few books; bookshops are innumerable in both the big cities of California, but generally prices are high. Dorothy and I combed San Francisco from one end to the other; the site of that town is superb, but Los Angeles, to my surprise, really is more picturesque—the great fire wiped out everything in Frisco. With Dorothy, I went over to the University of California, where the Rose is to enroll next term; and I saw six art galleries, altogether. The crowding and bustle of California is scarcely imaginable; when the economic crash comes, the suffering there will be great. San Francisco is jammed with drunken sailors, tens of thousands or hundreds of thousands of them every night, and both cities are full of soldiers just back from the Pacific. Discharged men have been looking for a room in which to live for weeks, some of them, and the prices of houses are extravagantly high; a four-room, jerry-built place in a standardized suburb is worth more than eleven thousand dollars—the price the Shaws are getting for their home.

Now to other letters, although I'd like to write more. I hate the thought of going back to barracks, after this night's letter-writing; for the night is bitter cold—the coldest December we have had at Dugway. Alas for the poor souls who must spend February here! I won't. More soon, Mom.

Love,
RAK Jr.

Letter to William C. McCann

January 26, 1946

Dear Bill,

Four days more, and I shall have departed from Dugway forever; a week, and I shall be free. How many letters have we exchanged since I became a soldier, I wonder? My military life has been remarkably pleasant, in comparison with that of most soldiers—although most of them, whose ideal camp is Fort Dix, would not much relish being exiled to the regions that I have been. It has been an enervatingly easy life, indeed; now I shudder at the thought of rising at six each morning, punctually, as a laboring civilian. Another job-opportunity for me is that of separation-counselor; for the soldier-counselors are being replaced by civilians. These are lucrative and interesting jobs, and I meet the requirements. I have written to Percy Jones General Hospital to see if they need me; any other separation-center would be too far from home.[24] . . .

Have you seen the new magazine *Tomorrow*? It endeavors, with but slight success, to be a lively literary monthly; it is published by the Creative Age press, and has money behind it, apparently. The editors are chiefly a crew of scribbling, ignorant women. There are a few good things in it—among them, a department about forgotten books. With an intelligent man to edit it, it could really amount to something.[25] . . .

Last Sunday, four of us crossed the Cedars by way of Beckwith Pass and the Beckwith Trail—the old route across the Great Salt Desert. I should like to have an old map of this region. I took many snapshots, and you shall see them, and I shall give you an account in full of the trip, when I get to Michigan. The snow had drifted deep in the gullies, and a desperate time we had crossing the mountains; the day was very mild, fortunately. We climbed White Rock, a seven-hundred-foot crag of smooth stone in the middle of the Cedars, and ate a hearty lunch in its shadow; then we proceeded to the Skull Valley Indian Reservation. (All this was in a jeep, you understand—nothing else could have gotten through, the trail being too narrow and sharp-turning even for a command-car, probably.) At the Reservation (three inhabited hovels, a dozen abandoned places), we conversed with a bulky brave, hoping to buy moccasins or gloves. "Got glove," he said. "No pinchum." I surmised, a good while later, that "no pinchum" meant "no finish 'em." Promising to return next week when the gloves were done, we took our departure, having bestowed four Hershey bars upon a shy, doll-like Indian boy not quite so old as Jane. I believe ours was the first motor-vehicle ever to cross through Beckwith Pass in winter.

I have been fraternizing with a German prisoner of war—a young fellow of twenty-six (looking much younger) named Ralph. He is Alfred Cutler's assistant at the library, and is to have charge of the place after Alfred is discharged next week. Ralph studied in Paris and Rome, and intended to enter the German foreign service. He is pale, slight, and blond, with that queer woodenness of gait and manner I have observed in almost every German soldier; he is extremely nervous and hesitant with us, as if incredulous that he is to be treated as an equal, although he has tea, cookies, and chocolate-bars nightly with us at the library. One could hardly ask for a young man of more liberal, impartial principles; possibly he is endeavoring to establish a "liberal" reputation, particularly since he expects to be sent back to his home in Leipzig, which is in Russian hands. He says he cannot understand why American soldiers prefer Germans to French; he denounces Franco as a "Fascist criminal"; his comrade (while he was at large, in disguise, in California) was a Zanzibar negro; he says his half-brother informs him that the Russian prison-camps are extremely decent; he condemns the Catholic Church as "a tool of reaction," although, with pleasing open-mindedness, he praises highly the talents and sincerity of Pius, whom he has seen and heard; he says all Europe will go Communist, and the prospect seems neither to displease nor to please him. Germany had no choice but between Fascism and Communism, he says; apparently he would have preferred the latter, although he seems to have understood those who made the opposite choice; and America, too, will have to choose thus—he insists there is no alternative. Indeed, his whole attitude is one of placid despair—typical enough of educated Germans of the better sort, no doubt. Alfred, an enthusiastic advocate of American capitalism, is endeavoring to win Ralph to the principles of the Right. Private Cutler, himself a regular jack-in-the-box of mannerisms and nervous gesticulations and speech, is forever railing at French emotionalism and praising Teutonic stolidity. "The French, you know," he says to Ralph, "don't admire courage, like *us*." "I suppose that may be true," says Ralph, with polite insincerity. On the other hand, Ralph is no turncoat, and does not sneer at his country. He seems embittered only against the French, for their conduct in the German occupation; he says that all the men in his stockade hope President Truman will force the French out of their occupation-zone. He is not given to racial-superiority nonsense of any sort, however. If there are many like him in Germany—and I doubt not that his sort is more numerous there than it is in America—where is all this necessity for "re-educating" Germany? I fear the problem of re-educating ourselves is a good deal more urgent. Questioned as to his family, Ralph replied, with a swallow, that he is sure he is the only survivor. Having spoken of the French Riviera, he added, swallowing hard again, with a melancholy grimace, "But I may see the Russian Riviera, instead. Somehow I can't get that conviction out of my head." He has nothing to go home to, no prospect in life but grinding poverty and servitude.

Ralph's innocent and youthful appearance, together with his shyness, is deceptive. He was an infantryman in the invasion of Crete, and remained in garrison there until shipped off to the Afrika Korps by his commanding officer, who disapproved of his affair with a Spanish girl. In Egypt, he, with a few others, was captured by British Indian troops. He fraternized with the Indians, however; they taught him how to say "India must be free!" in their tongue, and, one night, allowed him and a companion to escape, clad in British officers' uniforms. They made their way across the desert to the Nile, where they fell in with suspicious Egyptians; but they managed to get aboard a train for Cairo. On the train, they passed themselves off upon the British troops as Free French officers, and persuaded British officers to lend them money for their train-fare. (Ralph can speak excellent English and flawless French, incidentally.) Once in Cairo, they headed west for El Alamein, and crossed into the German lines; but only two days later, Montgomery's great offensive came, and Ralph was recaptured.

Not long after coming to America, Ralph escaped from his camp, obtained clothing, and made his way to San Francisco, where he obtained a job in a print-shop. He worked with a French-Canadian, but passed himself off as a Frenchman without difficulty. He acquired a disgust for America while in San Francisco—which I can well understand. After seven months of freedom (during which he obtained forged naturalization-papers), he grew homesick, and determined to get back to Leipzig via Mexico, Central America, and probably Brazil. He had intended to enter Mexico through Arizona; but on reaching the California line, he read in a paper of the escape of a group of German officers from the Phoenix camp. Alarmed at the hunt, he hurried down to Tijuana, and attempted to cross. There he was taken into custody—not as a German, but on suspicion of being a Frenchman who had entered illegally. Three days later, he was identified by his fingerprints. I know not if he has any intention of escaping from Dugway; it would be simple enough, for the prisoners wander about virtually at will, at all hours; there is no fence around the camp; and I noticed that already he is wearing army clothing with *no* "PW" printed upon it. Visitors at the library take him for an American private. Were I he, I think I'd chance it, in preference to being sent to the Russians two or three months from now; he could go back to Germany after matters had quieted down in Europe. He has several skills, and probably could get a job in this country without much difficulty.

So ends your last letter from Sergeant Kirk, Bill. I'll send you a card or two before I get home, however; I'd write, were I not to be constantly on the move spying out the land as I travel eastward and northward.

Yours,
Russell

Letter to William C. McCann

Kirk wrote the following letter during his first term at the University of St. Andrews.

October 18, 1948

Dear Bill,

"At the top of a high old house, a man had sat reading Russian novels until he thought he was mad." Thus Coppard, at the beginning of "Arabesque." I'm not quite in that state, but I have been sitting here before my great windows looking on the gardens, by my little electric heater, writing letters, until I am bemused. Tomorrow I shall be thirty years of age. I have done better in life than ever I really expected

I would, but not one-tenth so well as I would like to do. How rapidly the twenties went! Most of those years were wasted. This year, I think, will be as well spent as any in my life—time for reading, time for writing, time for wandering, with few distractions and no gnawing need for money.

What word of you and Isabelle and Jane? I would like to transport you all hither, for no one would enjoy this place more; and if ever I be a rich man, I shall uproot the McCanns and carry them off to Ireland and Scotland for a long sojourn.

What had Richard M. Dorson to say of his wanderings in foreign parts?[26] Rosemary will be more travelled than I, for she, growing uneasy at the idea of studying in solitude at Dublin, decided to spend her money touring instead, and, having visited Dublin, Killarney, Cork, Blarney, Liverpool, Chester, Edinburgh, and St. Andrews with me, has now gone to London and thence flown to Rome.[27] She will wander back to English ground via Florence, Milan, Mentone (on the Riviera), Avignon, Paris; and I shall meet her at Bradford, in Yorkshire, where she will stay for a week with an English girl. Then she'll take ship for the Air-Conditioned Nightmare once more.

If I have time, I shall get the back-installments of my journal caught up and send you a copy, today, or tomorrow. I neglected it all during the trip, of course, being either ill (aboard ship) or having too many things to see. Meanwhile, these few notes.

Everyone in St. Andrews is proud of the little old city; and that includes the thousand students (twice the old enrollment), all of whom swear by the gray town, even though they've been here only a week or two. I believe there could be no pleasanter place for a man to loll away his days. I am comfortably situated—much more so than most, for even here there is a mighty shortage of lodgings, despite the fact that there are sturdy medieval houses empty and derelict which could be refurbished for a comparatively small sum; but I suppose the difficulty lies in getting permits from Government. (The grocers and drapers seem to have no difficulty obtaining permits to scarify their shop-fronts with black, glazed, American-style, dime-store-type facades, all the rage with them just now; but the principal café here, a fine place, cannot get a permit to put in a new floor, despite the fact that it has the lumber lying ready in its garden.) The Government appears to prefer to build hideous little new bungalows and villas in the suburb below the hill, each with a silly little strip of lawn about it and a sillier name above the door. Ah, Cape Cod, Ranch House, and Contemporary! Even thou walk in beauty beside the Suburban Villa for the Laboring Poor! Well, I live in one of the newer houses of St. Andrews—i.e., about as old as the Wiest House. Queen's Gardens is a socially acceptable address, and my chamber has a mighty marble fireplace, a moulded-plaster ceiling, and other amenities; the MacLeods, who occupy this granite house with its front garden (across the street) and kitchen garden, are very pleasant people. Mr. MacLeod was the manager of a rubber plantation in Sumatra, and was imprisoned by the Japanese from 1942 to 1945; he has a bad limp, and walks with a cane—probably a souvenir of the prison-camp.

Good talk is the rule in Britain, I find. For every person in America who can talk interestingly on general subjects, one will find twenty here, I think. And the faces are interesting—not that curious monotony one observes on the street in Lansing. Every single person I have talked with is a bitter hater of the Labour government—which indicates, doubtless, that the political struggle is drawn up along lines of class and occupation much more rigid than those in America—and much more clearly delineated than ever before in Britain, I suspect. Probably the next elections will show that the middle-class people who voted for Labour just after the end of the war have now shrunk back into the Conservative and Liberal folds. The division between the parties is now closer than in America—the narrowness of the margin, I mean. At a by-election near Edinburgh last week, in an industrial region, the Conservative candidate got 13,000 votes, the Labour 14,000, the Scottish Nationalist 1,500. Had not the last candidate run (and the Nationalists are ultra-conservatives, for the most part), Labour would have lost. Franklin Roosevelt is remembered with gratitude in Britain, and tributes to his memory are often proffered to me, as an American—

43

which, you may imagine, I do not wholly relish. The British have reason to thank him, of course, and to thank the Truman Administration, as well; for our present administration has co-operated with the British in maintaining for the pound an artificially high ratio with the dollar, which makes my money worth less here than in Michigan. The pound is worth $2.80, on the free (and illegal) market; $4.03, official rate. Accordingly, an American can live much more cheaply in France or Italy. Congress is expected to grumble about this, next session.

I had a pleasant conversation yesterday with Miss Sutherland (lecturer in zoology, and actual head of the Department of Natural History, since the much-beloved Sir D'Arcy Thompson died last summer) and her brother, in their handsome apartment in Greyfriar's Gardens.[28] Handsome though your shelves at 117 Gunson are, they would shrink back abashed [at] the beautiful array of shelving and books arranged round the fireplace at 7 Greyfriars. M. S. C. Zoologists ordinarily are either dull or annoying when they talk of anything save zoology: but what a difference here! Mr. Sutherland is an administrator of some sort in Tanganyika, home for a while; he is in charge of irrigation, soil reclamation, and the like, on an enormous scale—for privately-owned plantations, I think. He seems to be contemplating his own T. V. A.[29] And what a difference between that sort of administrator, in America, and the Sutherlands of this country! We talked on everything under the sun—old armour, witchcraft, the laws of wages, architecture, American politics, old families, savagery and civilization, the social consequences of the Great Wars, etc., etc., etc.

Sutherland revealed that he had heard the most grievous reports of racial prejudice in America. I fear I did not calm his apprehensions, and maintained that the problem is not simply one of prejudice—it is a very real one that won't [die] down just because a couple of laws are passed. He commented that the negroes are fine fellows, although he laments the passing of the old tribal order in East Africa. "A few years ago, it was the custom for a young fellow to travel around from village to village—Africans are great travelers—for the fun of it; he was given food and a place to sleep, without question, by the people of any village he came to—so long as he would sit by the fire and give them the gossip of his place until it was time to go to bed. It was great fun for him and for them. But now, whenever a stranger appears in a town, it's 'Bukowayo?' (or whatever Swahili word Sutherland used)—'Where's the money?,' if he so much as asks for a drink of water. They've caught that from the Europeans." . . .

Later, I had tea (a most pleasant institution, which must be introduced into East Lansing) at the home of Professor Williams, who is to supervise my work.[30] He lives in the Roundel, one of the oldest houses in ancient St. Andrews, a great grey mansion just opposite the haunted Pends (the half-ruined gateway of the medieval priory of St. Andrews). He's a tall, disordered Ulsterman, bitter against Eire, and more conservative than R. A. Kirk, if such a thing be possible. He is more than austere, and greatly dreaded by the student body, having passed only seventeen students out of his class of 103, last year; but once he found what we both thought of Burke and Lecky, we got along splendidly. He has a Wiest-like library, up to the ceiling; and in the chief parlor he has a tremendous wall lined with old books in beautiful seventeenth-and eighteenth-century bindings—every single book on the wall. College people here receive lower salaries than they do in America; but I think they manage with them much more ably. Few automobiles, of course. There's really no place to keep automobiles in a medieval town like St. Andrews, anyway. The Roundel takes its name from a curious round tower at the street corner—a tower empty and grim, as I found from a glance into it as I passed through the lower hall.

Sutherland (a stout, short Scot of fifty years, the Retired Major incarnate) and I are planning an expedition to Glamis Castle: he is going to write to the factor, so that we can be shown through. I have seen it from the bus—properly ghostly. The Earl of Strathmoor resides there, and his line descends right from Malcolm Canmore—perhaps the oldest house in Britain. But they are come upon hard times, and last week there occurred a sale of "surplus furniture" from disused rooms at Glamis. Sutherland attended; the furniture brought good prices. He talked with people in the village of Glamis, and found that the

Castle has difficulty in finding maids and serving-men; the passages are damp, etc. "It's a sad thing," said Sutherland, "when old loyalties die. Those people in the village have been living from the table of the Castle for eight hundred years." He and Miss Sutherland agreed that Government ought to do something to assist such ancient families. "But not the present Government," they chuckled grimly.

As Rosemary remarks, in both Ireland and Britain one sees the end, perhaps, of an age of leisure and wealth. One sees it in the elaborate table-services, the plentitude of forks and spoons provided at each place even in small tea-rooms, the elaborate coffee-pots and tea-pots and water-jars of good silver than one encounters everywhere. [There] is no longer very much food to go with all this admirable apparatus—although enough to suffice me.

Write, Bill. More anon. Life here is not so austere as one might imagine: there is much more butter than in America, and more sugar, and more bread, and bigger breakfasts. I shall be content.

Yours,
Russell

The 1950s

. . . to conserve the spiritual and intellectual and political
tradition of our civilization.

from a letter to Henry Regnery, July 31, 1952

Letter to Fay Jewell

In a newsy Christmas letter to his Aunt Fay, Kirk discourses on many things, including his ongoing work on his doctoral thesis, which he already envisioned as a book—not knowing that this yet-unfinished book would establish his name as a world-renowned scholar.

December 22, 1951
5 John Street
St. Andrews

Dear Fay,

By the time this letter is in your hands, doubtless you will have gorged yourself all holiday season, and your diet will have come to naught. I do not seem to be shrinking nowadays, nor yet gaining; but a month of walking, which I should be able to undertake soon, should slim me. It would have been good to be with you at Christmas and New Year's. What interesting presents did you receive? Thus far, I have a food-parcel from Holland (sent by the agency of the McCanns) and a handsome bowl of blue glass from the Lorimers. Your packages probably will reach me between Christmas and New Year's.

Thank you for paying the taxes. Eventually, 873 Mill Street should give me a thousand dollars clear a year, in rent, so I am not sorry to own it.[1] Only about a thousand dollars remain to be paid on the mortgage. When that is vanished (which will be only a year or so), I shall commence to buy Mecosta from Potter, if he'll let me.[2] What with my depleted bank-balance, the ice-box for Plymouth may have to wait, unless they can get a good old-fashioned ice-box or a mere window-box. If they want to advance the money, however, I could repay them before long.

I plan to deplete my bank-balance still further. The several sums due me are slow in coming, and my expenditures are heavy this season. Will you send me an additional hundred dollars (in the same form of check as before), then? Air-mail will be best. As I believe I told you in an earlier letter, the first check reached me safely. This will leave only $34 in the bank; but I shall proceed to build the dollar-balance back up again, before long.

In February, I may go to Sicily for a month. My friend Lewis Engel and his wife plan to sail for Sicily and Italy early next month; but perhaps I have told you this. I shall return to Scotland attired like a brigand. At present I am wearing my Inverness cape, of a mulberry hue—which is the cynosure of many eyes, being the only Inverness cape in St. Andrews (although worn by an American), not to mention its color. It is a most picturesque garment.

I work desperately hard on the last section of my book. On December 27, I go to a grand tea at Kellie, for the grandees of the East Neuk, probably taking Anne Thomson with me.[3]

Yesterday I bought a very handsome holly wreath for my window, at a florist's shop. I had noticed an abundance of wreaths in the shops, but had been vaguely puzzled to see none in homes; I thought perhaps they were too expensive this year. The florist tucked my ten-shilling note hastily into his box, and then inquired, "Ye'll be wanting this for a windae?" I assented. "Aye, that's what ye do in America," said he. "In Scotland, we put them on graves." The wreath hangs in my window; last night the three spinster Miss Robertsons, who live down the street, inquired of Mrs. Duncan who was dead.

I may give some of your dried corn, when it comes, to Lady Crawford. They still have no servants at Balcarres House, except for a woman who comes days. They are to have eight guests for Christmas; and if I weren't invited elsewhere on that day, I would volunteer as a scullion. I am invited to Durie House for Christmas dinner, too, but have already told Miss Myres I would dine with her.

Before long—Monday, like enough—I shall have several more packages of books shipped off to you. Don't forget to forward the Osbert Lancaster books to Rosy (706 South Sixth Street, Bozeman, Montana) when you have looked at them. Carolyn tells me that you were much taken with those volumes. I don't know Osbert Lancaster personally, although the Crawfords do.[4] The cartoon of Lord and Lady Littlehampton setting off to the Continent is ruefully reminiscent of their own expeditions to the Earl and Countess of Crawford, no doubt. They hope to go to Greece next year, if they can manage it with their travel-allowance.

I shall be glad to get the photographs of Mecosta. Pray don't bother about that education-number of *Life,* however; we have turned one up in these parts. I hope you didn't take too much time looking for it. The book I need most is *Richard Hooker and Contemporary Political Thought*—a slim English volume, in dust-jacket.[5] Merry Christmas.

Love,
Russell

Letter to Margaret Pierce

January 18, 1952
5 John Street
St. Andrews

Dear Marg,

Many thanks to you and Frank for your package of various candies, which I shall gobble in short order; it came today. Your letter of December 12, came two days ago, taking more than five weeks to reach me. I was glad to have the picture of your cabin, and the description of life therein; I have shown the photograph to several people, and read them select passages. I don't think you ought to have a porch on the cabin: its lines are very harmonious just as they are. Or if you do, the porch-roof ought to slope at just the same angle the main roof does. You look a thousand miles away from civilization in this picture; I could use it as an illustration for my story "Skyberia," which I sent to the *American Mercury* recently.[6]

How is the remedial reading for the children coming? I should hate to undertake that most difficult task. The Michigan Education Association is chiefly an organization for extortion from the teachers and the state, and should be abolished, I think; it is about as educational and as liberal as John L. Lewis' Mine Workers Union.

Were I Jane, and had my college years to spend over, I think I should go to the smallest and most old-fashioned place I could find—Olivet, perhaps. One might get an education there; certainly none of the big places are educational institutions any longer. . . . [G]reat colleges now are turned out like ready-made suits.

I hope that the "defense" program in general bogs down. There is no danger to anyone, really, from Russia: she is sunk deep in poverty, suspicion, and apathy. The chief danger is from our own hysteria and boastfulness. The abolition of the UNO would be a step toward calmness of mind and enduring peace, I think.

Aye, my great book is done.[7] Now I am contracting with the old firm of Batsford, probably, to write a book on St. Andrews; it should bring me some much needed ready cash. I can get the script to them by May, I hope, if they decide definitely to publish it. I shall be made a doctor of letters, in gown and tippet of the style of the chancellor of the University of Paris, next July 4. . . .

Robert Hutchins recently remarked, "Astronomers at the University of Chicago have discovered what appears to be a moss-like substance existing on Mars. I believe that Mars once was inhabited by rational beings who had the misfortune to invent television."[8]

This week I shall go over to Balcarres house to help the Countess of Crawford and Balcarres chop down some shrubbery along her grand drive. The gardener and his boys have quit, and her whole staff of servants now consists of one cleaning-woman who comes days, to keep the great house of a hundred rooms in order. Lady Crawford superintends her home farm, raises pedigreed cattle, is starting to raise pigs in a big way, does wood-carving, and cares for the finest private library and the best collection of paintings in Scotland, in addition to her other duties. The enormous park at Balcarres still is splendid. In the midst of it stands Folly Hill, topped by an artificial ruin of the early nineteenth century and by some curious pre-Christian inscribed stones. One of the paths leading down the side of the hill is haunted dreadfully: something invisible treads on your heels and peers over your shoulder. Even poodles are affrighted.[9]

Early next month, I set out for Sicily, there to rendezvous with my friend Lewis Engel and his wife. I expect to see Locarno, Bellinzona, Bologna, Florence, Siena, and other ancient Swiss and Italian towns on my way down. I shall be back here early in March.

Now to some urgent literary projects. I am growing industrious, and may turn out four books in the space of one year. I accomplish this by dint of staying up until six in the morning, typing while others sleep, and refraining from eating any meals out, except when I invite people to dine with me.

Meat and coal grow steadily scarcer here; otherwise, there's not much additional austerity. The Ministry of Transport wants to go ahead with plans to drive a great coastal highway straight through all the charming little ports of Fife—leading nowhere, and serving no purpose. This is typical enough of modern bureaucracy. It is in such matters that Britain should economize; but no one suggests it.

Write when you can, O Marg. Compliments to Frank and Jane.

Yours,

Russell

Letter to Sidney Gair

Near the end of his years of study at St. Andrews, Kirk wrote to Gair, a friend and book marketer who worked for Henry Regnery; it was he who told Regnery about Kirk and suggested the possibility of publishing his work. In the following letter, Kirk apprises his friend of his recent walking trips through Scotland and other goings-on. At this point in his life, Kirk had not yet met Regnery face to face and indicates that he welcomes the chance to meet the conservative publisher.

May 6, 1952
5 John Street
St. Andrews, Fife

Dear Sidney,

Aye, I shall be here in Scotland until early September, though most of July will be spent in an expedition to the Rhineland. I am not particularly anxious to make that trip, however; so if Henry Regnery should come to Britain during that month, just let me know, and I will be here to receive him. I have told Lord Crawford that he may come, and the Crawfords tell me that I am to invite him to Balcarres. There he will see the finest private library left in Britain, and probably the best collection of early-Renaissance Italian paintings. Probably I have told you that Bernard Iddings Bell is to visit me here in August. Let me know if I can do any errands for you.

During the latter part of next month, I shall be laird of Kellie Castle's splendors, with three Scots and two imported Italian servants to wait on me hand and foot. Mail addressed to St. Andrews will be forwarded to me.

Miss Barbara White sends me pleasant letters from Rome. She is reluctant to believe that will and work have almost wholly deserted the British race; I am endeavoring to convince her of this melancholy truth.

I have requested *Time and Tide* to send you three successive free copies of that admirable weekly. Any news of the quarterly?[10] . . . You certainly have been travelling, these past few weeks. I see that Regnery has brought out an American edition of Wyndham Lewis' *Rotting Hill*.

My talk on the mind of Burke, at Scarborough, was well received, though I startled some radical parsons by my faith in Providence and my abhorrence of Rousseauistic sentimentality. The archbishop, a bishop, and the dean, not to mention rectors, vicars, and curates, have promised to re-read Burke. Old Scarborough is being uglified by super-cinemas, beach-amusements, and trippers. Good bits remain, all the same. The fine Georgian house in which the Sitwells used to live now is a Sitwell museum, its chief piece the noble Sargent portrait of the Sitwell family upon which Sir Osbert dwells in his memoirs. Downstairs is a vivarium. We were pleased to observe the intense interest in zoological studies displayed by the youth of Scarborough, thereat, until we found that their fascination was solely with snakes swallowing the live little frogs being thrown to them. Nothing charms like morbidity. Sir Robert Peel (in his speech at the opening of the Tamworth Reading Room, for which he was so crushingly denounced by Newman) asserted that the study of the physical sciences "will be a consolation even at the time of death."[11] Perhaps; but not for the man who is dying.

On my way southward to Scarborough, I walked the ninety miles from Edinburgh to Alnwick, in Northumberland, over the desolate Lammermuirs and along the Northumbrian coast—a matter of three days. Many an adventure had I. I saw the noble seventeenth-century house of Yester, the seat of the Marquis of Tweeddale, now disfigured by chicken-runs on its front lawns, in these times of great poverty for great gentlefolk; but the house and its ogival-capped wings are fine still. Making my way through the grand, decaying park, I found out the wreck of Yester Castle, and penetrated to the Goblin Ha' beneath it— the vast subterranean vault where Alexander III met the Knight of Elfland.[12] Then I pushed on into the empty Lammermuirs. Appropriately enough, that evening, as I descended the hills toward the douce old county town of Duns, I beheld a bogle sitting motionless and malevolent by a fence-post, in the misty gloaming—or what indubitably would have been taken for a bogle, not many years syne. I saw Bamburgh Castle, too, now flats; and Alnwick Castle, now a training college, dominated by professors of education worse in character and influence than the most violent of the medieval Percies who were masters here.[13]

Write when you can, Sidney; and let me serve you and our cause, if I may.

Yours,
Russell Kirk

Letter to Henry Regnery

In his initial letter to the conservative publisher, Kirk makes it known that he sees Regnery as a kindred soul in terms of publishing interests and expresses his hope that the two can work together in the future. The two developed a lifelong friendship along with a strong (though occasionally stormy) author-publisher relationship.

June 5, 1952
5 John Street
St. Andrews, Fife

Dear Mr. Regnery,

I hope that you can indeed manage to come to this side of the Atlantic before September. I must go home on September 6 or 7, although I would like to stay some months longer; but Michigan State College pretends to need me. (In point of fact, of course, all universities and colleges in America would be much better off if half their staffs spent their time in vagabondage abroad, instead of bondage at home.) The time of my Rhineland expedition can easily be altered, should you find yourself able to come in July. Here in Fife, I can show you dry rot aplenty; but thus far it is restricted chiefly to the buildings, having infected very few of the people. From the Earl of Crawford, the magnificent virtuoso of the seventeenth-century stamp, to Christie of Durie, the eccentric Scots laird of whom Lord Monboddo was the archetype, the old families of Fife are sound still; and there is much more to be said for the towns than for those of most of Britain.[14] Fife continues a civilized county, though the roofs are coming off the big houses with dismaying velocity.[15] Everyone would be very glad to see you. Would that you could have come during the past fortnight, when I was laird of Kellie Castle, that quaintly beautiful ancient house, and had a host of Caliban-like retainers, Fifers and Italians, to do my bidding. . . .

I shall indeed endeavor to seek out Mr. Schnitzler, when I go to the Rhineland; it is very good of you to suggest it.[16] I speak no word of

German, but no doubt he has the English. I rather dread the idea of my German expedition, what with the thought of the ruin I shall see; but the ruins of war are less dreary than the ruins of apathy and misgovernment which litter Britain.

Just now I am in desperate haste to finish a book on this old gray town of St. Andrews for the firm of Batsford. It will aid in the preservation of the place, I trust. When I get home, I shall set about seeing if I can work into shape any of my literary projects which might suit you. I am mightily flattered that you should be at all interested in seeing my work. My great fat book *The Conservatives' Rout*, on which I have been working for more than three years, is now in the hands of Alfred A. Knopf, to whom I more or less promised it, and I think he will publish it, though his editor in chief was aghast at the length of my manuscript.[17] If it shouldn't suit Alfredus Magnus, however, I shall have it sent on to you. There never has been a book like it, so far as breadth of subject is concerned, whatever its vices may be. The subtitle is *An Account of Conservative Ideas from Burke to Santayana*.

From the inception of your publishing enterprise, I have been a humble admirer of your energy and intelligence, and in deep sympathy with your aims. The Henry Regnery Company has done much good already; and I know it will do a great deal more. I wish you would manage to publish a volume of the letters of my old friend Albert Jay Nock, some day; as you probably know, one of his sons has been collecting his letters with such a book in view. What with the great interest in Nock that *Memoirs of a Superfluous Man* created, I think the volume would pay.

The roof was taken off another ancient house in St. Andrews, today—a pleasant little place by our only surviving medieval gate. The Scots have an accursed custom of taxing houses if they have a roof on them—whether they are empty or not—but of exempting them from taxation if they are roofless. Thus half—really half—of the old houses, great and small, have been demolished since the end of the First World War. Scotland is even more callous than America in such matters; I am sure the very Russians give more thought to historic and architectural tradition. This is the "ding it doun" legacy of Knox. I shall show you decay enough to break your heart, if you come over. But Britain is not beyond redemption yet; and if the remnants of the old order can win through this generation, it may be possible to make England and Scotland better countries than they have been since 1800.

Best wishes.

Yours,
Russell Kirk

Letter to Henry Regnery

July 31, 1952
5 John Street
St. Andrews, Fife
Scotland

Mr. Henry Regnery
Chicago

Dear Mr. Regnery,

Mr. Sidney Gair informs me that probably you will not be able to reach Britain before I leave for America. I'm sorry that we sha'n't meet here; but I count on showing Fife to you when next I am residing in the Kingdom of Fife—during 1953, that is, for I expect to return within a year. I was in Bonn only briefly, and so had no opportunity to pay my respects to your friend there, but I shall be sure to seek him out when next I visit the Rhineland. Canon [Bernard Iddings] Bell will be here with me for four or five days, about the middle of August.

I hope you received my postcard of the Porta Nigra, sent from Trier. Probably you have been there since the war; otherwise I would give you some description of the city now. Despite its terrible wounds, Trier will be beautiful again, and already is cheerful. I was much struck to find under the floor of the basilica a layer of ashes and fragments of wood that, very probably, were left from the burning of the building by the Franks. But the walls of Roman brick have withstood the block-busters better than the Renaissance walls of the electoral palace. Concerts are held daily in St. Simeon's cloister. I think the Liebfrauen the most beautiful church I have seen anywhere. Regnery is a name frequently encountered in the Moselle, I find: at Berncastel, I drank a bottle of wine from a Regnery vineyard.

In my previous letter to you, I mentioned the possibility that I might send the manuscript of my *Conservatives' Rout* to you; and now I am doing just that. Alfred Knopf wanted me to reduce the length of the book drastically, and I intend to do nothing of the sort; so I have requested him to send the typescript to you. It should arrive not many days after this letter. . . .

I shall be grateful for your opinion of my manuscript. Should you think it worth publishing, it would be well if it could be got into shape between September, 1952, and July, 1953, since I am sure to be in Michigan the whole of that period. It is my contribution to our endeavor to conserve the spiritual and intellectual and political tradition of our civilization; and if we are to rescue the modern mind, we must do it very soon. What Matthew Arnold called "an epoch of concentration" is impending, in any case. If we are to make that approaching era a time of enlightened conservatism, rather than an era of stagnant repression, we need to move with decision. The struggle will be decided in the minds of the rising generation—and within that generation, substantially by the minority who have the gift of reason. I do not think we need much fear the decaying "liberalism" of the retiring generation; as Disraeli said, "Prevailing opinions generally are the opinions of the generation that is passing." But we need to state some certitudes for the benefit of the groping new masters of society. More than anyone else in America, Mr. Regnery, you have been doing just this in the books you publish.

It is good to see your first college list; and most impressive it is, as a beginning. I shall do whatever I can, in my small way, to advance the distribution of these books. The course which I teach at Michigan State College, formerly called the history of civilization, now is being reorganized into a course in the "humanities," including Lord knows what not; and it is my belief that this ought to be taught through the use of certain of your College Readings, together with certain Pelican volumes. During the next year, we shall see what can be done about it. I am about to exchange the frock coat of Guizot for the astrologer's robes of Pico della Mirandola.

Cordially,
Russell Kirk
D. Litt.

Letter to Henry Regnery

In December 1952, after considering many possible alternatives, Kirk and Regnery agreed on the title of Kirk's upcoming book: The Conservative Mind.

December 1, 1952
Department of the History of Civilization
Michigan State College
East Lansing, Michigan

Mr. Henry Regnery
President, Henry Regnery Company

Dear Henry,

Your servant is hard at work amending *The Conservative Mind*—for such, pending your approval, I am calling the book. I fear it is going to be difficult to abridge it by fifty pages, as I had hoped; but it will shrink a little, at any rate, and be strengthened here and there. I should be able to return it to you within the week.

Do you plan to make your trip to England soon? If so, and if you are to get to Scotland, you ought to call on some of my friends there, provided you have the time; I have told them that you may make your appearance. Here they are:

Mr. George Scott-Moncrieff
6, James's Court
Edinburgh 1, Scotland

(George, one of the liveliest of Scottish men of letters, dwells in
the building in the Old Town where Boswell, Hume, and Adam Smith
once lived. You would like him immensely.)

Mr. Hew Lorimer
Kellie Castle
Pittenweem, Fife
Scotland

(Hew is one of the best of the Scottish sculptors—probably *the*
best; and his ancient house, Kellie, is in some respects the noblest ancient Scottish mansion remaining. Its plaster ceilings are particularly
fine. Kellie stands on the north side of the Forth, looking down to the
Bass Rock. Hew is a man of great presence, and Mary, his wife, a woman of much charm. They have three remarkable children.)

The Earl and Countess of Crawford and Balcarres
Balcarres
Colinsburgh, Fife
Scotland

(Lord Crawford, the premier earl on the Union Roll, is the glory of the peerage, redolent of what Burke calls "the unbought grace
of life"; and, like his ancestors for many generations, he is a patron
of the arts and a scholar. Lady Crawford, a Cavendish and a Cecil, is
extremely simple and pleasing in manner, and often seems like a girl
of sixteen. The Crawford collection of paintings and of early printed
books is among the best remaining in Britain.)

If you have time in London, you might look up Peter Quennell,
the old-style many-talented man of letters, at present editor of *History*

Today, and for many years editor of *Cornhill.* His recent book, *Spring in Sicily,* might well suit you for the Regnery list; he has no American publisher for it, but would like one. He says that his publisher (Nicholson and Weidenfeld, I think) intends to speak to you about it, when you come over. It is a very good book; I would send you my copy, but it isn't here; I have lent it to I know not who.[18]

I have made the requisite calculations concerning our Burke project. Length may be a difficulty. The Regnery Readings are set in uniform type, aren't they? Basing my calculation on the one I have to hand, the Pico della Mirandola, I find that Burke's *Reflections* will require almost exactly three hundred printed pages; and I do not think it can be satisfactorily abridged; what few passages could be omitted would only injure the sense without saving much space. The *Speech on Conciliation* would occupy some sixty pages, unabridged, but I could reduce this by a third without hurting it. The *Letter to a Noble Lord* would require forty pages, and could not be much reduced. As for the Indian speeches, I think our best course would be to choose Burke's final speech in the impeachment of Hastings (ninth day of the general reply, June 16, 1794); this runs to some fifty printed pages, but could be reduced to forty or less.

All in all, then, should we print the *Reflections,* the *Conciliation,* and the Hastings summary, the volume would run to something close to four hundred pages, including my introduction and notes. Will this be practicable? The *Reflections* then could make a separate fat Regnery Readings volume, and the *Conciliation* and the *Hastings* slim little volumes by themselves, or else a combined volume. We would have included something on three of the four great topics of Burke's career (the fourth being the Economical Reform), and have printed his greatest work in full. What think you of all this? Shall I set to work so soon as I am able? . . .

Don't forget to come to Michigan if you can.

Cordially,
Russell Kirk

Letter to T. S. Eliot

On June 30, 1953, Kirk wrote to T. S. Eliot for the first time, from aboard a ship bound for England. Kirk sought to interest Eliot, a director at the London publisher Faber & Faber, in publishing a British edition of The Conservative Mind.

T. S. S. Canberra
June 30, 1953
off Labrador

Mr. T. S. Eliot
Faber and Faber, Ltd.

Dear Mr. Eliot:

Our friend Mr. Henry Regnery has suggested that I call on you when I am in London, July 13–19. I believe he has sent you a copy of my new book, *The Conservative Mind*. If you have time to see me, a note will reach me in care of B. T. Batsford, Ltd., 4 Fitzharding Street, London W.1. (They are publishing my new *St. Andrews*.)

We have some other friends in common—Bernard Iddings Bell, and the Earl of Crawford, who enjoyed your recent visit to Balcarres, where I have spent many pleasant months. It was good to read that St. Andrews University had made you a doctor of laws. I have the honor to be a doctor of letters of St. Andrews. I am a Michiganian, by the way.

Cordially,
Russell Kirk
I land at Southampton on July 5.

Letter to T. S. Eliot

Kirk handwrote the following letter aboard RMS Queen Elizabeth, *on his way back to the United States after two months in England and Scotland.*

He recounts his first meeting with Eliot at the Edinburgh Festival, where the latter's play The Confidential Clerk *had debuted on August 25 at the Lyceum Theatre.*

R. M. S. Queen Elizabeth
September 10[, 1953]
Off Cherbourg

Dear Mr. Eliot,

Very good it was to talk with you in Edinburgh; and I hope to have you to my stump-country of Mecosta one day, where the life of the Michigan of yesteryear is not wholly departed. I suppose you are off to Geneva now—not so good as it once was, alas, though the streets round about the cathedral still are handsome. Fribourg is my favorite Swiss town.

Henry Regnery writes to me that the sales of *The Conservative Mind* are unabated, praise be; I now feel reasonably sure that we shall get through ten thousand copies by Christmas, which is doing amazingly well, for seven months or a bit more! We are moving toward the six-thousand mark now.

I shall be mightily pleased if Faber and Faber brings out the book. A good-sized English edition would pay[?] your firm, I think, especially if the price can be made less than the American. Let me know if you want that revised last chapter and by what date.[19]

The Regnery people tell me that four copies were sent in error to English journals: to J. E. Morpurgo (for the *Times*), *The Month, The Dublin Review,* and *The Fortnightly.*[20] Perhaps Christopher Hollis got his copy from the House of Commons library.[21] Anyway, they have made sure that these other reviews will not be published until an English edition appears.

I don't think I told you that I once intended to call my book *The Conservative Mind: From Burke to Eliot.* I decided, however, that it would be improper to deal at such length with a thinker whose work is not yet complete; and this was a fortunate decision, as matters are turning out, for it would have been rather embarrassing for you to publish a book with such a title.

The Confidential Clerk has been going through my mind ever since I saw it; and I am deeply impressed with it; but you shall see my opinions, for what they are worth, in the October *Month*.

Lord and Lady Crawford scolded me for not having compelled you to come to stay at Balcarres; but perhaps you have seen them since I left Fife.

More from Michigan. Some day, by the way, I am going to write a critical account of twentieth-century letters called *The Age of Eliot*—and perhaps before long.²² But first I shall probably have to finish my great fat book on the history of humanism (the Greeks onward), *The Humanist Tradition*.²³

Respectfully,
Russell Kirk

Letter to T. S. Eliot

October 21, 1953
237 Valley Court
East Lansing, Michigan

Dear Mr. Eliot,

Very good it will be to have Faber and Faber bring out a separate edition of *The Conservative Mind*. I shall set to work promptly on my revising for it, so that it can be published as soon as possible; various journals appear to be straining at the leash to review it. The reviews are now appearing in the quarterlies in America, and will continue to be printed there until well into next year, of course. Thus far, out of some fifty reviews I have seen, only three are hostile to the book; and only one, that in the *Partisan Review* (by a Hegelian professor of philosophy) deliberately misrepresents it. That is doing very well indeed in our time. Mr. Nisbet, whose book probably has reached you by this time, tells me that I have accomplished what he thought could not be done—

broken through the barrier against conservative books.[24] *Harper's* and the *Atlantic Monthly,* however, have conspicuously ignored *The Conservative Mind.* I was asked to address a good many colleges and associations, on the strength of the book.

I have asked the *Sewanee* people to let me review the Niebuhr book, but haven't heard from them yet; I am anxious to read it.[25] One or two people who have read my book have written to ask me why I make no mention of Niebuhr therein; I may do so in the Faber & Faber edition. In other respects Mr. Niebuhr is a genuine conservative, and very good it is to find him beginning to appreciate Burke. We have also, in America, however, a number of people who pretend to an anxiety for the revival of *conservatism,* by which they mean Hegelianism and the paternal state; they want to capture the word "conservative" for their own purposes, and my book seems to have appeared just at the right moment to have frustrated their efforts. My reviewer in the *Partisan* is a man of this sort, and I am delighted to have vexed him and his.

Probably you have seen my review of *The Confidential Clerk* in *The Month,* by this time—and of *Fotheringhay,* too. I could have done a little better had I possessed a printed text of the play, perhaps, but I listened to it closely, and have tried to catch the essence of it.[26] I look forward to Mr. Dobree's review in the next *Sewanee.*[27]

I hope that you may get to Michigan in the next year; or that we may meet in England or Scotland when I am over, which probably will be next September—and for a year. My best wishes.

Cordially,
Russell Kirk

Letter to E. Victor Milione

Writing on behalf of the newly formed Intercollegiate Society of Individualists (later known as the Intercollegiate Studies Institute), E. Victor Milione (1924–2008) approached Kirk about the possibility of his serving as a speaker on the society's behalf. He also sent Kirk a copy of the first issue of ISI's short-lived flagship periodical, the Individualist. *Kirk's icy rebuke far pre-dates the era when ISI became an organization much more to his liking: one that became and remains conservative rather than libertarian.*

May 24, 1954
Mecosta, Michigan

Mr. Victor Milione, Executive Assistant
Intercollegiate Society of Individualists

Dear Mr. Milione:

It is very good of Mr. Harper of the Foundation for Economic Education to have mentioned me to you, but I am afraid I cannot be of service.[28] At present I am desperately busy with a program of writing; and in the autumn I go abroad for several months. Moreover, I have severed myself from the world of universities; and I am an individualist in this, if in nothing else, that I play a lone hand, and so do not know many people who might be able to do some speaking for you.

And—if you will forgive such an answer to your courteous letter—I am afraid I scarcely see eye to eye with you people, despite my esteem for Mr. Chodorov and Mr. Buckley as persons.[29] On particular issues, we are very close; on philosophical postulates, a great gulf is fixed between us. I never call myself an individualist; and I wish that you people hadn't clutched that dreary ideology to your bosom. Politically, it ends in anarchy; spiritually, it is a hideous solitude. I do not even call myself an "individual"; I hope I am a *person*. I am all in favor of individuality, and all against individualism. The enclosed piece on censorship may suggest some of our differences.[30]

The first number of *The Individualist* shocks me. You might as well choose Marx for your prophet as Cousin.[31] There are several great realities, Cousin notwithstanding, in addition to the individual, and superior to him; and the greatest of them is God. As for your pantheon, if you chose Moses in place of Lao-Tsu, Aristotle in place of Zeno, Pascal in place of Spinoza, Falkland in place of Locke, Dante in place of

Milton, Johnson in place of Smith, Ruskin in place of Mill, Burke in place of Paine, Adams in place of Jefferson, Stephen in place of Spencer, Hawthorne in place of Thoreau, Brownson in place of Emerson, you might succeed in capturing the imagination of the rising generation. You won't otherwise. I am quite willing, however, to consent to the inclusion of my old friend Albert Jay Nock. I think you people really are conservatives in your prejudices, not "individualists"; and you may as well confess it, and get the credit for it.

Mr. Henry Regnery and I are endeavoring to get up a monthly journal intended to preserve the traditional values of our civilization; I enclose a prospectus. If we are to salvage anything from the modern flux, we shall do it through persuasion, not through defiance. I hope for better things from you.

Respectfully,
Russell Kirk

Letter to B. E. Hutchinson

Bernard Edwin Hutchinson (1888–1961) was a longtime automotive executive at Maxwell Motor Company and Chrysler Corporation. Legendary for his superb skills in corporate finance and his likeable, easygoing manner, he made Kirk's acquaintance during the mid-1950s. For his part, Kirk hoped to interest Hutchinson in helping to fund the Conservative Review, *but nothing came of this endeavor.*

July 10, 1954

Dear Mr. Hutchinson,

I have been about the country speechifying, but I haven't gotten to Detroit yet. Miss Owtram, it turns out, won't be coming until August; so perhaps we can come down to see you sometime that month, or in September.[32] I have finished my book *A Program for Conservatives*, which will be published this fall.

Here's a recent piece of mine you may not have seen. Possibly you saw my "Debacle of the Fabians" in the last number of the *Freeman*, before it underwent its metamorphosis—an article written at the suggestion of our friend Dr. Leo Wolman.[33] Incidentally, Mr. Regnery and I omitted Wolman, Garrett, and others from our list of possible contributors to the journal not because of any hostility, but because we thought it might seem presumptuous, since they were already contributing to the *Freeman*. Regnery is publishing a good book by Mr. Garrett in the spring, I believe.[34]

I have little hope for the metamorphosed *Freeman*, and am sorry the previous regime went under, just as they were getting into stride again. Mr. Frank Chodorov is a crotchety old anarchist, quite impractical, and can influence no one but a small coterie, *entre nous*.[35]

We are going forward with plans for *The Conservative Review*, our present title, and we hope to bring out the first number late in September. I should be able to send you a tentative table of contents before long.

I must turn my hand soon to my book on academic freedom. Life at Mecosta is very pleasant now, and everything is very green, including my ten thousand little new trees. My telephone here is No. 8. I hope to see you soon.

Cordially,
Russell Kirk

Letter to T. S. Eliot

Handwritten from Balcarres, the home of Kirk's friends the Earl and Countess of Crawford, the following letter to Eliot has the tone of a respectful man who is entirely at ease in his friendship with the great poet.

January 4, 1955
Royal British Hotel
Perth

Dear Mr. Eliot,
I shan't get down to London until almost the end of this month; I shall let you know the date in advance, though. What plans have you for a foreign expedition? It would be rather splendid to be stoned in Cyprus.[36] There's glory for you.

My review of *The Heresy of Democracy* is to appear in *The Month* soon.[37] I'm to discuss the book with Lord Percy when I'm in London. I hope Henry Regnery publishes it.

Lord and Lady Crawford hope you will come up to stay in Balcarres whenever you can contrive it. They have been left servantless recently: Lady Crawford washes the dishes, Lord Crawford wipes them, and Dr. Kirk carries them to the cupboard. The end of an old song.

A Program for Conservatives, though it hasn't yet got so much attention as Henry Regnery Company had hoped for, has sold six thousand copies in eleven weeks and at present is selling better than before. *Academic Freedom* will appear in March.

I think the Regnery Company has sent you a copy of Richard Weaver's *Ethics of Rhetoric.* I am taking the liberty of suggesting that the University of Chicago Press send you a copy of his *Ideas Have Consequences* (not Weaver's title—a different title in England would be agreeable to him, I think), of which seven or eight thousand copies were sold in 1949. Possibly Cambridge U. Press distributed a handful of copies in England— I'm not sure. I'm suggesting to Henry Regnery that he include *Ideas Have Consequences* in his revised and enlarged Gateway Series of paperbacks.

More presently. I may be reached at Balcarres.

Cordially,
Russell Kirk

Letter to T. S. Eliot

Kirk wrote the following letter after returning home to Mecosta from an early spring journey to the United Kingdom, where he had lunched with Eliot in London.

April 17, 1955

Dear Mr. Eliot,

Here's a recent piece of mine in which you will find yourself pictured in good company.

Academic Freedom is doing very well, though Robert Hutchins pouts and mutters that he may sue for libel—though he says he hasn't read the book.[38] I wish I could judge books for libel without bothering to read them. The first printing was sold out in ten days, and we now have eight thousand copies in print. There has been no adverse review as yet. I hope a copy has reached you. Only a small part of the book is concerned with Mr. Couch's case at Chicago.

Have you had any time to think about *A Program for Conservatives*?[39] The book continues to move along steadily here, and should eventually catch up with *The Conservative Mind*. I see the latter has infuriated Mr. R. J. White, at Cambridge—simply, I suspect, because I forgot to include his anthology *The Conservative Tradition* in my bibliography. To judge by his previous writings, he really agrees with me in everything, including the relation of theology to politics. A world of vanities.

I sent you a note just before I sailed, or intended to—but I put it, inadvertently, into an envelope addressed to Mr. Colin Clark, who returned it to me. Perhaps I sent you his note. It was of no consequence.

Mr. Couch hopes you can write the piece on tradition for *Collier's Encyclopedia*. He would like to get it not later than August, if possible—earlier would be better. About 2,000–2,500 words would be a good length. Mr. Couch would like you to take up European tradition, if that suits you, while I would deal chiefly with American.[40] He probably would use the pieces a little later in *Collier's Yearbook*, also. Crowell-Collier pays a decent honorarium. If you don't feel like undertaking this, I can write to Gabriel Marcel to see if he will take pen in hand.

I hope you're feeling pretty well. I thought you looked better when last we lunched together than at any time I had seen you before. I expect to call on Canon Bell in a few days.

Prospects for the projected conservative review are fairly bright just now. What think you of *The Modern Review* as a title?

More soon. Many thanks, again, for your kindnesses.

Cordially,
Russell Kirk

Letter to Felix Morley

One of the founders of the conservative weekly Human Events, *Morley (1894–1982) was a limited-government, antiwar constitutionalist whose views were close to Kirk's own. He contributed articles to several early issues of* Modern Age, *including the very first, and served on the periodical's editorial board.*

June 9, 1955

Dear Mr. Morley,

For some months, I have been meaning to write to you about *The Conservative Review*, the bi-monthly journal that Mr. Henry Regnery and I have been planning to publish. Perhaps you have seen my tentative prospectus; but I enclose a copy, anyway. A revised prospectus and a table of contents of the sample issue will be ready soon.

As an old admirer of yours and a reader of your books and articles, I have hoped to persuade you to be one of our editorial advisors, if we achieve regular publication. You would be in good company: Rudolf Allers, Bernard Iddings Bell, Brainard Cheney, Kenneth Colegrove, Leo R. Ward, Eliseo Vivas, Richard Weaver, Lynn Harold Hough, Donald Davidson, Nicholas Joost, Wilhelm Roepke, Eugene Davidson, Anthony Harrigan, Frederick Wilhelmsen, John Lukacs, Francis Graham Wilson, W. T. Couch, Douglas Bush, and Ross Hoffman. I've selected people from various disciplines, religious affiliations, and sections of the country. We hope that the advisors will find some good people to write for the journal, and will criticize our general policies. I hope that you might find time to advise us especially on foreign relations and the like. We shall be grateful if you feel able to help us.

Just now I am endeavoring to collect three or four thousand dollars to pay for printing and distributing the sample issue, which we would publish in September. Then we would appeal for support on the strength of that accomplishment. Two or three small foundations may give us five hundred dollars apiece, and the rest I hope to obtain in contributions of $100-$500 from individuals. I have made a beginning. I do all the work, and Mr. Henry Regnery will bear much of the overhead. I have my materials on hand for the sample issue, and a good many pieces which, I hope, will appear in subsequent issues. If you know of anyone who might give us a little money toward the undertaking, I should be grateful for the information.

Mr. Brainard Cheney has written for us a very good piece on the potential conservatism in the Democratic party. Can you suggest anyone who might write a similar article on the Republicans? I may try Richard Weaver.

We hope, of course, to print things by you from time to time. Is there any book which we might persuade you to review for the sample number?

I shall be here at Mecosta for the whole summer, except for brief sorties. If you should get to Michigan, I hope you will come over to visit me in my stump-country. We always have plenty of room. . . .

Here are some recent pieces of mine. Please don't bother to return them. I hope to hear from you.

Respectfully,
Russell Kirk

Letter to W. T. Couch

In the following letter, Kirk speaks of recent articles he has written for Collier's Year Book, *for which Couch was editorial director.*

July 11, 1955
Mr. W. T. Couch
Crowell-Collier Company

Dear Bill,

I think my piece on Conservatism from the *Year Book* has been adapted very well to the *National Encyclopedia,* and I have made no change therein, except to insert two commas. I return it herewith.

Here, too, is my piece on Censorship, with which I have taken considerable pains. I'm glad to be able to get it to you before the deadline, anyway. . . .

Pacific Spectator wants me to write for them a piece of 4,500 words about "The American Intellectual."[41] I hope to make it principally an essay in definition, tracing the history of the word, its usage in America, etc. I don't suppose they'll publish it before next winter. If you can use anything of the sort in either encyclopedia or yearbook, you might let me know, for I could adapt it.

I think that Bill Buckley has got much of his hostility toward freedom of expression from Willmoore Kendall, but that he has in part misunderstood Kendall, who seems to be working his way toward something deeper.[42] Kendall's devotion to Rousseau, however, attaches to him the concept of The General Will, and therefore he is always in peril of subscribing to what Tocqueville calls democratic despotism. Buckley is amazingly inconsistent in the matter; he says, for instance, that there should be no prohibition of the sale of narcotics, because that would interfere with "freedom of choice."

Mr. Mullendore, one of the chief supporters of the *Freeman*, has sent me a hundred dollars toward the trial number of the *Conservative Review*.[43] I am inclined to think that some men of means will come over to a more intelligent journal once they see it in print. A Texan is approaching Roy Cullen and others on our behalf.

More soon.

Yours,

Russell Kirk

[P.S.] Mr. Anthony Kerrigan, Fine Arts editor of the *American Peoples Encyclopedia,* 179 North Michigan Avenue, Chicago 1, would like to write an encyclopedia-piece on Spanish literature—or a yearbook piece. He is an accomplished translator (his Unamuno's short stories will be published by Regnery this fall) and knows much about the subject. He doesn't want to do it for his own encyclopedia because he already has a good man doing it there. Therefore he has suggested that I inquire of you whether you would be interested in having him do it for *Collier's Year Book,* since you have no such entry at present. You might let him know, if you like the idea. I am doing "Burke" for them, by the way.

Letter to William F. Buckley Sr.

Will Buckley, father of National Review *founder William F. Buckley Jr., wrote to invite Kirk to a symposium of conservative figures at the Buckley home in Sharon, Connecticut. He had in mind an event in which several debates would take place, with Kirk tentatively scheduled to take on Willmoore Kendall. Not long after this letter was written, Kirk hosted Will Buckley's famous son at his home in Mecosta and agreed to write a column for* National Review, *which began publication in November 1955.*

July 13, 1955
Mecosta, Michigan

Dear Mr. Buckley,

It is an honor to have your letter of July 11. I enclose some recent pieces of mine, by way of thanks.

Very good it would be to visit Sharon and talk with you all; but I have no money, and—to make an Irish bull—less time. I shall have to husband my resources for my expedition to the American Political Science Association, in Denver, early in September, where I am to fight the good fight for American liberties and American justice. Last year, when I addressed the same body, a great wave of "liberal" execration burst upon me. It is amusing, while waging such battles on the frontier at my own expense, to be knifed in the back by such chairborne condottieri as Frank Meyer and Frank Chodorov.[44]

Please give my friends Mr. Burnham, Mr. Schlamm, and Mr. Kendall my best wishes. I am rather surprised that you juxtaposed me with Mr. Kendall, since I was his principal sympathizer and defender in a recent conference at Buck Hill Falls. I never have called myself a New Conservative, and no one ever has called me that to my face.

I have been meaning to write to your son, but have been trapped by a multitude of literary obligations. I wanted to suggest that he see a friend of mine, Mr. Lewis Engel, Wilton, Connecticut, about support for his weekly magazine. Mr. Engel, at one time, at least, would have put up money for just such an undertaking. It would do no harm for

Bill to write to him or call on him. Ironically enough, all this silly business about my debate with Schlesinger at Harvard was caused by my defending *McCarthy and His Enemies*! But the story is too complex to be worth recounting here. A mad world, my masters. I am amused to find myself denounced in the current number of *Reporter*, by Schlesinger, as a "raging Manchesterian," and by Peter Viereck, in the current *Antioch Review*, for venturing to write about politics at all.[45]

Best wishes for your conference; I hope it is most fruitful. My apologies for not being able to come.

Respectfully,
Russell Kirk

P.S. Please tell your son, if you see him soon, that I shall be very glad to entertain him at Mecosta whenever he can come. There are no trains or busses to this heart of darkness, but there are busses from Lansing to Mt. Pleasant, where I could arrange to have him met.

Letter to T. S. Eliot

Writing less than a month after the appearance of the first issue of William F. Buckley Jr.'s National Review, *Kirk confides to Eliot about the need for intelligent magazine journalism in America, among other matters.*

December 22, 1955

Dear Mr. Eliot,

Your servant now plans to cross over to England in June, and to be abroad for the summer; so probably we shall meet next in London. I hope to have the *Conservative Review* well launched by that time. If all goes well, despite our eleventh-hour obstacles we shall go to press next month.[46]

Mr. Buckley is very free with his use of people's names; you're fortunate that you didn't appear on the masthead of the *National Review*.[47] I have told him to take my name off, though I'll write occasionally for the magazine. I don't think he consulted Roepke at all, or even knows Roepke's address—which is Geneva, not Zurich. I am afraid there may be too much Yale undergraduate spirit in the *National Review*. But we could use some weeklies like the *Spectator* or *Time and Tide* in this country, for our journalism certainly is far gone in decay. . . .

Mr. Henry Ford II has substantially disavowed Mr. Hutchins now.[48] Clinton Rossiter seems to be much embarrassed nowadays at his sinecure with the Fund for the Republic. The notorious bibliography on communism had at least his nominal approval.[49] He says this is his last academic WPA. The Ford Foundation has loosed a golden shower upon the universities and colleges to atone for its sins. And our university presidents are so many Danaes. I go to preach unto them in St. Louis at the convention of the Association of American Colleges next month. May I quote you on the moral responsibilities of teachers, and on the alleged line of demarcation between thinking and being?

I have a finger in the practical politics of Michigan nowadays. Walter Reuther and the CIO will have converted this state into a kind of labor dictatorship, within three or four years, if the dull people who still have money don't oppose them intelligently; and then they will proceed to extend their domination to the nation.[50] Events are moving very rapidly. The old political system of Michigan, with its cast of what Brownson called "territorial democracy," is being swept away by deliberate consolidation. The legislature is manipulated by the PAC and the NEA.[51] In my role as the last bonnet laird of the stump-country, I am trying to drive some sense into the heads of the Detroit industrialists who are the only surviving counterpoint to the strength of the union leaders.

William McGovern and I are thinking of writing, jointly, a book on conservative foreign policy.

I'm sending you copies of my little Gateway editions of Brownson and Gentz.[52] All in all, I soon will have written introductions to twenty volumes in that series.

Faber and Faber never have sent me or the Regnery Company any remittance for royalties on *The Conservative Mind*, nor any report thereof, though fifteen months have passed since publication. Do you know if there will be a reckoning at the end of this year? I suppose that a few hundred dollars are due me, and most handy that sum would be to me at the moment.

More presently. I hope that the London winter won't send you to the clinic. I hope that the Crawfords will entice you to Balcarres while I'm in Fife; I'll be at Balcarres and Kellie and Durie for some weeks early next summer, probably.

Cordially,
Russell Kirk

Letter to Brainard Cheney

Typing on Conservative Review *letterhead, Kirk laments to Cheney that his long-planned-for quarterly has yet to be launched, largely due to lack of sufficient funding.*

April 20, 1956

Dear Lon,

It is a long time since I have written to you. I was very sorry to learn that you had to return so suddenly from Rome, especially with such a cause. I suppose you have been mightily busy ever since you got back.

The *Review* hangs fire still; and since it appears that we won't be able to get out the trial number until fall, I return your manuscript to you, in the hope that your article, now so timely, can be published somewhere else before the election. I should have liked to print it. I'm sorry, though, to have held it so long in vain.

We now are seeking university or college sponsorship for the *Review*, which would make it easier for certain foundations to pour money into the venture. I hope something comes of our negotiations.

What news of your novel? If your agent hasn't accomplished anything yet, would you let me send the copy I still have here in my files to Henry Regnery? Or should I return that carbon-manuscript to you?

I'm still heavy-laden with work. On June 24, Glenn and Fay and I fly to Ireland, and proceed to Scotland and to Spain. We'll be back early in September. Is there any chance of your paying another visit to Mecosta in June or September, or earlier or later? My new library, converted from a brick factory, will be completed soon; and my lake-cottage (on Lake Mecosta, not Blue Lake) will be ready for you and Fanny to occupy it.

John Crowe Ransom (I stopped at Kenyon recently) tells me there is to be a formal conference of the Fugitives at Vanderbilt soon—paid for by the Rockefeller Foundation, I believe!

Certain people in the American Library Association are trying to get my articles excluded, in future, from *Collier's Year Book* and *Encyclopedia*. If Fanny has the time—and her librarian friends, too—it might do no harm for them to send P. F. Collier Company some commendation of my articles. The one on "Colleges and Universities" is under fire from the educational imperialists. . . .

My Aunt Fay may possibly get down to Nashville and Columbia this spring, on her way to visit my sister. I doubt if I will. Fay has had her gall-bladder removed, and is still rather ill from it.

Compliments to Fanny. More presently.

Yours,
Russell

Letter to Herbert Hoover

During the 1950s, Kirk corresponded periodically with Herbert Hoover and mailed the former president his books as they were published.

January 3, 1957
Mecosta, Michigan

Dear Mr. Hoover,

It was an honor and a pleasure to receive your note in re my *Beyond the Dreams of Avarice*, last May. I have been abroad since then, most of the time, but am now back hard at work. Among other things, I am busy helping to organize the Association for Rural Education, to resist the centralizers.

I have followed the campaign to make effective the recommendations of your Hoover Commission, and it is heartening to see some recommendations taking on form. If only the whole could become reality! But I see not one sign of a directing intelligence in Washington at present. Subsidizing everybody in every country seems to be the present administration's remedy for all the discontents of the age; and the failure will be swift and disastrous. Intelligence will tell in the long run, even in a university, someone said at the beginning of this century; and it is quite as true of national polity; but by that time. . . .[53]

In April and May, I shall be giving some lectures in Long Island for eight weeks; and I cherish a hope that it may be possible for us to meet sometime during that period. I hesitate to intrude upon a gentleman so industrious as you are, however, feeling rather like Alice: "Don't keep him waiting, child, for his time is worth a thousand pounds a minute."

Although I spend most of my time on my desolate acres here in Mecosta, I am nominally research professor of politics, Long Island University. At Post College, Long Island University, we are endeavoring to establish an intelligent Institute of Politics, and we hope to find the funds to make Professor Kenneth Colegrove the head of this Institute.[54] So I am looking for some foundation or individual who might give ten thousand dollars for a year to make Professor Colegrove's initial appointment possible. Do you happen to know of anyone who might help?

Mr. Henry Regnery and I are planning to publish a quarterly review, beginning this spring. Possibly you may find the time to write something for us, when we get underway; or we might reprint one of your speeches.

In the spring, Devin-Adair will publish my little book *The Intelligent Woman's Guide to Conservatism*, a species of retort against Bernard Shaw. I shall see that a copy is sent to you.

Respectfully,
Russell Kirk

Letter to T. S. Eliot

In a letter written on the letterhead of his long-hoped-for periodical, the Conservative Review, *Kirk encouraged Eliot to prepare for the* Review's *long-awaited first issue, which would appear soon. In reality, the periodical appeared somewhat later in the year under a different name,* Modern Age. *Kirk also fills in his friend on his doings as a visiting professor at C. W. Post College and other matters.*

January 15, 1957

Dear Mr. Eliot,

Our *Review*, after many wearisome delays, now will achieve publication of its first number—as a quarterly—this spring. I think you may find much to approve in it. Essays by Donald Davidson and Frederick Wilhelmsen may be especially interesting to you.[55]

Once upon a time there was a professor of natural history at St. Andrews who was a free man. For the professorship was endowed—this was about 1870—but the subject simply did not fit into any student's course of study in those days. So at the commencement of each term, the professor appeared in his appointed lecture-room; and no students came; so the professor went away to Egypt, annually, for the rest of the year. This went on for decades. At last some waggish students became aware of the professor's sinecure, and a hundred of them appeared for his lecture—which he delivered undisturbed, on a most abstruse topic. They came the second day; and again he lectured, on a more abstruse and utterly unrelated topic of natural science. And they came the third day; and once more he lectured, as learnedly and spontaneously as before, and on a subject even more bewildering. On the fourth day, no students appeared, and the professor went off to Egypt, and his life passed pleasantly away without further annoyance. Well, my sinecure at Long Island is like that, though I do have to give lectures there for eight weeks, in April and May, to air-force personnel. My chief contribution to the success of Post College, Long Island University, I suspect, is to cast an aura of conservatism about the place: trustees and benefactors are astounded, and sometimes delighted, to encounter a professor in America who does not take it for his appointed task to gnaw at the foundations of society.

Lord Crawford should arrive in New York soon now; he fears he won't have time to penetrate to these northern fastnesses, for the "leisurely" schedule of lecturing arranged by his hosts is leisurely only as that word is abused in New York and Chicago.[56] I shall go down to Chicago to hear him speak, however.

Last week I went to Washington to talk with Huntington Cairns about his American All Souls, which he tentatively calls a "residence in humanities."[57] I believe he has discussed the project with you. Very promising it is. He doesn't know who to choose for master or principal. Stanley Pargellis tells him he can't find the books for the library, but I am inclined to think that they still can be scraped up, with some difficulty.

The ice lies thick on our lakes, and my uncle caught thirty-five bluegills through that ice this day, and could have caught a hundred. A bear makes tracks in the snow about my lake cabin; and the beaver have dammed the stream scarcely more than a hundred yards distant from it. I shall be up here without interruption, writing books, for some two months.

Do you know Flannery O'Connor's recent book of short stories, *A Good Man Is Hard to Find?* Very good, and terrifying.[58] I don't know whether it has been published in Britain. Harcourt, Brace, publishes it here. And have you seen Geoffrey Wagner's novel *The Dispossessed?* Also very good, and terrifying. Probably it has been published in England; Devin-Adair has it here.

How have you been? I shall be coming over in June, if all goes well, and ought to be able to call on you in September, if not before. Then I'm off for Syracuse, to moon about among the ruins. They say the movie people are growing fond of Syracuse, accursed spite.[59]

Best wishes for 1957 to you; and many thanks for the handsome Christmas card.

Cordially,
Russell Kirk

P. S. I haven't forgot about that little book on education you suggested I might write.

Roy Campbell has suffered some sort of stroke, I hear, and is in a bad way.

Letter to T. S. Eliot

May 20, 1958

Dear Mr. Eliot,

Your servant has been giving lectures about you, particularly with reference to *On Poetry and Poets*. Most recently I spoke to the philosophy society at the University of Chicago, on "T. S. Eliot and the Restoration of Norms," and thoroughly bewildered most of them. The vocabularies of pragmatism and logical positivism can't cope with Virgil.

By the way, doubtless you have seen the Roman altar, under the high altar at Santa Maria Ara Coeli, said to have been erected by Augustus to the unknown god to be born in his reign, in accordance with the prophecy of Virgil. The Franciscan friar who showed it to me, and who had studied at Ascot, said in broken English that "it is only what you call a myth, of course; it is not so." Rationalism on the Capitoline. The friar was nervous about showing us the celebrated Bambino there, but we were properly respectful, much to his relief, and did not ask him if it was but a myth. The Bambino is supposed to have been carved by angels in the first century; but, though it may be ancient, in its present state of carving it cannot be earlier than the sixteenth century, if indeed so old.

I find that the American typesetter (and American typesetters, bad though they are, generally seem to be better than English typesetters nowadays) made a blunder on p. 207 of the American edition of *On Poetry and Poets*, and quotes Johnson thus:

"a barren strand,
A pretty fortress, and a dubious hand."[60]

This is rather like the celebrated case of a misprint in a volume of Scott, which produced the celebrated archaic word "andwere," much discussed in *Notes & Queries,* and generally concluded to ban an archaic form of "handware," or armour for the hands. As a matter of fact, what Scott wrote was "and were . . ."; the printer did the rest.

I don't know whether the last number of *Modern Age* reached you; I'm sending a copy under separate cover, anyway. In it you will find an interesting article by Thomas Molnar, "Intellectuals, Experts, and the Classless Society."[61] Mr. Molnar, a Belgian-Hungarian now living in New York, spent most of the war in Dachau and Buchenwald concentration camps, a topic on which he is very interesting. He has a first-rate mind, and is writing a book on the intellectuals, and another on "The Future of Education."[62] He will be in London early next month, and I have suggested that he call on you, if you are to be in town. I never have bothered you with any letter of commendation before, but I mention Molnar because you would find him worth talking to, and because he would like to discuss with you the future of the higher learning.

I hope you have been well; and that I may see you in the autumn.

Cordially,

Russell Kirk

Letter to W. T. Couch

July 14, 1959

Dear Bill,

Many thanks for the information about the *Chicago Review,* Chancellor Kimpton, and the *Saturday Review.*[63] Perhaps I can write something about the whole question; I will think about it. I have known for some time that there were strong objections against the nihilistic and pornographic tone of the *Chicago Review,* and that Mr. Kimpton was disturbed at all this. He has been saying some good things lately, and I have some of his speeches on hand. I may write a piece about him for *National Review.*

For months—more than a year, indeed—Norman Cousins kept a piece of mine entitled "The Common Inheritance of America and Europe," protesting that he wished very much to publish my work.[64] He paid me for it, and set it in type. Then, when it was ready to appear, he wrote to me urging me to delete all the references to Christianity. This would have been historical falsification, and of course I wouldn't do it—though I said I was willing to add a footnote remarking that I did not attribute to Christianity an *exclusive* possession of the merits and ideas I described. I got no answer to this, and the piece never was published; only a fortnight ago, with difficulty, I extracted from the offices of *Saturday Review* galleys of my article, so that I might publish it elsewhere.[65] Apparently they threw away the manuscript. So much for their far-ranging liberality of opinion.

More of these matters another time.

Mr. Herbert Hoover seems to have removed the name of Eugene Davidson from his list of possible directors of the Hoover Institution, I am sorry to report. I have been giving him some more advice on particular candidates. Your name still stands, at least alphabetically, at the head of the list.

It is good to learn that matters go smoothly just now in the editorship of *Collier's Encyclopedia*.

For my part, I am having most serious troubles with *Modern Age;* indeed, I have sent Henry Regnery my resignation as editor. What will come of this, I cannot predict just now. But if you could find time to send Henry a note on the general subject, it might do considerable good.

The trouble, in essence, is this: that curious creature David Collier has gained an ascendency over Henry Regnery, and Collier seems to aspire to be editor of *Modern Age,* in name, in fact, or both. I should be delighted to turn over the editorship to any reasonably competent person, but Collier is not such a man.[66] He is violently anti-Jewish (believing in the *Protocols of Zion*), badly educated in a social-science way (though with a doctor's degree from Northwestern), given to hysteria, and possessed of a passion of petty intrigue. Henry has a taste for oddities—which does little mischief, so long as those oddities are not invested with power. As I needn't tell you, Henry has fits and starts of admiring and detesting people, and I am the only person closely associated with him and his firm whose connection goes back so far as seven years.

Collier repeatedly has tried to intervene in the editorial policies of the magazine, though he is supposed to be only business-manager. His most recent act was to remove from the summer number of the magazine, without informing me at all, Hilaire du Berrier's article on Viet Nam, and to substitute something else, an article I never had seen. Collier intervenes simply for the sake of grasping power, primarily, but he also hates anything favorable to France, as Hilaire du Berrier's piece is, in some incidental degree: for the French cooperate with the Israelis in the attack on Egypt, and all Arabs are perfect—because they hate Jews. Therefore nothing by anyone who ever has said anything in defense of France must be published in *Modern Age*—such is Collier's chain of reasoning.

Now Henry sustained Collier in this—Henry notifying me, indeed, of what had happened, because Collier did not condescend even to mention the matter to me. Henry added in his letter that the magazine seemed to him to be getting progressively poorer, and that editorial direction hereafter ought to be in the hands of a committee—although I (Russell Kirk) still would be nominally editor, would do all the editorial work, and would take public responsibility—without salary, of course, as before.

Now no man in his right senses would remain editor under such conditions; yet Henry seems surprised that I resigned, and asks me to reconsider. I may add here that it is quite impracticable to form a committee to determine what goes into the magazine, since I do not reside in Chicago, and since both Henry and I are very busy men. My editorial decisions must be made fairly swiftly, and manuscripts cannot be passed about for months among members of a committee, and sometimes lost.

So I think it might do some good if you could write Henry a note about these matters: (1) whether you think *Modern Age* has been declining in interest and influence; (2) what, in the nature of things, must be the function and responsibilities of an editor; (3) your opinion of du Berrier on Viet Nam.

More before long. Compliments to Elizabeth.

Yours,
Russell

Letter to Henry Regnery

The following letter was written after a telephone call to Regnery in which Kirk resigned as editor of Modern Age *because of what he deemed intolerable interference by his managing editor, David Collier. Tensions had been simmering between the key editorial figures at the quarterly almost from its launch, with Kirk working from his office in Mecosta and Collier working a few feet away from Henry Regnery at the publisher's Chicago headquarters. As executive director of the Foundation for Foreign Affairs, which provided sponsoring support of* Modern Age, *Collier insisted on exercising editorial control over any articles dealing with international relations, a stance that Kirk found intolerable. Below, Kirk crisply clears the air with Regnery about the future of* Modern Age *and his own role in it.*

August 8, 1959

Mr. Henry Regnery
Rockywold
Ashland, New Hampshire

Dear Henry,

I think it would be best for us not to confer until I return from abroad—that is, in January. Meanwhile, you can think about our problems from time to time, and decide whether to seek a new editor, or else a new managing-editor-cum-business-manager. You cannot possibly retain both the present ones. If, when I return, David Collier has anything whatever to do with *Modern Age,* I cannot have anything to do with it—as editor, editorial advisor, or contributor.

In order that you may not be left with nothing to publish meanwhile, I am preparing for you two complete issues of *Modern Age;* and you are sure to approve of them. I enclose a table of contents of the next (winter) number. I will send you the manuscripts and everything else necessary for both issues before this month is out. These will be sent to you personally, at Chicago. With Collier I will have no communication.

Now in return for my doing this work, may I ask the following things of you, as favors?

(1) That I be *not* listed as editor in either of these issues. I do not desire to be held publicly responsible for a periodical over which I have no effective control.

(2) That Collier *not* be listed by his self-conferred titles of "Publisher and Associate Editor"; nor yet as editor. I do not desire him to have the credit for my work. Perhaps you could list yourself as editor; otherwise, Van Wissink, as assistant or acting editor. [67]

(3) That there be no bowdlerizing or re-writing of the articles which I send you. Collier has tried his hand at this before. If I am to take the moral responsibility in the eyes of the contributors, I must be assured that their work will not be tampered with. I will take pains that everything is in apple-pie order for the printer, aside from Van Wissink's necessary typographical notations.

(4) That Hilaire du Berrier's lively article on Viet Nam be printed in our winter number. By this time, doubtless, you have Couch's opinion of du Berrier.[68] Du Berrier is a courageous—physically and intellectually courageous—journalist, with a record of heroism. From other sources, I have hearty endorsements of him. I know something of the subject of which he writes—more than that ass Collier does. I enclose a copy of du Berrier's latest newsletter. Collier demands, snarlingly, articles which will rouse discussion; and when I supply one, he suppresses it. Further, du Berrier is to be paid $150 for his article.[69]

(5) That Curtis Cate's article "Integration in Algeria," one of the best pieces ever sent to us, be printed in our winter number, if Collier excludes it from the fall number; he already excluded it from the summer number, in which it was supposed to appear.[70]

(6) That the poems on hand and in Van Wissink's files be printed, as space allows, in both numbers. Although space was available for the two short and very good poems I had scheduled, as a minimum, for our summer issue, Van Wissink excluded them, presumably on Collier's orders.

If I can secure these favors from you, there may be some point to our meeting in January; if not, it would be vain for us to discuss the future of *Modern Age* together.

I shall see that sufficient book-reviews are included with the manuscripts or are sent to you by the reviewers before publication-dates.

Yours sincerely,
Russell Kirk

Letter to Henry Regnery

Several weeks after submitting his resignation from the editorship of Modern Age *to Regnery, Kirk wrote the following letter to his friend and publisher to clear the air about his experiences working with David Collier. Throughout this letter runs a faint but discernible strain of forlorn hope: that Kirk would yet be willing to again serve as editor of* Modern Age *if Collier were no longer associated with the periodical.*

August 27, 1959

Dear Henry,

I fear that we will not be able to meet in England. I don't sail until September 9, and will go first to Ireland, and won't arrive in London, presumably, until after you have left there. About October 7, I will arrive at Durie, Leven, Fife, Scotland, where I should be addressed for the following month or so. . . .

In a few days, I will send you the manuscripts for the winter numbers of *Modern Age*, completely in order. I may be able to send you the numbers for the spring number, too, before I go. These will be strong numbers. Don't allow Collier to ruin them, and permanently offend some of our best contributors, by throwing the manuscripts into his wastebasket or bowdlerizing them.

You suggest that *Modern Age* might be much improved by having someone in Chicago competent to handle day-to-day decisions and technical matters. Quite right! This is what I have been urging you since before we embarked upon the magazine. With a competent managing editor, any person in whom I could feel confidence, few of our difficulties would arise. But Collier has regularly refused to allow us to have a managing editor, fearing that his own authority might be diminished: instead, he has hired a string of office-boys, at whom he can scream several times a day.

One reasonably competent man or woman, with any sort of experience in proofreading, advertising, and circulation, could do a better work than Collier and all his crew. Collier is unable himself to write or rewrite a complex-compound sentence without making errors of syntax and punctuation.

As for an editorial committee to determine the contents of the magazine, I already have two committees, members of which I frequently consult: my committee of editorial advisors, and our steering committee. I am no Organization Man, to be committeed to death. I am always glad to have the recommendations and remonstrances of Henry Regnery and Charles Lee, though you have not found time these past two years to send me many. But why do you need some grand new committee to undertake that? I have always sent Collier and his people the manuscripts of each issue about three months in advance; apparently Collier has taken care not to show you anything until the magazine is almost ready for printing and binding. To try to have four or five people read and judge all the manuscripts submitted to me is simply silly: you and Charles, at least, are very busy men, and the manuscripts would be lost or mislaid from time to time, and many of them wouldn't get properly read for months, badly injuring the management of the review. I take it that this whole notion is some project of Collier's designed to increase his own power, he being in Chicago and able to wheedle the members of the projected committee. . . .

I have refrained from telling you, over the past two years, of his incessant silliness and obstruction, which has done us mischief with contributors, potential advertisers, and some foundations. Let me give you just two small examples now, however, to suggest the impossibility of my continuing to be editor if he were left in a position of authority.

(1) I had published two lengthy manuscripts by Harry Elmer Barnes; he sent Collier a third manuscript. Without consulting me, Collier mailed this on to me with a carbon-copy of his letter to Barnes: "I have instructed Kirk to publish this article as soon as possible." I had no space for it and cannot satisfy everyone who has a piece to print in *Modern Age*. If I am editor, Collier is not; if I am, Collier is not. He has caused much confusion by such tactics with our contributors.

(2) Lyle Munson, The Bookmailer, kindly offered to advertise in our pages. He had his advertising-agent, a person with a Jewish or quasi-Jewish name, write to us.[71] "We can't do business with that *Jew!*" Collier snarled at me. We didn't.

In short, if you want Collier around, you can't have Russell Kirk associated with you.

Apropos of the du Berrier article on Viet Nam, du Berrier's general thesis now has been sustained by a series of articles in the *New York World-Telegram*, by their special correspondent; and by a Congressional investigating sub-committee. I think some of the criticisms of du Berrier's approach and vehemence are justified, however. If you will have the kindness to send back the manuscript or the galleys to me—supposing that Collier has not burnt both—I will return the manuscript to du Berrier, and will try to persuade him to improve it and bring it up to date.

By the way, Collier did not condescend to send me proofs of my own review-article on Roger Freeman's educational studies, which— I suppose—is to appear in the fall issue of *Modern Age*.[72] For some months now—beginning long before I had resigned—Collier's people, presumably on his instructions, have *not* informed me what articles are to be included or excluded in approaching numbers; and, despite my repeated requests, they would never send me galleys of the cover. Collier made repeated hideous blunders with the covers, including misspelt names and labeling as "symposia" mere sets of two articles on some general subject. . . .

We need quite a different person as managing editor. Whenever I have made concessions to Collier, he has at once demanded more, arrogantly; and whenever I have tried to find some intelligent part for him in the magazine, he has simply failed to do the work. I suggested, for instance, that he might contribute to, or edit, our "News and Notes"; he did absolutely nothing. He demands powers, in short, which he is quite incompetent to exercise; and his demands upon me are so inconsistent, from one month to another, that it is impossible to satisfy them. He will demand simultaneously, for instance, that I publish many more articles on foreign affairs, more book reviews, and more short-short stories; and at the same time will complain that I send him more manuscripts than can be printed in 112 pages.

What has been worrying you principally about *Modern Age,* I take it, is Collier's allegation that subscription-renewals have dropped to thirty per cent. But Collier has bragged to me, more than once, of how he gave both you and me and the Relm Foundation exaggerated or depreciated circulation-figures, from time to time, to hearten or frighten you people. He enjoys fancying himself a Machiavelli. His thirty-per-cent figure was deliberately chosen at a natural low point in renewals, and arrived at by excluding certain types of renewals. If you could check yourself into the actual renewals at present, I think you would find that nowadays renewals are running nearly double Collier's figure. In any event, it is silly—and I needn't remind you that you have said so yourself—to assume that one can hastily build circulation of a serious quarterly to a self-sustaining level, by direct-mail promotion, and expect most readers, or nearly all, to renew automatically. *Yale Review* has taken more than fifty years to attain a circulation less than that we hope to have after the end of three years. We must find our permanent audience gradually. It is no solution to blame an editor of a serious quarterly for not attracting the public of the *Saturday Evening Post*—or to appoint a ponderous committee to handicap him. If Collier were running the magazine, you would have some ten or twenty subscribers left at the end of a year of his editorship. If you can find a better editor than I am, employ him, by all means; I'd be delighted. I make no claims to editorial competence, and never did. But don't try to convince yourself that five squabbling, busy men could do a better job of editorship than could one tolerably intelligent person who is willing to devote most of his time to the work. And let me suggest, finally, that the mission of a serious quarterly is not, and cannot be, to the masses. Vulgarizing will not bring you a crowd of new readers; it will simply alienate the present subscribers, and fail to influence the formers of opinion.

If you people had allowed me as much time for improving the magazine as I have had to spend simply in defending my own position over the past several months, we might have achieved something by now. As things have been, I have been unable to seek new contributors or to interest new foundations and individuals in helping us.

Cordially,
Russell Kirk

The 1960s

Surely we have a hard row to hoe. And we may fail. But we are put into this world to do battle.

from a letter to Jerry Pournelle, April 20, 1963

Letter to Brainard Cheney

In a candid letter to "Lon" Cheney, Kirk summarizes the reasons for his departure from the editorship of Modern Age. *Kirk divulged his perception of a "strong anti-Jewish and anti-Catholic prejudice of David Collier" only to his intimate friends and never shared it otherwise.*

February 12, 1960
Post College
Greenvale, L.I.
New York

Dear Lon,

What a pity we couldn't contrive to meet in Ireland![1] I'll be here at Post College most of the time until April 11. I'll be home at Mecosta all spring and summer, and you Cheneys should come up. At present I have no prospect of a Tennessee expedition.

Aye, I fear *Modern Age* will sink deep into dullness. The controversy over the editorship was mostly a matter of many cooks wanting to spoil the broth. When a magazine has a fair success, all at once all sorts of people desire to edit it—and this is especially true among conservatives. There now are eight or nine people who hold vetoes over the contents of each number of *Modern Age!* Another trouble was the strong anti-Jewish and anti-Catholic prejudice of David Collier, the nominal publisher.

The next book I'll get ready for publication will be my *Inhumane Businessman,* my collected educational essays.[2]

Compliments to Fanny. More before long, I hope.

Yours,
Russell

Letter to William F. Buckley Jr.

Buckley was bemused by F. A. Hayek's essay "Why I Am Not a Conserva-
tive," which was published as the afterword to the distinguished Austrian's
book The Constitution of Liberty *(Chicago: University of Chicago Press,*
1960). Having extemporaneously debated Hayek on the question of libertari-
anism versus conservatism at a meeting of the Mont Pelerin Society in 1957,
Kirk held a fairly strong, unfavorable view of Hayek, which he confided to
Buckley.

December 20, 1961

Mr. William Buckley Jr.
National Review

Dear Bill,

While I can't account fully for Hayek's distemper, in general he is
a vain and impractical person, rather doctrinaire, who thinks that he is
the law and all the prophets, and that nothing is needed for the salvation of humanity but the obedient reading of Hayek's works. He is not
a man of much resolution, and perhaps all the agitation about "extrem-
ists" impels him to make some gesture of dissociation.

I fancy, too, that all this is somehow connected with troubles within the Mont Pelerin Society. You may have noticed the strange letter
which Director, Friedman, and Stigler wrote in reply to my "From the
Academy" piece on the Mont Pelerin Society.[3] They seemed aggrieved
that I had happened to mention Roepke's *Humane Economy*, rather than
Hayek's *Constitution of Liberty*. Within that Society, at present there
is a struggle between the Christians and more tolerant people on the
one hand, and the rigid quasi-Benthamite liberals on the other. Fritz
Machlup, a civil libertine of Princeton and the most disagreeable sort
of conceited academician, is attempting to oust Roepke from the presidency; and he is said to have won over Hayek to his side by playing
upon Hayek's own vanity.[4] I enclose some papers from Roepke which
explain some of this.

How *National Review* comes into this internecine strife, I know not, except that Roepke has written for it in the past, and that I, innocently enough, praised the present direction of the Mont Pelerin Society for its breadth of view and friendliness toward Christians, conservatives, and even Spaniards. . . .

Doubtless we will rasp their delicate sensibilities still further when you publish my "From the Academy" piece, now in your bank, on Hunold's anthology *Freedom and Serfdom;* for they dislike Hunold even more than Roepke.[5]

I look forward to seeing you in Florida.[6] This meeting, as I understand it is to help formulate general principles of action in various fields—foreign policy taxation, labor legislation, education, etc., etc. We want to have in mind some sort of agenda, so as not to waste time. Senator Goldwater is the only politician of note who has real respect for ideas and people with degrees—perhaps because he didn't finish college himself. In foreign policy, particularly—the field with which he has had [the] least experience—I think we may help to outline a policy at once sound and popular.

The only person coming whom you do not know already is Jay Gordon Hall, I think, Cicero and Machiavelli rolled into one. He and I are two minds with but a single thought, two hearts that beat as one, so you now know his general principles. He deliberately worked his way up from the assembly-line of the big motor companies to entrench himself in a post where he could advance conservative causes—and he has succeeded. *Entre nous,* he says that if the people at the top of General Motors knew what he really does, they would fire him, terrified. He is a doctor of philosophy in history of the University of Chicago, and also a hard-fisted practical political manager. . . . He hopes to retire from General Motors one day and become a professor of classics.

Yours,

Russell

Letter to Robert Drake

Kirk enjoyed the short fiction of Robert Drake (1930–2001), a Tennessee-born English professor whose stories were set in a small railroad town in West Tennessee similar in some respects to the town in which Kirk grew up, Plymouth, Michigan. At the time Kirk wrote this letter, Drake had recently transitioned from a post at Northwestern University to one at the University of Texas. He had written to ask Kirk to support his application for a Guggenheim Fellowship to compile a bibliography of works by and about the English short story writer Saki (Hector Hugh Munro).

December 30, 1961

Dear Bob,

A happy new year to you! I have heartily endorsed your Guggenheim application. I look forward to seeing the Saki bibliography. It's good to hear that Texas suits you. I might get down that way in March, just conceivably. . . .

The world goes well with me. In the spring, my collected ghost-stories will be published: *The Surly Sullen Bell.*[7] I have written twenty periodical pieces since I returned home in October, and have given sixty speeches. Next week I fly down to Palm Beach for a conference with Senator Goldwater—just four or five of us—so Jacqueline and Caroline had best plan to pack.

Nowadays I am justice of the peace of Morton Township, Mecosta County. In pursuance of my duties as master of the high justice, the middle, and the low, recently I dug in the cellar of Jingo Cracky, the dead Miser of Mecosta, for a treasure-trove. (We found eight thousand dollars in half-pint jars; all in all, the dirty old man, who had lived on stale bread and honey for more than seventy years, had saved half a million, by going without running water, and baths, and the like.) As we labored, my uncle and the undersheriff and I, a hulking figure loomed in the doorway. We were wearing our six-guns, for robbers have been active (unlike everyone else) at Mecosta recently, and the Miser's House stands lonely on the marge of Hughes Swamp. So, suffused with dreams of glory, I reached happily for my holster; but the undersheriff murmured, "He is a federal man"—and so, alack, he was.[8]

Cordially,
Russell

Letter to Jay Gordon Hall

Hall was a longtime friend of Kirk who worked as a publicist and lobbyist for General Motors Corporation. "Suave, humorous, and very gentlemanly, Hall had taught history and was a considerable Latin scholar; his exemplar was Marcus Tullius Cicero," wrote Kirk in The Sword of Imagination: Memoirs of a Half-Century of Literary Conflict *(Grand Rapids, MI: Eerdmans, 1995), adding that Hall was also a quiet but significant force in the Goldwater-for-president movement in the early 1960s, when Lyndon Johnson was the candidate of General Motors (255).*

January 14, 1962

Dear Gordon,

A good and profitable time we had at Palm Beach. We must meet again soon, the lot of us. I'm in process of improving my facilities for conferences at Mecosta, including the enlargement of the library, and I hope that in the spring or summer we can contrive a similarly leisurely session here.

Do send me any materials that would be useful for the two speeches of the Senator's with which I am to help. I take it that the Notre Dame one is the more urgent, and will get my draft done in the next five or six days, if that's all right.[9]

Peter Stanlis is in grave difficulties about keeping his *Burke Newsletter* going; it costs little enough—about $350 a quarterly issue, in direct costs—but there is no benefactor for even that, and besides Peter has to handle all the correspondence, mailing, addressing, billing, and the like himself. The University of Detroit appears unwilling to go on with the project without a subsidy from some quarter. The *Newsletter* has done much good, and actually has stimulated conservative opinions among professors of history, and others. I enclose some copies of correspondence which suggest how this scholarly *Newsletter* stimulates immediate political action on either coast of these United States. These are *Burke Newsletter* people.

Now do you know of any source from which Peter might get some help? Is there any chance that Alvin Bentley's new foundation might make a small grant in aid?[10] A mere thousand dollars a year would save the undertaking, I think; two thousand would put it on a sound footing, for the time being. And the grant could be made to the University of Detroit, and so be impeccably respectable. I am suggesting to Peter that he write to you about this.

Peter, by the way, is a thorough Goldwaterian now. Here are some passages from recent letters of his:

"I hope that as soon as I complete my Relm book and book on Frost that I can take an active part in bringing about a counter-revolution on traditional grounds in the next national election. Alma has said that I must stay out of practical politics until I complete the work I have scheduled; and she is right. But the criminal folly of Kennedy in not helping the anti-communist Cubans, in intervening when we should have kept hands off in the Dominican Republic, and in destroying the only anti-communist group in the Congo has me too worked up to sit on the sidelines. Isn't it odd that Kennedy and the State Department morons can accept gladly a divided Korea, a divided Germany, and a divided Indo-China, but insist that "Unity" compels their insane policy in the Congo. You and Jay Gordon Hall can count on me, not just now but when the time comes, in both a Michigan and national campaign, to help however I can. I have voted consistently Republican . . . in recent years, so I might as well work with you on the big campaigns. . . . I hope that you have laid some good plots for meshes in which to entangle the silken sophistries of doctrinaire liberals. My feeling is that history is about to catch up to them with a crash in the next congressional and presidential elections."

More soon. I'll make some speeches in Chicago on January 22, 23, and 24, but will be back at Mecosta thereafter for a fortnight.

Yours,
Russell

The 1960s

Letter to Jerry Pournelle

Pournelle (1933–2017) was an American science fiction novelist, essayist, and journalist at large. He is best known for the dystopian Lucifer's Hammer *(1977), cowritten with Larry Niven. During the early 1960s, as a graduate student struggling with the questions of contemporary American culture in a time of revolutionary transition as well as searching for a thesis for his doctoral dissertation, he began corresponding with Kirk. In the following letter of encouragement, Kirk provides a candid look into his own thoughts on the state of conservatism and its role in American culture.*

April 20, 1963

Dear Mr. Pournelle,

Very good it is to hear from you. I enclose a recent piece of mine; also a copy of a speech by Senator Goldwater, which you may not have seen.[11]

My national newspaper column prospers, a straw in the wind: I now have seventy-five dailies carrying it, my latest big-city conquests being Detroit, Houston, Salt Lake, Atlanta, and San Francisco.

Your letter is full of interest to me. I am going to write for *Commonweal*, in the near future, a piece—requested by them—on the general subject; and I may quote you.[12]

Your model of the political world is good. Nazism, and to a lesser extent Fascism, are combinations of socialism and nationalism, I think—so far as their theoretical origins can be squared with their practical performance—and perhaps something of the sort should be indicated on your plan, if possible. Nothing very good has been written on Hume's Toryism: I think it would be difficult to demonstrate there is any kinship between it and anarchism. Hume most distinctly was no Whig. The thesis should be very provocative.[13]

One often grows discouraged, of course, at the confusion of American politics, practical and theoretical. But all this is part of the nature of things. In any time, the great mass of men are moved only by self-interest and prejudice. Of that small minority who think seriously

103

about the problems of their society, most are badly schooled; and there is a lag of a generation between the slogans of the politicians and the new concepts of men of intellect. Besides, the non-ideological character of American and British politics—in part a considerable blessing—tends to slow and confuse the development of theory in a time of crisis.

"Individualism" was a lost cause from its beginnings—and little pity. In America, it remains only as the dogma of a small sect, whose influence is almost negligible. One ought not to fancy that the abler practical politicians like Senator Goldwater, or the better men in American business, really are influenced by such fallacies—even though some of their more vocal supporters may repeat the slogans like incantations, and even though the leaders themselves, from time to time—as with the leaders of all political factions—tend to utter some of these phrases. For one thing, the American businessman generally is a Christian, and rejects "individualism" once he understands what it means.[14]

In general, the student conservatives and their clubs grow more sensible, and turn toward more genuine political theory. Take, for example, the Intercollegiate Society of Individualists. They began, a decade ago, by uttering the individualist and old-liberal slogans; but they have learned and reformed. Burke is now their mentor, and your servant is their chief living authority. This disturbs some of their financial backers, and people like Mr. Frank Meyer; but as they lose the support of such people, they will attract that of more intelligent people. They are turning out some really admirable pamphlets and other publications nowadays. Are you in touch with them?

Similarly, Senator Goldwater has learnt much since he entered politics, almost in a fit of absence of mind. I know him well. My friend Clinton Rossiter's neat categories, or stereotypes, rarely apply well in reality. You will get a different view of Mr. Goldwater from the enclosed speech. And do you know his "Forgotten American" statement? Mr. Goldwater's closest advisers are your servant, Professor Gerhart Niemeyer (a genuine conservative), Dr. Jay Gordon Hall (a disciple of Cicero and a classical scholar, who has created himself political agent of General Motors), and Mr. William Baroody, of the American

Enterprise Association, a good economist and a Lebanese Catholic. None of these people have any truck with FEE sloganizing or "individualist" notions.[15]

There remains in this country a large body of support for an imaginative conservatism. Though the odds are against us, we may succeed in saving a good deal from the wreck of the modern world; and, as Henry Adams liked to say in his mordant way, "The fun is in the process."

Much depends upon establishing some sort of model or standard for conservatives. The silliness of the people you describe will be eclipsed if sound sense is displayed by others—and expressed with some power. The "right" will follow whoever speaks most clearly and persuasively, as one with authority. Thus one does not compromise with the silly people, but rather overawes them or leads them into ways of wisdom. It is necessary, in fine, to speak from a position of strength. Fortified as I am by my newspaper column, my books, my good standing with serious quarterlies and journals of opinion, and the approbation of the *New York Times, Time,* and *Fortune,* it is difficult for extreme people of any sort to do me mischief. Thus one gradually makes gains, for nothing succeeds like success.

It is true enough that often there is better chance of converting the liberals of the humanitarian sort than of leading the doctrinaire zealots of the "Right" into paths of wisdom. I find Senators Humphrey and Eugene McCarthy, for instance, much more agreeable than certain people we could name—and also it is easier to come to a practical understanding of them.

But one need not despair of a good many of the enthusiasts for the slogans of nineteenth-century liberalism. Most of these gentlemen do not quite understand what they say; their real sentiments are something better. It is a matter of improving them.

Eric Voegelin says that the great line of demarcation in modern politics does *not* lie between the liberals on the one hand the totalitarians on the other, but rather between the immanest sectarians on the one hand, and all those who believe in a transcendent order on the other.[16] Adventitious labels sometimes conceal an underlying agreement on first principles. Possibly better terms than "conservative" and "liberal" will come out of our present time of troubles. Meanwhile, of course, one has to employ what words lie ready to hand.

The necessities of modern America require conservative measures—both parties will be forced to understand this, unless we come to disaster first. A Spanish friend of mine, in Spain a liberal, tells me after some residence in America that the United States needs conservative thought and polices more than anything else—being in this different from Spain. (Though he more and more distrusts Spanish liberalism, too.)

Surely we have a hard row to hoe. And we may fail. But we are put into this world to do battle. "Things are in the saddle, and ride mankind," more than ever before. I suspect, indeed, that the modern age will come to smash; and then we will have to build afresh, upon old principles. Meanwhile, we guard what Mr. T. S. Eliot calls "the enduring things."

Already you have done a good deal in the cause of order, justice, and freedom. It will not do to become altogether disheartened now—even though I, too, often have my hours and days and weeks of discouragement.

The conservative revival is weakest, at least among students, on the West coast. Elsewhere, matters are looking up now—especially among Southern students. Cheerfulness will keep breaking in.

Best wishes for your dissertation. Do let me know if I can be of help in any way. I remember you very well. I will be at Los Angeles State College, as "distinguished professor of American Studies," for the whole of July and a little of June; just possibly we may contrive to meet during that period.

More another time. Thanks for writing.

Cordially,
Russell Kirk

Letter to T. S. Eliot

In his final letter to Eliot, Kirk brings his friend up to date on his immediate publishing and travel plans.

June 9, 1963

Dear Mr. Eliot,

You are in good spirits, I trust. Many thanks for the several Christmas cards I owe you: I seem always to be abroad at Christmas, and so never get around to sending cards. (This last Christmas, I was at El Escorial.)

Here, enclosed, are some pieces of mine you probably haven't seen. My next book will be a fat new edition of my first book, *Randolph of Roanoke,* with a good many of Randolph's speeches and letters included.[17] I'll see that a copy is sent unto you. Also this autumn I'll publish a collection of my autobiographical sketches, travel pieces, and newspaper columns, *Confessions of a Bohemian Tory.*[18] And a new edition of my *St. Andrews* is coming out.

I have heard nothing for some months from our friends the Earl and Countess of Crawford; but I suppose other Fifers would let me know, were they not well enough.

What have you been doing? Are any more plays in prospect? My assistant has written a book—not yet published—*The Death of Theatre,* which I think you will like. He is Mr. Kenneth Shorey; when, eventually, the book appears, we'll send you a copy.[19]

My Italian publishers, Centro di Vita Italiana, are holding a big conference in Rome, at the end of September. I'll be there, as will Gabriel Marcel, Thomas Molnar, Wilhelm Roepke (probably), and others you know of. The director of the Center, Giano Accame, hopes very much that you may be able to come; presumably you have heard from him. They want to get together conservatively-inclined folk from all parts.

The Goldwaterians, of whom your servant is of the inner circle, are going great guns nowadays.[20] I enclose a speech of Senator Goldwater's, which doubtless contrasts remarkably with the account of the Senator given by most of the English press.

A tornado is brewing in Mecosta County. . . . And the plague of summer cottagers is upon us.

More another time—with less of an interval, I trust. Best wishes to you.

Cordially,
Russell Kirk

Letter to Annette Y. Courtemanche

On March 19, 1964, after being courted by Kirk for roughly four years, Annette Courtemanche wrote a lengthy letter to him in which she stated, "I have decided that our marriage is inevitable." Learning of the letter's contents during a phone call later that day, Kirk replied jokingly, "Like death and taxes?" But her broaching of the subject opened the door to the fulfillment of one of his life's goals: to marry for love and, in time, to rear children who would come to know that the service of God is perfect freedom. Kirk was seriously smitten with the young woman to whom he devoted a great many pet names, such as Pocahontas (in honor of Annette's Native American heritage), Hypatia, Persephone, and Best Beloved, among many others. As a result of their conversation, Kirk wrote the following letter, which reveals an exuberant, playful side of him not often seen by those outside his immediate family.

March 20, 1964

Darling Annette,

I'M GOING TO MARRY ANNETTE! What a thought! She isn't quite sure about it yet, though more or less resigned to the horrid prospect. But I think I may succeed, and so I'm all in a whirl, and probably will continue to be vertiginous until, years from now, that splendid event occurs. I know I should write so tender a letter in holography; but you knowing, Pocahontas, what my scrawl is like, my sentiments will be better preserved for our posterity via this typewriter.

Of course you will often have doubts about all this, and times when you are dissatisfied with me, Beauty. Don't let such misgivings worry you overmuch. For you obviously have had serious doubts about all the men you ever have known: otherwise you wouldn't be single, though so desirable at twenty-three. Like all the others, I have bad flaws. But so will any other men in whom you are interested from time to time. It is not a question of what man is perfect, but rather of what man would, in the long run, be best for you.

I am rather frightened at the prospect, I confess: I feel as a mortal man must have felt who won the favors of one of the Olympian goddesses. For you really have been my goddess, Annette girl, ever since I first saw you at the Wellington Hotel.[21] (We must put a bronze plaque on the facade of that building, to celebrate our first meeting.) As I told you before, I thought at once, sitting opposite you, "Wouldn't it be wonderful to know her! But of course I never will." I confess now that the thought passed, too, through my mind, "Wouldn't it be wonderful to *marry* her!" But that reflection was too absurd for words, and I tried to dismiss it. (Though you were very beautiful, it wasn't physical attraction, in any considerable degree, that made me want to marry you on the spot, you understand, A.Y.C.: rather, it was some mysterious affinity and rapture of spirit, that made you outshine at once all the other women I ever had known.) So this is all like a dream for me—your tender letter that gives me hope, Beauty. Don't wake me too soon. . . .

What a day it will be—if ever, for I still am afraid to count too much upon you, lest I be overwhelmed with sorrow—when you let me give you an engagement-ring! (I think, by the way, that ring ought to be something unique, not just the dull diamond that the commercial jewelers promote; but we can cross that bridge when we come to it.) (In fact, I ought to get a Florentine jeweler, for example, to make a unique ring especially for you.) . . .

If you think of me all the time, you lovely thing, then you do love me, Annette—after a fashion, at least. Pleasant preoccupation with one person is the surest sign of real love—if that preoccupation endures. And you and I have been thinking about each other for a good long while.

The people that we can't get along without—supposing our relationship to them is honorable—are the ones we truly love. That being so, you do feel love for me, Annette. Whether it is enough love for you to want to be united with me always, I cannot decide for you; it must be your own heart and mind that give you the answer. But caring as much for me as you do already—and knowing how you are all the world to me—I don't think you could be unhappy as my wife. . . .[22]

I won't ever fail you, Pocahontas. Even if you decide against me, I will try to serve you always, so far as I may. (I can't promise everything, of course, for husbands of beauties sometimes have a strange way of resenting the presence of the Beauty's old chums, even when those chums are as learned as myself.) But I would try my very best, even should I lose you. Mercurial though you are in small things, Best Beloved, you are sound and true in great things: so I know now that you never will drive me away by any light or selfish action of your own. . . .

You are still growing in spirit and mind, as I have told you often, Persephone: and indeed you will feel more thorough affinity with me in a matter of a year, or even of months. We are never going to be identical twins: but that's good, because husband and wife ought not to be exactly like each other—that would be boring, and almost incestuous. . . .

Yes, your (our) children certainly should go to a Catholic school, for religion is the essence of education; I would want this, even were I not—what I am—a kind of strong auxiliary of the Church. And we must make sure that they are not snobs. Long Island, by the way, is one of the least ideal places in the world to rear children: I marvel at your parents' strength of character, therefore, in turning out you three young Courtemanches so successfully.[23]

Do you know what? This is only a tentative suggestion, of course; but if you and I should marry, Annette darling, I should like to bring your parents to Mecosta and settle them in a house here. They love country life, and the Springfield Gardens they knew in their young days is gone forever. Despite your taste for city life (its better pleasures, that is) you soon would grow to appreciate the country and the village; and with me, of course, you could travel to all sorts of interesting cities and lands. We would have our little Scottish house as a European base. And I think that between us we could rear such children as this time rarely sees.

You must tell me all about your child-rearing designs when next we are together, Hypatia.

And we could work so well together, in so many fields! Few husbands and wives have such an opportunity. . . .

Even husband and wife should retain some little mysteries of their own. I don't expect you to tell me everything, always, Pocahontas: really, it's more fun if you don't. Besides, as you know, usually I can guess accurately enough at what isn't uttered, for all practical purposes.

I think I would be good for you. Henry James has a short story about two men—one splendid and imposing in company, the other scarcely noticeable. But it turns out (this is a kind of supernatural story) that the obscure little man, when observed in private, fills the room with his strong personality and charm; and when one glances into a room in which you expect to find the important man—why, he isn't there at all, because he has no internal life: he exists only in the sight of others, really.[24] So it is with externals and internals, the outer life and the inner life. What I offer Annette is the inner life, the life of spirit—not that our outer life would be altogether lacking in dignity or interest. The dashing young rake-type offers you externals, of body and of existence; but he turns out to be only a whited sepulchre, a hollow shell—fun to dance with, doubtless, but hell to marry. (For Hell, in essence, is an empty place, blind and hollow, with only the simulacrum of life—God cannot be known there.) . . .

Mickie—who, of course, surveys the Courtemanche-Kirk romance with close attention and interest, even though I don't confide wholly in her (or in anybody) about it—remarked to me a month or two ago, "Well, Russell, whether you win or lose Annette, there are compensations. If you win her, you will be deliriously happy—and will worry a lot. If you lose her, you still have the even tenor of your ways."[25]

Though Mickie likes me so much herself, I think she wonders whether Annette is serious about me, and rather wants to protect me. She's not really seen the serious side of Annette, for one thing, and probably thinks you are less mature than you actually are. She approves of you, but wonders, I suspect, whether you may not break my heart. You and Mickie really are a good deal similar in character and charm, as well as political convictions.

Now I must get to work on much duller letters, Indian Princess. I'd like to write to you all day, every day—and all night, too. But then you'd have to read all my infatuated ramblings. I'll telephone on Wednesday, anyway, and will be with you—though Hell should bar the way—on Sunday afternoon. Meanwhile, some four more letters, rapturous and dithyrambic, or perhaps five, should make their devoted way to you, my darling dearest Annette girl, Conservative Beauty.

Do you know, I think I'm in love?

Write, if you should have time; I don't have to get another twelve-page epistle for a while, though, much though I should relish it. I think of nothing but you, Pocahontas—which isn't good for my work, but fun. I send you innumerable ritualistic kisses.[26]

Much love,
Russell

Letter to Frances Cheney

Frances Neel Cheney (1906–1996) was the wife of the southern novelist and essayist Brainard "Lon" Cheney and a close friend of short story writer Flannery O'Connor. In October 1955, the Cheneys introduced Kirk to O'Connor when they came individually to visit the Cheney home, Cold Chimneys, in Smyrna, Tennessee. In the following letter, Kirk provides a whirlwind summary of the goings-on in his life since the late summer of 1964, when he joined the Roman Catholic Church and married Annette Courtemanche.

April 23, 1965

Dear Fannie,

Very good it is to hear from you. What have you and Lon been doing in recent months?

Your servant has been most active. On August 19, I was baptized a Papist; on September 19, I was married to Annette Yvonne Cecile Courtemanche. We wandered, in this country, Scotland, and South Africa, for some seven months. We will now get some serious work done at home for two months, and will be in California during late June and the whole of July.

My collected critical essays, *Fulminations of a Nocturnal Bookman,* will be published in two or three weeks.[27] In the autumn, the Louisiana State University Press will publish my essays on modern culture. I am working on a baroque romance of modern Africa, *Memoirs of a Creature of the Twilight.*[28] Then I turn my hand to a sober book on Robert Taft in Congress, and to a short life of Edmund Burke.

Artie Shaw means to make *Old House of Fear* into a film.[29] Aye, the book has had a remarkable sale for "young adults." (It even was on tape for auditors at the World's Fair, in the *Encyclopedia Americana* exhibit.) . . . I scarcely thought it publishable myself.

Annette and I do hope to see you and Lon before many months are out. I will probably speak in Chattanooga about the beginning of June, though I don't know whether I can get to Nashville. Best wishes.

Cordially,

Russell

Letter to Harvey Shapiro

Shapiro (1924–2013) was the longtime editor of the New York Times Magazine. *He respected Kirk as an intelligent voice of American conservatism and published several articles by him. In 1966, during a period of cultural and political upheaval in the United States, he telephoned Kirk to ask if he would write an article on the current political atmosphere in America, especially as it concerned conservatism. Kirk provided the following prospectus in reply.*

June 21, 1966

Mr. Harvey Shapiro
The New York Times Magazine

Dear Mr. Shapiro,

Thanks for your telephone call today. Here is a brief synopsis of my possible piece on the political drift of the country.

The conservative element increases in strength, for two reasons: (1) the frustration in Viet Nam; (2) the threat of inflation and financial instability. Ronald Reagan's success is a symptom.

The "New Left" damages its own cause: "extremism" has passed to the left, and the American public disapproves. All "peace" candidates were defeated in the primaries, and "peace" leaders in Congress and elsewhere will be in trouble this fall. The real public pressure upon President Johnson is for military success and financial soundness. Democracies demand, sometimes imprudently, speedy victory.

The Goldwater defeat in 1964 had little connection with the strength of conservative or liberal opinion in American. As the Louis Cheskin poll in depth indicated, the primary question then was the "trigger-happy" issue—now obsolete.[30] Aside from that, many who voted against Goldwater felt that he was "some sort of radical" who would upset the applecart. Thus the presidential election of 1964 obscured the real drift of things.

The "radical right," though still noisy, is only a minor factor in this drift. We will *not* see the triumph of the "Right" in American politics; but we may see success for the genuine conservatives, who begin to appear as the middle-of-the-roaders. For instance, Mr. Nixon now appears as the central choice of the Republican party, between Reagan on the one hand and Romney on the other. The Democratic party and the national administration also move, if confusedly, toward more conservative attitudes.

The old issues are passing from the scene. "Civil rights," strictly speaking, no longer is a burning question. There will be strong public reaction, probably, against the actual functioning of the "Medicare" and "Medicaid" programs. The complexion of Congress, after this November, will be distinctly more conservative.

The situation of President Johnson is distinctly like that of President Truman during the Korean War. But the situation of Senator Robert Kennedy is curiously like that of Henry Wallace; if he continues to shift to the left, he enters the political wilderness. The American public is nearly prepared for a change to a conservative leadership prepared to make hard decisions and restore stability. But as yet it is not clear where adequate conservative leaders are to be found.

So much for hasty jottings. I would make all this more coherent in a regular article, of course.[31]

Cordially,
Russell Kirk

Letter to Ralph Christie

Described by Kirk, in his memoir The Sword of Imagination, *as "the surviving archetype of the eccentric Scots laird of the old school—generous, hospitable, humorous, and omnivorous reader, a seeker after occult knowledge" and "always an accomplished raconteur," Christie was one of the lifelong friends Kirk met during his early sojourns in Scotland during the late 1940s and early '50s (115). Kirk spent many evenings at Christie's mansion, Durie House, enjoying the hospitality of the laird and his wife, Margret, often spending late hours in the business room of the house listening to Ralph tell hair-raising ghost stories. Early in his marriage, Kirk took Annette to visit the Christies and all his other Scottish friends, and she too was enchanted by their friendly graciousness.*

December 2, 1966

Major Ralph Christie
Durie

Dear Ralph,

Soon Durie will have its Christmas tree up, I take it. We shall be at home in Mecosta for Christmas and New Year's, and thinking of all at Durie.

I hear that you are reading, puffing at your pipe, and spending two hours a day in the business room. Well done! Does the grandson increase in strength and wit?

I am virtually finished with my book about Robert Taft, and a copy will be sent unto you when it is published in the spring. My story

"Balgrummo's Hell" should appear within a month or two, in a magazine, and you will receive a copy of that, too.[32]

The temperature has fallen to ten degrees below zero at Mecosta, this night. Today we visited our two growing yaks on their ranch, and near froze to death while feeding them slices of dry bread.[33]

I'm engaged in a newspaper campaign, through my column, to prevent America meddling ignorantly in Rhodesia and Southwest Africa. For once, I have powerful allies.

More soon. Best wishes for all at Durie at Christmas—though I'll write again before then.

Cordially,
Russell Kirk

Letter to Ray Bradbury

Bradbury initially wrote to Kirk to thank him for publishing "Count Dracula and Mr. Ray Bradbury" as his "From the Academy" column in the April 4, 1967, issue of National Review. *That column and Bradbury's gracious letter of thanks began a lifelong friendship between the two writers, who deeply admired each other's work.*

April 14, 1967

Mr. Ray Bradbury
10267 Cheviot Drive
Los Angeles

Dear Ray Bradbury,

Very pleasant it is to hear from you. Now I may have an opportunity to see *Dandelion Wine* in New York about the time it opens. I will be there on the evenings of April 26 and 28. Would either do? If so, what theater is it in Lincoln Center?[34]

I may try to persuade the *New York Times Magazine* to let me do a piece about you, on the strength of the new play—though they may feel that I am poaching on the ground of the *Times'* dramatic critics, such as they are.

Recently I have been speaking to groups of clergymen on the lively topic "The Renewal of Church and State through Fantasy." You have a conspicuous place therein, along with C. S. Lewis and others.

After closer study of all your books, I may find time this summer to undertake a long serious essay for *Kenyon Review* or *Sewanee Review* on your work. It's lamentable, but perhaps not strange, that even the well-inclined literary reviews haven't taken you up; for you have more of the moral imagination than anyone else now writing in America, and a more wondrous style. With the stamp of approval of *Kenyon*, you will be forever a Major Writer. By the way, do Simon and Schuster publish all your books?

Just the other day I came upon *Something Wicked This Way Comes*, in paperback, which I hadn't read before. You are at your best therein. I always have wanted to build my own Hall of Mirrors. By the way, did you ever pass through John Betjeman's Cave of the Winds, in what's left of the pleasure-grounds of the Festival of Britain, Hammersmith, London? You'd like it. . . .

The first buds of the season are now appearing on our trees and shrubs in the haunted land of Mecosta. I shall plant a thousand Norway spruces late this month.

Cordially,
Russell Kirk

Letter to Margret Christie

From the late 1940s through the mid 1960s, Kirk enjoyed visiting Scotland and staying at Durie House, a massive structure owned by his friends Ralph and Margret Christie. Learning of Ralph's death in April 1967, Kirk wrote the following letter of consolation and encouragement to Margret.

April 23, 1967

Dear Margret,

Today George Scott-Moncrieff's letter arrived here, telling of Ralph's death. We had expected that, of course; yet somehow Ralph seemed as enduring as Durie. If any man be made for eternity, such is Ralph, and you and I shall know him again.

I have written some paragraphs about Ralph that will be published in my syndicated newspaper column, and we will send you a copy, in print, within a few days. He would be pleased to read them.

Annette and I hope that you may be able to visit us at Mecosta, some time this year. We will be at home for the whole of the next twelve months, very probably, except for my own speechifying-expeditions; and summer would be a very good time to come unto us. The future Wizard of Mecosta should be born in July; visit us before that, or at that time, or thereafter, for it will be a good season.[35]

A few years ago, Ralph was startled to discover that I was so comparatively young; he always had taken me for a man of his own years. I wish, indeed, that I had known him from his youth; our eighteen years of friendship seemed like one summer. As Plato says, no natural desire is without the possibility of fulfillment, and this is true of the hunger for immortality. "Plato, thou reasonest well." In those brief years, a conscience spoke to a conscience, over glasses of gin, and those voices will not be forever silenced.

Much more might be said, but we will not trouble you with words just now. Annette sends her love to you and the children—children still to me, for I consider myself Ralph's contemporary, in defiance of the tooth of time—and so do I. Write when you can, Margret.

Affectionately,
Russell Kirk

Letter to Ray Bradbury

July 8, 1967

Mr. Ray Bradbury
Los Angeles

Dear Ray,

Very good it is to have your news of the provisional success of *Dandelion Wine.* I do pray that sponsors may be found.

Our Heir should be born this week, and the old house at Mecosta has been restored—for the first time in ninety years—in celebration of his coming. Annette is in good spirits. I'll not get to California until September, if then, but I count on seeing you before the year is out.

My brief life of Edmund Burke is just published, and my *Political Principles of Taft* will appear in September. Now I turn my hand to *The Recovery of Norms*, which I have promised to my publisher by September.[36] Then I should be able to sit down to writing something carefully about the work of Mr. Ray Bradbury, whether for the *New York Times Magazine*, or *Kenyon Review*, or both. I may try to include that intended piece in *The Recovery of Norms*, indeed.

I have lectured at one or two churches—aye, even from the pulpit—on angels and devils. Your *Something Wicked This Way Comes* was one of my chief illustrations. And I have given copies of most of your works to the Newman Center at Ferris State College . . . , our nearest institution of the higher learning in America.

A friend of mine who edits *Practical English* (one of the *Scholastic Magazine* publications) told me recently of how a female librarian was enraged to find *Fahrenheit 451* among a shipment of books for children, and proudly announced that she had burnt that evil book.[37]

I may soon write a piece for *National Review*, and a shorter one for my syndicated column, on the subject of Librarians and *Fahrenheit 451*. Some months ago, I gave nearly a thousand books from my library to our new local public library. These were sent to the nearest agency of the State Library system for classification and the like. Nearly half of them never came back to our local library; and when we inquired, it turned out that they had been burnt, quite literally. The bureaucrat responsible had discovered that Russell Kirk, donor, was a Wicked Conservative, and therefore he destroyed virtually all the books on politics, current affairs, and economics, to be quite safe. (Actually, I gave more radical and liberal works than conservative, but he was unable to distinguish, and so destroyed the lot, except those he was sure were not conservative. I even have his confession in writing; he was proud of his holocaust. In the process, incidentally, he got rid of all the *better* books by radicals and liberals.)

119

Also he destroyed much else—on what principles, if any, I still am trying to discover. A complete set of O. Henry's works, in good print and well bound, was among the victims. Why? Written too long ago? Only Best knows. (That's the librarian's name.)

But he has caught a Tartar, since I am on friendly terms with the Librarian of the State of Michigan, and with the Speaker of the House of Representatives. Also I have a typewriter, and am published daily by several Michigan newspapers. Best complained that he didn't know we had made a list of the books donated—we ought to have warned him.

There seems to be some dim possibility that my baroque African romance *A Creature of the Twilight* may be made into a film, especially now that Nigeria is fulfilling my prophecy almost to the letter.[38] I have told some folks that they ought to try to persuade you to write the film script, if you have any leisure for that sort of thing nowadays. I think you'd be rather fond of Manfred Arcane, my picaresque hero. Though the political circumstances are more nearly Nigeria, the physical background is mostly Moroccan, with a dash of the Danakil Desert or the Spanish Sahara thrown in. People didn't believe that a war could be concluded so abruptly as it is in my book, until the Israelis began to move.[39]

More another time. Best wishes.

Cordially,
Russell Kirk

Letter to Henry Regnery

August 14, 1967

Mr. Henry Regnery
Henry Regnery Company

Dear Henry,

Aye, I know Eric Voegelin's books well.[40] My several reviews of them, published in the quarterlies, are supposed to appear in my collection *The Death of Art: Fulminations of a Nocturnal Bookman*. But the intended publisher of that volume, Peter Ruber, seems to have been carried off by the princes of the air. I don't think I even have a carbon-copy handy! Anyway, in some sense I endeavored to make Voegelin intelligible in that series of review-essays.

Now one of Voegelin's most earnest disciples is Gerhart Niemeyer, of Notre Dame. He himself is not perfect in English style, but perhaps could make Voegelin's important work more understandable. Jeffrey Hart might be a possibility for what you have in mind.

Yes, I think Doellinger's book would be worth republishing. The whole affair was most interesting, with Acton much involved, and Baron von Hugel. You would need an introduction by someone learned in the field, I think. Perhaps Father John Courtney Murray might be interested.[41]

I think that good Rhine grapes could be grown in Michigan; anyway, Rhine is the best of the wines which Michigan wineries try to sell. (They try every variety, and produce in large quantities, sold very cheaply, of course—but mostly to impecunious alcoholics.) The grapes of Jerez certainly don't do well in this state. I wonder if anyone has tried planting the Mosel grape; but perhaps we're not quite warm enough.

More another time.

Yours,
Russell

P.S. You might see if Avon would be interested in *John Randolph*. I have sent Avon a revised final chapter of *The Conservative Mind*, and also corrections to the earlier chapters.[42]

Letter to Peter W. Schramm

Schramm edited the short-lived conservative periodical Phalanx: An Interdisciplinary Review, *which was published from 1967 to 1968 under the auspices of the Southern California Collegiate Conference. He acquired a printed copy of Willmoore Kendall's article "What Killed the Civil Rights*

Movement?" which was written shortly before Kendall's death, and sent it to Kirk for editorial advice.

November 4, 1967

Mr. Peter W. Schramm
Phalanx
3853 Reklaw Drive
Studio City, California

Dear Mr. Schramm,

Thanks for sending me Willmoore Kendall's article.[43] I think his point is sound, and the piece ought to be interesting to many readers. Your only difficulty is that Kendall's style—at least in his later years—was almost unreadable, in print. It was effective as a spoken style, at least as he delivered such sentences and paragraphs; but put on the printed page, the sentences are too long and confusing, even for a person accustomed to, and fond of, long sentences—like myself; and his paragraphs are no better.

Possibly you can contrive to break up the sentences somewhat, and certainly the paragraphs, without too much editorial labor, and without doing mischief to the author. But it will not be incomprehensible if you print it as it stands; indeed, it is more readable than some of his other late writings.

Has the Conservative Book Club, or Arlington House, advertised with you at all? If not, I should think they might be persuaded to do so, since they have advertised in other student-edited journals, I believe. They might try a page advertising my *Burke*, or their special offer in connection with my *Creature of the Twilight*. Should you people write to them, you can say I suggested that you do so.

Cordially,
Russell Kirk

Letter to Michael Oakeshott

Oakeshott (1901–1990) was a highly respected English scholar of philosophy, religion, politics, and history who served at the London School of Economics as professor of political science for twenty years. In 1953 he reviewed Kirk's The Conservative Mind; *and in his 1956 essay "On Being Conservative," he described the typical conservative as one who has the disposition "to prefer the familiar to the unknown, to prefer the tried to the untried, fact to mystery, the actual to the possible, the limited to the unbounded, the near to the distant, the sufficient to the superabundant, the convenient to the perfect, present laughter to utopian bliss." ("On Being Conservative" was originally a lecture delivered by Oakeshott in 1956; it was published six years later in his* Rationalism in Politics, and Other Essays *[London: Methuen, 1962], 168–96.)*

January 17, 1968

Professor Michael Oakeshott
The London School of Economics

Dear Professor Oakeshott,

Mr. Richard J. Bishirjian informs me that he has been in correspondence with you concerning the possibility of study at the London School, presumably with the doctorate in view. I commend him to you.

I have known Mr. Bishirjian for several years, and have corresponded with him frequently. He is a very serious and able student, who has gone to much trouble and expense to prepare himself in the classical languages, among other disciplines. He is both highly intelligent and sensible, and deserves whatever help he can obtain. Recently he has been studying with Eric Voegelin, at the University of Notre Dame. You would find him a superior sort.[44]

I continue to quote from your admirable *Rationalism in Politics* in my writings and lectures. Just now I am about to commence my long-postponed book *The Age of Eliot.*

Cordially,
Russell Kirk

Letter to Warren Fleischauer

Kirk met Fleischauer (1916–1982) during his undergraduate years at Mich-
igan State College, during the late 1930s; later they were fellow members
of the George Ade Society in East Lansing. Having earned his doctorate in
English, Fleischauer served for many years in the English department at
Frostburg State College (now Frostburg State University) in Maryland. He
was an authority on the works of Samuel Johnson and worked for much of
his life on a never-completed biography of Johnson. Fleischauer and his wife,
Frances, kept a home in Mecosta just a short walk from Piety Hill. The two
families maintained close ties that ended only with Fleischauer's death after a
heart attack on the front porch of his Mecosta residence in 1982.

April 29, 1968

Dr. Warren Fleischauer
Frostburg, Maryland

Dear Warren,

What are the plans of the Fleischauers for the summer? I go to
Scotland on June 1, and Annette may join me there later; anyway, we'll
be back in Mecosta shortly after the middle of July. I trust that you
people mean to sojourn in your Mecosta house during the latter part of
the summer.

Monica is full of energy, and recognizes some seven or eight
words. She will have a sibling late in September, it appears. Aunt Nor-
mie is cheerful in the convalescent home at Millbrook. Yesterday we
took her to the Sugar Bush Festival at Shepard. Fay is in better spirits
than before.

An eighteenth-century man, much attached to Samuel Johnson,
is now on the faculty at Central Michigan: a Dr. Fuller. He and his
wife visited my library today.

I am to review a new book called *The Morality of Scholarship*, with
contributions by Northrop Frye, Stuart Hampshire, and Conor Cruise
O'Brien. In his essay, Frye commences thus: "In the eighteenth century

there was some confidence that, in Samuel Johnson's words, no new discoveries were to be made in the field of morality."[45] Now doubtless this
was Johnson's sentiment, but were such his *words?* Or is Frye confusedly
referring to the famous passage in Burke's *Reflections?* "We know that
we have made no new discoveries. . . ."[46] Is there a very similar passage
somewhere in Johnson's works? Let me know, if you have time.

How goes the world with you? I speechify incessantly nowadays,
and must be off to the University of Minnesota early tomorrow morning. More another time. Compliments to Frannie.

Yours,
Russell

Letter to Dan Rottenberg

*In early September 1968, Kirk received a letter from editor, author, and jour-
nalist Dan Rottenberg, then a staff writer at the* Wall Street Journal, *asking Kirk to participate in a survey of public affairs columnists to share the
manner in which he gathered information and arrived at his conclusions. In
response, Kirk wrote the following lengthy letter, which provides insights on
his life as a columnist—especially during national political campaigns.*

September 13, 1968

Mr. Dan Rottenberg
The Wall Street Journal
711 West Monroe Street
Chicago, Illinois

Dear Mr. Rottenberg,

Thanks for your letter of September 3; I would have replied sooner,
had it reached me promptly. But it was addressed to General Features,
in New York—where I never call. General Features has been bought by
the Los Angeles Times Syndicate, and your letter may have wandered
out to the editorial offices in Los Angeles. Anyway, it reached me here
only yesterday. I should be addressed simply at Mecosta, Michigan.

I look forward to the *Journal*'s survey of columnists on their method of gathering information. I don't know whether I can be classified as a "public affairs columnist," since for the most part my column is a more leisurely and reflective affair, dealing often with books, travel, education, interesting characters, general ruminations, and the like. As conventions and elections approach, however, I become more current. I suppose that only one out of four columns, throughout the year, deals directly with public affairs in the immediate political sense.

From the nature of my column, I am able to depend upon personal observation, conversations, and serious reading to a greater extent than can those columnists who must publish tomorrow their account of today's events. I make almost no use of the wire services, or of television and radio, except for matters of indisputable fact. I am on the road literally about two days out of every three, throughout the year, in part speechifying at universities and colleges. Also I usually go abroad, chiefly to Europe and Africa, about two or three months a year. I hardly know how to estimate the percentage of my columns, so far as personal observation and information obtained from news-reports are concerned, but I suppose it is about 90 per cent personal observation to 10 per cent second-hand.

I may add that I carry on a large correspondence regularly with public men of both parties, newspaper editors, clergymen, professors, men of business, and others, and obtain much information from them. But I almost never am to be found at cocktail parties in Washington or New York—the curse of serious journalism, these.

Again because of the character of my column, and my own background as historian and political theorist, probably I read a good many more serious books annually than does the typical columnist; also I review such books for the learned and critical quarterlies. I subscribe to some one hundred such serious journals, many of them foreign ones, and obtain from such sources much information which the wire services, newspapers, and other popular media cannot supply. I also subscribe to several of the more respectable foreign dailies, particularly British. I have correspondents in several European, Latin American, and African countries.

It being unnecessary for me, in "To the Point," to comment on every political event that occurs, I tend to write about those events and men with which and whom I have personal acquaintance. Recently, for instance, I analyzed the Republican convention in Michigan as an example of the new Republican unity; I attended that convention as a delegate, though I didn't mention the fact in the column itself. Similarly, recent columnar character-analyses of mine concerning Nixon, Humphrey, and McCarthy were founded on personal acquaintance and conversations extending over the past several years.

In general, I feel that many of my columnar colleagues are too eager to write *ex cathedra* of matters concerning which their knowledge is somewhat superficial, and to depend too heavily upon gossip and polls and wire-services. In an urgent column concerned wholly with public affairs, however, some of this superficiality is inevitable, for lack of leisure to reflect and investigate.

Now some words about my criticism of the public-opinion polls in 1964. (I have no higher opinion of most of those polls in 1968.) I think the polls sometimes are malicious or biased, and often do not go deep enough or wide enough in ascertaining sentiments—which frequently, anyways, are ephemeral sentiments.

Throughout the primary and state-convention period of 1964, I find on consulting my political columns for that year, I was a good prophet. I argued that the pollsters generally underestimated Goldwater's appeal to Republicans, and that was borne out by primary and convention results. My chief triumph occurred in connection with the California presidential primary. On May 28, 1964, at a press conference I held in Los Angeles, I predicted unequivocally that Goldwater would win the primary—by a margin of one-half of one per cent. (Actually, he beat Rockefeller by about one per cent, four days later.) The polls all had shown a contrary result, some by considerable margins; and I think I was the only columnist to predict a Goldwater victory there.

From June until November, 1964, I wrote about three times that the polls still did not reflect Goldwater's appeal. This changed as the election approached, nevertheless. For one thing, polls themselves can have a cumulative effect, if they are virtually unanimous. (Thus, today, they work for Nixon.) The pollsters can become prophets who work the fulfillment of their own prophecies, for many voters fear to run against what is said to be the conviction of the majority, and others wish to back a winning horse. To this influence was added the ineptitude of the Goldwater organization, as the campaign reached its later stages; in the last three or four weeks, Goldwater lost ground very speedily.[47]

My own estimates of Goldwater's earlier strength were founded chiefly upon conversations with newspaper editors and public men, and upon my travels in some seventeen states during the course of the campaign. I addressed some seventy audiences during that period.

About a fortnight or three weeks before the election, it became clear to me that Goldwater would lose, and probably lose very badly, though not necessarily so badly as the polls predicted. I encountered one poll which is not widely known, but which I perceived to be probably very accurate. This was the poll of Cheskin Associates, in Chicago, concerning which I conversed at length with Mr. Louis Cheskin. The Cheskin polls are conducted in depth, and discriminately, since Mr. Cheskin believes rightly that it's no use asking people for whom they are going to vote, well in advance of an election; most of them really don't know. The Cheskin method is to try to ascertain the underlying *prejudices* of the representative voters, through a long questionnaire—sometimes of a hundred questions, some with several parts—administered to a limited sample. In the Johnson-Goldwater contest, the Cheskin survey in the key states of Illinois and California revealed a prejudice against Goldwater on the "trigger-happy" issue so strong that no possible prejudice in his favor, or against Johnson, could countervail it. One question in particular was significant: "Suppose that Johnson and Goldwater were out hunting deer. Do you suppose that either of these gentlemen would fire at the first movement in the brush?" Of those responding, 17 per cent said that Johnson would; 37 per cent, that Goldwater would. "You see," Mr. Cheskin commented, "it's all over." He was quite right.

Polls of a sort, then, are fairly reliable indicators; but not the usual nose-counting ones, unless taken with a good many grains of salt and close analysis. I did not give Goldwater any chance in my column after talking with Mr. Cheskin, though in my November 3 column I did outline how election-return listeners should analyze the significance of returns from various states, regardless of radio and television commentators, and of pollsters. I pointed out that if Goldwater did badly in Ohio, he must lose the country; that if Johnson should slip in Texas, Goldwater would carry the South; that if Goldwater should carry Maine, he would make a better national showing than had been expected; that if Johnson would take New York, New Jersey, and New England; etc., etc. In fine, my own analysis was more accurate than that of the polls in the pre-nomination period, and I think continued more accurate until the last month of the contest, during which closing period I abandoned the forecasting game. While I used popular polls as very rough indicators on occasions, and respected a few polls in depth, in general I depended on a large amount of conversation and correspondence with local politicians, information from newspapers editors and the like, and my own meetings with lecture-audiences and the general public in my travels.

I do find some monthly and weekly magazines of value in such matters, and a few newspapers—the *New York Times* (which allowance for a certain preference and hope, on occasion) and (without any intention to flatter you Dow-Jones people) more particularly the *W. S. Journal* and the *National Observer;* also, often the *Washington Post.* One more thing: I gather a good deal of reliable information from the political agents of large corporations, and sometimes from labor-union agents.

In all the preceding, it should be remembered that I am a ruminative columnist who is only incidentally and occasionally political; and that, strictly speaking, I am an essayist, novelist, and critic, rather than a political journalist. Therefore I lack both some of the virtues and some of the vices of the representative "public affairs" commentator.

So far as forecasting this season goes, incidentally, fortune has favored me. I predicted all of Mr. Nixon's primary and convention victories, regardless of polls (though often the polls confirmed my judgment); and also I predicted Mr. McCarthy's strength in New Hampshire, Wisconsin, and elsewhere—and Mr. Humphrey's easy nomination. My estimates of the real strength of Mr. Rockefeller and Mr. Romney were upheld by the results. The performance of the best-known pollsters just before the Republican convention substantiates my suspicions of those gentry, I believe.

For the record—though I've not yet done this in my column, and I write before detailed polls have been published—I venture to predict now that, as matters are drifting, Mr. Wallace will carry four to six states of the lower South; Mr. Nixon will take nearly everything else; Mr. Humphrey's defeat probably will be worse than Goldwater's, at least in number of states carried, and may be as bad as Hoover's.[48] My sources of information, again, are travel recently in a good many states; tips from editors, political activists, clergymen, and the like; and a wide reading of local newspapers, not simply the New York and Washington press. Also I have a useful acquaintance with various people in the splinter factions.

My reply to you at this length may suggest the character of the correspondence which my assistant and I carry on; surely it has satiated your interest by this time, anyway. Do let me know if I can be of more help in any way. I will be at home most of the time (what with the anticipated birth of our second child, tomorrow or the next day) until the latter part of October. . . . Best wishes for your project.

Cordially,
Russell Kirk

Letter to Ted Humes

Kirk was a longtime friend and correspondent with Ted Humes (born Theodore L. Huminski, 1922–2002), a former CIA officer, attorney, Republican congressional candidate in Pennsylvania, and GOP political operative in Arizona. For a time, Humes worked at St. Francis College, where he served as director of development and founded the short-lived St. Francis Quarterly, *for which Kirk submitted to a short interview.*

October 18, 1968

Mr. Ted Humes
Saint Francis College
Loretto, Pennsylvania

Dear Ted,

It now appears that I can spend the night after my talk with you—whether you are living in Towson or near Loretto by that time. The following day, I must proceed to New York.

If it's not too much trouble for you, I will plan to arrive at Pittsburgh airport at 1:25 p.m., Friday, October 25—TWA Flight 69. The two flights which reach Johnstown are at impossible times—3 a.m. and 4 p.m. (The last is cutting matters too close, I think, and for the first, I should have to start a day early from Mecosta.)

I enclose my succinct replies to your inquiries for the *St. Francis Quarterly.*

So I'll be with you a week from now.

Cordially,
Russell Kirk

1. Dr. Kirk: To what do you attribute the present campus unrest and disorder?

The principal cause, I think, is boredom and anonymity: that is, the typical mass campus is far too big, and has attracted a great many students who have no real interest in the real intellectual concerns of the academy. The rootless are always violent, and the lonely and bored find riot a welcome diversion. Until—if ever—the humane scale is restored on the campus, and until some comparatively strict standards for entrance are re-established, we may expect disorder to continue. In addition to this condition, the permissivism which the rising generation has known, in the average home and the average school, throughout their young lives, leads to a demand for total liberty—which, like everything else carried to an extreme, is absurd.

2. What is your theory behind the "alienation" from society of the children of good middle and upper class families, and their alleged rejection of what we regard as traditional and respectable values?

The rising generation, it seems to me, rebels against the absence of norms and order. In Santayana's phrase, "Freedom from what? Freedom from the consequences of freedom." Indulgently treated in the average affluent household, denied by the laws the possibility of purposeful work even if they had desired it, kept in a kind of compulsory idleness which has amounted to moral and intellectual stagnation, the rising generation hungers after some challenge, and tries to defy a stifling materialism. In such circumstances, the most violent demagogue or ridiculous freak can attract a following among the undisciplined and confused young people. The alienation is genuine enough, in many instances; but the causes embraced by radical young people lead to an alienation yet more thorough.

3. Do you see an abatement or an exacerbation of the student disaffection and unrest in the near future?

I fancy that the present unrest will subside somewhat during this academic year, particularly after the election. It will be clear to even the most radical undergraduate that America is not bound for revolution: the public tendency is altogether in another direction; the shallow talk of "revolution" no longer will be "in." The probable termination or dwindling away of the war in Viet Nam, and the prospect of curtailment of military conscription, will remove one great cause of protest: while the tendency of the "black power" people increasingly will separate the Negro organization from naïve white students.

4. What might be the ultimate consequences of a failure to arrest the student disturbances?

As Professor Seymour Martin Lipset suggests, student disaffection could be a most serious problem, were it really to affect the mass of American students. Colleges and universities would sink to the intellectual level of the institutions of Egypt, India, or many Latin-American states; serious study would become nearly impossible; student radicals would try to use campuses as sanctuaries for assaults upon the political order. Repressive measures by public authorities would follow, necessarily.

5. *Do you agree that secularizing influences in our society seem to be holding sway—does this augur bad for the future of Church related institutions like St. Francis?*

Aye, the tendency of the time in this country is to break down the remaining institutions and bodies of principle which distinguish between the things of Caesar and the things of God. A straw in the wind is a recent decision by the federal Bureau of Public Roads that chapels cannot be erected along highways built with federal subsidies, because this would violate the separation of church and state, allegedly! Church-connected colleges increasingly would be pushed to the wall, if this tendency were to continue; and the whole social order would be increasingly bored and violent, and the realm of the transcendent should be closed to the mass of men.

6. *Do you see any profound changes in the national government as a result of Mr. Nixon's election? Do you see, for example, a complete overhaul of our policies vis a vis Rhodesia and South Africa?*

Perhaps the most important changes may result from change of governmental personnel, rather than from fresh legislation: the prospect of four or five new appointments to the Supreme Court will suggest what differences in attitude and policy may become manifest; this is as true of the National Labor Relations Board, for instance, and the federal Office of Education. (We may expect an end to Washington pressures to compel school "busing," for instance.) Foreign policy will change considerably, into an endeavor to present firmer resistance to Russian and Chinese imperialism. Little attention will be paid to the United Nations, and ties with actual or potential allies strengthened. There should be less cajoling of the petty "emergent nations" of Africa, for example, and friendlier relations with the Republic of South Africa; one may expect abandonment of sanctions against Rhodesia, and possibly recognition of that country, if present negotiations be-tween the Wilson and Smith governments collapse—though some time-lag will intervene.

Letter to Paulina Piedrahita

Paulina Piedrahita was a university student who came from Bogotá, Co-lombia, to Mecosta to be academically mentored by Kirk during the mid-1960s, boarding with Kirk's uncle and aunt, Potter and Fay Jewell, in their cabin at Piety Hill. In the following letter, written after Piedrahita's return to Bogotá, Kirk writes familiarly about Colombian politics and other, more everyday matters.

January 3, 1969
Mecosta

Senorita Paulina Piedrahita
Bogota

Dear Paulina,

How good to have your Christmas card! All's well here amidst the deep snows of Mecosta. Monica and Cecilia are lively but well-behaved. Annette is in good spirits, as am I.

I follow your Colombian politics with mystification. Recently I re-proved, in print, a local priest who delivered a sermon, in our very own parish church, rebuking the Pope for not staying in hovels while he was in Colombia, and traveling in helicopters "used to kill guerrillas fighting for freedom." We had a Latin-American visitor some months ago: Senator Jorge Siles Salinas, from Bolivia, who saw here a side of America to which otherwise he was not introduced by our Department of State.[49]

The Nixon administration will be honest, if cautious; at least there will issue from Washington no great follies during the next four years, in foreign affairs or domestic. I see Mr. Nixon now and again, and am friendly with the most powerful man in the embryo cabinet, Mr. Robert Finch.[50]

My book *Enemies of the Permanent Things: Observations of Abnormity in Literature and Politics* will be published in March. I am hard at work upon my long-postponed *Age of Eliot*.[51] This year I speechify everywhere, especially against Black Power zealots. The cities of Kabul or Fez are far safer, nowadays, than any city in Michigan; but Mecosta is immune to criminality. (In the past eighty-five years, there has been not one instance of unlawful entry into an occupied house!) . . .

Would we could come unto you in Bogota! Shall I have myself appointed ambassador to Colombia?

Our little ancient house in Scotland already is too small for my swelling family.[52] Possibly we may lease the Prior's House (c. 1500 A.D.) of Pittenweem Priory, one of the oldest continuously-inhabited residences in Scotland.

More another time. Annette sends her love. Do let us have news of you from time to time.

Cordially,
Russell Kirk

Letter to Anne Thomson

Thomson was among Kirk's circle of friends during his years studying at the University of St. Andrews. A medical doctor by training and profession, she lives in Aberfeldy, a small town in Highland Perthshire, though she served for a time treating the sick in Kenya.

June 29, 1969

Dr. Anne Thomson
Aberfeldy

Dear Anne,

No place could be more different than Aberfeldy than is Nairobi, I fancy. When are you coming over to see the wonders of Mecosta? We are in the process of building Fortress Kirk, a vast addition to our Old House—really a separate building (virtually a tower) of brick, connected with the Old House by subterranean and superterranean passages. We have fallout shelters, steel doors, oaken shutters, and all, in readiness for the dawning age. So you will be lodged in splendor when you come.

I'll be in Scotland, briefly, late in September or early in October; but Annette and the babies will stay home. During the latter three weeks of July, friends of ours will occupy our Pittenweem house and will wander somewhat in Scotland; they may stop by to see you in their Perthshire explorations. They are Mr. and Mrs. John Emmons, of Big Rapids, our county seat. Mr. Emmons is the chief dairy-farmer of our county, and will be much interested in rural Scotland. They are pleasant, youngish people.[53]

Little Cecilia crawls most vigorously now, and climbs. Monica, her elder sister, talks much—whole sentences—and has taken to beholding Patti, one of our ancestral spirits or genii here at Mecosta. Today she led Annette to the spot by the old cistern where Patti (masculine) is wont to stand, and patted his head (invisible), and kissed him, and embraced him—little arms in a circle round vacancy. "Hi, Patti," Monica said. She waves to him, and calls to him, from a parlor window; he doesn't seem to move much from his station by the cistern, and evidently is of dwarfish stature, though much taller than Monica.

I think you should have received, by this time, a copy of my most recent book, *Enemies of the Permanent Things*. Do let me know if you haven't.

We are endeavoring to sell our Pittenweem house, grown too small for our present household: price, seven thousand pounds, furnished. The key can be got from the National Trust Office in Pittenweem High Street, if you think of anyone who might be interested. Later we may lease the Prior's Palace, Pittenweem Priory, which will lodge us adequately.

Henry Lorimer and his wife, Didi, are stranded in Canada, with visa-trouble, too complicated to explain here! They were coming through Ontario to visit us, but were turned back at the American frontier, and now can't get back to New York, where they have been living. I have sent off a special-delivery letter to the White House, in an endeavor to rescue them.

Hew Lorimer thinks of giving Kellie to the National Trust, but is fifty thousand pounds short of a sufficient endowment, I believe. Mary Lorimer doesn't want to leave Kellie, but her health and their finances no longer can keep up the castle, I fear.[54]

Send us news, pray. More before I come to Scotland.

Yours,
Russell Kirk

Letter to Hew Lorimer

Esteemed Scottish sculptor Hew Lorimer (1907–1993) is perhaps best known for crafting the sculpted figures that adorn the exterior of the National Library of Scotland: figures representing theology, history, law, science, medicine, poetry, and music. Hew and his wife, Mary, were longtime friends of Kirk who met the younger man during his student days in Scotland. In the following letter, Kirk speaks recurrently of Kellie and his own Scottish property: a small house at 40 High Street in Pittenweem, Fife.

July 2, 1969

Hew Lorimer, Esq.
Kellie Castle

Dear Hew,

Many thanks for your letter of 28th June. Here's much news for you and Mary.

Aye, Mr. And Mrs. Emmons will be in 40 High Street from *July* 8 to 27. Should they pick up the key at the National Trust office?

I think we must abandon any intention of letting 40 High Street this summer. Various friends of mine talk of staying there from time to time; what's more, already seven people have answered my advertisement of sale in *National Review,* and some doubtless will call to see the house in the course of the summer. One gentleman, connected with the ancient American silversmith firm of Samuel Kirk & Son, proposes to live there for a week in August, to see how he likes it, at my invitation—supposing we don't sell it first.[55] Soon we'll send you a schedule of intended invaders of 40 High Street.

My friend Dr. Paul Gottfried, a professor of history, and his bride—now in the Continent on their honeymoon—may come to 40 High Street for a week in August, if nobody else is in the house at that time. I have suggested that he call you from London in advance. He telephoned you while you were away, but will try again when he and his bride return from Dalmatia. . . .

I think that probably Annette and I will wish to lease the Prior's Palace for a term of years, when it becomes available. The big walled garden is an additional attraction, with small children. We may undertake some restoration elsewhere in Pittenweem, too; but probably that must wait until we come over as a body, next summer. . . .

My secret agents in various quarters of the globe continue to send me reports on Monica and her fiancé. . . . [56]

But we shall discourse of all this with Henry and Didi, when they arrive about five hours from now, here at Mecosta![57] Probably you will hear from Henry of his tribulations, and of how Sir Russell the Wizard Knight rescued him. To put matters very briefly, he and Didi decided to drive through Canada to Mecosta, against my advice. There happened what I had feared might happen: at the farther frontier, they were stopped; their visas were not in perfect order; they were deprived of their visas and told to visit an American consulate-general, the one in Toronto; arrived there, they were treated with great hauteur, scolded, and told that they could not even apply for new visas for at least three months! They were badly scared, and feared they would have to return penuriously to Britain, forever, when first they telephoned your servant.

Indeed, this was a pretty kettle of fish, for various reasons—and one not to be remedied by law, the younger Lorimers being indeed somewhat in the wrong, so far as immigration technicalities go. But

I spent two days—while they wept in Toronto—on their business; and here is a list of the people to whom I wrote or telephoned:

Mr. Patrick Buchanan, Special Assistant to the President of the United States.
The Honorable Elford Cederberg, member of Congress from my district.
The Honorable Robert Griffin, senator from Michigan.
The Honorable Barry Goldwater, senator from Arizona.
The Honorable Gerald Ford, Republican leader of the House of Representatives.
Mr. Jay Gordon Hall, national political agent of General Motors.
Dr. Richard V. Allen, Special Assistant to the Secretary of State.

This morning, I obtained a special decree from the Honorable Richard Milhous Nixon, President of the United States, exempting Henry and Didi from the usual requirements and procedures of the Immigration and Naturalization Service. Hurrah! I hope Henry doesn't contrive to get into more trouble before he arrives at Mecosta. His difficulty was his honesty and excessive frankness of speech; the world, as I wrote to him, belongs to the disingenuous. By the way, I think that I have succeeded in assuring that he and Didi will receive immigrant visas before the end of this month, and so will be able to labor in the American vineyard so long as they please.

What legalistic travail it was! I cajoled and indulged in veiled menaces. Probably I am the only man in this century to enjoy an unqualified victory over Divine Bureaucracy. And Henry and his spouse now rise above the law, admitted to aristocratic privileges and exceptions in this decadent democracy. I might not have behaved with such unwonted (in me) speed of action, had not Annette insisted that Henry and Didi must arrive at Mecosta, governments or no governments, in time for the grand beaver buffet reception we have planned for them. (Yes, real beaver from our swamps.)

I do hope your sojourn in hospital will not be very unpleasant, Hew, and that Mary has a good time in England. More when you are back at Kellie. . . .

Do let me know if I can help with the National Trust Scheme for Kellie, or whatever is going forward. I can pledge a thousand pounds now, and could pay it before long, if need be; probably I could help more later, particularly when we sell 40 High Street. Is there a pledge-form I could fill out?[58]

Cordially,
Russell

Letter to Henry Kissinger

Kirk first encountered Kissinger when the latter was serving as editor of Confluence, *a political science journal he founded while serving on the faculty at Harvard during the 1950s. Kissinger accepted for publication an essay Kirk had written on Woodrow Wilson; this was reprinted in* Enemies of the Permanent Things *and in* The Essential Russell Kirk. *(See* Enemies of the Permanent Things: Observations of Abnormity in Literature and Politics *[New Rochelle, NY: Arlington House, 1969]; rev. ed. [Peru, IL: Sugden, 1984] and* The Essential Russell Kirk: Selected Essays, *edited by George A. Panichas [Wilmington, DE: ISI Books, 2007].) In 1969, when the following letter was written, Kissinger was serving in the Nixon White House as national security advisor. In this role—and, later, as secretary of state—he was an influential advocate for a policy of détente with the Soviet Union.*

September 12, 1969

Dr. Henry A. Kissinger
The White House
Washington, D.C.

Dear Dr. Kissinger,

As I need hardly inform you, your servant is much comforted by your presence in the post that you have taken; conceivably you may have noticed my remark to that effect in the *New York Times Magazine*, some weeks ago.[59] But how you must be laboring!

Some years ago, in the late lamented *Confluence,* you published my essay on Woodrow Wilson.[60] It has been included, that piece, in my latest book, *Enemies of the Permanent Things;* and so I am sending a copy of the book to you, with my compliments: not that I expect you to find time to read it, this side of the tomb.

From Rome, Dr. Francesco Leoni writes to me inquiring whether I might be able to speak of him to you. Dr. Leoni is the editor of a small magazine, *Relazioni,* and a serious and well-disposed gentleman. I think he would write to you offering some information upon the growth of the Communist influence in Italy. Anyway, should you hear from him, I commend him to you. His address is Piazza Navona 23, Roma—hard by my favorite Roman restaurant, Tre Scalini.

I'm off three days from now for a fortnight in Dalmatia (Diocletian's palace, chiefly) and another fortnight in Britain (seeking out places mentioned in Eliot's *Four Quartets*). Best wishes.

Cordially,
Russell Kirk

The 1970s

. . . an attempt to wake some of the rising generation to
awareness of their own cultural and institutional roots.

from a letter to Irving Kristol, December 26, 1972

Letter to William F. Buckley Jr.

Mr. William Buckley
National Review

Dear Bill,

I enclose a copy of a letter I have sent to the USIA people, concerning a piece of mine on Ray Bradbury that they wish to reprint. This may be of a little interest to you, what with your USIA connection.[1] Actually, the USIA bureaucracy wished to eliminate from my piece all references to liberals, librarians, conservative writers, and God! Talk of censorship! I have let them take out the liberals and the librarians, as not being essential to this particular essay (and because they pretend they must shorten it, what with considerations of space); but God they shall not take—neither Ray Bradbury's God, nor mine. This Civil-Liberties-Union mentality in the USIA must seem curious to the Moslems or the Buddhists (even) of Indonesia, say: they must take it, if they bother to read the USIA's outpourings, that the United States is quite as godless as Soviet Russia.

Cordially,
Russell

Letter to Andrew Lytle

A self-described "Northern Agrarian," believing in smallholding and a humane economy, Kirk deeply admired the group of southern academics and writers who formed the Agrarians and published the influential treatise I'll Take My Stand *(New York: Harper & Brothers, 1930), a defense of traditional southern culture. One of the group's number, Lytle (1902–1995)*

145

became friends with Kirk and eventually agreed to speak at a seminar at Piety Hill along with Cleanth Brooks in 1989.

February 11, 1971

Mr. Andrew Lytle
Editor, *The Sewanee Review*
Sewanee, Tennessee

Dear Mr. Lytle,

Do let me know of any way in which I might be able to help to obtain financial support for *The Sewanee Review;* I should be glad to write directly to foundations or individuals, should that seem desirable.

I have long believed that *The Sewanee Review* is the best critical quarterly surviving in the world. Recently I read through almost the whole run of T. S. Eliot's *Criterion*, down to its end in 1939; and I was reminded of how necessary such publications are for any high culture. Throughout its long continuity, *Sewanee* has been a powerful force to sustain the moral imagination, the traditions of civility, and the canons of right reason. Through its criticism of letters and thought, it has provided—as did *The Criterion*—a standard for mind and conscience, in a time when mass appetites have threatened to submerge modern culture. Courageous and perceptive, *Sewanee* has not yielded to leveling pressures. Of the many magazines to which I subscribe, *Sewanee* is the one to which I turn first. At a very modest cost, *The Sewanee Review* does much to sustain the continuity of civilization.

Cordially,
Russell Kirk

Letter to Valerie Eliot

Russell and Annette Kirk, along with all four daughters, were on friendly terms with Valerie Eliot (1926–2012), widow of the distinguished poet and executrix of his literary estate. This longtime friendship began in earnest when Kirk wrote the following letter to Mrs. Eliot, asking permission to reprint portions of her late husband's published and unpublished writings in his forthcoming book Eliot and His Age.

March 22, 1971

Mrs. T. S. Eliot
c/o Faber & Faber
Russell Square
London

Dear Mrs. Eliot,

Some eighteen years ago, I told your husband that I would write, one day, a book to be called *The Age of Eliot*. At last I near completion of that study, although the title has changed from the original to *Eliot and His Age: T. S. Eliot's Moral Imagination in the Twentieth Century*. Random House will publish the book here in America; nothing has been arranged yet about British publication.

I discuss both the poetry and the prose, though the latter at greater length than any previous critics have. The character of the book, as a critical study, probably is sufficiently suggested by the sub-title.

Now I should like to obtain your permission to quote both from some of your husband's letters to me, and from his published writings. Of course I am applying also for permission, so far as the latter are concerned, to Faber & Faber and to the two American publishers. My quotations are for critical purposes, of course.

I enclose a list of the passages I would quote from your husband's letters. As you will perceive, I mean to publish only extracts, and most of those very brief; no letter is published in its entirety; nothing of a personal character is included.

As for the quotations from your husband's writings, these are somewhat less numerous, the length of my study considered, than is usual in critical studies of T. S. Eliot's work—in part because I do not belong to the "lemon-squeezer school of criticism," nor yet to the legion of those enamored of alleged "sources." I do quote from *The Criterion* more frequently than do other critics, because I pay some attention to his views of events during his time.

I rather think you will like this book, which is better calculated to inform the common (though educated) reader than most such studies have been; and of course I will send you a copy once copies are available—which may be late this year. Incidentally, I have sent to Mr. T. S. Matthews, at his request, copies of my correspondence with your husband; I look forward to his biography, and to Mr. Sencourt's. My own book, of course, is no biography—and still less does it resemble an anthology. It does contain a number of interesting remarks by Canon B. I. Bell, Wyndham Lewis, Roy Campbell, George Scott-Moncrieff, and other friends whom your husband and I had in common.

Possibly you have seen Mr. Marion Montgomery's admirable little study *T. S. Eliot: a Study of the American Magus,* published a few months ago. If you haven't, I would be glad to send you a copy; it is one of the more perceptive essays.

My wife and I, with our three girl-babies, will be in Scotland for about six weeks during June and the first half of July. My wife would like very much to talk with you—as, of course, I would, too. So if you should have any leisure to see us, we will descend into England briefly for that express purpose; I'll write from Scotland once we are established there. (I have had a little ancient house in Pittenweem, but am selling it, my household now being too large for its five rooms.) Probably we will be staying from time to time at Balcarres, Kellie, Durie, and other Fife houses, but I will send you a precise address later. My wife, Annette Yvonne Cecile Courtemanche Kirk, is thirty years old (to my fifty-two); the babies—Monica, Cecilia, and Felicia, the first two names somewhat suggestive of Eliot plays—are three years, two years, and ten months old, respectively.

I made my way to East Coker, for the first time, about a year and a half ago, and attended service in that fine old church, and said my prayer before the oval stone.[2]

We still are deep in snow at Mecosta; doubtless spring has come to you, but my hundred-odd lilac bushes won't be in bloom for a month yet, or more. I am busy with all sorts of concerns, including an endeavor to obtain an endowment for *The Sewanee Review*. Best wishes from all Kirks.

Yours cordially,
Russell Kirk

Letter to Mickie Teetor

In 1971, the Kirks' close friends Chuck and Mickie Teetor traveled to Portugal and Spain with their two daughters.

June 26, 1971

Mrs. Charles Teetor
Palace Hotel
Busaco, Portugal

Dear Mickie,

Much do we wish we could be with you in your peregrinations. Have Sintra and Busaco been as wondrous as the descriptions in Santiago de Compostela?

Annette's mother died more than a week ago. The funeral was held in Long Island, but she was buried at St. Michael's, Remus, a few days ago.[3] Regis the elder has come unto us now, and we will endeavor to keep him happy and busy at Mecosta. It will take some time to settle his various affairs, so we'll not go abroad at all this summer. But do think about an expedition to Madeira with us in December.

There was a good deal of attention in the Long Island papers to Mary Courtemanche's death—a good long obituary in the *Long Island Press*. She died with fortitude and hope. Annette was thoroughly worn out by her long vigils. Now she is spending much time with the three little girls, all of whom welcomed her home cordially. She could scarcely recognize Cecilia, what with changes in the course of five weeks.

Henry Lorimer has departed or is departing from Nettle Creek, I am told, and will return to Britain to enter upon training in the retail trade—which seems to me an unpromising prospect. I think that Didi and baby are coming to Mecosta while Henry is in Scotland seeing Hew. There are not many occupations satisfying in themselves; mine is one of the few that are both interesting and eminent.[4] I fancy that I could have been content as a tolerable potter, though. . . .

Has Chuck found opportunity to inspect the strange fishing-vessels of the Portuguese? What do Victoria and Christina say about Portugal? Have you all been to lively festivals? . . .

Soon I will have page-proofs of *Eliot*. I must turn my hand to the rather dreary work of writing *The Roots of American Order*.

We look forward to thorough accounts of your travels when all Teetors return.

Love,
Russell

Letter to Rev. Martin D'Arcy

Father Martin D'Arcy, SJ (1888–1976), was a Roman Catholic priest, prolific author, and an influential friend of several key literary figures, including T. S. Eliot, Evelyn Waugh, Dorothy L. Sayers, J. R. R. Tolkien, and W. H. Auden. He was also a friend of Russell and Annette Kirk, who were influenced by D'Arcy's views of the Four Last Things: death, judgment, heaven, and hell.

July 12, 1971

The Reverend Martin D'Arcy, S.J.
Farm Street
London

Dear Father D'Arcy,

My wife and I meant to send you our congratulations on your eightieth birthday; but events descended upon us then; and only now do we send to you the letter we had intended. I find on my desk a letter that my wife began to write to you, and I quote from that unfinished missive, dated February 2, 1969:

"Dear Father D'Arcy,

"You may recall our meeting in Los Angeles during the summer of 1965. Father Lucy of Loyola University introduced us." (You and I had met earlier in New York, of course.)

"At present my husband is at work on a book about the age of Eliot. Since we saw you, he has published *Edmund Burke: A Genius Reconsidered; The Political Principles of Robert Taft;* and *Enemies of the Permanent Things: Observations of Abnormity in Literature and Society.*

"I never did have the baby I was expecting that summer we met, and since then we have had two beautiful little girls who are the joy of our life. I thought you might enjoy reading the columns Russell wrote about them as well as one about your remarks to me concerning heaven. (I hope this was remembered correctly!)[5]

"If the opportunity ever arises, we would love to have you visit us here in the 'stump country' of Michigan, or at our little house in Pittenweem, Fife. We hope to be there the next summer. . . ."

Here endeth my wife's note; but to Annette's fragmentary epistle I add that we now have three baby girls, the announcements of whose births we enclose; that my book *Eliot and His Age: T. S. Eliot's Moral Imagination in the Twentieth Century* will be published by Random House in February; that we have sold our house in Pittenweem; but that we have vastly enlarged my ancestral house here at Mecosta; and that we do dream of luring you here one day. I do hope that you might contrive to come to see us when next you are in America lecturing.

Your writings are much cited and quoted in my book about our old friend TSE. In one chapter, I point out that those who have difficulty in understanding *Four Quartets* would do well to read certain sections in your *Death and Life,* written about the same time. Of course you knew Eliot well in those years. Did you happen to discuss questions theological with him while he was at work upon the *Quartets?* It would be very interesting to Eliot's readers if you directly influenced Eliot's thought and expression in the *Quartets.* You quote Eliot therein, of course. By the way, I have the fourth impression of your book, 1948—"war economy standard." Has there been a later edition, on either side of the ocean?

I have reports of you now and then from your many friends. I do hope that you and Annette and I may contrive to meet again before many months are out. We'll not be going to Britain until next summer; but perhaps you will be over here; we pray so.

Some photographs are enclosed for you, as well as copies of my columns that Annette mentioned.

Cordially,

Russell Kirk

Letter to Eric Voegelin

Kirk harbored a deep and open respect for Voegelin (1901–1985), a distinguished German-born political philosopher, to whom he devoted a chapter in his Enemies of the Permanent Things *and quoted aptly in* Eliot and His Age.

July 19, 1971

Dr. Eric Voegelin
The Hoover Institution
Stanford, California

Dear Eric,

Here, tardily, you will find what I meant to send to you a year ago: announcements of the births of my three little daughters; also here is a picture of the three with their mother.

Much do I wish I had been able to participate in the great Voegelin affair at Notre Dame; but I had to speak elsewhere on those days. I should have liked to hear the exchange on gnosticism. Are the papers to be published?[6]

I have read carefully the Voegelin-James number of *The Southern Review*.[7] *The Turn of the Screw* always had puzzled me, but I find much more meaning in it now. Henry James was a man with Swedenborgian forebears who didn't believe in ghosts; I am one with Swedenborgian forebears who *does* believe in ghosts; indeed, everybody who stays here in my ancestral house of Piety Hill becomes a more fervent believer than even I am.

Except for some of his short stories, everything of James' I have tried to read only puts me to sleep. T. S. Eliot, though the successor of James in London, seems to have been little attracted to James—though for that matter, he had no relish for any New England authors except Hawthorne. I should have the page proofs of my long *Eliot and His Age* book any day now, and Random House will publish it in February; you will find yourself quoted and cited therein. Two memoirs or biographies of Eliot are in preparation—by Robert Sencourt and T. S. Matthews—but they may be rather odd affairs, since Mrs. Eliot (obeying her husband's will) sets her face against all biographies, and will permit no quotation from his letters for such a purpose, or perhaps from his works, so far as the laws of copyright are involved. Although, my book being on a chronological plan, some thread of biography must run through it, in essence it is a critical study of his moral and social thought—as the subtitle, *T. S. Eliot's Moral Imagination in the Twentieth Century*, sufficiently suggests.

Hegel is another writer I never could bear to read much of; but I am mightily enlightened by your "Study in Sorcery."[8] It will sustain me against various Hegelian friends either side of the Atlantic. (I used to quote Tocqueville to them, but now can quote Voegelin, too.)

Incidentally, one of the small symptoms of the historical and theoretical illiteracy of this century, which you may or may not have noticed, occurs in what was, until recently, the most widely-used short history of political thought in American colleges—George Sabine's.[9] Sabine says solemnly that Burke was strongly influenced by Hegel—which is rather like Henry James being strongly influenced by T. S. Eliot. Or I think of a slip-of-the-tongue phrase of a friend of mine, unintentionally effectively: "He smoked so rapidly that he lit one cigarette from the butt of the next."

I've no immediate prospect of getting to Stanford, but some such expedition may occur before many months are out; I hope so. Best wishes to you and your wife.

Cordially,
Russell Kirk

Letter to Clinton Wallace

Clinton Wallace was the Kirks' famous "burglar-butler," whom Russell and Annette first met in late 1966. Between then and the time the following letter was written, Wallace had wandered the roads of America, providing for himself by doing odd jobs and panhandling. At some point, he was arrested (not for the first time in his life) and imprisoned for pilfering from a church poor box, his reasoning being that the money was intended for the poor, he himself was poor, so the money was rightly his to take. A harmless man, though large and fierce looking, Wallace was sent to the maximum-security prison in Graterford, Pennsylvania. In 1971 he wrote to Kirk, who promised to provide the handful of conditions necessary for the man to be eligible for parole: a sponsor, a place to live, and a job.

September 7, 1971

Mr. Clinton Wallace
No. H-9912
Box 244
Graterford, Pennsylvania

Dear Mr. Wallace:

Thank you for your letter of August 30, 1971. As you requested therein, I am sending a copy of this reply of mine to the Board of Probation and Parole, in Harrisburg.

I am now able to assure you that we will be glad to receive you here if you obtain parole. We can give you work in gardening and maintenance of my properties, and will be able to provide suitable lodging for you. (I am now endeavoring to arrange for the lease or purchase of a large house near our own, as a kind of overflow-house for my under-takings, and you could have a pleasant room there; anyway, something adequate will be found for you before you are released.)

Today I conversed with my friend Mr. Dale May, our local—that is, county—probation-parole agent, who is familiar with your case. When you come here, you will meet him: a pleasant, sensible gentleman. He believes that you would find Mecosta a good place to be. He and I are arranging that no one in Mecosta need be aware of your terms in prison.

Mr. May believes that your release is unlikely to occur before No-vember. Once we know more or less precisely when you will be placed on parole, we will send you an airline ticket from the airport nearest to you to either Tri-City Airport (Saginaw) or Kent County Airport (Grand Rapids), depending on what flight may be most convenient. We will send a car to meet your flight at the airport; either airport is about seventy miles distant from Mecosta. At the same time, should you need any cash on hand, we will send you a remittance of a few dollars to cov-er expenses incidental to travel.

You, or the prison or parole authorities, will need to let us know some days in advance, if possible, as to precisely when you are to be re-leased; you or they are welcome to telephone us collect at Mecosta for that purpose. . . .

The employment we have in prospect for you is neither very ardu-ous nor very exacting, but will suffice for your support, and will carry with it future Social Security benefits, of course; if all works out satis-factorily, probably you could have a permanent situation with us, should you desire it. There are thousands of good books for you to read in my library, at your disposal whenever you wish, and there will be several people about with whom you can have conversations when you desire. At present, our household consists of my wife and our three babies; my wife's father, Mr. Regis Courtemanche; my assistant, Mr. Boyd Cathey; our maid, Mrs. May Cole, whom I believe you met when you were here twice before; our cook, Mrs. Cecilia Nadjowski; and vari-ous youthful part-time helpers, indoors and outdoors, boys and girls.

We are employing also a highly-skilled carpenter, Mr. John Mulcahy, practically full time, for some months; and you may be able to lend him a hand, even though you have no especial skill as a builder, in various enlargements and improvements of my properties that we are carrying on. Also there lives with us our young friend Miss Gracia Virgo, a university student, with whom you once exchanged letters.

I am writing tonight, concerning you, to the Board of Probation and Parole. I do hope that they may consider your application favorably.

Yours sincerely,
Russell Kirk

Letter to Richard M. Nixon

Nixon was a regular reader of Kirk's syndicated newspaper column "To the Point," and in late September 1971, he wrote to commend Kirk on a recent column in which the writer had agreed with the president regarding a recent speech in which the latter discoursed on the rise of new economic powers in the world and warned against cultural decadence.

September 28, 1971

The Honorable Richard M. Nixon
President of the United States
The White House
Washington, D.C.

Dear President Nixon,

Very good it is to have your kind and interesting letter of September 21, referring to my column in which I touched on your remarks, at Kansas City, about decadence.[10] (I shouldn't be surprised if you are the first president to have been associated with Livy in a newspaper column.) Cheerfulness will keep breaking in, and I think we will make headway against the grim forces of decadence. Just now I am hard at work upon a project of this character, my long-delayed book *The Roots of*

American Order. Pepperdine College plans to make documentary films based on that book, when it's published.

I am lost in wonder at the success with which you deal with a thousand difficulties. What a task you have! I fancy that some rather doctrinaire conservatives of our acquaintance will return before long to hearty approval of the Nixon administration. They tend to forget, from time to time, that conservatism is not a strange set of immutable rules of policy, fixed as the laws of Lycurgus, but instead a way of looking at man and society: a cast of mind and character, governed indeed by certain sound general principles, but capable of prudential application in different ways in varying circumstances. You have our prayers.

Cordially,
Russell Kirk

Letter to William F. Buckley Jr.

September 29, 1971

Mr. William F. Buckley Jr.
National Review
New York City

Dear Bill,

Many thanks for the copy of *Cruising Speed.* I have even read it! (I had to take time off from Polybius and Pausanias.) I like particularly your remarks on the students who head lecture-committees, knowing well such afflictions.

The Los Angeles Times–General Features Syndicate people tell me that they have resumed sending you my "To the Point" regularly, and even offer to supply you with a complete file of whatever period you may have missed; but I don't propose to afflict you with such a mass of mimeographed materials unless you are making vast collections of Buckley Papers for posterity. (I am doing something of the sort: already a large part of my papers repose in the Clarke Historical

Library, Central Michigan University.) Your scoundrelly syndicate hasn't reciprocated, though, and the Grand Rapids *Press* seems *never* to publish you now. But of course I keep up with you in *National Review*, so don't bother to prod your syndicate.

I have lost some papers recently, though no big ones—chiefly because I'm writing little about practical politics in a time when nothing very important is occurring, I suspect. Editors love political gossip, even when—as with Tom Wicker and Max Lerner—the gossip is promptly and almost invariably undone by the event. Nothing could be [more] boring for me—and, I fancy, for my readers—than analyses of the prospects of Birch Bayh and John Lindsay for assuming the presidency of these United States. I did cudgel Bayh, though, for being the only real impediment now to a Prayer Amendment—and reminded folk how very like he looks to Robert Mitchum. . . .

More another time.

Cordially,
Russell

Letter to David Lindsay, Earl of Crawford and Balcarres

As a doctoral student who spent six months every year in Scotland, studying at the University of St. Andrews, Kirk spent many pleasant days as a guest of David and Mary Lindsay, Earl and Countess of Crawford, at their ancestral home of Balcarres House. As Kirk later wrote (in the third person) of his time spent at various Scottish estates, "His Fife years of peace and charm, spent among old books, in old houses, in discourse with urbane and kindly men and women a generation older than Kirk, gave him such an education as is not to be bought in the graduate schools of Harvard or of Yale, and such a detachment from the ephemeral as had become most difficult to attain in a sensate age" (The Sword of Imagination: Memoirs of a Half-Century of Literary Conflict [Grand Rapids, MI: Eerdmans, 1995], 120).

November 4, 1971
as of Mecosta, Michigan

158

The Right Honourable the Earl of Crawford and Balcarres
Balcarres
Colinsburgh, Fife

Dear David,

Very good it is to have your letter of October 20, and to learn that you have not been used to build an Empire for Science, a la Dr. Nock, the film that we once saw together. My father has had a troubled heart for the past thirty-five years or so; it gives less trouble as the years pass. My doctor told me yesterday that I must reduce my consumption of wine and chocolate; perhaps I will be delightfully slim when I come to Balcarres next.

I receive a good many long and interesting letters—usually from people quite unknown to me—in my enormous volume of mail; but it is too true that the art of letter-writing is sadly decayed. Telephone and television have much to do with this degeneration. Telephones are tremendous wasters of time: people call me and ramble on in desultory fashion, and I can't make head or tail of what they desire. If only they were capable of writing ordinary notes, I might be able to handle their business with dispatch. Leisure is necessary for good letter-writing, of course, and I wrote my best and longest letters when I was a soldier in desert or jungle. I remain amazed at the volume of correspondence turned out by public and literary men in the eighteenth and nineteenth centuries, despite their having no typewriters and no carbon-copies; also they had only bad light to write by. Journal-keeping is nearly extinct; I have given it up myself, but my newspaper column, four times a week, provides a kind of substitute—particularly a column like mine, often of a meditative or anecdotal character.

Hew Lorimer wants my friend Charles Teetor to buy Innergellie.[11] I have urged Chuck to do so, and I think somewhat of combining forces with Chuck in a joint purchase. I always have dreamed of dwelling in a House by the Churchyard! There are curious sculptured fragments of an earlier Innergellie House in the gardens, and of course the place generally is very handsome, or could be made so. Had I been a

Lumsden, I never would have thought of parting with the house, which really cannot be very costly to maintain, being compact and in good structural condition.

In my last letter, I mentioned to you a silly "memoir" of T. S. Eliot by the late Robert Sencourt. There is nothing of consequence in it about Eliot, but it is a damning self-portrait of Sencourt, who appears to have been a loathsome snob. Now I find that the book contains a reference to your father (properly footnoted, or rather chapter-noted, by the equally abhorrent American Ph.D. who edited Sencourt's manuscript: "12. Lord Privy Seal 1916–1919 and 27th Earl of Crawford from 1913") in connection with the Garsington set, viz.:

"The iron gateway of Garsington Manor opened on to a little courtyard above which rose its Elizabethan gables. Taking this over from a farmer, Lady Ottoline rapidly transformed it by making its atmosphere as sumptuous and exotic as that of any house in Oxfordshire. Tapestries, satins and brocades stood out against the vivid colours painted on its panels and walls. Alongside it was a hedged path on which peacocks moved the scintillating blue of their necks and the array of their outspread tails. The garden led down to a swimming-pool from which naked forms would emerge on to the paths. Lady Ottoline seemed to some of her guests not unlike one of her peacocks as she floated among them in coloured shawls and nurtured genius. Men and women from politics and high society, such as Margot Asquith and Lord Crawford, . . . mingled with her literary discoveries of whom the chief at that time was Lytton Strachey, already busy with the vivid ironies of *Eminent Victorians*. . . ."[12]

Did your father really frequently mingle with the "literary discoveries" at Garsington, or is this a bit of Sencourt's fondness for associating himself, even at considerable remove, with Rank & Fashion? Lady Ottoline is preserved in amber by your old tutor Aldous Huxley, of course, in *Those Barren Leaves*.[13]

No, I don't think you ever showed me your great-grandfather's passages on the transmission of knowledge through old families. I hope to see it when I come unto you next. Most of my own education came from my grandfather's good books (and my grandfather himself) in his house by the railway station.

Will Pittenweem and Anstruther be ruined by the Common Market's open door to the fishermen of the Continent? George Scott-Moncrieff says so.

Now I must write off to decline a university vice-presidency. I suspect that I was offered it not because of my quasi-learned works, but because of my syndicated newspaper column, popular in the city where that university stands!

More before long; compliments to Mary.

Yours,
Russell Kirk

Letter to Margret Christie

November 22, 1971

Mrs. Margret Christie
Coldstream
Durie
Leven, Fife

Dear Margret,

Only yesterday I learnt that we are supposed to send you a cheque for seven pounds to pay for something you wove for Annette's sister Marie.[14] Here it is; I'm very sorry it wasn't sent sooner.

When are you coming to see us? If you like snows, this is a good season now. We'll not be over until next summer, although almost certainly we will spend weeks or months in Fife then. We do hope you will make a sojourn with us at Mecosta before long.

Didi Lorimer is here now; Henry and Didi will be returning to Scotland about a fortnight from now, and Henry is to become a director of a brewery in the Canongate. We have bought their furniture from the Ohio farmhouse, and I believe they intend to buy, once settled (preferably in Fife), the furniture from 40 High Street that Peter has kindly lodged at Durie for us.

Didi saw a most effectual ghost here in our old house two nights ago! She was awakened by the sound of her bedroom door bursting open (it ordinarily being difficult to open, the door being out of plumb with the doorjamb); then there was the scraping of the door on a carpet (a carpet that doesn't exist); then a man stood by her bed briefly, with a white expressionless face, wearing a checked gray coat. At once he began to dwindle, in the sense of contracting, and vanished altogether. Baby Hew Lorimer, in the same room with Didi, wasn't alarmed, but Didi was—thoroughly. She telephoned me (we having an elaborate internal telephone system) and I dashed up to her quarters; but of course nothing was to be found. Somehow I fancied the figure might be that of my great-uncle Raymond, who died in the house after a long sickness from [a] brain-tumor (having been hammered on the head by a madman), and who was a member of the Spiritualist circle here in the old days. We had Didi look through a venerable photograph-album that she never had seen before, and which I had forgotten. Sure enough, she identified Raymond Johnson's face—three different photographs—as the one she had seen! And in two of the pictures, Uncle Ray was wearing a gray checked coat! Raymond died only a few weeks after I was born; my mother saw his spectre by her bed at the time of his death—a second-sight apparition.

In some other respects, our phantoms have been active lately—the non-existent baby crying in the attic above the kitchen, for instance: Annette and Didi heard the phantom baby simultaneously. This has happened on other occasions, beginning about seven years ago, but not for past two years, until now.

I'm hard at work on my *Roots of American Order*. What news of you? Annette, Monica, Cecilia, and Felicia send you their love. More another time.

Yours,
Russell Kirk

Letter to Oscar Collier

Collier was Kirk's longtime literary agent. In 1972, Kirk discovered by accident that one of his own ghostly tales had been adapted for television and telecast on Rod Serling's series Night Gallery. *Although he considered television a tool of cultural blight, Kirk saw it as his responsibility (and that of other traditionalist conservatives) to "take up the tools—the weapons, if you will—effective in that age" and work to leaven the culture if possible. "Sentiments . . . may yet be raised up in the Waste Land—conceivably through the innovating weapon called television," he later declared, in one of his most important essays, "The Age of Sentiments." (This essay was originally published in* Modern Age *27 [Summer–Fall 1983]: 228–35, and republished in his collection* Redeeming the Time, *edited by Jeffrey O. Nelson [Wilmington, DE: Intercollegiate Studies Institute, 1996], 140.) In the following letter, Kirk alerts Collier of the* Night Gallery *discovery and urges him to approach Serling with another possible story, "Balgrummo's Hell."*

January 24, 1972

Mr. Oscar Collier
Seligmann and Collier
280 Madison Avenue
New York, N.Y., 10016

Dear Oscar,

Under separate cover, I mean to send to you a photostatic copy of my short (and uncanny) story "Balgrummo's Hell," on the chance that you might be able to sell it to Rod Serling's NBC television program *Night Gallery*. Last week, to my surprise—I having had no forewarning—*Night Gallery* showed "Old House of Sorworth," "adapted from a story by Russell Kirk." They may be interested in others.

Who let them have "Old House of Sorworth," from *The Surly Sullen Bell*, I don't know; but presumably Fleet gave them permission. (There was also some Californian agent trying to sell *Creature of the*

Twilight, etc. to Hollywood; perhaps he had a hand in this.) I have written to Doris Schiff, inquiring.[15] They rather butchered the story, especially in giving it an even nastier ending than it was supposed to have, but presumably they are able to pay decently for the "adaptation."

Anyway, the rights to "Balgrummo's Hell" belong solely to me. This story, published in the magazine *Fantasy & Science Fiction* in 1967 and reprinted in *The Best from F&SF, Seventeenth Series,* 1968, was not included in *The Surly Sullen Bell,* naturally—not having been written when that volume was published. *Fantasy & Science Fiction* acquired only first serial rights and an option of first anthological rights—both of which have been exercised. The story, therefore, is yours to sell to television on my behalf, if opportunity offers. Rod Serling presumably knows about me from common friends. . . .

Any word from Random House about *Roots of American Order?*[16] I sent copies of the first four chapters of that typescript to Mr. Sherwood Sugden, at Open Court; he writes to me that I should hear from them about a week from now as to whether they are interested in taking it on our terms. (I mentioned that we'd have to have a minimum advance of $6,000.) I shall let you know what he reports; he wishes to take it himself; meanwhile, perhaps you will hear something from Random House.

From internal evidence in the *Night Gallery* version of my "Old Place of Sorworth," I judge that the Serling people are familiar with the whole of my *Surly Sullen Bell,* not merely with that one ghostly tale—though "Old Place" has been anthologized by Fontana and its American distributor, as well as included in the Paperback Library edition of *Surly Sullen Bell.* Anyway, "Balgrummo's Hell," which seems much in the Serling vein, is my only ghostly tale not included in *Surly Sullen Bell.*

Various prospective reviewers write to me enthusiastically about *Eliot and His Age,* advance copies of which have gone out.[17] We shall see whether the reviewers for the more mass media are of such opinions.

Cordially,
Russell Kirk

Letter to Max Ways

Ways (1905–1985) was a writer and editor who worked for many years at Henry Luce's publications, notably Time *and* Fortune. *In 1953, he wrote the lengthy unsigned review of* The Conservative Mind *for* Time *magazine that brought Kirk's book to a wide audience.*

February 13, 1972

Mr. Max Ways
Fortune
Time-Life Building
New York City

Dear Mr. Ways,

Noticing in a wire-service story today your recent remarks at a conference on the Future, it came into my head that I am nineteen years tardy in thanking you for that review of my *Conservative Mind*, in 1953, which did so much to attract public attention to the book. (There is no future at Mecosta—only the past.) Anyway, Random House has just published my fat book *Eliot and His Age*, my greatest labor since *The Conservative Mind*, and I am asking Random House to send you a copy, with my compliments. My editor there, Mrs. Charlotte Mayerson, would be grateful for any comments on the book that you might find time to jot down, since she is collecting such remarks to put on the jacket of the second printing, and such places.

I enclose a recent textbook-review of mine that may amuse you. One might as well laugh with Democritus. Just now I am busy with a textbook endeavor of my own, *The Roots of American Order*, an innovating approach; film documentaries may be made on the basis of it.

All's well at Mecosta, where we now have three girl-babies—Monica, Cecilia, and Felicia—to romp in my ancestral haunted house. Best wishes.

Cordially,
Russell Kirk

Letter to George H. Nash

While writing his doctoral dissertation on postwar conservatism at Harvard University, George Nash contacted Kirk with a list of specific questions related to the McCarthy era and the presidential aspirations of Senator Barry Goldwater. Nash's dissertation was published by Basic Books in 1976 as The Conservative Intellectual Movement in America since 1945, *a work that is considered a touchstone of conservative history.*

April 20, 1972

Mr. George H. Nash III
115 Richards Hall
Harvard University
Cambridge, Massachusetts

Dear Mr. Nash,

Thanks for your letter of April 1. Yes, my *Eliot* receives much attention in the reviews; so far, the most perceptive longer reviews have appeared in *The Nation* and *The Progressive!*

Here are replies to your inquiries.

(1) Yes, some of us met with Senator Goldwater at Palm Beach, the Breakers Hotel (known as God's Waiting-Room, because of the advanced years of most of its guests, late in 1961, I believe—a few weeks before *National Review* flogged the Birch Society. One decision arrived at, at Mr. Buckley's suggestion, was that it should be made clear that Senator Goldwater's views were not those of the Birch Society, or rather of Robert Welch. There were present the Senator, Mr. Buckley, Mr. William Baroody of the American Enterprise Institute, and Dr. Jay Gordon Hall (a classical scholar, among other things).[18] We talked of political principles in general, and of campaign prospects. One by-product of the meeting was my piece in *America* on political fantastics, chiefly the Birch Society.[19] (I can still supply you with a copy, I think, if you need it; but I believe it's in *Confessions of a Bohemian*

Tory.) Senator Goldwater said that he would make it clear to the New York *Times* that he was not leagued with the Birch Society. Some weeks passed, and no such statement appeared in the *Times*. I wrote to Senator Goldwater to ask what had happened. He replied that he had given such a statement to a *Times* reporter on a plane flight, but that the *Times* had not published it. I then printed his statement in my *America* piece—and the *Times* carried a news-item reporting what I had reported of Goldwater!

(2) No, I had no connection, one way or the other, with the Joe McCarthy affair. Most of that time I was abroad—in Fife, usually. I never met Senator Joseph McCarthy, nor corresponded with him; nor did I know anyone connected with him, except William Buckley, whom I then knew only slightly. I never wrote anything about McCarthy, except a passing reference in a piece of mine in Kissinger's *Confluence* quarterly.[20]

(3) The only conservative politician for whom I ever wrote aught was Senator Goldwater. His speech at Notre Dame, in 1962, was my work; also his formal lecture at Yale (Chubb lectures?) in that year (though the latter may have been reworked by someone else; I never saw the final version). If you mention this, however, it would be best not to say that I *wrote* the addresses—rather, that I had a hand in them.

(4) I have spoken at a good many ISI summer schools and meetings of ISI chapters, but never have been a trustee or advisor of the organization.

(5) *The Death of Art* was to be a collection of my essays, but the intended publisher never brought it out, and then collapsed. Practically everything I intended to include in the volume was published later in *Enemies of the Permanent Things*, instead.

(6) Edmund Opitz once asked me to review a book by [Romano] Guardini, I think, for the *Freeman;* but someone at the FEE monastery meddled with the review, adding a sentence or two, so I withdrew it.[21] I believe the *Freeman* (FEE) has reprinted abridged versions of one or two pieces of mine published elsewhere. Earlier, the *Freeman* edited by

Florence _____ published a piece of mine on the Fabians.[22] I never had any editorial connection with the *Freeman* in any of its metamorphoses, nor was I asked to.

(7) Yes, there was a plan—got up mostly by Republican citizens of Ripon, Wisconsin—to establish an institute of conservative studies at Ripon College, in 1955 or so; the president of the college was warmly in favor of it, and the chairman of the department of political science. But radicals on the faculty objected vehemently; the president was frightened, and dropped the proposal. I was supposed to have been appointed head of the institute, but had no hearty relish for the idea, and did not attempt to revive the undertaking. No liberals were favorably interested in the plan: at Ripon, they all opposed it, but not so vituperatively (and obscenely) as did the radicals and left-liberals. The president of Ripon then was Dr. Fred Pinkham. I give some account of the affair in *Collier's Year Book* for 1955 (published in 1956); my article therein on academic freedom.

Yes, you are welcome to quote me in your dissertation.

I spent an hour in private conference with President Nixon, in the White House, less than a fortnight ago. He had re-read *A Program for Conservatives* (very carefully, it appeared), and had passed out copies to various people on his staff. We talked about social decadence, problems of leadership, religious faith as the basis of social order, reform of education, etc. He had spoken of that book with me late in 1967, too, in his New York office; it clearly influences him not a little.

Do let me know whenever I can be of more help.

Cordially,

Russell Kirk

Letter to Harold L. Weatherby

"Hal" Weatherby (1934–) served for many years as professor of English literature at Vanderbilt University, where his scholarship focused upon the traditional canonical works of English and American letters. He respected Kirk as a fellow scholar of normative literature; and in 1972, he wrote to ask him

about whether there exists any evidence indicating a definite influence by John Cardinal Newman on T. S. Eliot's thought and work.

May 15, 1972

Professor Hal Weatherby
Department of English
Vanderbilt University
Nashville, Tennessee

Dear Mr. Weatherby,

Very pleasant it is to hear from you, and to have your kind words about *Eliot and His Age.* I've no present prospect of getting to Vanderbilt again, but I should like to I enclose a review-piece of mine that may at once amuse and sadden you. . . .

I have written to the Archbishop of Portland, Robert Dwyer, to see if he has some suggestions concerning the influence of Newman upon Eliot; he knows Eliot's work well. I haven't any letters from Eliot that mention Newman, and I don't believe that we ever discussed him in our conversations. As I worked upon my book, however, I found several passages in Eliot—perhaps some in *The Criterion*—that had Newman's ring; it's a pity I didn't keep notes on those, for your subject is an important and interesting one. Now and again Eliot paraphrased Newman, without acknowledgment—doubtless on the assumption, which he made often, that his readers would recognize the source, or perhaps in part unconsciously. Take the following example.

There is a passage in *Apologia pro Vita Sua,* Chapter V, beginning, "Starting with the being of a God, (which, as I have said, is as certain to me as the certainty of my own existence, though when I try to put the grounds of that certainty into logical shape I find a difficulty in doing so in mood and figure to my satisfaction). . . ."[23] Compare Eliot's passage, in his introduction to Pascal's *Pensees,* beginning, "The Christian thinker—and I mean the man who is trying consciously and conscientiously to explain to himself the sequence which culminates in

169

faith, rather than the public apologist—proceeds by rejection and elimination. He finds the world to be so and so; he finds its character inexplicable by any non-religious theory. . . ."[24] But probably you are aware of this and other parallels.

One person who may know much about all this is G. H. Bantock, who had an article on "Newman and Education" in the *Cambridge Journal,* August, 1951, and who recently published a good little book, *T. S. Eliot and Education.* He is a professor of education at the University of Leicester.

And possibly Father Martin D'Arcy may know something of all this. Just now he is at Loyola University, Los Angeles.

I shall keep my eyes open for more information on this matter.

Best wishes,

Cordially,
Russell Kirk

Letter to Sydney J. Harris

Common-sense liberal columnist Sydney Harris (1917–1986) was a favorite of the Kirks, and Harris respected Kirk's column, as well. As Annette Kirk has said on more than one occasion, "Conservative liberals and liberal conservatives admire Russell Kirk"—meaning that men and women of principle, whether of the left or the right, can find common ground in matters of decency, friendship, and respect.

May 18, 1972

Mr. Sydney J. Harris
Publishers-Hall Syndicate
401 North Wabash Avenue
Chicago, Illinois

Dear Sydney Harris,

My wife, like myself, was happy to receive your kind note this morning; for you are the favorite columnist of Annette Yvonne Cecile

Courtemanche Kirk, aged thirty-one summers. She reads your column much more devotedly than she does mine. Incidentally, various newspapers transpose our names and even our photographs from time to time, if they carry both your column and mine; they know birds of a feather when they see them. I enclose a clipping from the Ada, Oklahoma, paper, sent to me by a reader—in this instance, my name on your column; it occurs as often the other way around.

My fat *Eliot*'s most kind reviews so far, interestingly enough, have appeared in *The Nation* and *The Progressive*.[25] I have had some pleasant letters about the book from (among others) Robert Speaight, who knew Eliot earlier and better than I did; and I am much relieved that he has no fault to find; indeed, to my considerable surprise, he asks *me* for some information: I thought that the Eliot book would interest you. Best wishes.

Cordially,

Russell Kirk

P.S.: I enclose a recent piece of mine on a language & literature textbook series, to amuse and sadden you.

Letter to Ray Bradbury

In 1972 Bradbury sent Kirk a copy of a recently published volume containing the notes and texts of three plays—The Wonderful Ice Cream Suit, To the Chicago Abyss, *and* The Veldt—*he had written for his Pandemonium Theater group in Los Angeles.*

August 5, 1972

Mr. Ray Bradbury
10265 Cheviot Drive
Los Angeles, California

Dear Ray,

Many thanks, tardily, for your little "Pandemonium Theater" book. I do hope that will make possible many performances of your marvelous plays. . . .

171

I have finished my vast book *The Roots of American Order*, and now possibly may find time to write some fantasies for and about my three little girl-children. . . .

If you have had opportunity—though probably you've not had time—to write anything about my *Eliot* among your reviews, I'd be glad to have a copy, especially because I am getting together reviews to be used in connection with the possibility of a London edition of my book. Random House is dreadful about sending me copies of reviews—and about everything else, for that matter. Have you ever found a satisfactory publisher—satisfactory even in the sense of being tolerably efficient, I mean? I haven't, neither great nor small. It's no wonder that in America the dog-food business does twice as much volume as does the book business (not counting, I believe, the anti-intellectual textbook business).

All's well in my haunted house at Mecosta. The ghosts have been obliging visitors in recent months. The Crying Baby has been heard again, most distinctly. (The crying apparently comes from a room where one of my grandmother's children died within an hour of birth.) And the Man in the Checked Coat and High Collar visited an Englishwoman who was staying with us—and who, until then didn't believe in the least in the existence of apparitions; he really terrified her, perhaps maliciously. (He seems to be my great-uncle Raymond, who died of a brain tumor, caused by a madman who beat him on the head with a hammer.) My great-grandfather's generation were Spiritualists and Swedenborgians, and the influences seem to linger on at Piety Hill. You must come unto us one day to sample our ghostly wonders; but perhaps the phantoms won't divert you, for they seem to relish afflicting Infidels.

I'll be out your way for a few days in October, speechifying, and I hope we may contrive to meet then. More when my schedule is better arranged.

Cordially,
Russell Kirk

Letter to Thomas Chaimowicz

A distinguished visiting professor at the International Academy of Philosophy in the Principality of Liechtenstein and honorary professor of Roman law at the University of Salzburg, Chaimowicz (1924–2002) was a key force in reinvigorating interest in the works of Edmund Burke on the European Continent during the decades immediately following World War II. He and Kirk were friends for many years, until the latter's death in 1994.

September 4, 1972

Dr. Thomas Chaimowicz
Salzburg-Aigen

Dear Tommy,

Tomorrow I'm off to Scotland, for much walking; I'll be back here about October 3. Annette and the three girl-babies must remain at home. Would that you and Rosemarie would let me lead you on a Scottish tour! Annette wishes to spend the Christmas season in Austria, perhaps in 1973; we'll see. When are you people coming to America to overturn the stock market?

Aye, the Kaltenbrunner volume has reached me; a big fat impressive thing. I hope it is well reviewed, and that you resurrect Burke among German-readers.[26]

Henry Kissinger does brilliantly; I talked with him briefly in a corridor of the White House, a few months ago, and then had an hour with President Nixon. Annette came along. The President is full of confidence, and acts as if he had all the time in the world. He is fundamentally a Quaker. It now appears that he will defeat McGovern two to one, in the popular vote, carrying nearly all the states. The second administration will be distinctly conservative. Mr. Nixon asked me what one book he should read: I told him Eliot's *Notes towards the Definition of Culture.*

Did you receive a copy of my big book *Eliot and His Age*? You were supposed to. If not, let me know, and I'll send one. It has been widely reviewed, but it becomes harder and harder, with every year that passes, to reach a wide public in America with a serious book.

But you ask my opinion of Dr. Kissinger. He is a disciple of Metternich primarily, a well-read and clever man, sound on all counts, so far as I can tell; personally ambitious, but that ambition has been gratified; he has more influence upon Richard Nixon than do all others combined. . . .

Mecosta is verdant now. More once I return from Scotland.

Cordially,
Russell

I have finished writing my big book *The Roots of American Order*.

Letter to Montgomery Belgion

An English man of the right, (Harold) Montgomery Belgion (1892–1973) was a friend of T. S. Eliot and a frequent contributor to the Criterion *during the 1930s. Eliot introduced Kirk to Belgion during one of his visits to the United Kingdom. In late 1972, Kirk sent a copy of his recently published* Eliot and His Age *to Belgion, who found it a worthy study of the great man of letters' work and significance.*

November 6, 1972

Mr. Montgomery Belgion
Highfield
Titchmarsh
Kettering, Northants

Dear Mr. Belgion,

Many thanks for your kind letter of October 6. I'm happy that my fat book arrived so opportunely. It is lengthily and cordially reviewed in this land; there is such a review by Malcolm Muggeridge in the current *Esquire*, I understand, but I've not seen it yet.[27] Do you know of any London firm that might care to publish it? My New York agent has commissioned a London agent to see about a British edition, but both seem to be languid in the business.

Henry Regnery Company now is run by Henry's son-in-law, Harvey Plotkin, and is altered out of recognition. The Illinois firm of Open Court, however, seems to intend to occupy somewhat the position that Regnery did formerly. Once Henry Regnery mentioned to me that you suggested it might be well to republish Wilkie Collins' *Armadale*. The hour is better now for such publication in America—though the Regnery firm isn't set up for that sort of undertaking.

I visited Kettering a decade or more ago, when its chief surviving charm was an old inn—since thoughtfully demolished, I understand. The destruction now proceeds apace in Scotland, where I spent the month of September. Glasgow is utterly ruined, and much damage has been done in Edinburgh—though there is some resistance in the New Town.

Here in Michigan, my wife and I have been contending furiously—and successfully, it appears, against the evil proposal, on the ballot, for abortion on demand.[28] Recently I persuaded President Nixon to read *Notes towards the Definition of Culture*.[29]

Best wishes to you.

Respectfully,
Russell Kirk

Letter to Irving Kristol

Called by some commentators "the godfather of neoconservatism," Kristol (1920–2009) was a prominent voice in promulgating a right-leaning ideological vision of American domestic and foreign policy. He founded or was associated editorially with several key periodicals, including Commentary, Encounter, *the* Reporter, *and the* National Interest. *At the time Kirk wrote the following letter, Kristol was in a senior position at Basic Books, a major New York publisher. Kirk hoped to interest a large publisher in the manuscript of his most recent book,* The Roots of American Order. *Kristol was on pleasant terms with Kirk but had no use for the latter's emphasis upon the moral imagination and the role of prudence and high character in historical conservatism, and he rejected the book. Many years later, in his Heritage Foundation lecture "The Neoconservatives: An Endangered Species," Kirk said, "Deficient in historical understanding as in familiarity with humane letters, most of the Neoconservatives lack those long views and that apprehension of the human condition which forms a basis for successful statecraft. Often clever, these Neoconservatives; seldom wise." (Kirk's lecture was reprinted in* The Politics of Prudence *[Bryn Mawr, PA: Intercollegiate Studies Institute, 1993], 172–90.)*

December 26, 1972

Mr. Irving Kristol
10 East 53rd Street
New York, N. Y. 10022

Dear Mr. Kristol,

The pleasant piece about you in the latest *National Observer* reminds me that I have been intending to write to you for some time. For one thing, Thomas Molnar suggests that I ought to interest you in a fat book I have completed, *The Roots of American Order*—about which, more below. Also I have been meaning to send you a copy of my *Eliot and His Age,* that being a book you might like. (Random House was supposed to have sent you one months ago, but that firm has a genius for not doing such things.) Anyway, I'll dispatch a copy, inscribed, under separate cover. I enclose with this letter the latest lecture-agents' brochure about your servant, to let you know what I am up to nowadays.

I marvel that you accomplish so very much in various fields, living as you do in Manhattan. T. S. Eliot said once that the worst form of expatriation for an American writer was to live in New York City. Some day you must come to visit us at our haunted house here—where, on this icy night, at four in the morning, I write beside a roaring fire of great elm logs.

Peter De Luca, at whose house in Los Angeles we had some pleasant talk about two years ago, is doing very well with his little Thomas Aquinas College, near Malibu: a very sound undertaking in general, although a bit too purely Scholastic for my taste; still, I'm on the board of visitors.

About my new book: I think that Basic Books might find it worth publishing. *The Roots of American Order* is intended chiefly for use in colleges—though not, I trust, in the typical "history of civilization" survey. Rather, it is meant for special courses, and should have considerable use in the "orientation" courses now common, perhaps especially in community colleges. Also it should have a considerable trade sale, and not only to my usual fifteen-thousand-or-so readers.

Pepperdine University persuaded me to write the book, and paid me $20,000 cash for doing so; but the rights belong to them; I act, in effect, as their agent. Pepperdine plans to use the book, and to get it used in other Evangelical colleges; also it has excellent prospects of being used in Catholic colleges, wondrous to say, and in various state institutions. (It already has been read and approved, in various developing versions, by professors at that congeries of institutions.) Pepperdine plans to make a series of documentary films based on the book, to be used in conjunction with the book itself: they will be filmed chiefly in Jerusalem, Athens, Rome, and London. The USIA is seriously interested in sponsoring such films.

In general, my approach is historical; yet I am concerned not with civilization in general, but rather with the institutions and beliefs which underlie the American personal and social order. The limitations of space considered, I endeavor to make the book lively and even picturesque, so as to appeal to the imagination of college students and others; most such works are catalogues of names and arid descriptions of abstract concepts, as I needn't tell you. It needs to be remembered that this book is not a kind of history of ideas meant for professors, but an attempt to wake some of the rising generation to awareness of their own cultural and institutional roots.

If you think that Basic Books might be interested in seeing this endeavor of mine, I will send a copy of the typescript to you. It is in twelve chapters, beginning with the Hebrew prophets and finishing not long after the Civil War, with some brief concluding reflections.

All's well in these northern fastnesses. Best wishes to you.

Cordially,
Russell Kirk

Letter to Marguerite J. Reese

In the following letter, Kirk seeks in a collegial manner to straighten out a perceived copyright infraction with the copyright director of Holt, Rinehart & Winston.

July 17, 1973

Miss Marguerite J. Reese
Director, Subsidiary Rights Department
Holt, Rinehart and Winston, Inc.
383 Madison Avenue
New York, N.Y.

Dear Miss Reese:

Thanks for your letter of June 7, which arrived here while I was abroad, but which was acknowledged by a member of my staff. In it, you refer to an essay of mine entitled "The Courage to Affirm," in which some lines from Frost's "Black Cottage" were quoted.

I do not possess a copy of the issue of *New Guard* in which this piece of mine apparently appeared, nor one of the new Holt book, *The Conservative Alternative,* in which it is reprinted, according to your letter. But I take it that we have here something of a comedy of errors.

I take it that the piece in question is a lecture which I delivered, as part of a series, at the New School of Social Research, more than a decade ago. I am not at all sure that the *New Guard* had permission, formally, to reprint it; but someone in my office may have given them permission, for all I know at this date; anyway, I have no objection to their having printed it. Had I known that you at Holt desired a request for permission to quote some illustrative lines from Frost, however, I would have so requested permission from your office—or have deleted the lines from the *New Guard* piece, had I been aware that any difficulty was involved. I received no payment for my essay from *New Guard,* so far as I know, and my quotation was merely of a critical and illustrative nature, authorized by the copyright laws. Incidentally, this is the first occasion in my four decades as a published writer that any permissions department has made such a complaint to me.

But now for the second act in the comedy of errors. It is obvious that Holt, Rinehart, and Winston have infringed upon my own literary property: for your firm printed this whole essay of mine, "The Courage to Affirm," without having obtained permission from me, it appears! If *New Guard* possessed any rights at all in the matter, those would have been only first serial rights; permission to reprint should have been requested from me, the author, whose property the essay is. Have you any record of having made such a request of me? I have no correspondence of that sort from your office in my files.

I suppose that the sensible thing for us to do is to call it quits. If you will forgive me, I will forgive you; and you are welcome to use my essay without payment, if you and yours will forget about my lecture-quotation from Frost. I will be grateful, however, if you can send a review-copy of this Viewpoint Series anthology to me—both for my file of my own publications, and because I might be able to comment on it sympathetically in my syndicated newspaper column or elsewhere.

Yours sincerely,

Russell Kirk

Editor, *The University Bookman*

Letter to Sherwood Sugden

As the publication date of The Roots of American Order *approached, Kirk wrote to editor Sherwood Sugden at Open Court Publishing to provide information crucial to the volume's final production.*

March 23, 1974

Mr. Sherwood Sugden, Managing Editor
Open Court Publishing Company
LaSalle, Illinois

Dear Sherwood,

Many thanks for your letter of March 15, and your later telephone call. I reply below to your various paragraphs.

1. Aye, let the title stand as *Roots of American Order*.

2. Rather than turning to Professor Fairbanks for the preparation of questions for a teachers' manual, I have decided that we might get the thing accomplished sooner if we have it done by my brother-in-law, Dr. Regis Courtemanche, Department of History, C. W. Post College, Greenvale, Long Island, New York. I have telephoned him, and he is willing to do so. He will have a week free—a college recess—early in April, so he should be able to do the work fairly promptly. His wife, an experienced teacher too, can help him. He already has read the typescript of *Roots*, but of course will need a complete photostat of the typescript to work from. Will you send him one such? I will go over the questions he prepares. I have suggested a payment of Open Court for $300 for his work; would this be all right with you? The photostat of the typescript should be sent to Dr. Courtemanche at his home address. . . .

3. I have completed the draft of the copy for the jacket and the catalog, and enclose both.

4. I have replied to all your observations and jottings, and enclose your original thereof, with my notations; I hope everything is clear. You will find that I have responded affirmatively to nearly all of your suggestions.

5. I have done the same with the Jim Johnson observations, and return the list, with my notations.

6. I am drawing up a chronology, and will enclose it with this letter if I finish it today; if I don't finish it today, I will send it along in a day or two.

7. I am drawing up a synopsis of each chapter, for the teachers' guide (or for the book itself, should you think it well to make it part of the table of contents or to append it to the main book); I will either enclose it with this letter or send it on in a day or two. Thus all that Regis Courtemanche will need to do for the teachers' guide is to prepare the questions.

8. Writing a *Lives of the Saints* properly would require a real knowledge of Hebrew and Greek and Latin, which I don't possess and never will have time or patience to acquire; also access over a period of years to a splendid library like the Newberry, which I don't have. But somebody certainly ought to do it.

9. My assistant is now inserting the names of publishers in both the bibliography and the chapter-notes, and I will send to you today, or soon, copies of the bibliography-pages with those names inserted—or, in the case of the chapter-notes, copies of the pages of notes at the end of each chapter, with the data inserted.

10. When I have got all the above out of the way, I will see if I can write a few pages about Job, to insert in Chapter II for the sake of dramatic relief.

11. Did you ever have a more prompt and cooperative author?

12. Both Mr. Romuald Gantkowski and myself have sent to J. Campaigne's office a list of people to whom review/complimentary copies of *Roots* should be sent, with a view to quotable commendations and textbooks adoptions; these include a list of the Church of Christ colleges associated with Pepperdine University, at most of which there should be a good chance of adoptions.[30] Should I send copies of those lists directly to you?

13. Mr. Gantkowski would like to know what the price of the book will be. Can you tell me?

More before long; best wishes.

Cordially,
Russell

Postscript: If Irving Kristol hasn't time to do a brief preface for *Roots*, as probably he won't have, I don't think it would be well to have a preface or foreword at all. With such a book, a preface is rather an impediment both to the general reader and the textbook-user. And if the author of the preface is less well known than the author of the book, and writes less well, what is the point of it?

—R. K.

Letter to Gerald R. Ford

On August 9, 1974, on the verge of impeachment for his role in the Watergate cover-up, President Richard Nixon resigned. He was succeeded in office by his vice president and fellow Republican Gerald R. Ford of Grand Rapids, Michigan.

August 10, 1974

The Honorable Gerald Ford
President of the United States
Washington, D.C.

Dear President Ford,

As the original Ford-For-President zealot, I am grateful to Providence for your elevation. You may recall my syndicated column of some months ago, in which I mentioned my endeavor about 1962 and 1963 to rouse some national interest in the possibility of nominating you for the presidency in 1964; in which I mentioned, too, my several recommendations to Mr. Nixon, over the years, that you would be the best candidate for the vice-presidency. Apparently through chance; but actually through, as Tocqueville says, what we call chance, but what really is the combination of many small causes which are providential, you have become President. We pray that you may be given strength to bear all your high responsibilities.

Having been one of those small instruments of Providence in your case, I now venture to try my hand again at nomination of vice-presidents. It appears to me that the gentleman who would best complement you is Mr. Elliot Richardson. You know his abundant qualifications better than I do. It appears to me that his power of persuasion, his administrative experience, and his fertile mind would serve you better than the qualities of any other among the various able public men who might be nominated for that office. I correspond frequently with Mr. Richardson (though I have not mentioned this possibility to him), and I am convinced that he would add much strength to your administration.[31]

Let me offer you once more my thanks for the integrity and ability which you have given to American politics.

Yours sincerely,
Russell Kirk

Letter to Richard M. Nixon

Writing a little over a month after Nixon resigned the American presidency over the Watergate Scandal, Kirk sought to comfort and encourage his long-time friend.

September 17, 1974

The Honorable Richard Nixon
San Clemente, California

Dear Mr. Nixon,

How I wish I could relieve you of some part of the burden of your disappointment! Yours was a most successful presidency, in so many fields. In the long run, I believe, the historians will decide that you were treated with injustice, as was President Andrew Johnson; and Johnson did not have television to prejudice the public against him.

In my syndicated column and elsewhere, I did what I could to oppose the tide of the mass media; but it was somewhat like the endeavor of King Canute to turn back the North Sea. My wife and I pray that your sorrows may diminish.

With your fortitude, so often tried, you may yet do good and great things. As John Adams said of his own defeat, unpopularity fell upon him like the Tower of Siloam: "*Sic transit gloria mundi.*" But I think, too, of John Quincy Adams, the Old Man Eloquent, returning from his catastrophic defeat undiminished in vigor, and taking once more a seat in the House of Representatives, to exercise a strong influence upon the Congress.

There is no need to reply to this note, which is simply to tell you that all your actions have been understood by some few, at least. I do not mean to trouble you with correspondence when you have so many tribulations and doubtless are so much in need of rest.

Respectfully,
Russell Kirk

Letter to Elliot Richardson

Richardson (1920–1999) was an attorney and Republican political figure who served American presidents in four cabinet-level positions. He is perhaps best known as one of the principal figures in the so-called Saturday Night Massacre: in 1973, after serving roughly five months as Richard Nixon's attorney general, he refused Nixon's directive to fire Watergate special prosecutor Archibald Cox, choosing to resign rather than interfere in the Watergate investigation. Although he was a self-styled moderate in politics, Kirk liked and respected him as a man of character and integrity.

October 11, 1974

Mr. Elliot L. Richardson
Woodrow Wilson International Center for Scholars
Smithsonian Institution Building
Washington, D.C.

Dear Mr. Richardson,

Many thanks for your good letter of October 7. For your amusement between lecture-expeditions, I enclose a series of special columns I wrote about Taiwan and Quemoy. I'm speechifying much myself this month—Michigan, Indiana, New York, South Carolina, Alabama, and California early in November.

If, as I take it, you are endorsing candidates during some of your addresses, I hope you may have opportunity to say a good word for Richard Lugar in Indiana: the best of mayors opposing the most repellent of senators.[32] . . .

A real copy of my *Roots of American Order* should reach you some time this month.[33] I detest reading galleys myself, so I don't wonder that you haven't gotten to mine. There should be a second big printing soon after formal publication (I take it that Open Court has orders for 15,000 copies already of the first printing), so if you think of aught to say about the book, your observations might well be recorded on the jacket of the second printing. We have kind remarks by an interesting congeries of people already—Northcote Parkinson, Ray Bradbury, and I don't know who all.[34]

Recently I spent an evening with an old friend, the Archduke Otto von Habsburg. (Do you know him?) His observations on Russian economic difficulties are very much like yours.

I wrote to President Ford that you would be the ideal vice-president, and he might have paid some attention, had he ever seen the letter; we have been acquainted some years. But no sooner had I put my letter in the postbox than Mr. Ford's people announced their silly (and disingenuous) plan to urge virtually all Republicans to send in their nominations for the vice-presidency. Doubtless my missive was lost in the shuffle. As you say, on narrow margins do great events turn. Presumably Providence was reserving you for something happier.[35]

The nomination of Mr. Rockefeller may turn out to be disastrous, for a variety of reasons; I am writing a column about that tonight, though I abstained from such observations until now out of kindliness toward the new President.[36] *Entre nous*, I speculate on what implicit great expectations may have been held out tacitly to certain folk close to the White House by Rockefeller people. The Rockefeller putsch was conducted while you were abroad by the Rockefeller publicity apparatus: many stories planted in the wire-services and elsewhere, easily recognizable by such as myself, but of course accepted more or less at face value by the public and presumably by the President's staff, which is not competent. The argument used by the Rockefeller people about Mr. E. Richardson was that "he's too liberal" (!) The argument did have some weight with those numerous folk who fancy that conservatism or liberalism is rigorous adherence to a set of ephemeral but sacred secular dogmas, rather than a general cast of mind and character.

As things are moving, nevertheless, Mr. Rockefeller may be hoist by his own petard. Nominations for Supreme Court justices having been rejected, so may nominations for the vice-presidency. What would occur then, Lord only knows. Whether Mr. Ford will stand in 1976, as things are developing in public and private life, Lord only knows. Incidentally—a question you needn't answer, of course, if you aren't so inclined, and which answer, if any, I sha'n't publicize—did the President offer you a cabinet post? You've occupied half of them already, so I don't imagine any would much attract you; but I wonder whether the civility had been extended; if it wasn't, it's odd. I don't fancy that any of the Nixon people remaining about the White House would have opposed such an offer, or that their opposition would have counted for much if they had set their faces against it. Mr. Melvin Laird, perhaps?—a gentleman I've not met, but in whom, I suspect, Mr. Ford ought not to repose overmuch confidence if (as some have told me) Mr. Laird's dreams of glory are lofty as Mr. Rockefeller's. For all I know, however, I impugn a dear friend of yours.

More another time. I do hope you find some time to work upon your book.

Cordially,
Russell Kirk

Letter to Kirby McCauley

Literary agent and editor McCauley (1941–2014) founded the Pimlico Agency in New York during the 1970s and became highly respected representing writers of science fiction, horror, suspense, and dark fantasy. He served as Kirk's literary agent for many years. McCauley's horror anthology Frights:

New Stories of Suspense and Supernatural Terror *(New York: St. Mar-tin's, 1976) contained the story Kirk considered his best: the award-winning "There's a Long, Long Trail A-Winding."*

January 18, 1975
as of Mecosta, Michigan

Mr. Kirby McCauley, Literary Agent
220 East 26th Street
New York, New York 10016

Dear Mr. McCauley,

Here is my longish short story for you—perhaps my best. It has been eight or nine years since I wrote any fictions, but my hand has not lost its cunning. I hope "A Long, Long Trail A-Winding" will serve your turn. My earlier "St. Anthony Help" idea I abandoned; it wouldn't turn out suitably for me, though there are touches of my original intent in in the enclosed story. "Frank" is drawn accurately enough from the life.[37] I am pleased to have been able to develop a genuine character in an uncanny tale—something rarely done, I think. There are a half-dozen interpretations of the story possible, which is all to the good.

Do you have any good word from publishers of paperbacks concerning my earlier works? Best wishes for *Frights,* and to you for 1975.

Cordially,
Russell Kirk

Letter to Blouke Carus

Today serving as Chairman Emeritus and chief technical advisor of the Carus Corporation, a chemical conglomerate specializing in permanganate, manganese, oxidation, catalyst and blended phosphate technologies, Carus (1927–) was for many years president of Open Court Publishing Company, publisher of Kirk's The Roots of American Order *(1980). Kirk had a high opinion of Open Court and its mission as a publisher of tradition-oriented educational material.*

June 28, 1975

Mr. Blouke Carus, President
Open Court Publishing Company
LaSalle, Illinois

Dear Blouke,

You will find enclosed a letter from a lady at Our Lady of Sorrows Academy, in Montana—an enthusiast for the Open Court program. As she justly points out, Open Court had best not get entangled, even nominally, with NOW, the lunatic "feminist" outfit. I transmit to you herewith, with my endorsement, various documents about NOW which she sent to me. In *National Review,* about a month from now, you can read a piece of mine on the silly and baneful "Sexist Task Force" which NOW and similar zealots are trying to inflict upon state systems of public instruction. As some of the enclosed material suggests, NOW is trying to dominate both publishers and television stations, and to exercise censorship. It would be very foolish indeed to give ground before these fanatics, because they are freaks who represent only a handful of American women, but make much belligerent noise. The NOW endorsement applied to Open Court's program would be the kiss of death at decent schools, particularly Catholic ones. . . .

It is good that the second printing of *Roots* will appear in the immediate future. Many reviews are yet to appear, and college adoptions are coming in—though there will be no flood of such adoptions until Open Court either gets a paperback edition published or else brings out a jacketless "text edition" (actually the same book, jacketless, at short discount and much lower price). As the book is priced now, most students simply cannot be asked to buy it. I am trying my own hand at raising funds for Pepperdine to begin production of a film based on *Roots.* If the film comes to pass, you will have on your list one profitable book in addition to the Open Court readers—profitable in a large way.

Best wishes to you and yours; more another time.

Cordially,

Russell

Letter to William F. Buckley Jr.

Buckley had been solicitous of the Kirk family's well-being after the Ash Wednesday Fire of 1975, and Russell Kirk was grateful for the concern of his longtime friend.

July 3, 1975

Mr. William F. Buckley, Jr.
National Review
150 East 35th Street
New York, N.Y.

Dear Bill,

Did I ever reply to your two kind notes of condolence on the destruction of Piety Hill? Our troubles ran me five hundred letters into arrears in my correspondence. Anyway, many thanks from Annette and me for your thoughtfulness.

We were in New York about ten days ago, and tried to seek you out, but found that you were in mid-Atlantic.

Late this month we will commence the rebuilding—in a properly archaic Italianate style, restoring some architectural features of the Old House. Only one thing was raked from the ashes: a tiny ancient saucer with roses upon it.

"You may break, you may shatter the vase, if you will,
But the scent of the roses will cling to it still."

We dwell in the New House—the massive wing, with fire-doors, we built five years ago. Any day now there will arrive to reside with us two families—or the remnants thereof—of Vietnamese; doubtless they are inured to ruin.

The Roots of American Order has gone into its second large printing already. Pepperdine University hopes to make an hour-and-a-half film based on it, for both television and theater showings; Bruce Herschensohn would direct it. Pepperdine is looking for foundation or corporation money to finance the film. Do you have any suggestions? Conceivably Clement Stone may be induced to put up half the money.[38] Pepperdine needs a total of about $450,000.

I cease to write—or rather, publish—my syndicated column about August 1. Thirteen years is long enough for such a chore, and I had grown increasingly bored with it. All sorts of conservatively-inclined columnists are turning up nowadays, so there is less need for me in that field. This should give me time for more satisfying and enduring work.

Annette, Monica, Cecilia, and Felicia send you their love. Our fourth child should be born in October, God willing.

Cordially,

Russell Kirk

Letter to Albert Hunold

Along with Friedrich Hayek, Swiss economist Hunold (1899–1981) was one of the founders of the Mont Pelerin Society, in 1947. Over time, tensions developed between the two men regarding the direction of the Society, leading to Hunold's departure after he published an essay, "How the Mont Pelerin Society Lost Its Soul" in 1962. He was a friend and ally of Wilhelm Roepke, himself admired by Kirk for his advocacy of smallholding and a humane economy.

July 31, 1975

Dr. A. Hunold
Ch-9056 Gais/Swislen

Dear Dr. Hunold,

Many thanks, tardily, for your letter of July 8. Alas, I shan't be able to join you, Thomas Molnar, and others for a meeting of the Roepke

Foundation on August 10; for I'm not going abroad at all this summer. As possibly you may have read, my ancestral house was burnt to ashes on last Ash Wednesday, and since then our affairs have been in considerable confusion. We commence some rebuilding next month, and I must be at home for that. Our fourth child is to be born in October, so my wife can't travel this summer, anyway. We do expect to venture to Scotland, and perhaps so far as Switzerland and Austria, next summer.

Yes, I am acquainted with Irving Kristol: a force for good. The present Congress of the United States is perhaps the feeblest we ever have endured: I look for little improvement of domestic or foreign policy. I believe that the Democrats will nominate Governor George Wallace for the presidency—a man more decisive than any recent incumbent, but almost utterly ignorant of statecraft on any grand scale. Our chief hope, in international concerns, is that Russia and China will commit grand blunders too.

My very best wishes to you: I hope we may contrive to meet either in Gais or in Mecosta before many seasons are out; more another time.

Cordially,
Russell Kirk

Letter to Mary Lindsay, Countess of Crawford and Balcarres

Beginning in the late 1940s, when he was writing his doctoral dissertation at the University of St. Andrews, Kirk was a frequent guest at Balcarres, the ancestral estate of David Lindsay, 28th Earl of Crawford and 11th Earl of Balcarres. As a bachelor, and later as a married man in the company of his wife and daughters, Kirk enjoyed the kind hospitality of the Lindsays. In late December 1975, Kirk was informed by letter that David Lindsay had died.

December 30, 1975

The Countess of Crawford and Balcarres

Dear Mary,

Only yesterday there came a letter from Sheila Christie, and we learned that David was gone. I do hope he received, before the end, the letter which I wrote early this month. His letter to which I replied had been full of kindness; and if you have seen my answer, you know that, providentially, I expressed in it my gratitude to you both for your goodness to me all these years.

Annette said, so soon as we heard, that our afternoon with you a year and a half ago was one of those timeless periods; and it was so good that David was well and most cheerful that day. She had taken a long stroll along the drives and paths that day, and has sung his praises ever since.

It is merciful to him that the end came quickly; I know he had dreaded the possibility of increasing enfeeblement. We shall not look upon his like again, here below. But David was made for eternity, and you shall know him always; and so, I pray, shall I. He has been spared much, in this bent age of ours.

My head is full tonight of the countless good and wise things he said and wrote to me from time to time; and full of cheering memories of days and evenings at the Enchanted Palace of Balcarres. I shall write something for publication about him, and of course will send you a copy so soon as it is printed.

Perhaps Hew [Lorimer] will carve his stone. So much should be graven upon it, did we now follow the epitaph-mode of yesteryear. David did immense good in standing up for the permanent things, the guardian of beauty and dignity. That the soul may endure always, a certain discipline and self-awareness are required, I suspect; and those David possessed. We pray for you in this hour of loss, which is not final.

I am not sure that I sent to you earlier the enclosed announcement of the birth of our fourth daughter. Perhaps we may show her to you next summer.

I think and think and think of you both.

Yours,
Russell Kirk

Letter to James Turner

One of the most satisfactory and cordial relationships Kirk enjoyed with a publisher's editor was with James Turner, managing editor at Arkham

House, which published Kirk's ghost story collections The Princess of All Lands *(1979) and* Watchers at the Strait Gate *(1984). In his initial letter to Turner, Kirk orients Turner to where matters stand with the stories that would together form the volume* The Princess of All Lands.

January 7, 1976

Mr. James Turner
Managing Editor
Arkham House Publishers
Sauk City, Wisconsin

Dear Mr. Turner,

I learn from Mr. Kirby McCauley that he, Mr. Hartmann, and Mr. Meng conferred on the project of having Arkham House publish a collection of my stories, and that all went well.[39] I understand that you prefer that the projected "Princess of All Lands" be not published in periodical form before the intended book appears; and that is satisfactory to me.

For your interest, I enclose copies of three stories of mine that will appear in the book. These form a trilogy of sorts, although they fall into place more or less accidentally. "Balgrummo's Hell" is an infernal tale; "There's a Long, Long Trail A-Winding" is a purgatorial tale; and "Saviourgate" is a paradisical tale. The first one you may have read in *Fantasy & Science-Fiction* or in *The Best from Fantasy and Science-Fiction;* the second will appear before long in the anthology *Frights,* edited by Mr. McCauley. "Saviourgate" I wrote a few days ago—or finished and polished, rather—and I have sent off to Mr. McCauley a copy of it for possible publication in some periodical. I think that probably "Balgrummo's Hell" and "Long, Long Trail" are the best of the baker's dozen of ghostly tales that I have written.

So it remains only for me to write "The Princess of All Lands." I am not quite sure of the length of that, but if you wish you can count upon it being somewhat longer than the longest other story—"Long,

Long Trail," which is nearly twelve thousand words. Would you want anything as long as twenty thousand words, the total length of the enclosed trilogy considered?

Now I could have "The Princess of All Lands" ready for you this summer, if not sooner. In view of that, you may wish to list my book for publication *before* the catalogue to be distributed two years from now. Just let me know. . . .

Best wishes to you for 1976.

Cordially,
Russell Kirk

Letter to R. Emmett Tyrrell Jr.

In 1972, during a period of radical leftist dominance on American university campuses, Tyrrell founded the irreverent right-wing periodical the Alternative: An American Spectator *while an undergraduate at Indiana University. The magazine steadily grew in reputation because of the Menckenesque ridicule it brought to bear on progressivism's favorite causes and public figures. (Eventually Tyrrell renamed the magazine the* American Spectator.*) In early 1976, on the eve of a trip abroad, Tyrrell telephoned Kirk to ask his opinion of the best places to lodge while in Rome.*

February 2, 1976
as of Albion College
Albion, Michigan

Mr. R. Emmett Tyrrell
Editor, *The Alternative*
Box 877
Bloomington, Indiana

Dear Mr. Tyrrell,

At precisely the time you telephoned Mecosta to inquire about Roman hotels, your servant, at Albion, was discussing with his assistant, Mr. Christopher O'Brien, the wondrous success of Mr. Tyrrell with his *Alternative.* Do you know Arthur Koestler's book *The Roots of Coincidence?*

It has been some years since last I was in Rome, but I can offer some comments on the hotels you mention. The De Ville, in the Via Sistina, is in the heart of the "English quarter," rather near the Spanish Steps; convenient enough, but somewhat noisy and crowded there. The Raphael is near the Vatican, I believe—mostly a modern quarter nowadays, alas, of no great interest. I think I have stayed at the Albergo del Pantheon; indeed, it is improbable that there are two hotels of that name. It looks directly on the Pantheon, in the very heart of medieval Rome, a fine picturesque situation, with many *trattorie* about. It is a simple place, but clean, and some of the rooms have private baths. That is the quarter of Rome in which I always stay—though usually at the Albergo Minerva, a few rods distant from the Pantheon. The Minerva, nominally a first-class hotel, has very hard beds and large though gloomy chambers; it is frequented by the clergy, and is the oldest hotel in Rome—that is, a palace-building erected, in the seventeenth century, deliberately as a formal public hotel. The Minerva, like the Albergo del Pantheon, is a "mueble"—that is, it serves no meals but a simple breakfast. That is all to the good, for it is much more fun to take one's meals in the *trattorie,* and the food is better and more genuine outside the big hotels. The rates at both the Pantheon and the Minerva are relatively low. The address of the Minerva is simply the Piazza Minerva (the small piazza opening off the Piazza del Pantheon). You will understand that ordinarily I stay in ancient and relatively cheap hotels, far from the madding crowd of tourists.

I am here at Albion College four days each week, during February. Restoration of the ruined house of Piety Hill, at Mecosta, proceeds grandly but slowly. We are incorporating all sorts of architectural features snatched from the jaws of the urban renewers of western Michigan. You must come to see it one day, when it is done: the last of America's Italianate villas.

Best wishes to you and the magazine, which is full of good things, and is spoken of everywhere. Do let me know if I can give more advice about the Italian expedition.

Cordially,
Russell Kirk

Letter to Canon Reginald Cant

Canon Reginald Cant (1914–1987) was chancellor of York Minster and a colleague of the late Canon Basil A. Smith (1908–1969), a friend of Kirk, treasurer of York Minster, and writer of ghostly tales. As a friend of Smith's widow, Phillis, Cant was aware that Kirk was an admirer of Smith's stories who might be in a position to publish them. With her permission, Cant sent Kirk the stories that were eventually published in the volume The Scallion Stone *(1980). "Into these stories," Kirk later wrote, in* The Sword of Imagination, *"Smith had woven fragments of local legends and of personal experience. Canon Smith knew that the whole of human existence is suffused with mysteries, and that pitfalls have been dug for the vagrant erring soul. A man of light, he was aware of the brooding unregenerate darkness that has menaced mankind from the beginning of human existence. After a fashion, these tales are parables of that fascinating perilous darkness, which suddenly may envelop the unwary or the fallen"—words that accurately describe many of Kirk's own ghostly tales (235).*

May 16, 1976

Dear Canon Cant,

Somewhat tardily, I thank you for having sent me the five stories by our friend Basil Smith; they arrived safely, and I have re-read them all, and have sent them to my literary agent in New York, Mr. Kirby McCauley, who specializes in ghostly tales—perhaps the only such specialist in the world. Perhaps he can publish one or two in anthologies of the uncanny which he gets up; one such book, *Frights*, will be published by St. Martin's Press in New York this month, with a purgatorial story of mine, "A Long, Long Trail a-Winding," as the first piece in the volume. Also he may be able to get some published in the monthly *Fantasy and Science-Fiction,* or some other decent magazine of the sort. And there is some possibility that we might persuade Arkham House—which is to publish in a year or so a new collection of my own tales—to make a little volume of the tales of B. A. Smith.[40] We'll see. Publishing of nearly all sorts is in decay in this land just now.

If we do succeed in arranging publication, the rewards will not be great: about $125 for a story in a magazine, perhaps $300 for one in an anthology. Royalties for a slim volume are not impressive, either. But there always are some chances of television or film adaptation: perhaps the delusory hope which emerged from Pandora's box. Anyway, it would be good to see Basil's ingenious stories in print. Many thanks for your kindness in forwarding the stories; I will keep you informed of developments, which may not be speedy. I'll write to Phillis about the matter, too. Best wishes.

Cordially,

Russell Kirk

Letter to Brigid M. Boardman

Boardman (1931–) is the foremost modern authority on the life and works of the Catholic poet and critic Francis Thompson (1859–1907), best known for his poem "The Hound of Heaven." With Kirk being an admirer of Thompson's signature poem, he and Boardman corresponded, and eventually the Kirks and Boardman became friends and mutual admirers.

December 5, 1976

Miss Brigid Mary Boardman
Bath

Dear Brigid,

Many thanks for your letter of October 12. No, we've not managed an English expedition. It appeared possible that I might fly over next month, in connection with a plan to establish a new "private" university in Britain, I being a trustee; but that plan has been postponed.[41] We may all travel to Scotland next summer; I hope so.

I read that the baths of Bath are closed: what a pity! There's the last of an old song.

How goes the study of Francis Thompson?[42] If you see Phyl Smith soon, pray tell her that I will write to her so soon as I have word of prospects for American publication of Basil's ghost-stories, of which she sent copies to me at my request. It appears possible that we may get a little volume of them published. My own new collection of uncanny tales will appear next year; I just finished writing the final one of them, "The Princess of All Lands," about Annette's being kidnapped last year; we will tell you about that adventure some day.

I don't know anything of the Ann Arbor Pentecostals in particular; the Pentecostal movement is spread across the face of America.[43] In general, I think the movement something of a sham. Our Bicentenary wasn't celebrated so thoroughly as I might wish, but many of the local projects were sound, and there has been a good deal of historic preservation and restoration in connection with the Bicentenary. I am on the Michigan commission for the Bicentenary. I trust that the big years are yet to come: 1987 and 1989 the anniversaries of the Constitutional Convention and of the inauguration of the first president.

Five days from today, I fly out to California to confer with Mr. Ronald Reagan and others about the possibility of making a film based upon my fat book *The Roots of American Order*. Soon I will commence writing my long-postponed book about decadence and renewal in the higher learning in this country.

Annette, Monica, Cecilia, Felicia, and the ever-cheerful Andrea (now a trifle more than a year old) send you their best wishes. We hope that your mother and you will have a merry Christmas. Restoration of the house moves along: most of the interiors should be in tolerable shape by Christmas. In the spring we will commence building a two-story loggia-wing.

Cordially,
Russell Kirk

Letter to Jeffrey Meyers

Meyers is a prolific American literary scholar and biographer. He has writ-
ten full-length studies of Katherine Mansfield, Ernest Hemingway, D. H.
Lawrence, Joseph Conrad, Edgar Allan Poe, F. Scott Fitzgerald, Edmund
Wilson, and George Orwell, among others. In 1977, as he researched a study
of Wyndham Lewis (1882–1957), he wrote to Kirk to request an interview,
knowing that Kirk and Lewis had been friends. Eventually Meyers invited
Kirk to write the introduction to his book, but this fell through after Meyers
asked Kirk to make extensive revisions to his contribution, which Kirk re-
fused to do.

October 13, 1977

Mr. Jeffrey Meyers
Associate Professor of English
The University of Colorado at Boulder

Dear Mr. Meyers,

Thanks for your note of October 9. I should be glad to talk with
you about Lewis. I expect to be at home in May, at least for the first half
of the month (except perhaps for a commencement-address or two), and
would be happy to entertain you here; we always have room for guests.
Mecosta is rather a remote place, more than seventy miles from either
the Grand Rapids or the Saginaw airport; we could send a car to meet
you at either airport, if need be.

Meanwhile, I reply to some of your inquiries. All my surviving
correspondence with Lewis, I believe, appears in that volume of his
letters which was published a few years ago.[44] I did write a vignette
about him which is included in my book *Confessions of a Bohemian Tory*
(Fleet, 1965), which has just gone out of print. Probably you can find a
copy in the university library; but if not, probably I could track down a
reading-copy to lend to you. Also I wrote an obituary notice (unsigned)
which appeared in *National Review* a fortnight or so after his death—
"Wyndham Lewis, R.I.P.," in the editorial pages, I believe.[45]

Henry Regnery, now writing his memoirs, includes considerable information about Lewis, and possesses a number of letters from him, I believe; you might be able to obtain copies: Mr. Henry Regnery, President, Gateway Editions, 180 North Michigan Avenue, Chicago. Mrs. T. S. Eliot now is preparing a collection of TSE's letters to 1926, and must have a good many Lewis items in her collection; I hear from her now and then.

You might get some information from Mr. Geoffrey Stone, Igls, Tyrol, Austria. Mr. Stone once told me an amusing anecdote of a visit to Lewis, who had invited Stone and his wife to dine.[46] But Lewis grew increasingly uneasy as the food was consumed, complained about inflation, was about to offer them brandy—and then said, "But of course you must be going"—and virtually pushed them out the door.

With me, contrary to his reputation, Lewis always was kindly and generous. At his repeated urging, I once consumed almost his entire bottle of brandy, in an afternoon of talk—though it is true that he was then blind. At the time, he could drink only champagne, and T. S. Eliot recently had brought him a case of little bottles of champagne, from the Continent. I found him talkative, alert, and humorous, despite his blindness. He was interested in the practical politics of America, and especially in the character of American financial difficulties about 1955. He detested and suspected all publishers, and arranged to have me visit him alone, rather than in company with Henry Regnery. When going out, he would dine only at the Hyde Park Hotel Grill— "It's very expensive," he declared—as someone's guest. This he inflicted upon Henry Regnery. When I invited him to join me there on another occasion, he agreed; but when, a few days later, I turned up at the Grill, he wasn't there; as I looked about, a phone call came through for me, and it was Lewis, who said he was feeling indisposed, but that I must come instead to dine with him and his wife, the next evening—which I did. I suspect that he, or his wife, had experienced second thoughts about putting me to the cost of dinner for three—though at the time, being a bachelor, I was quite able to bear such trifles.

Blindness did not seem to affect his mind or even to dishearten him, except that he could not paint, of course. I never discussed his American wanderings with him.

You might obtain an anecdote of an abortive lecture of his at Michigan State University (during his Canadian sojourn) from my friend Mr. W. C. McCann, 1156 Sabron, East Lansing, Michigan. At a gathering before the lecture, Lewis drank too much, locked himself in his host's bathroom, and would not come out for the lecture. I believe he finally was dragged to the lecture-hall, but was incoherent there.

Doubtless you have thought of consulting Geoffrey Wagner, one of Lewis' critics, who lives in New York City.[47]

Probably I could think of more, in reply to questions of yours in the course of conversation. I hope we may contrive to meet. Best wishes for your undertaking.

Cordially,
Russell Kirk

Letter to Folke Leander

Leander (1910–1981) was a Swedish philosopher and academic who wrote extensively and favorably about the New Humanist thought of Irving Babbitt and Paul Elmer More. His doctoral dissertation, originally published in 1937 as Humanism and Naturalism: A Comparative Study of Ernest Seillière, Irving Babbitt, and Paul Elmer More *(Göteborg: Elanders boktryckeri aktiebolag), provided a thoughtful counterbalance to the prevailing philosophical opinion of the day and set the pattern for much of his later work. Leander and Kirk corresponded in a respectful manner periodically throughout their careers.*

January 28, 1978

Mr. Folke Leander
Rosgangen 37
602 11 Norrkoping
Sweden

Dear Mr. Leander,

The copies of your admirable dissertation are being passed out slowly and prudently to libraries and individuals who will value copies;

so the book will achieve some influential circulation in this country at last.[48]

Was the Spanish expedition your first one? I used to know much of Spain fairly well. I think that Segovia is my favorite city, though the South has much of interest; I haven't yet seen Cordoba.

Mecosta, like your town, lies in the clutch of a great blizzard—the fiercest since 1914.

Claes Ryn's *Democracy and the Ethical Life* is published now, although I've not yet received my copy.

I will have six books published this year, it appears—three new, three new editions of earlier works, viz.:

Decadence and Renewal in the Higher Learning
The Princess of All Lands (tales)
John Randolph of Roanoke (third edition)
Old House of Fear (third edition)
The Conservative Mind (sixth edition)
Essences (a mystical romance) (if I get it done in time for publication this year)

What good news about your daughter! I always have thought it strange that anyone could be enraptured by Marxism: it is like making a religion out of Bimetallism or Social Credit. The end, *per impossible,* would be wondrously dreary. We now have at Piety Hill thirteen refugees from Marxism: eleven Vietnamese, one a Boatperson, arrived last week; two young Ethiopians. One thinks of Henry and Brooks Adams' prediction that all the world would become Marxist, and then rot away.

Have you seen A. J. Ayer's autobiography? I reviewed it recently.[49] What a shallow, vain man, much like Bertrand Russell—and, unlike Russell, a total bore!

More another time; best wishes to you for 1978.

Cordially,
Russell Kirk

Letter to Henry Regnery

In the midst of writing his Memoirs of a Dissident Publisher *(published in 1979), Regnery sent Kirk a photocopy of one chapter in the making regarding several legendary literary figures Kirk had known personally.*

February 15, 1978

Mr. Henry Regnery
70 East Cedar Street
Chicago, Illinois 60611

Dear Henry,

Many thanks for having sent me the Campbell-Lewis-Eliot-Pound chapter of your memoirs. I will comment upon it later in this letter; a very interesting piece.

This day I received a telephone call from the Liberty Fund bureaucracy, demanding that I send to them immediately the document formally transferring copyright of *John Randolph of Roanoke* from H. Regnery Company to Russell Kirk. They say they can't proceed to any printing until they have that precious piece. Any undertaking directed by lawyers is doomed to dissolution. What frustrations David Franke must endure![50] Anyway, will you send back to me, signed, that formal transfer-of-copyright form which I posted to you a fortnight ago, so that poor David Franke can push ahead with the new edition of *Randolph*, which he intends to have out before Memorial Day?

I have sent back to the younger Henry R. the galleys of *Decadence and Renewal*: a considerable job it was to correct them. I already am drawing up the large index, on typed sheets, which I can fill in with numbers once I have the page proofs to collate. . . .

Now for some comments on your admirable chapter on the four men of letters:

(1) P. 9, reference to the "young American poet who apologized . . ." I was there with you on that occasion, you may recall. The "young poet"—

not so young, actually—was the late Robert Lowell, of the large but un-justified reputation, a ritualistic liberal of the first water. You may wish to mention his name.[51]

(2) P. 26, reference to Victor Stamp, in *Revenge for Love*: did Roy ever tell you, as he told me, that he was Lewis' original for Victor Stamp, and that Lewis had tried to kill him (Roy) off in at least three of his novels? Actually, later Roy did die much as Lewis had made Stamp die in *Revenge*: in a car with his wife, going over a cliff in Spain.

(3) P. 36, statement that Lewis came out of his experience intact, unlike his character Harding: Lewis wasn't really "intact" during his Canadian years, I suppose, though he survived them and recovered af-terward. He drank very heavily indeed, it appears, and when he spoke at Michigan State during that period he became hopelessly intoxicated before his lecture, locked himself into a bathroom, and was incoherent on the platform.

The chapter is a lively and valuable one. My copy ends rather abruptly, p. 54, with a quotation from Pound; perhaps there is more to come; if not, perhaps you need a page or two of summary to conclude the chapter.

We still are deep in snow at Mecosta. The Kerrigans plan to come to us some time in March; Annette is arranging the date. Perhaps you and Eleanor can come up with them then; the Kerrigans have no mo-tor transportation, of course, and so might ride up with you. I'll let you know soon the tentative date, and see if it happens to coincide with your plans. More then.

Cordially,
Russell

Letter to Ramsey Campbell

Described as "Britain's most respected living horror writer" by the Oxford Companion to English Literature, *Campbell (1946–) is a horror writ-er and anthologist. He and Kirk admired each other's fiction; and in 1978,*

Campbell approached Kirk about contributing to one of his upcoming editions of short horror fiction.

May 5, 1978

Mr. Ramsey Campbell
Liverpool

Dear Mr. Campbell,

Very good it is to have your letter of April 19. I hope you will yet find a publisher for *A Pantheon of Terror*. Aye, I can contrive a story for your *New Terrors*, I think, and get it to you by December.[52] Yet I am heavy laden: recently I wrote three ghostly tales, at Kirby McCauley's urging, and all have been snapped up, one by Kirby himself. There are four more standing requests for tales, besides yours; but I shall do my best. I shall even cudgel my brains, if possible, to do a contemporary story for you—though quite unlike the usual thing of that sort. The other day I sent off to Kirby one such, for his anthology; it is my boldest tale, in that the ghost himself, in effect, is both the narrator and the principal actor—something difficult to accomplish and yet retain some probability. This is "Lex Talionis."[53] My principal character therein, like the chief characters in almost all my tales, is drawn from the life—or death.

Arkham should publish my long-delayed *Princess of All Lands* next month, I suppose.

I look forward to seeing your stories—your own, I mean. I'm a connoisseur of carnivals and ghost-trains myself, as in "The Companion."[54] One of the weirdest I encountered [was], of all places, at Wigtown, in Galloway, years ago; a companion and I were the only customers. (A perfectly solid American companion, though.)

More another time; now I must turn my hand to writing a learned essay on the early and present reputation of my old friend T. S. Eliot. Best wishes.

Cordially,
Russell Kirk

Letter to Kirby McCauley

June 7, 1978

Mr. Kirby McCauley
310 East 46th Street
New York, New York, 10017

Dear Kirby,

Thanks for all your news of June 5. Here are some comments and business.

(1) Aye, do use "The Peculiar Demesne" in your anthology; the advance of $350 is quite all right.[55] I think "The Peculiar Demesne" will do as a title. I don't say "domain," for, as in the body of the story, I use the word "demesne" as still widely employed in Ireland and formerly in England; that is, the extensive grounds or (Scots) policies in the neighborhood of the residence of a landed proprietor, as distinguished from farms, etc., which he lets out. The word "domain," on the other hand, has an imperial or kingly connotation, implying a realm or much of a realm, which is not intended in the story.

(2) If I keep to my schedule, the romance should be finished by July 4—that's right, less than a month from now. I will need the other half of my advance precisely a month later, on August 4, to meet a mortgage-payment; so I am likely to get the finished product into your hands about the end of the first week of the next month. It will amount to more than a hundred thousand words. Was that the revised extended length which you suggested some months ago? There should be eighteen chapters, approximately. What title shall we use—*That Archaic Smile, Essences, Balgrummo Lodging,* or something else? What does our St. Martin's editor think about titles?[56]

(3) The romance being finished, I may be able to get off three or four more ghostly tales to you before the end of the year, thus satisfying immediate demand. We then will have enough, with the unused tales from *Surly Sullen Bell,* to make up a second volume of my ghost-

stories.[57] I should have the galleys from Arkham House before long, I take it.

(4) As I mentioned in my previous letter, it would be well if you could return to me, for the present, the original typescript of the first six chapters of my Gothick romance—supposing that they are in your possession, and not at St. Martin's. This would enable me to insert and collate various revised pages for the first six chapters which I have prepared here—changes necessary, in part, to reconcile the first six chapters with the developing chapters which I have written in recent months. Alternatively, of course, I could send you my revised pages for the first six chapters, and you could insert them; but I would save you that chore, and be able to check for any inconsistencies or omissions, were we to follow the first method. I do have here a pretty good copy of the first six chapters, but there may be some small changes I made in the original copy which were not indicated on my photostat-copy.

More before long; best wishes.

Cordially,
Russell

Letter to Thomas Howard

Howard (1935–) is a Roman Catholic layman, literary scholar, and retired English professor who is the author of numerous well-received books, including Narnia and Beyond: A Guide to the Fiction of C. S. Lewis *(1987, 2006),* The Novels of Charles Williams *(1991), and* On Being Catholic *(1997). For a time, he was part of a close circle of scholarly Catholic friends who sometimes styled themselves "the Junior Inklings," whose number included Sheldon Vanauken, Peter Kreeft, and Dom Julian Stead. In June 1978, Howard wrote to Kirk about a proposed interdisciplinary Christian Studies Program at Hillsdale College, offering several courses each term to be taught by distinguished Christian clergy and scholars. Howard suggested Vanauken and Kreeft as possible instructors.*

August 6, 1978

Dr. Thomas Howard
Department of English
Gordon College
Wenham, Massachusetts, 01984

Dear Dr. Howard,

Thanks for your recent note about our Revised Version of the proposal for the Institute for Christian Studies. We will commence in a modest way this autumn, with a half-dozen courses offered (by people who would be at Hillsdale anyway; and the Reverend Sheldon Smith, of Washington Memorial Chapel at Valley Forge, who has a leave of absence from his church this year, will be able to give us two or three months of his time to get us organized. No, although I know Sheldon Vanauken's name, I've not read his *Severe Mercy;* I must do so, and will get in touch with him, when our plans make headway; also Peter Kreeft.

In my capacity as editor of *The University Bookman,* may I persuade you to review my forthcoming book *Decadence and Renewal in the Higher Learning* (Gateway Editions)? If you can undertake this, be as cruel to the book as you like. I think you may find it lively, or at least mordant; it is a kind of chronological denunciation. It was supposed to be published this month, but it won't be out until next, I suppose, what with difficulties with the printer. I am asking Gateway Editions to send you page-proofs, if they are available (you may receive *uncorrected* ones, for everything is in process right now), and to send a bound copy to you later. The reason for such haste is that I should like to get a review into the autumn number (November) of my little *University Bookman,* if possible; I already have sent off the copy for the rest of that number. About 1,500 words, more or less, would be a good length; and we would pay an honorarium of $75, and supply some free copies—and more free copies should you request them in advance. Just let me know whether you could undertake this soon, pray.

I enclose a sample copy of the *Bookman,* in case you don't see it ordinarily. . . .

I hope we may contrive to meet somewhere before long.

Cordially,

Russell Kirk

Letter to David Adam Bovenizer

Bovenizer was a friend of Russell and Annette Kirk. In mid-1978, he wrote Kirk a letter that appealed to his love of all things Scottish, including a news item about the influential Scottish clergyman and man of letters George MacDonald (1824–1905), a native of Huntly, Scotland, whose imaginative works—with their element of sehnsucht, or spiritual yearning for the source of joy—exercised a profound influence on the minds of C. S. Lewis, G. K. Chesterton, Madeleine L'Engle, and many other writers Kirk admired.

November 16, 1978

Mr. David Adam Bovenizer
Barnesville, Ohio

Dear Mr. Bovenizer,

My tardy thanks to you for your kind and interesting letter of July 6. It is good to have Duncan Williams' contribution to the *Times;* I shall pass it on to the Hillsdale people, in case they've not beheld it.[58]

And how good to have news of MacDonald and Huntly! Just now, at Hillsdale, I am discussing his *Phantastes* and *Lilith* with a class of mine. From time to time, I have entertained vague notions of writing a book about George MacDonald, and of residing in Scotland for a year or two to do it—at Huntly, much of the time. Did you happen to see the MacDonald collection or room in the town library at Huntly? I passed through the town once, but not at an hour when—I was afoot—I could visit the library. And where did you stay—perhaps at the Huntly Arms, Family & Commercial? I hope to track down the bogies of Glenbogie, to the south of Huntly. Yes, I certainly will take the liberty of calling upon Mr. and Mrs. James Black, and seeing the Farm, when I get to Huntly—which possibly might be next summer.

A mystical Scottish romance of mine own, tentatively entitled *Essences,* will be published next May by St. Martin's Press. Meanwhile I have other books appearing—a notice of one of them enclosed. Best wishes to you.

Cordially,
Russell Kirk

Letter to Ross J. S. Hoffman

A distinguished historian long associated with Fordham University, Hoffman (1902–1979) was, according to fellow historian John P. McCarthy, "one of the key figures in the revival of American academic interest in Edmund Burke in the late 1940s and 1950s—a revival closely related to the development of the modern American conservative intellectual movement." Kirk and Hoffman first met at a meeting of the George Ade Society in East Lansing during the late 1940s, when the latter addressed the group. Over time, the two became friends and traveling companions, with Kirk occasionally visiting Hoffman and his wife, Hannah, during trips to New York.

January 19, 1979
as of Piety Hill
Mecosta, Michigan 49332

Dr. Ross J. S. Hoffman
Helen Avenue, Hix Park
Rye, New York

Dear Ross,

Very good it is to have your letter of January 15, which arrived here despite our enormous snows. I had been thinking often of you lately: so the arrival of your missive is something for Arthur Koestler's *Roots of Coincidence*. And only the other day I moved that handsome set of Scott which you so kindly gave to me to a new and more accessible shelf, and thought of you then.

During the next twelve months I will have fourteen books published—that is, new books, new editions of earlier Kirk's Works, books with long contributions by me, books with prefaces by me, foreign translations, etc. And, like you, I must set to writing my memoirs, but for publication, under the title *An Obscurant's History of His Own Time*. The book just now published is *Decadence and Renewal in the Higher Learning* (leaflet enclosed); my collected tales, *The Princess of All Lands*, will appear any day now; and my mystical romance, as yet untitled but perhaps to be called *The Hollow Dark*, will be published by St. Martin's Press in September. There is a possibility of making my *Roots* into a film, and also my romance *A Creature of the Twilight*. Under separate cover I am posting to you, inscribed, a copy of the new (third) edition of my *John Randolph of Roanoke*.

Our house is not wholly rebuilt since the Great Fire of Ash Wednesday, 1975; but it is sufficiently imposing to be mistaken for a monument of antique times. It ordinarily is crowded with people: until recently, our extended family consisted of thirty-five people (including the eleven Vietnamese who dwelt with us for three years), and even now, in addition to [my] wife and four daughters, we have with us one aged aunt, one schoolmistress, one novelist acting as my assistant, two young Ethiopians, and often others; and we have in immediate prospect (tomorrow, for the first comer) one Eritrean, two young Vietnamese, and perhaps a Chinese (Taiwan) family. As yet, no Rhodesians have applied. No unwed mothers dwell with us at present.

The youngest daughter, Andrea, now is aged three. Annette Yvonne Cecile Courtemanche Kirk, my spouse, remains marvelously beautiful and vigorous, and runs everything in Mecosta County, included the Board of Social Services. Between Christmas and New Year's, Malcolm Muggeridge and his wife, Kitty, were with us; and fifty-five people joined with us for three days to listen to his words of wisdom and to mine.

As for worldly goods, we are poorer than church mice, and I never know how the monthly bills will be paid; but we have survived, so far, by selling land and houses, and by my working twelve hours a day, seven days a week. There has been an immense load of debt since the Great Fire; I have been compared with Sir Walter [Scott] at Abbotsford, and the analogy is closer than people think.

I hear from Tom Vincitorio now and again.[59] A female professor of history at Boston University, Aileen Kraditor, is getting up a collection of essays by historians of a politically conservative bent, to be published as a book with a preface by me; I have suggested to her that she try to persuade you to contribute a piece.[60] My talk on Brownson, given at Fordham last year, is to be included in a book edited by Brother Gilhooley at Fordham (Fordham University Press).[61] . . .

How much more I should write! I think often of our days together, in Ireland especially. As Eliot knew, there really are eternal moments; and some of those we shall share beyond the end of time.

Meanwhile, I do wish you and Hannah a good Anno Domini 1979. More another time.

Cordially,
Russell

Letter to James Turner

April 11, 1979

Mr. James Turner
Editor, Arkham House
R. R. 2, Box 70
Collinsville, Illinois, 26634

Dear James Turner,
Various items of news and inquiry for you:
(1) I have sent to Ray Bradbury an inscribed copy of *Princess*, lest your review-copy be slow in reaching him, and have asked if he can find

time soon to review it for *The University Bookman*. A commendation of the book by him would be useful in various ways, of course.

(2) There is a new senior editor at the Conservative Book Club, Dr. Richard Bishirjian; I am acquainted with him. Although the odds still are against an adoption in that quarter, you might send him a copy of the book, now that copies are available, and a letter. Soon they will be distributing my *Decadence and Renewal*.

(3) Have you thought of a simple one-page, or quarter-page, mailing-piece in connection with *Princess?* I mean a piece of paper describing the book, preferably with an order-blank (perhaps on the reverse), which could fit easily and lightly into an ordinary envelope? Because of my many divers activities, I carry on a tremendous correspondence every week, and could send out such a flyer with all my envelopes. Also I could take such flyers with me on lecture-expeditions, sometimes; and perhaps you can think of some select lists of people to whom such advertisements could be sent.

(4) I regret to report that the jacket-drawing and the frontispiece meet with universal disapproval from the people to whom I have given copies or to whom I have shown the book. My wife is particularly hot against these; and I disapprove myself. For the sort of book this is, these illustrations are remarkably inappropriate—indeed, dreadful in the wrong sense of that word.

So far as Arkham House has bookshop sales, the misleading jacket-illustration will kill sales to all except those browsers who already are familiar with my work.

But your first print-run, I understand, is of merely three thousand copies. So it occurs to my mind that this lamentable burden might be lightened by altering the jacket for the second printing; I take it there will be such. There still is time for such action.

What we might do is to use a quotation about the book, from Ray Bradbury or some other well-known person in this occult field, to cover up at least the upper portion of the jacket-illustration. The quoted sentence or sentences could be set in large type upon a blank white space, thus blotting out most of the figures in the illustration without requiring complete redesigning and reprinting of the jacket. (Otherwise, the jacket, including the spine, is quite satisfactory.) What say you to this? Also the remarkably uninteresting and child-like frontispiece should be eliminated altogether—whether by simply not printing the picture on that page, or deleting that whole page from the next printing, neither side of the page being essential to the book.

This jacket, by the way, scarcely can be what you had expected from its designer, for whose work you delayed so long. Had I known that you required a good illustrator, I could have provided you with the work of friends of mine who know all my stories and how to illustrate them. I don't know why editors and publishers are afraid to consult authors on such important matters. I do hope that the sorry jacket won't deter all reviewers from bothering with the volume.

(5) I shall be speaking for several-day sessions at three colleges this summer, and the people in charge want to have copies of my books on display for sale; sometimes they sell twenty or thirty copies of one or the other of my books at each college. So you may wish to notify the several people in charge that *Princess* now is available. They are, respectively—

Dr. John Sparks
Department of History
Grove City College
Grove City, Pennsylvania

Mr. Larry Reed, Director, Summer Seminar
Department of Economics
Northwood Institute
Midland, Michigan

Dr. Charles D. Van Eaton, Chairman
Department of Economics
Hillsdale College
Hillsdale, Michigan

(6) If and when you get around to more advertising, two of the magazines which especially attract readers of my work are *The Intercollegiate Review* and *Modern Age*. The first has the largest circulation of any serious quarterly in America. The business addresses of the two are the same, happily: 14 South Bryn Mawr Avenue, Bryn Mawr, Pennsylvania. Their advertising rates are low.

(7) Your idea of sending review-copies to practically all Michigan papers is a good one; no publisher of mine ever has taken that trouble before. But doubtless you know that I am better known nationally—in New York and California, especially, and in the South—than I am in Michigan. Therefore you will get better results, I am sure, if you take the trouble to send review-copies to the two-hundred-and-fifty odd daily papers throughout the country which carry regular book-review sections. This is the cheapest and most effective form of advertising possible; and in the past this method has gotten many, many reviews in biggish papers which otherwise would not have noticed the book; and sometimes the local reviewers are better and more quotable than the reviewers in what remains of the national book-review media. The West Coast reviewers have been particularly cordial.

More another time; best wishes.

Cordially,
Russell Kirk

I take it that you will nominate *Princess* for the Fifth World Fantasy Convention award; notice of that convention next autumn has been sent to me, together with a nomination-blank and presumably a nomination-form has been sent to you, too.

Letter to Henry Regnery

On May 25, 1979, publisher Henry Regnery's second son and namesake, Henry F. Regnery, was among 273 persons who died in the crash of a commercial airliner upon takeoff in Chicago. A rising figure within his father's company, he was traveling with Regnery Gateway sales manager Dennis Connell—a former student assistant of Russell Kirk—who also died in what

*United Press International described at the time (according to the online UPI
Archives, July 19, 1989) as "the worst air disaster in U.S. history."*

May 26, 1979

Mr. Henry Regnery
Three Oaks, Michigan

Dear Henry,

Bill Buckley telephoned us last midnight to tell of the crash. We
did not know until this morning, however, that Dennis, as well as Henry, had been on that plane; of course Bill did not recognize Dennis'
name, and knew which Henry Regnery only because of the South Bend
identification.

What vigor so suddenly ended! In his last letter to me, Henry remarked that we must meet before long to talk of old times. I saw him
last in Pittenweem. How well I remember him as a little boy, in Hinsdale!

He has Annette's prayers and mine; and we pray for you and
Eleanor, too.

We will write to Jan Connell. Dennis was everything to her; she
is a very good young woman, and I hope that her Christian faith will
be of some comfort now.

And yet it was a merciful death, and the one I would choose for
myself; it's likely enough, with all the flying that I do. But for Henry it
came too soon, and for Dennis.

Do let me know if I can be of help in any way with the firm's undertakings; I hope you have people immediately available who know
something about book-publishing.

We hope that you and Eleanor will come to visit us as soon as you
may; we will be at home most of the summer.

I'll write more later. Just now I am going to pray.

Yours,
Russell

Letter to Arianna Stassinopoulos

Long before her marriage to Michael Huffington and her ascendancy as a major media figure in the world of progressive politics, Arianna Stassinopoulos was a rising conservative figure and an author of several serious books. Russell and Annette Kirk met her during the mid-1970s; and in 1979, Russell reviewed one of her books for a major southern newspaper.

August 3, 1979

Miss Arianna Stassinopoulos
12, Cadogan Gardens
London, S.W.3

Dear Arianna,

For some time I have been meaning to send this review to you: I did it for the *Birmingham News,* the largest paper in Alabama and Mississippi. You will perceive that your book has no more cordial admirer.[62] Someone or other wrote a silly piece about it and submitted it to me for *The University Bookman;* but I rejected that review.

Annette and I are sorry you weren't able to visit us when last you were this side of the Atlantic. We thought of telephoning you in California, to see if you might be persuaded to appear after all; but we decided not to press you, knowing how many people one has to see on such an expedition. Do come to us whenever you can; we would collect you at either Grand Rapids airport or Saginaw airport.

Upon what are you at work now? Two books of mine are published recently, and in September will be published my mystical romance *Lord of the Hollow Dark.* Best wishes to you.

Cordially,
Russell Kirk
P.S.: A suggestion or two—
On p. 91 of *After Reason,* you write that Pound sanctified Hitler. Presumably you meant to write "Mussolini"; so far as I know, Pound never applauded Hitler.

Also there was some quotation from Burke, I think, which—so it seemed to me—needed to be better understood in its context; but I cannot find it at this moment.

Letter to Richard P. Rosser

Rosser (1929–2007) was a friend of Kirk and a political science professor who served as president of DePauw University from 1977 to 1986. On September 4, 1979, he wrote a cordial letter to Kirk in which he mentioned that he had recently approached the Moore Foundation in search of funding for a proposed Center for Management and Entrepreneurship at DePauw. He reported to Kirk that the foundation insisted on having control over the sort of courses the center should teach and who should be allowed to teach them—a problem because Rosser wanted Kirk to serve as a visiting professor and teach there.

September 7, 1979

Dr. Richard P. Rosser, President
DePauw University
Greencastle, Indiana

Dear Dick,

Very good it is to have your letter of September 4. It's a pity that you didn't have an opportunity to visit us on your way south; but we hope to lure you to our dark tower next summer, if not earlier. . . .

I look forward to your presidential position papers. Perhaps you will let us publish some portion thereof in our *University Bookman.* I'll send you a copy of the current number. It gets a surprising amount of serious attention, our slim volume.

I don't know the Moore Foundation; so I cannot sit in judgment of them. But in general the endowed zealots for "free enterprise" are a narrow and eccentric lot, nearly as blinkered and inflexible as New Left gentry. The Free Enterprise people generally take one of two attitudes:

(1) A defiance of the state indistinguishable from an anarchism which would efface, very swiftly, all forms of private property, let alone large commercial and industrial corporations;

(2) An attitude of "great corporations are holy and do no wrong," which helps to justify the predictions of Marx that consolidation of "capitalism" will reach the point at which seizure by the proletarian dictatorship becomes very easy, there being almost no brave defenders of "capital" remaining—merely a managerial class.[63]

I shall be at Calvin College during January—the only person ever permitted to profess there who does not swear to abide forever by all tenets of the Synod of Dort. I have an invitation from Indiana University to become the first distinguished Visiting Professor of newly-endowed establishment, for the term commencing in February; I've not arranged the details of this yet. In January, 1981, I will begin to be distinguished visiting professor at Pepperdine University, Malibu, for a term—this excites the Kirk daughters. I do hope that the Center for Management at DePauw comes to take on flesh, and that some sojourn of mine there can be sandwiched in.

More another time; best wishes to you and your wife. I'll send you some pieces of mine under separate cover.

Cordially,
Russell

Letter to Edward S. Babbitt

Babbitt (1903–1997) was the son and literary executor of one of Kirk's conservative heroes, New Humanist champion Irving Babbitt (1865–1933).

September 30, 1979

Mr. Edward S. Babbitt
10 Skinner Lane
South Hadley, Massachusetts, 01075

Dear Mr. Babbitt,

Aye, very good it is that the Liberty Press edition of *Democracy and Leadership* is published at last: a handsome job of book-production.[64] One day I may persuade them, or some other publisher (probably the latter) to undertake the publication of one or two more of your father's books; but as yet I have no definite prospects for that. I am endeavoring to make sure that some reviews of *Democracy and Leadership* appear soon.

It is heartening that you are in shape to write letters again. I must enter a hospital on October 19, for the first time since I was three years old; but it is merely an ailing gall-bladder.

My assistant posted off to you the promised copy of Folke Leander's *Humanism and Naturalism*. If you've not received it by this time, do let me know, and I'll send you another copy.

James T. Farrell happened to write a longish letter—the first one he ever sent me—only a few days before his recent death. I suspect that he was unaware of my rather harsh comments on his comments on your father's writings.[65] I met John Dos Passos only once, and never mentioned to him P. E. More's "explosion in a cesspool" comment.[66]

More another time; best wishes to you, and to your sister.

Cordially,

Russell Kirk

Letter to William F. Buckley Jr.

In the letter below, Kirk brings Buckley up to date on everyday matters before clearing the air about an issue that had disturbed him for some time: his belief that the literary editor of National Review *had chosen not to review his books for several years.*

November 2, 1979

Mr. William F. Buckley, Jr.
National Review
150 East 35th Street
New York, New York, 10016

Dear Bill,

You should have been here for Hallowe'en—four hundred trick-or-treaters being tricked! Our capers father rumors. Recently a pretty young Evangelical came to see Annette on some educational business, and was surprised to discover that we're Papists. "I'm so glad!" "Why?" "Because downtown they told me that you were pagans, and sacrifice living cats."

I'm just out of the hospital, where I underwent the first surgery of my sixty-one years: my friend Dwain Cummings removed my gall bladder, repaired an hiatal hernia four times the size of any such deformity he had beheld before, and made other repairs. I recover rapidly, and must be off for a week's travel only two days from now. Annette and all the girls thrive.

Strange to say, my fulminations in *Decadence and Renewal* seem to have won me much favor in the academy. I am invited to spend time at all sorts of establishments. Just now, for some months, I am flung into a breach: appointed director of the social-science program of the Education Research Council of America, temporarily, my friend Raymond English having resigned; this will keep me in Cleveland much of the time. Then I'm to spend most of January at Calvin College, lecturing on Eliot—the first person ever permitted to profess there who does not swear to abide always by the dogmas of the Synod of Dort. In March and April, I am to be the Patton Lecturer (in history) at Indiana University—more or less succeeding Henry Steele Commager. . . .

Despite the success of *Decadence* in certain quarters, I am lost in wonder at the difficulty of getting books reviewed anywhere—especially books by notorious conservatives, of course. The little literary cliques narrow and narrow, and every person seems to read but one magazine. You will recall a time when the *Chicago Tribune,* the Washington papers, and the *Los Angeles Times* reviewed books more or less independently, even if the quality of most reviews was shabby enough; nowadays they will not review a book unless it has first been reviewed, and approved, in the *New York Times* and the *New York Review of Books.*

And my experience with *National Review* in recent years, I'll have you know, has been discouraging: I get more attention in *The Nation* or *The Progressive!*[67] In the past two years, or somewhat less, I have published the following several books, the most productive literary period of your servant's life. Some of these books, of course, were new editions of earlier books of mine; but even the earlier editions, for one reason or another, never had been reviewed in *National Review*. I called all these books to the attention of your people; they were studiously ignored, in favor of the sort of books which the *New York Times* reviews—Tuchman, et al.[68] Here is the catalogue:

	N.R.'s treatment
John Randolph of Roanoke, third edition, enlarged	never reviewed at all
The Conservative Mind, sixth edition	never reviewed, any edition
Decadence and Renewal in the Higher Learning	reviewed only in Stanton Evans' column
The Princess of All Lands	not reviewed—though the *Wall Street Journal* gave it much attention[69]
Lord of the Hollow Dark (published a month ago)	not yet reviewed; presumably no review scheduled
Babbitt, *Democracy and Leadership*, edited by Kirk	not reviewed

What a record of inattention! I don't think these books of mine are uninteresting to your readers, though they may bore your present staff. Why this silent treatment? Only the *New York Review of Books* is equally oblivious to Kirk's Works. . . .

Perhaps it will be said that my books are reviewed in *The University Bookman*. Well, some are, some aren't. But there isn't supposed to be any coordination of reviews between the two magazines; we're not supposed to be the same publication, at law or in any other sense; I review books, or choose them for review, quite regardless of whether or not they have been, or will be, reviewed in NR. (As it turns out, there are very few duplications of reviews between the two magazines.) In any event, if on this ground my books are to be excluded from the book-review pages of NR, am I expected to exclude all contributors to

NR from the review-pages of the *University Bookman?* What a strange notion!

Presumably you never have noticed the gradual exclusion of the Wizard of Mecosta from your magazine's pages. It was otherwise in the days of Meyer.[70] What is occurring?

I'm to speak at the installation of the new President of Southampton College, in Long Island, on November 11–22. I'd have an invitation sent to you, were it not such a long dreary way out to Southampton, especially now that the better trains with the club cars have gone down to dusty death. But perhaps we can get together for an hour or two, if you're to be in the city. We'll be spending a night or two with Charles and Mickie Teetor, 1030 Fifth Avenue.

More another time; best wishes.

Cordially,
Russell

The 1980s

But the question remains as to whether conservatively-inclined people possess imagination and resolution sufficient to contend tolerably well with our present discontents and difficulties.

from a letter to Robert A. Waters, March 20, 1989

Letter to William F. Buckley Jr.

In early January 1980, Kirk suffered a heart attack that left him weakened and in low spirits. This may have contributed to the substance of the "missing holograph communication" he mentions in which he announced his desired separation from National Review *as a regular columnist. After Buckley kindly asked Kirk to reconsider—and perhaps begin writing regular book reviews for the journal—Kirk wrote the following letter, in which he displays an approachable tone and stance while still maintaining his desire to end his regular column, "From the Academy."*

January 28, 1980
as of Mecosta, Michigan, 49332

Mr. William F. Buckley, Jr.
National Review
150 East 35th Street
New York, NY

Dear Bill,

Much thanks for your recent, though undated, letter. By this time you may have received my missing holograph communication to you, written from a hospital in Grand Rapids about January 12—the one in which I announced my weariness of "From the Academy."

Aye, I can keep "From the Academy" going until, and including, your twenty-fifth anniversary number. On what date will that occur? And I can continue to contribute to *National Review* on various topics, I suppose—six two-page printed pages a year, perhaps, rather than my previous twelve one-page printed pages for the past several years. Your "Books Arts & Manners" section undoubtedly would be improved, if 'tis meself that says it, by the contributions of a seasoned literary critic like R. Kirk. (By the way, I am beginning to get up a collection of my critical essays for book publication—*Sewanee Review, Kenyon Review,* etc.; doubtless *National Review* will refuse to review the volume when it appears.) I find the January 25 number's "Books Arts & Manners" particularly disappointing. Mr. Sobran's rambling article doesn't belong in that part of the magazine, if it belongs anywhere.[1]

Apropos of all this, I enclose a letter I received yesterday from Devin Garrity.[2] The Burke book to which he refers did deserve mention in *National Review,* though it is no vast definitive biography; the fact that it was reviewed in the *New Yorker* makes my point that good books seem almost automatically rejected for review by *National Review,* your journal taking the judgment of the *N. Y. Review of Books* and Madison Avenue literary cocktail parties for the laws of the Medes and Persians.[3] And I suppose that my introduction to this Devin-Garrity Burke book contributed to NR's rejection of the review. . . .

What mean you by presenting me with a telephone credit-card? Why, that's like thrusting upon me a color television set: I do loathe and abominate the invention of Alexander Graham Bell, and almost never resort to it. . . . After all the trouble you went to, it would be graceless to return the accursed card to you; therefore I shall bury it in the depths of my passport case, to be resorted to only in some inconceivable emergency.[4]

More another time. I seem sufficiently recovered from my hospitalization earlier this month, and will be on the road again about February 4. My illness did cause the cancelling of all but one day of my Calvin College seminar. I may cancel most of my Indiana University professorship, too.

The appearance of Edward Teller on your program has produced generally favorable comment in these parts.[5] But I refuse to watch even Ray Bradbury's *Martian Chronicles* on television; indeed, Ray says the production is no good.[6] By the way, Ray Bradbury would like to meet you some time. He won't fly in planes, and trains to New York are slow nowadays, so you might find time for a pleasant talk with him some day when you are in Los Angeles. He has great charm, and is full of ideas.

More another time.

Cordially,

Russell Kirk

Letter to Peter Kreeft

Kreeft (1937–) is a professor of philosophy at Boston College and The King's College. A formidable apologist for the Christian faith and Roman Catholic orthodoxy, he is the author of numerous well-received books, among which Love Is Stronger Than Death *(San Francisco: Harper & Row, 1979) was his first. Kirk greatly admired Kreeft's books, and the two men were on cordial terms.*

April 7, 1980

Dr. Peter Kreeft
Department of Philosophy
Boston College
Chestnut Hill, Massachusetts, 02167

Dear Mr. Kreeft,

As you may have noticed, your *Love Is Stronger than Death* is one of the five books nominated for the American Book Award's prize for "religious and inspirational" books, to be awarded at the beginning of next month. I suspect that the prize actually will be given to that radical-chic book about the Egyptian Gnostics; but at least your good book is recognized as being in the first rank for 1979.[7]

The reason why it appears as a surviving selection is that I nominated it rather late in the game, after I had had an opportunity to read it. I then arranged for the American Book Awards people to have copies of it sent to the other selectors (whose identity I know not), and, wondrous to relate, they concurred in my judgment in this one important instance. Your book was called to my attention by Dr. Louis Vos, of Calvin College—where I very nearly succeeded you as interim lecturer, but was prevented by being hospitalized only half an hour before the first reception was scheduled for me at Calvin!

I think that the American Book Awards people are trying to be more honest than were the notorious . . . National Book Awards gentry, whom I denounced in print about two years ago.[8] Still, I suspect that the final choice of the Gnostic book has been virtually rigged.

We thank you for so good a book on so grand a theme. Best wishes. I hope that we may contrive to meet some day.

Cordially,
Russell Kirk

Letter to Ray Bradbury

The Kirk family lived in Malibu, California, during the fall of 1980, while Russell lectured at Pepperdine University and negotiated with numerous individuals to bring about a film version of The Roots of American Order. *He wrote the following undated letter in September, shortly after his arrival in Southern California.*

as of 20220 Inland Lane
Malibu, California, 90267
telephone (213) 456–8900

Mr. Ray Bradbury
10265 Cheviot Drive
Los Angeles, California, 90064

Dear Ray,

With five Kirk females, your servant is entrenched on a hilltop here, just above the Grand Landslip of 1979.[9] We will be in Malibu until December 15. I hope that we may contrive to get together during this season; address and telephone number are above; my formal duties are very light—though, as I needn't tell you, there always is plenty of writing to be done. I am lending a hand in the production of a pilot film, first of a series of thirteen one-hour films that National Public Broadcasting or, locally, KCET—means to base on my *Roots of American Order*, at last. Also, I give a seminar on the same theme at Pepperdine University—as Distinguished Visiting Professor of *Sociology* (!)

Yesterday I received a copy of McCauley's anthology *Dark Forces*, with a story therein by you, another by me. Your tale excepted (more about that below), I don't relish my company.[10] My feeling is similar about my company in two other anthologies, containing stories of mine, published in the past month or so. I don't think I will write any more tales for anthologies, or let my stories be reprinted therein except under especial circumstances and foreknowledge. For most of these "horror" tales are mere childish nastiness, anti-erotic when pretending to be sexually exciting. I suppose that the prevalence of the Naked Girlie magazines accounts for the pseudo-erotic . . . character of such writing by people (some of them, anyway) who know better; they want to be paid, and the girlie magazines pay. It would be better to fry chicken for Colonel Sanders' successors.

But "A Touch of Petulance" is up at least to your accustomed standard, of which I am the warmest admirer; I shall hand it to Annette to read. Did you ever have yourself that kind of experience: I mean the young self encountering the old self, literally or almost literally, and the old self (at another time) encountering the young self? I never did; but a friend of mine in Alabama (no credulous or superstitious man) had precisely that experience. As a boy, in deep sorrow, he became aware of a presence that comforted him stoically; and forty years later, walking the same street after decades of absence, he was aware of a sorrowful small boy walking invisibly beside him—his youthful self, from across the gulf of time. My friend himself had been his own comforter. The man recognized the boy he had been once, although the boy had not recognized in his invisible comforter the man whom he would become.[11]

If I write one more longish uncanny tale, I will have enough for a second volume: that is, a companion volume to *Princess of All Lands.* After that I shall rest on my laurels, so far as fiction is concerned.

On what grand designs are you engaged just now? Best wishes; more another time; do let us know, by note or telephone, if you think of a convenient time and place for us to rendezvous.

Cordially,

Russell

Letter to Ronald Reagan

In November 1980, Reagan decisively defeated incumbent Jimmy Carter for the United States presidency, an outcome Kirk had long predicted.

November 15, 1980

The Honorable Ronald Reagan

Dear Mr. Reagan,

Well done! Your servant was one of the few to predict a Ronald Reagan victory by a very large margin throughout the campaign, never growing fainthearted; and so it has come to pass. You now have the opportunity to do so much to renew and reinvigorate this country. I enclose a recent speech of mine to the Heritage Foundation, "The Conservative Movement: Then and Now," in which, incidentally, I predict your triumph.

For the present, I am a neighbor of yours, residing until December 12 here at Malibu—after that, back to Michigan. While we are here, I am lending a hand with the first stage of production of thirteen one-hour films to be based on my book *The Roots of American Order,* in which you have taken a kindly interest for several years. National Public Broadcasting expects to raise most of the money for the production, and to undertake national distribution. Se we begin to make headway in popular television, as in practical politics.

Recollecting your remark during the campaign that you mean to appoint a woman to the Supreme Court of the United States, I have a recommendation to make. Chief Justice Mary Coleman has just been re-elected to the Supreme Court of Michigan; possibly you are familiar with the record of her first term on that court. She is an intelligent conservative, learned in the law, especially experienced in cases concerning children and youth, and a staunch restrainer of bureaucracy. Also, incidentally, she is a beautiful woman—even at the age of sixty-three, I believe—who once upon a time was Miss Maryland; she has dignity and charm, and is married to another Republican judge of high reputation.[12] I was active in both of Mrs. Coleman's campaigns for election to the Supreme Court, and have followed her decisions with close attention, and have sung her praises in the pages of *National Review* and in my syndicated newspaper column. On the chance that you may need to fill a vacancy in the Supreme Court before many months are out, I commend to you without any reservation Chief Justice Mary Coleman. One could not possibly do better in appointing the first woman to sit upon the bench of the United States Supreme Court.

We are mightily grateful for your fortitude and diligence of these past several months; and we are praying for your eminent success in office.

Cordially,
Russell Kirk

Letter to John O'Sullivan

For much of his adult life, Kirk worked quietly to arrange extended visits to America by conservative-thinking figures from overseas as well as refugees from political oppression in foreign lands, often putting them up for weeks, months, or years at his home in Mecosta. In the following letter, Kirk sounds out John O'Sullivan (1942–)—British-born editor of Policy Review *and*

eventually William F. Buckley Jr.'s successor as editor of National Review—
*on the possibility of securing funding for visits by two European visitors to
the United States.*

January 6, 1981

Mr. John O'Sullivan
Policy Review
The Heritage Foundation
513 C Street, N.E.
Washington, D.C., 20002

Dear Mr. O'Sullivan,

You may recall that when I was with you last, I mentioned the possibility of sponsoring a visit to this country by a Polish scholar in politics and history, Professor Ludwikowski, of the University of Krakow. I may have mentioned also—though I'm not sure that I did—the possibility of a similar visit by Signor Mario Marcolla, an Italian conservative writer.

Now I should like to help these two conservatively-minded gentlemen spend some time in the United States. I don't know that either is a splendid public speaker in the English language; but conversations, meetings with select groups, introduction to editors, and the like would be of value to all concerned. Dr. Ludwikowski's trip will be sponsored for a month by the United States government—one of the State Department programs for distinguished visitors, doubtless—but he would like to remain a month or two longer in order to consult scholars, libraries, and other people and things. Mr. Marcolla would like to spend a month or two (bringing his wife with him) in visiting conservative circles in the United States; I can arrange some engagements for him without difficulty, in New York and elsewhere.

Would it be possible for the Heritage Foundation and the Marguerite Eyer Wilbur Foundation (of which I am president) to sponsor jointly the visit of these gentlemen? The Wilbur Foundation, of course, has no premises to be used for meetings, and is a Californian foundation. Perhaps it would be more suitable for the Heritage Foundation to act as official sponsor (what with your Washington situation), and for the Wilbur Foundation to make a grant to the Heritage Foundation toward the cost of these gentlemen's travel-expenses. (I would suggest to my colleague-trustees of the Wilbur Foundation an appropriation of four thousand dollars for Professor Ludwikowski, and another four thousand for Signor Marcolla.) Pray let me know your judgment on such matters. . . .

Below I summarize briefly the accomplishments of these two men.

Professor Rett Ludwikowski is the leading light of a whole school of Polish younger men engaged in political and historical studies. His and their especial interest is conservatism, particularly in its British and American forms. Dr. Ludwikowski has published several books in the historical and political disciplines, including one on John Stuart Mill; I possess copies of his publications. He has studied in Britain; and he has a good knowledge of conservative thought, about which he has written several periodical articles. He and his associates are endeavoring to publish the works of Edmund Burke in Polish. At this time particularly, conversations with Professor Ludwikowski would be of much interest. Incidentally, the survival of non-Communist professors and doctrines at the University of Krakow, at one time in open defiance of the Polish national government, is a lively and curious phenomenon. It would be well for people in America to be in touch with this group of Polish writers and thinkers. I have exchanged letters and publications with Dr. Ludwikowski for several years.

Signor Mario Marcolla, by gainful occupation an executive in a Milanese industrial firm, has long been active in movements to coordinate resistance to communism and socialism in Italy. He is an earnest Catholic, and a feature writer for *Osservatore Romano*. He organized and personally conducted my tour of Italian conservative circles some seventeen years ago. He frequently addresses gatherings of Opus Dei, the conservative Catholic organization which has branches in many countries—and which doubtless would be glad to have him speak in New York, Chicago, and elsewhere. Mr. Marcolla, accompanied by his wife, would spend about two months in the United States, meeting with interested groups and learning about present circumstances and movements of opinion in this country.

Although the needs and circumstances of these two gentlemen differ somewhat, I estimate that either would require a minimum of four thousand dollars for travel-expenses; if our two foundations together could make up a grant somewhat larger than that, and Heritage could provide Washington hospitality, the project might be accomplished. (Neither gentleman has private means sufficient to cover the basic cost of travel from his native country to New York, let alone other expenses; but Dr. Ludwikowski's transatlantic travel presumably will be paid for by the American government.)

In Michigan, I will be happy to extend hospitality to either or both of these gentlemen for as long as they care to stay. Also I can take a hand in arranging their meetings and possible lectures.

I present this proposal to you in the first instance; and if the Heritage Foundation becomes interested in the undertaking, I will present it to my colleagues of the Wilbur Foundation, either at an intended meeting in March (rather late for our purposes, perhaps) or, if necessary, by correspondence before then.

More another time; I write in some haste.

Cordially,

Russell Kirk

Letter to William F. Buckley Jr.

With the aid of W. Wesley McDonald, Kirk assembled a large number of representative essays and short stories representing conservative thought for Viking's Portable Conservative Reader *(1982). Here, writing shortly before the work's publication, Kirk apologizes to Buckley for the omission of the latter's representative essay and tells of his own upcoming travels and commitments.*

April 8, 1982

Mr. William F. Buckley, Jr.
National Review

Dear Bill,

My secret agents tell me that you will be speaking in Grand Rapids on April 20. I would endeavor to entice you to Mecosta then, were it not that I will be in California on that date; and Annette will be just back from Texas. It is a pity to miss you.

Under separate cover, I have sent you a copy of the *Portable Conservative Reader,* inscribed. Alas, you are not represented therein. Along with Richard Weaver, James Fitzjames Stephen, G. K. Chesterton, John Hookham Frere, George Canning, and many another friend of mine, quick or dead, you were pushed out by Viking's demand that I reduce my selections by a third. Albert Jay Nock was expelled, too. Also I had a problem of trying to fit my selections into a kind of pattern, within sections of the book. But I do wish your eloquent "Latin Mass" had survived![13]

Just now I am writing a ninth-grade textbook in economics. Also I have to prepare myself to witness at William Ball's latest important church-state trial, in Lansing.

I hope to hear and see you at the Philadelphia Society, between the Lansing trial and my Californian engagements. Best wishes.

Cordially,
Russell

Letter to Robert Walters

Nationally syndicated columnist Robert Walters published an article in mid-July 1982 in which he claimed, "Homosexual conduct in Congress dates back at least to the early years of the 19th century, when Rep. John Randolph of

Virginia, a leading opponent of President Thomas Jefferson's policies, became notorious for his erratic behavior in general and his kinky sexual proclivities in particular." (See Bowling Green [KY] Daily News, *July 18, 1982, 6A.) Upon reading this column, Kirk challenged Walters to substantiate his remarks, in a letter to which Walters did not reply.*

August 17, 1982
Box 4
Mecosta, Michigan, 49332

Mr. Robert Walters
Newspaper Enterprise Association
200 Park Avenue
New York, New York, 10017

Dear Mr. Walters,

My attention has been called to one of your syndicated columns, published approximately a month ago, concerning the scandals about congressional pages. I agree with you, incidentally, that it would be well to engage regular pages of tolerable years.

My inquiry, however, concerns your remarks on John Randolph of Roanoke—who, you imply, was a homosexual, and known for "kinky sexual proclivities in particular."

I am the author of the best-known book about Randolph still in print, *John Randolph of Roanoke: A Study in American Politics*. Probably I have read almost everything about Randolph ever published, and have gone thoroughly through his papers in the several archives where they may be consulted. Never before, anywhere, have I encountered any suggestion that Randolph was a homosexual or otherwise given to sexual excess.

Actually, the general assumption is that Randolph was sexually impotent before he was twenty years old, possibly as a result of venereal disease contracted while he was a student at Columbia College. Certainly he was impotent at the time of his death. While indeed there occurred occasional references by his political enemies to Randolph's *lack* of sexuality, these were sneers at his alleged impotence, not suggestions of sexual deviance. The most famous of these exchanges is said to have occurred when another member of Congress hinted in a speech at Randolph's impotence, and Randolph is said to have replied, "The gentleman boasts of the possession of qualities in which he is exceeded by the bull in his pasture and the negro in his field."

Henry Adams calls Randolph "that Saint Michael in politics"— not that Adams approved of Randolph's politics generally. Randolph's eccentricities, in short, did not extend to sexual excesses of any sort— quite the contrary. It would be about as plausible to accuse J.F.K. of obsessive chastity.

So I wish to inquire of you where you obtained this information about Randolph. What with the "gay" movement of recent years, various odd books have been published in attempts to prove, for whatever reason, that all sorts of famous people must have been gay. The allegation has been made, in the past decade, about T. S. Eliot and Edmund Burke, for instances. I have written books about both Eliot and Burke; and here, too, the arguments will not hold water. As an historian, I am interested in accuracy.

Did you, then, encounter this allegation in some printed source? For thirteen years the Los Angeles Times Syndicate published my thrice-weekly column, until I tired of the labor; so I am aware of the haste with which newspaper columns must be prepared, and of errors that slip in from time to time. You may wish to correct your remarks on Randolph. At any rate, I will be grateful if you can let me know the source of your information.

If you are not familiar with my Randolph book, originally published by the University of Chicago Press, I will be happy to send you with my compliments a copy of the present third and enlarged edition.

Yours sincerely,
Russell Kirk
Editor, *The University Bookman*

Letter to the Editor of the *Times Literary Supplement*

Kirk's Portable Conservative Reader—*an anthology of short writings by many British and American conservatives—was reviewed in a fairly large number of venues upon appearance. One of the most prestigious, the* Times Literary Supplement, *published a moderate-length, sour review by Tom Paulin, a Northern Irish poet and critic who considered the volume boring. Kirk responded to the review with a letter to the editor.*

November 7, 1982

The Editor
The Times Literary Supplement
Printing House Square
London

Sir:

In your pages on 8th October there appeared a review of *The Portable Conservative Reader,* edited by me. The reviewer, a Mr. Tom Paulin, appears to be a disciple of Clement Fadge of *New Grub Street.*[14] He complains of the "dullness" of the quick or dead contributors to this anthology—exempting, I take it, merely Burke and Kipling.

Among those dull contributors are Coleridge, Fenimore Cooper, Macaulay, Hawthorne, Stevenson, Gissing, Saintsbury, Conrad, Christopher Dawson, Eliot, C. S. Lewis, Betjeman, Freya Stark, Jacquetta Hawkes, Muggeridge. Whatever such authors may be accused of, never before have they been found dull. Who are the lively political writers favored by Mr. Paulin, of the deathless prose?

Does Mr. Paulin fear that people who happen to read this anthology might be influenced by it? And does he fancy that the best way to dissuade them from opening it (if indeed Mr. Paulin himself bothered to look at its table of contents) is to instruct them that they would find the book boring?

Some of us familiar for several decades with *The Times Literary Supplement* have noticed periods in which your periodical has descended into what Burke called "a licentious toleration"—that is, an indulgence of silliness, malice, and ideological prejudice among its reviewers. Then, after repeated complaints from authors and publishers, TLS has reformed its ways. Is such a salutary new reformation in prospect?

Yours sincerely,
Russell Kirk
Editor, *The University Bookman*

Letter to Mario Marcolla

Kirk held the conservative Italian industrialist and writer Mario Marcolla (1929–2003) in high regard. The following letter is colored by Kirk's reflections on the seasons of life and the social decay of both Italy and the United States.

November 7, 1982

Signor Mario Marcolla
Via Luigi Fossati, 7
10052 Monza (Milano)
Italy

Dear Mario,

Very good it is to have your letter of October 17, received today. I mean to enclose with this communication a copy of my lecture "Can Virtue Be Taught?," delivered at the Heritage Foundation, Washington. Also I am posting to you, under separate cover, a copy of the collection of my lectures (during 1981, chiefly) recently published by the Heritage Foundation.[15] Have you received already a copy of my book *The Viking Portable Conservative Reader?* If not, pray let me know, and I will post a copy to you.

Could you send me a copy of the issue of *Ulisse* containing my little essay on religion in America?[16] I did receive payment for the piece, but no copies.

Is there some particular publication, or kind of publications, that you desire from the Heritage Foundation? If so, I will prevail upon my friend Mr. Lawler (who now directs also a new Catholic association) to post them to you.

"Can Virtue Be Taught?" eventually will be published by the Heritage Foundation, in a second collection of my lectures.[17] Mr. Marion Montgomery now is revising his three lectures on the subject, delivered at Piety Hill; he means to make a small book of them.

Warren Fleischauer died most abruptly; no one had known that he had heart disease. His life was a melancholy one, for the most part, though he had a strong sense of humor. I do miss him.

Aye, the news from Italy depresses us here. The signs of social decay are strong in America, too; but there is also strong resistance to this drift. At least among us a major election, like that of last week, produces no disasters.

We have found a visiting professorship for our Polish friend Dr. Rett Ludwikowski—at Elizabethtown College, in Pennsylvania. We have even found an automobile for the Ludwikowski family. Now we must endeavor to bring over his chief student from Krakow, and that student's wife—a student and professor being ardent disciples of Burke.

I am now finishing a textbook in economics for the ninth grade— that is, for boys and girls some fourteen or fifteen years of age! And I must write two more ghostly tales to have enough for a second volume of my short fiction. Then I turn my hand to my ruminative memoirs. Annette whizzes about the country on the business of her Commission on Excellence in Education; she goes to Washington next week for a few days.

The season's first snow fell upon Mecosta yesterday. It is said that we are to experience the hardest Michigan winter in human memory. But how brief our lives are, and how short all memories! In our childhood, we assume that we will live almost forever, and that civilizations are eternal; yet even the existence of great cultures is brief enough, for they commenced to decay at the hour of their splendor. "Dark, dark, dark: they all go into the dark."

Yet be of good cheer! Annette and the four daughters join me in cordial best wishes to you and yours.

Affectionately,
Russell

Letter to David Scott

The late David Scott was a successful businessman and an admirer of Kirk. Below, the latter responds to a question regarding worthwhile conservative foundations to which to contribute and provides a frank summary of his own health and manner of life as master of Piety Hill.

December 15, 1982
as of Piety Hill
Mecosta, Michigan, 49332

Dr. David Scott
5800 Midhill Street
Bethesda, Maryland, 20817

Dear David,

You will find enclosed a piece about me that Henry Regnery wrote for the Kirk bibliography recently published by the Clarke Historical Library.[18] Did I send you a copy of the Bibliography itself? Did I give you, or did you happen to obtain elsewhere my recent *Portable Conservative Reader* (Viking)? If not, pray let me know, and I'll post one to you.

My next Heritage lecture will occur at 5:30, Wednesday, January 19, presumably at the Heritage Foundation. Perhaps you can come. The topic is "America's Augustan Age?"—a refinement and enlargement of a lecture of mine you may have heard before.

Now for your inquiry about possible benefactions. . . . If you wish to benefit a tax-exempt foundation, you could not do better than bequeath something to the Marguerite Eyer Wilbur Foundation, over which I preside. (The foundress died some months ago, at a very advanced age.[19]) The enclosed pamphlet tells something about our activities. Our principal and continuous program is the Wilbur Fellowships, by the terms of which promising writers and scholars (of various ages) reside at Mecosta as interns (or sometimes students-for-credit) with me. We generally select candidates of conservative inclinations. They stay here for anything from a month to two years. We own two houses in which they reside, and the overflow is lodged in my own residence. I have a half-dozen such at present. We accomplish something to counteract the influence of the various radical centers, and our "graduates" generally make their mark in the world. . . .

By the way, I too have diabetes; and heart trouble also. All I do about either is to reform my diet somewhat. I am supposed to have had a coronary, as you did, but I walked through it without knowing anything very serious was amiss. Apropos of finance, I never have owned a share of stock or a bond; have no regular life insurance; have no savings account in banks; never speculate (lacking the money, even had I the will); have no regular income from any source—that is, no salary or wage; and am content to lay up treasure in Heaven. Existence at Piety Hill is hand to mouth, month upon month, but debt certainly is a stimulant to literary production. My exertions are further stimulated by the presence at my long board of various Ethiopians, Vietnamese, Poles, impecunious students, and Lord knows who all, all of them desirous of being dined and wined. In short, I live very much the sort of life that Walter Scott did at Abbotsford. Both Annette and I spend a large part of our times in unremunerated charitable activities—including the labors for the Wilbur Foundation and its Fellows. . . .

I hope this week to finish one long ghost story, "The Invasion of the Church of the Holy Ghost." After that, I must write one more, long or short; and then I'll have enough for a new collection, *Watchers at the Strait Gate*. But tonight I must write Chapter 11 of my ninth-grade textbook on economics.

Be of good cheer, David; I do wish you and yours a merry Christmas.

Cordially,
Russell

Letter to Jacques Barzun

A longtime scholar of culture, literature, and the history of ideas at Columbia University, Barzun (1907–2012) is an often-cited authority on literary and cultural standards. He and Kirk were respectful acquaintances, having met and spoken together at various scholarly colloquia.

June 22, 1983

Dr. Jacques Barzun
597 Fifth Avenue
New York, New York, 10017

Dear Dr. Barzun,

My thanks to you, most tardily, for having sent me kindly the off-print of your good essay "William James, Author."[20] I must find me a copy of *A Stroll with William James*, which presumably is published by this time.

Your books have been of much value to my wife, Annette, in her work with the Commission on Excellence in Education. Without her wheedling and bullying, that Commission's much-discussed report would have been feeble. It has many flaws and omissions, as it stands; but at least it ventures some mordant criticism of the existing incompetence.[21]

I am finishing a ninth-grade textbook in economics (!), and now must turn my hand to my ruminative memoirs.

Best wishes to you.

Cordially,
Russell Kirk

Letter to James Turner

As Kirk prepared to publish his final collection of ghost stories, he wrote the following cordial letter to the managing editor at Arkham House, detailing his inclusion criteria and a portion of his publicity plans for the volume.

August 26, 1983

Mr. James Turner
Managing Editor, Arkham House
70 West Country Lane
Collinsville, Illinois, 62234

Dear James Turner,

Here is the final tale for *Watchers at the Strait Gate*. I sha'n't publish it in any magazine before the book appears: *Fantasy and Science Fiction* still has one story to bring out, early next year; and it would be well to have one previously-unpublished story in our collection, anyway.

"The Invasion of the Church of the Holy Ghost" was the longest of all my tales, I believe; "An Encounter by Mortstone Pond," enclosed, is my shortest. To prolong it would weaken its effect. The source of the experience is a real experience of my friend Dr. James Bowling, in Alabama; but the setting is my native town of Plymouth, Michigan: pond, miller's house, and store really exist.

I am sending a copy of the new story to Kirby McCauley, for his files, but am telling him not to sell it to a periodical.

Now we need to get in shape the remaining stories from *The Surly Sullen Bell* that we are to reprint in *Watchers at the Strait Gate*.[22] I enclose a typed list of a few printers' errors and small corrections that occur in some of those stories; doubtless your typist can correlate these with the text in *The Surly Sullen Bell*.

I don't suppose that you mean to include all the contents of *Bell* that didn't appear in *Princess*—though it is all right with me if you desire to do so.

Probably you will leave out "Skyberia" because it is not ghostly, though somewhat eerie. "Lost Lake" presumably will go because it is a true narration, rather than fiction. "A Cautionary Note on the Ghostly Tale" needs revision, if it is to be included. Do you think we should include it? And if you wish, I will write an introduction about the length of that in *Princess*.

When we have decided just how many stories we will include in the book, I think we should append a sub-title on the title-page, *Mystical or Mysterious Tales*.

On second thought, perhaps it would be well for me to combine portions of "A Cautionary Note" with some new remarks, and print the synthesis as my introduction. I may even have time to do something of the sort before posting this envelope to you.

Edmund Fuller probably will review the new book in *The Wall Street Journal*—if he still is reviewing by the time it is published; his health is poor. Later I will send you names and addresses of other likely reviewers and review-media—that is, periodicals and people to whom you might not send otherwise such a ghostly collection.

More before long; best wishes.

Cordially,
Russell Kirk

Letter to Karl von Habsburg

Archduke Karl of Austria (1961–) is the eldest son of Kirk's longtime friend Otto von Habsburg and Princess Regina of Saxe-Meiningen, as well as the grandson of Karl I, the last of the Austrian emperors. The younger Archduke lived and studied with Kirk in Mecosta for a time in 1984. Later, he wrote of his guest, in his memoir The Sword of Imagination: Memoirs of a Half-Century of Literary Conflict *(Grand Rapids, MI: Eerdmans, 1995),* "Adventurous, humorous, interested in everything under the sun, a hunter and a soldier and a navigator easy in manner—why, Karl fascinated everybody of all ages" (211).

September 21, 1983

Your Imperial Highness,

It is good to have your letter of September 8. My wife and I look forward to meeting you at Venice. Dr. Chaimowicz is making the reservations, I understand.

We will have everything in readiness for you at Mecosta next summer. In January, very probably the Marguerite Eyer Wilbur Foundation will make a grant in the amount of $1,500 to help defray your expenses in the United States. There will be rather simple but no unpleasant lodging for you in one of the houses owned by the Foundation here at Mecosta, adjacent to my library.

Now it should be understood that the sojourn at Mecosta is chiefly an opportunity to read in my library, write papers if you wish, and hold discussions with other advanced students and with people who come to visit us. Ordinarily there will be one formal seminar weekly. Also there may be one large seminar, lasting for three days, with students and others from various parts of the country. Mecosta is a small and fairly remote village, but we do have pleasant lakes and rivers.

We probably will have in residence while you are here a Croatian family of four: the father, Ivan Pongracic, plans constitutional studies with me. You may find that subject of interest to you. Mr. Pongracic is a budgetary official in Croatia—to which land he would prefer not to return.

We send our compliments to your parents and to your sister Walburga. Our youngest daughter, Andrea, asks especially to be remembered to the Archduchess Walburga; her coming to Mecosta was a very grand event for Andrea.[23]

Cordially,
Russell Kirk

Letter to Pope John Paul II

Russell and Annette Kirk had an exceedingly high regard for John Paul II, the Polish-born Karol Wojtyla, whom they met in 1983 in Rome. "With the election to the throne of Peter of Karol Wojtyla," wrote Kirk in The Sword of Imagination, *"there commenced a genuine renewal of authority, tradition, the sacred, and the Good News" (447). At the conclusion of their audience with the Pope, Annette reminded him that, many years earlier, he had joined in marriage two of the Kirks' friends, Rett and Marguerite Ludwikowski, he an eminent professor of legal and political theory who fled Communist Poland in 1982 to reside in the United States. To this news, the Pope smiled gently and said "Sì, sì, Ludwikowski."*

December 16, 1983

His Holiness John Paul II
The Vatican

Your Holiness,

Herewith I transmit to you a copy of the most recent book by Rett Ludwikowski; it has been inscribed to you by him.[24] This volume is difficult to obtain, having been suppressed in Poland not long after its publication.

My wife, Annette, meant to deliver this book to your Holiness on the occasion, last month, of the audience that you granted to us as members of the Seventh International Congress of the Family; but she neglected to bring it with her on that occasion, although she did present at the audience a note from Dr. Ludwikowski.

Also we enclose a copy of the recent report *A Nation at Risk,* issued by the National Commission on Excellence in Education, of which body my wife was one of the more active members. It was through her persuasion that there was included in the report the statement that parents are the primary educators.

Rett and Marguerite Ludwikowski, whom your Holiness joined in matrimony years ago, are with us at Mecosta at present. We have succeeded in obtaining for Rett a post at Catholic University, in Washington.

We do thank your Holiness most earnestly, as Christmas approaches, for your courageous words and your good works.

Respectfully,
Russell Kirk

Letter to Benjamin Hart

In March 1984, Benjamin Hart—one of the founders of the conservative Dartmouth Review *and, at the time, director of studies at the Heritage Foundation—asked Kirk for his perspective on the clash between conservatism and libertarianism in general and on his famous disputes with Friedrich von Hayek and Frank Meyer in particular.*

March 23, 1984

Mr. Benjamin Hart, Director of Studies
The Heritage Foundation
513 C Street, N.E.
Washington, D.C., 10002

Dear Ben,

Thanks for your letter, to which I reply with unaccustomed promptitude.

You have in my *Reclaiming a Patrimony* my only essay on that chirping sect the Libertarians.[25] I never have regarded that crew as worth bothering about, and so, always economizing on time, I always have refrained from replying to them; they are about as influential upon the general public as are the Bimetallists and the Prohibitionists and the Free Soil Party.

Henry Regnery, in his *Memoirs of a Dissident Publisher*, has an account (pp. 158–161) of my exchange with Hayek and related matters. The Mt. Pélerin Society exchange took place in 1957, at St. Moritz (in a hotel later purchased by the Shah).[26] I will have the relevant pages of Henry's book photocopied to send to you, if you don't have the volume available. Henry remembers the occasion much better than I do, and gives a fairly full description of my remarks; also of Frank Meyer's criticisms.

In addition to what Henry says in his summary, I recall remarking that Hayek referred to religion as "mysticism"; I retorted that such a notion merely reveals ignorance of religion. I pointed out that Hayek repeatedly acknowledges the influence of Burke; well, Burke is the founder of conservatism; indeed, it is adherence to Burke's principles that defines the term. Burke's "Old Whigs," fusing with Portland's Pitt's Tories, became the Conservative party of Britain—and the dominant influence in that party. Hayek remarked also that conservatism never could win over young people; I retorted that it was doing precisely that in America, apparently to Hayek's resentment; while the oldfangled doctrinaire liberalism for which Hayek spoke was confined to the generation that was passing.

Hayek dislikes being called either a liberal or a libertarian, but does not rebuff the praises of such libertarians as Murray Rothbard, perhaps because Hayek has been so unfairly assailed in many quarters that he is grateful for adulation from any quarter. He is no anarchist, but for the most part a disciple of Burke and Tocqueville; he grows more conservative in his later work.

The Conservative Mind and other writings of mine were somewhat bitterly attacked in 1954 and 1955 by Frank Meyer in *The Freeman* and (I think) the *American Mercury,* by Frank Chodorov in *The Freeman,* and by Murray Rothbard (writing under a pseudonym—Jonathan Russell, I think) in *Faith and Freedom* (a curious journal for a professed atheist to publish in).[27] The assault seems to have been concerted, but ineffectual. I did not trouble myself to reply to any of their pieces. They seem to have been motivated in part by an "underdog" mentality: that is, they assumed that anyone whose writing had received praise in non-libertarian publications must be a crypto-collectivist, to be denounced, because conservative views always have been opposed, more or less, in various magazines and papers that had approved *The Conservative Mind.*

Your father may remember all this better than I do.[28]

Probably you know Ernest van den Haag's demolition of the libertarians in the pages of *National Review,* three or four years ago. I concur.[29]

The libertarians' ignorant hostility toward religion, like that of village atheists who distribute still copies of Paine's *Age of Reason*, is a principal gulf separating them from conservatives. They are not skeptics—that would be well enough understood—but militant atheists, so claiming a positive knowledge of purposelessness that no one can possess.

In addition, my aversion to the libertarians is founded in part upon their hopeless impracticality and archaic attitudes. They postulate an absolute individual liberty that never has been attained anywhere— and never can be attained, it running counter to human nature and the necessity for order. They seem to dream of a fancied nineteenth-century utopia of freedom that never really existed anywhere. Their fantasy clearly seems unattainable and silly to most practical people; therefore association with such utopians tends to discredit real conservatives.

The libertarians obtain their support from, and try to please, old-fangled American doctrinaire liberals like the Kochs of Kansas. Such businessmen could not survive for a month without the protection of government against violence and fraud.

Yes, the defiant flouted hedonism of the Libertarians raises the hackles of most Americans, and especially of conservative Americans. Clearly the Libertarians oppose not merely the political order that secures freedom and justice, but also the moral order that enables men to restrain their own appetites and passions. Such Libertarians make a great fuss about the inalienable right of topless dancers to display their charms at the very time when they deny that Soviet Russia is a danger to anybody. They often are difficult to distinguish from the gentlemen and ladies of the American Civil Liberties Union. . . .

I have kept no files on the criticism of Frank Meyer and other people, but perhaps your father might secure them without much difficulty from very early numbers of *National Review;* some occurred there.

The Libertarians' notion that they can come to power(!) through forming a national political party is somewhat less realistic than the ambitions of Harold Stassen or John Anderson; they have as much prospect of national ascendancy as has the Rainbow People's Party. Perhaps they turn to such a strange expedient because they have failed to make the least popular impression by their publications. Libertarianism is merely a crazy political ideology, and ideologies go nowhere in America.

The one person Hayek could find to edit his *Constitution of Liberty*—a wise book, for the most part—was my then-young disciple Edwin McClellan, now professor of Japanese at Yale: an interesting little commentary on the attitude of the rising generation toward conservatism vs. oldfangled libertarianism.

Perhaps these desultory observations will be of some use to you; do let me know if I may be of more help. . . .

Best wishes for your essay.

Cordially,
Russell

P. S. . . . My piece in *Modern Age* and *Reclaiming a Patrimony* was written only at express request for a symposium sponsored by ISI and the Liberty Fund in Florida; I did not attend in person. I would not have bothered to undertake it otherwise, thinking the Libertarians too odd and powerless a political sect to drub; it would have been like breaking a butterfly on the wheel.

Letter to Christopher Derrick

Derrick (1921–2007) was an English Catholic author, reviewer, and lecturer who is probably best remembered for his reminiscences of G. K. Chesterton and his book C. S. Lewis and the Church of Rome *(San Francisco: Ignatius Press, 1981). In the Winter 1984 issue of* Reflections, *Kirk reviewed Derrick's book* That Strange Divine Sea: Reflections on Being a Catholic. *In this assessment, he took Derrick to task for his "nuclear pacifism," the question of nuclear disarmament being a hot topic during this particularly tense period in U.S.–Soviet relations. In a letter dated March 21, 1984, Derrick wrote to Kirk to explain his objections to Kirk's review. Kirk responded by commending the prospects of the Strategic Defense Initiative or a variation thereof: a purely defensive tool against incoming Soviet missiles.*

July 9, 1984

Mr. Christopher Derrick
25 Park Hill Road
Wallington, Surrey

Dear Mr. Derrick,

Thanks, tardily, for your letter of March 21, which reached me here eventually. I denounced the employment of the atomic bomb at Hiroshima and Nagasaki, in *The Conservative Mind* and elsewhere.[30] But it did Bronze Age folk no good to complain of the inhumane edges of the iron swords of the Hittites and the Greeks. The only way to avert the Soviet missiles is to build up "atomic shield" devices in the United States: it is adequate defence that prevents hideous aggression. . . .

Moral questions cannot be separated from political questions or vice versa: surely not when grim Luciferian dominations aspire to domination of the world.

I turn my hand now to a manual on modern theories of law. Best wishes to you.

Cordially,
Russell Kirk

Letter to Lorraine Swanson

Throughout his career, Kirk hated to have his written words changed needlessly. In 1985, he ghost-wrote Nebraska senator Carl T. Curtis's Forty Years against the Tide: Congress and the Welfare State *and secured Regnery Gateway as the book's publisher. Kirk's anger at the needless delay wrought by the actions of an overzealous Regnery copyeditor—*

which caused the book's publication to be pushed into 1986—led to the copyeditor's release.

October 9, 1985

Miss Lorraine Swanson
Regnery Gateway, Inc.
950 North Shore Drive
Lake Bluff, Illinois, 60044

Dear Miss Swanson,

The remaining galleys of *Forty Years* are enclosed. I have tried to undo all the mischief accomplished by your idiotic quondam copy-editor; and Miss Ellingwood has striven womanfully to the same end. [31]

Now you are going to have to change the arrangement of the book back to fourteen chapters, eliminating the silly "parts" and "chapters" invented by the discharged copy-editor. Otherwise the book would be a dreadful mess. For one thing, there are numerous references to "previous chapter," "Chapter Three," etc., which become nonsensical when we are giving instead an incredible number of little new chapters. For another thing, when sequential sections of a chapter are carved up into tiny separate chapters, continuity is lost, and the reader does not know what the beginning paragraph of one of the new chapters is meant to signify. For a third thing, some of the little new chapters are ridiculously brief—some of only two to four paragraphs! One would think that your abominable copy-editor had done this damage out of malice.

So you are going to have to eliminate the fourteen "Parts" and convert them back into Chapters. Then you are going to have to reset the present "chapter" headings as sectional headings within each chapter. This means that you must use a much smaller typeface for the restored sectional headings, and not flourish them as if they were banner headlines in a newspaper. There is no other way out of the mess the late executed copy-editor has made of the book.

I never was sent the marked-up typescript for the early galleys that were transmitted to me; nor, as you know, do any such marked-up typescripts accompany the enclosed remaining galleys. Whatever happened to that copy which was sent to the typesetters? Did the copy-editor destroy it in the hope that her hideous alterations might not be detected?

If only you people had not put the typescript into that idiot copy-editor's hands, we would not have all this last-hour bother. I had written to Mr. Regnery thrice that no copy-editing would be needed; I am an editor myself. I had so told him in conversation, too. The next time I entrust a book to Regnery Gateway, I will have my agent write it into the contract that no Regnery copy-editor will be permitted to look at it: it must be a matter between the typesetter and myself exclusively.

Now let me have page proofs so soon as you can. I shall be absent from Mecosta, and virtually unreachable, between October 13 and 23, inclusive.

Yours,
Russell Kirk

Letter to Wesley McDonald

Having written his master's and doctoral theses on Kirk, McDonald began transforming his materials into a book about his former teacher during the mid-1980s. In August 1985, he wrote a letter to ask Kirk several questions concerning the events of his life. The nature of McDonald's questions is plain from the substance of Kirk's replies.

November 24, 1985

Dr. Wesley McDonald

Dear Wesley,

Here are replies to your inquiries of last August.

(1) My mother died early in 1943, when I was at Dugway Proving Ground.

(2) Yes, John Clark was a disciple of Babbitt, and first introduced me to that writer.

(3) My thought already was pretty fully developed when I went to Duke. I did esteem, however, Charles Sydnor, the historian of the South, whose books I have in my library; and he liked my thesis on Randolph, and nominally was its supervisor. (I conferred with him only once on the subject, and then very briefly.) My interest in Randolph began in my high-school years.

(4) The Red Cedar Bookshop was born in 1946 and expired in 1947, only a year old, when I went off to Scotland. It was a partnership with Adrian Smith, a good friend of mine. With him, I purchased the huge and splendid libraries of Justice Howard Wiest (Supreme Court) and of Clarence Bement (an automobile pioneer of Lansing), and they supplied the stock for our enterprise; also we handled new books. Our purchase and transportation of Justice Wiest's library, and his house, are described in my story "What Shadows We Pursue": the characters therein are taken from the life. The shop being difficult to carry on in my absence, Adrian simply sold off the stock at a discount.

(5) As for Frank Meyer, I have no objection to having my work appear in an anthology in company with other writers with whom I disagree in considerable part.[32] My disagreement with Meyer was only one reason why I did not wish to appear on the masthead of *National Review*: the main reason was that writing for many magazines, I do not desire to have people think I am intimately associated editorially with any one magazine in particular.

(6) Stanlis' book reinforced, rather than formed, my understanding of Burke on natural law; you will note that Stanlis mentions my periodical essay on the subject in the bibliography of his book.[33] No, I don't think Burke's moral imagination inconsistent with natural-law thought of Burke's sort. The direct influence upon Burke was Ciceronian and from Richard Hooker, rather than from St. Thomas; but of course Hooker was influenced by Thomas.

(7) I exchanged one letter, I think with William Havard.[34] What I did was to commend his typescript to the University of Notre Dame

Press; he sent it to me for that purpose, or rather (I think) the Press it-self sent it to me. Perhaps there was no correspondence directly with Havard; I'm not sure.

(8) You'll get no comments from me on your Chapter III. Like my old friend Eliot, I never interpret my own writings for anybody; they must stand by themselves. . . .

Best wishes to you.

Cordially,
Russell

Letter to Charlton Heston

For over twenty years, Kirk hoped to bring his book The Roots of American Order *to life in a multipart film. At various times he contacted Ronald Reagan, Robert Speaight, and Charlton Heston about the prospects for their serving as narrator; however, funding never became available and the project languished.*

December 28, 1985

Mr. Charlton Heston
c/o Mrs. Carol M. Lanning
1369 Avenida de Cortez
Pacific Palisades, California 90272

Dear Mr. Heston,

In the course of our conversation at Bill Buckley's breakfast gathering, my wife, Annette, promised to send you a copy of my fat book *The Roots of American Order;* you recalled that the Pepperdine University people had hoped to persuade you to be the host or the narrator for a series of films to be based on that volume. So here it is, inscribed to you.

Neither Pepperdine nor Dr. Richard Bishirjian (who is now handling the business) has succeeded in finding funds adequate to produce the intended series of films. But hope springing eternal, conceivably the coming of the Bicentenary of the Constitution may rouse interest in the right quarters. However that may be, should the film-project ever take on flesh, you would be the perfect narrator, linking together dramatic episodes, and perhaps yourself participating in the drama.

Very pleasant it was to have some talk with you. Annette and I do wish you much success for Anno Domini 1986.

Cordially,
Russell Kirk

Letter to Henry Regnery

While Henry Regnery lived in Chicago, he also owned a home away from the city, in the village of Three Oaks, Michigan. From there he sent two letters to Kirk in early 1986 with news about a new edition of The Conservative Mind *and the future of his publishing company. Kirk, who had recently visited the Regnery family in Chicago, responded as follows.*

January 11, 1986

Mr. Henry Regnery
P. O. Box 4
Three Oaks, Michigan

Dear Henry,

P. O. Box 4, Little Cub Bear (translation of the Pottawatomi "Mecosta"), Michigan, is happy to receive the letters of January 4 and 7 from P. O. Box 4, Three Oaks, Michigan.

It is pleasant to learn that the Seventh Edition, *Conservative Mind,* soon will go off to the typesetters. I enclose some advance publicity, fresh from the press. I do hope that Clyde Peters, to his promise true, contrived to supply Hillsdale College Bookstore with at least fifteen copies of the book, in one edition or another, for it will be used for a special class, two sections, for the term beginning any day now. If only Peters had had a small paperback printing brought out several months ago as he said he would, that class, the class at the University of Colorado last summer, and a good many other would-be purchasers could have obtained the book, and there would have been a selling-out of the paperback printing before the Seventh Edition should appear. At least Regnery Gateway should sell the Hillsdale people what few copies remain of the hardbound edition, at paperback price, if they cannot supply paperbacks.

I do hope that the contract has been settled with Heritage Foundation for publishing my *Wise Men Know*. . . . It shouldn't be a financial problem, really, for the little book certainly should pay for itself through sales (including Conservative Book Club sales), what with all my publicity nowadays in conservative and other circles.[35]

John East is approached by the University of Illinois Press about his book, also. I shall write to him today that he would be wise to settle with you, for university presses take forever to decide on anything, having to submit proposals to hostile professorial committees, find readers for a typescript and then find more readers if one of the first lot is hostile or raises questions or doesn't submit his report, etc., etc.[36] . . .

As I wrote earlier, I think that the shift to Washington will have most happy results.[37] When I win ten million dollars in one of those magazine-subscription lotteries, I shall invest it all in Regnery Gateway. . . .

The University of Detroit wants me to be visiting professor of political economy in the fall term of 1986–87 academic year, visiting there once a week—one day and night, that is. They must find $18,000 for that purpose. I have told them to approach Henry Salvatori, who has given for similar Kirk purposes, in the past, to Olivet College and to Pepperdine University. If they don't succeed in that quarter, perhaps the Marquette Fund may hear from them. It seems that things are changing somewhat at the Olin Foundation—the John Olin Foundation, I mean. Do you have any good tidings of matters there?

Apropos of your remarks on Hawthorne, I have noted often, over the past thirty years, how that author is systematically omitted or barely mentioned in nearly all school textbooks in American literature: the textbook compilers and publishers' editors are bright enough to detect Hawthorne's views of human nature and politics. Walt Whitman, idiot democratist and homosexual, is their hero. But it is interesting that they have not been able to diminish respect for Hawthorne at the higher levels of education.

Our train-trip from Chicago to Grand Rapids went very well, when last we parted from you and Eleanor. Conductors are more civil than most of them used to be—surely the only improvement in American manners. If we go down the other way, Grand Rapids to Chicago, one day, we certainly will endeavor to call upon the Regnerys. . . .

More before long; best wishes to you and Eleanor.

Cordially,
Russell

Letter to Arnaud de Borchgrave

On January 13, 1986, the Washington Times *ran an editorial titled "Defund the Right," taking Kirk to task for accepting money from the National Endowment for the Humanities to support the writing of a book on Edmund Burke and the Framing of the Constitution. Kirk defended his position in a letter published in the Letters section of the paper on January 24. Kirk was answered a few days later by Martin Morse Wooster (Washington editor of* Harper's *Magazine) and Howard Phillips (chairman of Conservative Caucus), who basically supported the argument of the* Times' *original editorial: that while they deeply respected Kirk, he and other conservatives should take the lead in eschewing the practice of private citizens being paid for their work from federal coffers.*

January 17, 1986

Mr. Arnaud de Borchgrave, Editor
The Washington Times
3600 New York Avenue, N.E.
Washington, D.C., 20002

Sir:

My attention has been called to an ignorantly defamatory editorial, under the heading "Defund the Right," which appeared in your paper on January 13. Permit me to comment upon it.

Your editorial writer reproached me for having accepted a grant from the National Endowment for the Humanities for research and writing connected with Edmund Burke. This member of your staff did not trouble himself even to ascertain the full title of my project.

My subject is "Edmund Burke and the Constitution of the United States"—a theme on which not even an essay had been published until I took it up during the six months of my NEH grant, which is one of the grants awarded in connection with the Bicentenary of the Constitution. Your writer declares that my study must be "redundant"—because nineteen years ago I published a brief biography of Burke. On such ground, any writing connected with the Constitution must be redundant, various books on the Constitution having been published over the years.

Portions of my study of Burke and the Constitution have been the subjects of formal lectures to the Minnesota Historical Society and to the Heritage Foundation; other portions will appear in the immediate future in *Modern Age, The Intercollegiate Review,* and other periodicals; and the whole later will appear as a book.[38] I take up such matters as Burke's influence upon certain framers of the American Constitution; his still stronger influence upon such jurists and politicians, in interpretation of the Constitution, as John Marshall, Joseph Story, and John C. Calhoun; the changes in the British Constitution worked by Burke and his party; and Burke's attacks upon the several French constitutions of the revolutionary era. There never has been published any systematic examination of all this. Only an ignoramus could dismiss such studies in political history and theory as "redundant."

As for the writer's argument that people of conservative inclinations should not accept funds from the federal government—why, on that ground we may expect to encounter in your pages editorials denouncing President Reagan for being paid a salary out of the Treasury, and accusing Attorney General Meese of corruption because he occupies office space at public expense.

Yours sincerely,
Russell Kirk

Letter to William F. Buckley Jr.

February 26, 1986

Mr. William F. Buckley, Jr.
National Review

Dear Bill,

Many thanks for your thoughtful letter of February 18. However do you contrive to think of so many small details as reimbursement for travel for Annette and your servant?[39] That travel was charged against other accounts, both Annette's and mine, so that it cost you and *National Review* naught, or me; but thanks for thinking of it so kindly. Your dinner and breakfast made us both happy, and we met pleasant folk we had not encountered before, among them, Charlton Heston, the Divine.

Andrea Seton Kirk, aged ten, has much enjoyed your children's book, Goblin series, generously sent to her.[40]

Today I finished writing a preface to Louis Filler's volume *Dictionary of Conservatism*, which he wrote entirely himself in his quondam-church house, The Belfry, Ovid, Michigan. Dr. Filler is a kind of latter-day Isaac Disraeli, a discoverer and revealer of literary and political curiosities.[41] The book will be worth reviewing when it appears. I am prodding Henry Regnery into getting Greg Wolfe's *Right* book published.[42] Carl Curtis' memoirs, in which I took an editorial hand, will be published by Regnery in March. I should like to write more tales, but never will find time for them again. Burke, the Law, and my memoirs will take up the rest of this year, at least.

Annette joins me in best wishes to you in Switzerland.[43] We have more snow here at Mecosta.

Cordially,
Russell

Letter to Henry Regnery

Regnery published Bryan F. Griffin's Menckenesque takedown of the book industry's puffery and pretense, Panic among the Philistines, *in 1983. Three years later, he enlisted Kirk to assess a new manuscript by Griffin, titled "Book Wars"—which Kirk endorsed but Regnery did not publish.*

June 14, 1986

Mr. Henry Regnery, Chairman
Regnery Gateway, Inc.
44 East Superior Street
Chicago, Illinois, 60611

Dear Henry,

On the very eve of departure for Colorado, I send you this report on Mr. Griffin's *Book Wars*. Incidentally, I make much reference to his *Panic among the Philistines* in an introduction (125 typewritten pages!) I have just completed to Babbitt's *Literature and the American College*, the whole to be published by the National Humanities Institute. . . .

What a hard-hitting typescript Mr. Griffin presents you with! He writes with great skill and passion, and is right about everything. Even in Congress, people are outraged at pornography, or profess to be. The capture of book-reviewing and publicizing is a very strange phenomenon, really, not entirely explained by the silliness of ritualistic liberalism: it appears to be, though I'm no Fundamentalist, Lord knows—that this intoxication with horrid tortures, violation of children, and the like really is an explosion of the power of the Evil Spirit—who, like God, commonly works through human means.

I do hope you publish the little book, and I will do all I can to help to attract attention to it.

Thanks again for your tea and the tour of your garden. What a wondrous variety of things you raise successfully! My shrubbery is converting the house of Piety Hill into the enchanted palace of

Sleeping Beauty: the lilacs, the honeysuckle, flowering crabs, mock orange, beauty bush, and other species are becoming really gigantic hedges. You have missed them in bloom, but at least you shall see how they have grown, when you come up with Eleanor.

Have you acquired premises in Washington? With proper management, you may make a greater success of the new venture, in terms of sales and popular influence, than ever you were able to do in Chicago. I am eager for the new stage of Henry Regnery's bold publishing adventures to commence.

More from Colorado, possibly. Perhaps by the time I return from that state, a fresh set of page proofs for *The Conservative Mind* will be ready for me. Ah, the hideous task of doing the index all over again!

Compliments to Eleanor; and do give Alf my best wishes when you talk with him or write to him.[44]

Cordially,
Russell

Letter to Charles Teetor

In the centuries-old tradition of scholars in Europe and the British Isles, Kirk enjoyed taking long walks during his free time, sometimes covering between thirty and forty miles per day. The following letter to a longtime friend provides a taste of Kirk's enthusiasm for this Johnsonian pastime.

March 15, 1987

Mr. Charles Teetor
Westernesse Farms
Amagansett, Long Island

Dear Chuck,

Much thanks, tardily, for your letter of February 9. Some of my correspondence is six months in arrears. I was desperately busy getting out a textbook on the Constitution for high school students, but that is done now, the deadline met.

Your walker's guide concept is a healthy one. Some such guides exist in England and Scotland, but few elsewhere, I think; and the British ones are not widely sold. It takes much time to compile one such, nevertheless; and the sale is more limited than once it was, most people now thinking of walking as a penance for which they ought to be paid a dollar a mile, the receipts to be contributed to the poor persecuted Sandinistas.

And most of Spain is not very good country for walkers, the heat, aridity, and dust considered: it is like walking in Nevada. But of course there are good walks in the hills and mountains of the northern provinces paralleling the Bay of Biscay, and in the extreme south, too. I think of that wondrous walk for many miles, halfway down the sides of a great gorge, with tunnels and rope bridges, that I have glimpsed from a train: it appears to run all the way from Granada to the coast. Shall we walk that together in the spring of 1988? That looks possible for me. Cecilia Abigail Kirk, now accomplished in the Spanish tongue, might accompany us two ancient mariners.

By the way, my foot complaint vanished years ago—it was at its worst in Dalmatia—and I am up to walking forty miles a day, once more, except that sometimes my vascular system gives me trouble when I am going uphill for a considerable distance. That may be compensated for, however, by tiny nitroglycerine pills, which have the power of dynamite. And that particular trouble is much diminished from what it was a few years ago.

But I have something to propose for the near future. On April 11, Annette, Andrea, and I fly to Prestwick: for I am to be Fulbright Lecturer at St. Andrews during Whitsun term. We shall return to America on June 12. My duties at St. Andrews will be very light, I fancy.

Now if you are to be at Barcelona during April, May, and June, you might make an expedition to Scotland; then you and I could make some specimen walking expeditions in that country, which I know fairly well; and we could discuss the whole project. I know both wild and tame walks there. The two wildest I never have had time or reason to undertake, though I wished to; but I have done the third wildest.

We shall be staying at Durie House, Leven, Fife—which Georgian house you will remember. Probably I will give two or three lectures at Groningen University, in Holland, too; possibly one or two at Salzburg. Austria is a noble walking country, as you know.

Scottish walking now must be either by the hill-tracks or by the seashore. Automobiles, since my years at St. Andrews, have thoroughly spoiled the inland walks in which I engaged so regularly.

More of all this another time. We'll not have an opportunity to see the Teetors before we fly to Scotland, but we do hope to see you in Fife, or at least upon our June return to American shores.

Cordially,
Russell

Letter to Howard Baker

The day after Associate Justice Lewis Powell resigned from the U.S. Supreme Court, Kirk wrote to President Ronald Reagan's chief of staff to urge the nomination of Robert H. Bork as Powell's replacement. On July 1, 1987, Reagan formally nominated Bork, who was denied a seat on the High Court by Senate Democrats, who feared his presence on the Court would swing its philosophical balance to the right. Over time, Kirk came to have reservations about Bork's understanding of the natural law, especially as articulated in the latter's book The Tempting of America: The Political Seduction of Law *(New York: Free Press, 1990).*

June 28, 1987

The Honorable Howard Baker
Chief of Staff to the President of the United States
The White House
Washington, D.C.

Dear Mr. Baker:

Permit me to commend to you for appointment to the Supreme Court of the United States Judge Robert Bork. I have followed closely his judicial decisions, and find him to be a jurist of sound and temperate convictions, possessed of a philosophical habit of mind, and bent upon maintaining the Constitution of the United States impartially.

Some information about myself is enclosed, by way of suggesting that I know something about jurists and jurisprudence.

Yours sincerely,
Russell Kirk

Letter to George W. Bush

In late June 1987, George W. Bush—then a largely unknown figure— addressed a gathering of Michigan's Republican organizers at a meeting held at Canadian Lakes, a resort located a few miles west of Kirk's home in Mecosta. Kirk was present at this event, in which Bush appealed to the gathering on behalf of the soon-to-be-announced candidacy of his father, George H. W. Bush, for president of the United States. Kirk was an early and admiring supporter of the candidacy and early presidency of "Bush 41," although his opinion soured when Bush involved the United States in the First Gulf War, which Kirk considered imprudent, needless, and wasteful.

June 30, 1987

Mr. George Bush the younger
733 15th Street, N.W., Suite 800
Washington, D.C. 20005

Dear Mr. Bush,

Many thanks for your kind note following our conversation at the Republican gathering in Mecosta County. Very good it was of you to visit us in these wilds.

It was Mr. Paul Wisgerhof, formerly with the Heritage Foundation, now with the Department of State, who was arranging for me to meet in Washington with the Bush policy people. The date of that intended meeting is being moved up to July 8, 9, or 10.

I believe that Michigan will send a Bush delegation to the national convention in 1988. My wife and I take usually a covert hand in state politics; we both are local Bush delegates, though. For the time being, the principal power in Michigan Republicanism is my friend and ally Harry Veryser. . . .

How little thanks honest and able political leadership obtains! Venomous partisanship, ruthless special interests, and malice by the mass media seem to increase with every year that passes. The family of Bush has risen superior to demagoguery and special interest for generations; and some of us, at least, are grateful.

More another time; best wishes. I enclose a recent piece of mine that may be of some interest to you.

Cordially,
Russell Kirk

Letter to William F. Buckley Jr.

July 7, 1987

Mr. William F. Buckley, Jr.
National Review

Dear Bill,

Your kind note of invitation to contribute again to *National Review*'s pages reached me in Scotland; but I postponed replying until I should have my fingers on a typewriter and have some piece prepared for your inspection. Now yesterday I received also an entreaty from Mr. Richard Vigilante, possibly prompted by you, for a Kirk essay.[45] No sooner said than done: Here, enclosed, is my two-thousand-word "Lost Souls," executed last night.[46] I have sent a copy to Mr. Vigilante also. Possibly this may serve your turn.

However do you contrive to go on writing daily columns and running *National Review*? Plus Demon TV? A quarter of a century of writing thousand-word pieces for NR, and thirteen years of writing syndicated columns of some 750 words apiece, left me imaginatively desiccated. I will never recover from my aversion, since my withdrawal from that disagreeable species of journalism, to turning out short ephemeral pieces. Nowadays my most agreeable form of literary production is the formal lecture; and a second volume of my Heritage Lectures, *The Wise Men Know What Wicked Things Are Written on the Sky*, will be published by Regnery early this autumn.

Annette and I are much taken by your recent column on your interviewing of the seven Democratic presidential candidates.[47]

More another time; best wishes.

Cordially,

Russell

Letter to George H. W. Bush

Kirk was initially proud of having a hand in promoting the successful candidacy of George H. W. Bush in the 1988 election. After the election, his high regard for Bush fell dramatically as he came to see the truth of the president's claim that he lacked "the vision thing" and especially because of the Bush-led prosecution of the First Gulf War, which Kirk regarded as a needless and costly adventure in imperialistic overreach.

October 11, 1987

The Honorable George Bush
Vice President of the United States
Washington, D.C.

Dear Vice-President Bush,

Permit me to thank you for the announcement of your candidacy for the presidency of the United States. My wife and I know how high an attachment to duty and how much fortitude are required for such an undertaking. This Republic very rarely has known a presidential candidate so eminently qualified as you by experience, talent, and character. In recent decades especially, the presidential office has been assailed by the ignorant, the violent, and the false among the American people. You undertake a tremendous task, in adverse times; we are grateful to you.

In February, probably, a conference will be held at my house here of Michigan managers of the campaigns of several Republican presidential candidates. My wife and I are closely acquainted with the campaign directors for Mr. Dole, Mr. Robertson, Mr. Kemp, and yourself.[48] It has been suggested that only I am in a position to bring them into a friendly league—or at least to restrain their vehemence against other candidates. Whether or not Michigan delegates—the majority of them—endorse your candidacy in February, I shall do my best to ensure that the people of Michigan endorse it in November, 1988.[49]

What patience you exhibited in your interview by the porcine little Barbara Walters! How long can the Republic endure, when public opinion, in considerable part, is formed by such creatures?

Cordially,
Russell Kirk

Letter to Jay Gordon Hall

Kirk wrote the following letter during Hall's final illness; he died on December 22, 1987.

November 15, 1987

Dr. Jay Gordon Hall
Bloomfield Hills, Michigan

Dear Gordon,

How good it was to see you and have lively talk, a few weeks ago! I hope we didn't tire you overmuch. Ruth fed us with her accustomed skill and taste.

I enclose a recent piece of mine that will remind you of our European wanderings three decades gone—though I don't take up our Italian and Scottish expeditions in this particular essay.

I know how serious your physical condition is, and so write to you frankly about such concerns; after all, in the midst of life we all of us, at every moment, are in death. About two years ago I slid into unconsciousness in a car, and was very nearly transported to another realm of being—not so much by the heart-failure itself as by the ghastly narcotic the hospital used upon me as a purported means of revival (after I already had revived). So I am not unacquainted with the present precariousness of your existence.

We never know, actually, whether or not we will survive for a few more years. I ignored the advice of my physicians, and am in good shape now, probably in consequence of my obduracy. Thus for all we know, you and I may have many more good times together.

But supposing that you are not long for this world, Gordon, let me tell you now how memorable our friendship has been. You and I have enjoyed together what Eliot called "eternal moments." I think we will enjoy those always. When Annette asked Martin D'Arcy whether man and wife would know each other in eternity, he replied that heaven is a state of being in which all the good actions and reflections of one's life are forever present, whenever one desires them: and not in memory merely, not "re-experienced" merely, but experienced one for all. (Hell, on the other hand, is a state of being in which all the evil committed in one's life is eternally present to one's consciousness and inescapable.)

Or, to put matters in another fashion, we are *now* in eternity; our souls exist beyond time; and the so-called "life after death" is not a new existence, in which one acquires new friends and obtains a good job in a bank, but instead is *this* existence, we now know, for good or ill. That is why every day's decisions matter so much: they determine the eternal state.

Thus you and I will be friends beyond time; and what we have known together, in Bloomfield Hills or Mecosta or Rome or Edinburgh, we will know and experience always. One thinks of John Gay's inscription on his tombstone:

"Life is a jest and all things shew it:
I thought so once, but now I know it."

Then be of good cheer, Gordon. We do pray for you.

This letter would be longer, were it not that I must be off tomorrow for a week's speechifying in North Carolina. I'll write again before long. Annette joins me in best wishes to you and Ruth.

Cordially,
Russell

Letter to Henry Regnery

Looking ahead to his seventieth birthday, Kirk writes to his longtime publisher and friend to briefly review his accomplishments and then outline the books he hopes to complete before the end of his life.

December 6, 1987

Mr. Henry Regnery, Chairman
Regnery Gateway, Inc.
44 East Superior Street
Chicago, Illinois 60611

Dear Henry,

In reply to inquiries from various people as to how I mean to occupy myself, now that I have had twenty-five books published and approach the age of seventy—why, like my fellow Scot John Paul Jones, I've not yet begun to fight. The next action is to board the *Serapis.*[50]

What I have been undertaking, ever since I first was published nationally when I was sixteen years old, is the defence of what T. S. Eliot called "the permanent things." (My first prize essay was entitled "Mementoes," appropriately enough, as matters turned out for me.) My historical books, my polemical writings, my literary criticism, and even my fiction have been meant to resist the ideological passions that have been consuming civilization ever since 1914—what Arnold Toynbee calls our "time of troubles." Rather than singing hallelujah to the river god, I have rowed against the current of prevalent opinion. As I approach my seventieth birthday, I am somewhat surprised that I have not been swept out to the great deep; indeed, that I have made some headway against the tide of ideology and the fierce appetites of our age.

So the next (and perhaps final) decade of my life will be spent, as my earlier decades were spent, in contending against intellectual and social disorder. In particular, I hope to complete a well-written book about the causes of the afflictions of the soul and the afflictions of the commonwealth in this century that now draws to a close: a book innocent of the usual facile arguments about "capitalism" *v.* "Marxism." The completion of my memoirs, and of my two intended slim volumes about the Constitution, and of my book on contending theories of jurisprudence, will be closely related to this general end of analyzing our twentieth-century discontents and disasters. I mean to let some cheerfulness break in, if possible—to remind readers that the will, after all, is free; and to draw the sword against historical determinism, which Marcel (in a book of his published by you) calls "that armed ghost, the meaning of history."[51] Differing somewhat with my friend Malcolm Muggeridge, I have not abandoned hope for us confused creatures here below.

My study and writing will involve several disciplines: those of history, humane letters, political theory, theology, and even physics. I will need to diminish the volume of my serious journalism in order to make time for this large literary undertaking; also I will need to speak less often on the campuses, despite increased demand for my lectures.

Despite the analogy with which this letter commenced, I write not from the burning deck of the *Bonhomme Richard*, but from beside the fire on the hearth of my library, at three in the morning, the witching hour; and I must discharge three or four more shots from this typewriter before I sleep. Say not the struggle against the antagonist world naught availeth. Best wishes.

Cordially,

Russell Kirk

P.S.: I stacked five cords of firewood this day, against the blizzards that soon will howl round our Italianate tower and cupola. Annette and I plan to acquire snowshoes this winter and explore the snow-choked woods that still hem in this ancestral village.

Letter to Gavin Scott-Moncrieff

A son of Kirk's friend George Scott-Moncrieff, Gavin Scott-Moncrieff (1942–) is a successful Scottish hotelier, owner of the stylish Flodigarry Hotel and High Tide Restaurant on the Isle of Skye.

February 11, 1988

Mr. Gavin Scott-Moncrieff
Flodigarry Hotels
Staffin
Isle of Skye

Dear Gavin,

What a splendid present, the book on Eigg! I am learning much from my reading of it. Eventually I will put my essay on Eigg (already published in one of my earlier books) in the ruminative memoirs I am to write this summer; and your gift will enable me to enlarge that essay.[52]

I don't suppose you can recollect my month in Eigg, spent mostly with the Scott-Moncrieffs; you were too little then. I was then thirty-five years of age; in October I will be seventy. What shadows we are, and what shadows we pursue!

Henry Regnery definitely is going to republish your father's selection of Stevenson's essays; and I will make sure you get a copy when that little volume appears. Before that, I will send you a copy of my newest (twenty-sixth) book, *The Wise Men Know What Wicked Things Are Written on the Sky*. (You may recognize the title as borrowed from Chesterton's "The Ballad of the White Horse.") I don't yet have copies myself of that just-published slim volume.

How Annette and I yearn to behold your hotel at Staffin! We've no prospect of an expedition to Scotland (or anywhere else) this year, but possibly the funds and the time may be found before the century runs out. We pray for the success of your undertaking. . . .

And you and yours must come to visit us, if ever you have the opportunity; we've plenty of room for you. We're arranging for Ann Findlay to come unto us for the whole of summer, 1988. Alan Scott-Moncrieff was with us a few months ago, and we hope to get him here again this year, but for the present he is busily painting in Long Island.[53]

Now I must turn to wrestle with Demon Income Tax; so more another time. The strange denizens of the stranger house of Piety Hill do wish the Scott-Moncrieffs of Taigh-Osda Flodigarry all manner of good for Anno Domini 1988.

Cordially,
Russell Kirk

Letter to Benjamin Hart

The following tongue-in-cheek letter takes issue with Hart's article "The Evangelical Temptation: Why I've Stopped Attending the Catholic Church," which had appeared in the February 1988 issue of the Roman Catholic monthly Crisis. *In his article, Hart lamented that many Catholic churches he had attended during his adult life seemed given over to a left-liberal social gospel, with sermons consisting of scoldings and harangues on apartheid, militarism, gay rights, sexism, and other topics seemingly lifted from any liberal-leaning newspaper's editorial page.*

March 22, 1988

Mr. Benjamin Hart
The Heritage Foundation

Dear Ben,

Thanks for your letter of recent date. Have you had opportunity to confer with your colleagues at Heritage concerning publication of my several Heritage Lectures on the Constitution? Will Heritage desire to arrange publication? Or should I publish them by my own arrangements? I should get them into shape this spring or early summer, so that a publisher might bring them out so early as autumn, 1988.

Also I have five lectures on the Constitution and political economy, delivered recently (one a month) at the University of Detroit, the last to be delivered next month. These could be included in the same volume, if you like the idea.

I've not yet been paid for my Heritage Lecture on Cultural Conservatism by your fiscal people—although it has been five weeks and more since I delivered the lecture. Perhaps libertarians have infiltrated your treasure house.

Now for some observations on your essay in *Crisis*, which I already had beheld. Some of us discussed it in Drummond Island, indeed, where we foregathered with Cardinal Law some weeks ago.[54] It was determined by us Papists to have Ben Hart excommunicated and condemned, and put to the flames at an *auto-de-fe;* we mean to have Dinesh D'Souza put the match to the faggots.

I can well understand your dismay at the present state of the Catholic Church in these United States. . . . But if you go over to fundamentalism, you fall into feebleness; it cannot stand against modernism. On the question of Authority, pray recall the words of Newman in 1846:

"Conscience is an authority; the Bible is an authority; such is the Church; such is Antiquity; such are the words of the wise, such are hereditary lessons; such are ethical truths; such are historical memories, such are legal saws and state maxims; such are proverbs; such are sentiments, presages and prepossessions."[55]

To rely upon the Old and New Testaments through private interpretation of passages is to force every man to make his own religion—or to entice him to do so. Scripture is only one aspect of religious understanding. And Scripture cannot be understood and interpreted without the Authority of the Church. I possess a large library of theology, and the various dictionaries and commentaries upon the bible, and have long meditated and written upon these subjects. I could not possibly interpret any book of the bible for myself, without Authority to refer to. Consider such a passage as "Resist not evil." How are we to understand this without turning to Authority for ascertaining the signification of that simple sentence. I stand astounded at the presumption of persons who, though totally ignorant of Hebrew, Greek, Aramaic, or even the Latin of the Vulgate, fancy that they can spell out for themselves, infallibly, every symbolic or mystical line of the Bible. I had sooner trust a motorcycle enthusiast to be my pilot in a Concorde. Nay, Fundamentalists and the like cannot stand long against the sophistries of modernism.

Cordially,
Russell Kirk
Inquisitor of Heretical Pravity

Letter to Caroline Lecuru

Lecuru was a university student and Wilbur Fellow who studied for a time at Piety Hill during the mid-1980s, after which she wrote her master's thesis on Kirk's novel Lord of the Hollow Dark *under the guidance of M. E. Bradford at the University of Dallas. In early April, 1988, she wrote to Kirk to ask about the origins of the names and places of the novel.*

April 22, 1988

Miss Caroline Lecuru
P. O. Box 397
University of Dallas Station
Irving, Texas 75062–4799

Dear Caroline,

It is good to have your letter of April 4. Annette and I are mightily grateful for "Grim Irony."[56] The antique shop in the church has survived; I don't know whether it prospers, but must stop in some day. Cecilia didn't get the Truman Fellowship: three of her four interrogators were radicals or ritualistic liberals, demanding to know *her* program for South Africa, and asking questions about her father's opinions. Aye, she is happy at Sevilla; I wish I could have her guide me about the city. She lodges between the Giralda and the bull-ring.

Well, a master's thesis on Lord Balgrummo! Various dissertations and theses have been written about *The Conservative Mind*, but not about *Lord of the Hollow Dark*. You must come up here during the summer to confer with me. Meanwhile, I set down the following bits of information.

(1) The idea of the Weem comes from the medieval legends of Patrick's Purgatory, the cave on an island in Lough Dergh, in northern Ireland, where St. Patrick was said to have had visions, and others after him. A modern monastery and retreat-house, on a large scale, stands on the site; but there is dispute as to whether that really is or was the site. I have added to Patrick's Purgatory some details of the cave called St. Fillan's Weem, at Pittenweem, in Fife, on the Forth—a cave I know well. (The great stair still exists in St. Fillan's.)

(2) The original of Balgrummo Lodging is a great tower-house on the outskirts of Edinburgh, uninhabited when I saw it, and with all the trees in its part cut down; I don't even know the name of the castle. But I have added to that scenic quasi-ruin details of Thirlstane Castle, in the Borders, which is in very good order and open to the public. Forty years ago, the nobleman who lived there was under house arrest for life, within the walls of Thirlstane, because he "had been very naughty when young," and the only penalty the House of Lords can impose is death. My earlier tale "Balgrummo's Hell," included in my collection *The Princess of All Lands*, is the germ from which *Lord of the Hollow Dark* grew.

(3) Manfred Arcane, alias the Archvicar, is resurrected from my earlier romance *A Creature of the Twilight;* also from my earlier tale "The Last God's Dream." He haunts me, urging me to bring him to life and to the attention of the public again.

(4) The pseudonyms of the characters, obviously, are taken from *The Waste Land* and other Eliot poems, and are suited to their personalities.

(5) The elaborate water-arrangements under Balgrummo Lodging were suggested by a novel of Francis Marion Crawford's about Rome, and by Scottish lades and mills with which I am familiar.

There are other points worth talking about perhaps, O Caroline, you have some in mind that I could write to you about; if so, pray let me know. Otherwise we can explore the whole matter when you come unto us.

How like you the University of Dallas? You are often in our thoughts here, and many people inquire after you. Who was it spoke to me recently, in some city, about "That beautiful girl who drove us up from Grand Rapids"? Anyway, Piety Hill yearns after you.

Cordially,
Russell Kirk

Letter to Charles Heatherly

Currently serving as director of policy for the Colorado Senate GOP, Heatherly worked as director of special projects at the Heritage Foundation from 1987 to 1993.

April 22, 1988

Mr. Charles Heatherly
Vice-President for Academic Affairs
The Heritage Foundation

Dear Chuck,

Annette had arranged a breakfast meeting, I believe, with you next week; but now it turns out that she and I won't be able to visit Washington next week, though we will get to New York and Philadelphia. Anyway, we count on seeing you on the occasion of my next Heritage Lecture (in August), if not before.

One thing we had intended to talk with you about is the possibility of your arranging one of the Bradley Fellowships for Dr. Roger Scruton, the author of *The Meaning of Conservatism* and other books, and editor and founder of *The Salisbury Review*, that most admirable magazine. (I hope that Heritage subscribes to it.) Professor Scruton was with us last week for one of our ISI Piety Hill seminars (on Eliot and the Defense of Culture), and was much applauded; he is a remarkably intelligent and courageous man. (I had not met him before.) He expressed interest in spending a term or a year at Heritage. He was at Bowling Green University, in Ohio, for a few weeks, but has now returned to Birkbeck College, London University, where he is professor of aesthetics.

I find him the brightest of all English conservatives nowadays, and you would like him. He is little more than forty years old.

Cordially,

Russell

Letter to Forrest McDonald

McDonald (1927–2016) was for many years professor of history at the University of Alabama and a distinguished constitutional scholar and specialist on the early American Republic. He and Kirk were longtime friends and mutual admirers. McDonald held The Roots of American Order *in high regard and in 2003 contributed the foreword to a new edition of that work.*

April 24, 1988

Professor Forrest McDonald
Department of History
The University of Alabama
University, Alabama

Dear Forrest,

Two or three years ago, in your kind *Detroit News* review of my book *The Roots of American Order*, you mentioned that a few mistakes occur therein. I'm sure there must be more than you noticed; but I'll be grateful if you can recall and specify such slips as you observed.[57] For I am getting up a third edition, with an introduction, and want to make all possible corrections.[58] Probably it will be published in Regnery's Gateway paperbacks—a big one—but also made available in cloth. (ISI soon will have sold out its stock of the book, the only stock still available.) I'll be mightily grateful, then, if you can contrive to think of some of my absurdities.

I enclose my most recent piece, from the seventh volume of that gigantic reference-work *Literature Criticism from 1400–1800,* edited by James Person; it is just now published. It is pleasant to be able to re-store tolerable sense in such quarters. The huge Volume 7 is a well-compiled anthology of selections from Locke, Montesquieu, Hume, and Burke—or rather, for the most part, a selection of critical writings about those four.

Is *We the People* available anywhere?[59] On learning from the University of Chicago Press that they had no copy to sell me, I recommended to the Liberty Fund people that they beseech you to let them bring it out; doubtless you have heard from them. I have a borrowed paperback copy.

Annette and I are off to Washington tomorrow for the White House affair commemorating the fifth anniversary of *A Nation at Risk,* the report of the Commission on Excellence in Education. Annette, the most humane of the commissioners, has prepared a statement for the press; many of the members of the Commission are anti-Reagan, and may seize the opportunity to pronounce an anathema.

All's well at Piety Hill. I have been out transplanting saplings and shrubs today; our lilacs have commenced to bud. I have been arranging a meeting of several factions of Michigan's Republicans, here at my house, with your servant as conciliator; but like Tweedledum and Tweedledee, they prefer to quarrel. Most of the folk who are active in politics either get into it as an amusing spiteful game, or else expect to obtain loot. I find it more satisfying to plant maples and oaks.

Best wishes to you.

Cordially,
Russell

Letter to Edwin Meese

Having been investigated exhaustively during the Wedtech scandal of the mid-1980s, Meese resigned as attorney general in August 1988, although he was never convicted of any wrongdoing.

July 7, 1988

The Honorable Edwin Meese
Attorney-General of the United States
The United States Department of Justice
Washington, D.C.

Dear Mr. Meese,

We are grateful for the fortitude which you have displayed ever since reckless partisans began to attempt to drag you down. You have behaved throughout all this honorably and courageously, as a true public man should. Where will we find gentlemen of ability and honesty to carry on the government of the United States, if this denigration of the Executive Force is to persist? I have been telling people throughout the country, and foreign journalists, too, that your appointment as Attorney-General was the best appointment that President Reagan made.

Annette and I hope that some day, now that you are freed from the harassments of office, you may find time to visit us at Mecosta. Perhaps an ISI seminar might be arranged.

Cordially,
Russell Kirk

Letter to Harry Veryser

A longtime friend of Russell and Annette Kirk, Veryser is an adjunct professor of Economics at the University of Detroit–Mercy, having earlier served as chair of the Department of Economics and Finance. He also was an active member of

Americans for the Competitive Enterprise System (ACES) and the chairman of the board and owner of an automotive supply company for many years.

July 10, 1988

Mr. Harry Veryser
Mount Clemens, Michigan

Dear Harry,

Very good it was to have some time with you and Don in Washington.[60] You may recall—if you were present during my final lecture—that immediately thereafter I was carried off to the White House in a White House limousine driven by a sergeant of marines, and then whisked up to talk with President Reagan, who stood tall and high-spirited after his expedition to Moscow. He told me jokes, apparently original; I never have heard before any of his jests, so I suppose that he creates them all. Here is one—which, he said to me, he didn't tell to Gorbachev:

He and Gorbachev were riding in the countryside near Moscow, Reagan accompanied by a Secret Serviceman, Gorbachev by a KGB agent. Their limousine passed near a considerable cataract; Gorbachev had the limousine driver stop the car.

"Jump down that waterfall!" he commanded the Secret Serviceman. That person declined.

"Why don't you obey my order?" Gorbachev demanded.

"Because, sir, I have a wife and three children."

Gorbachev addressed the KGB agent: "Jump down that waterfall!" The man promptly obeyed.

Horrified, the Secret Serviceman clambered down to the foot of the waterfall, where he found the KGB agent, battered and bruised but alive, trying to wring out his clothes. "Why did you obey him?" the Secret Serviceman asked.

"Because I have a wife and three children."

Thus did Mr. Reagan convey to me the fact that he does not labor under illusions concerning the Soviet character.

Many thanks for the copy of your letter to the Earhart Foundation. If that grant is awarded, I think it might be well to write to Henry Regnery, asking if the Marquette Fund might grant an additional (supplementary) five thousand dollars for my book and lectures on jurisprudence.

Did you ever write to, and gain a response, from, Michael Joyce, Bradley Foundation, concerning our earlier lectures on the Constitution and political economy? I don't mean that we should approach him now, but it would be interesting to me to learn whether he rejected the application. . . .

The drought continues here, ferociously; I have lost some of the saplings and shrubs I planted this spring.

More before long. I enclose my speech against the Libertarians, on the chance that you'd not beheld it earlier.[61]

Cordially,

Russell

Letter to Gleaves Whitney

Director of the Hauenstein Center for Presidential Studies at Grand Valley State University, historian Gleaves Whitney was a graduate student at the University of Michigan in 1988. At that time, he was researching and writing his doctoral dissertation on European Catholic conceptions of decadence, believing (as he wrote at the conclusion of a 1991 article titled "Decadence and Its Critics," published in the Intercollegiate Review *26 [Fall 1991]: 21–25) "one of my tasks is to help university students understand just what the Western vision is; another is to help them recognize just what historical processes have blurred and blinded our knowledge of that vision over the centuries." Whitney wrote to Kirk to ask for advice on literature about conservative Western perspectives on cultural decadence and received the following reply.*

July 16, 1988

Mr. Gleaves Whitney
2488 Stone
Ann Arbor, Michigan 48105

Dear Mr. Whitney,

Thanks for your letter of July 6. . . .

I enclose various pieces of interest to you. And here are some responses to your inquiries.

1) Books about decadence, etc. Aye, you might look into my *Decadence and Renewal in the Higher Learning;* or, perhaps more pertinently, into my very recent book (Regnery) *The Wise Men Know What Wicked Things Are Written on the Sky.* I enclose a copy of the speech with which that book originated. Also have a look at my *Program for Conservatives;* I enclose an inscribed copy, which you may keep forever, forever and a day, until the walls shall crumble in ruin, and moulder in dust away.[62] Aye, Eliot is desperately concerned about decadence; read especially *Notes towards the Definition of Culture.* And obtain especially a copy of Tage Lindbom, *The Tares and the Good Grain;* Friedrich Georg Juenger, *The Failure of Technology;* and Malcolm Muggeridge, *Chronicles of Wasted Time,* the second volume particularly.

2) I enclose with reference to individualism and egoism, my latest assault on the Libertarians—my Heritage Lecture of April 19, 1988.[63] . . .

3) I enclose some pamphlets of mine about reading for the young, particularly my little tract on *Teaching History to the Rising Generation.*[64] The most pleasant way to learn history at the age of fourteen, though, is to read great historical novels—intelligible ones, of course. (As you have noticed, books written by people who write only for children are shallow and silly and boring books; they condescend foolishly, those authors.) Here are some such books for fourteen-year-old boys—or thirteen-year-old, as I note by referring to your letter. All will teach a good deal of history:

R. L. Stevenson, *The Black Arrow*
Walter Scott, *Ivanhoe*
J. F. Cooper, *The Last of the Mohicans*
John Masefield, *Martin Hyde, the Duke's Messenger*
R. Blackmore, *Lorna Doone*
Howard Pyle, *Men of Iron*
Howard Pyle, *Otto of the Silver Hand*
Kingsley, *Westward Ho!*

And there are many others; you should browse through our children's library, or libraries, on top and bottom floors, when next you come unto us at Piety Hill. And I have various books here that list and recommend such historical romances.

More another time; best wishes from the denizens of Piety Hill.

Cordially,
Russell Kirk

Letter to H. Lee Cheek Jr.

Cheek is dean of the social sciences and professor of political science and religion at East Georgia State College. He was a Wilbur Fellow who studied under Kirk from 1984 to 1985. In a July 9, 1988, letter, while attending the Straussian Claremont Institute, Cheek wrote at length to Kirk about the influence of Leo Strauss and Harry Jaffa at Claremont, noting that "Jaffa and company" were seeking to drive a wedge between Kirk's friend (and fellow Burke scholar) Francis Canavan and other traditionalist interpreters of Burke's thought.

July 16, 1988

Mr. Lee Cheek, Jr.
1040 North College Avenue
Claremont, California 91711

Dear Lee,

Thanks for your letter of July 9, with its interesting enclosures. In return, herewith—or rather, under separate cover—I am posting to you a mass of my recent writings and speeches on the Constitution, Burke, etc.

Nay, Father Canavan was with Peter Stanlis and myself at a very recent meeting of Burke scholars for three days in Chicago, and he is of one mind with us. He inscribed my copy of his book "To the Mentor of Us All."

I am sending you a copy of the new edition of my *Edmund Burke*, hot from the press; you may keep it forever, forever and a day, till the walls shall crumble in ruin, and moulder in dust away. Therein you will find remarks of mine on Strauss' distortion of Burke. Incidentally, in 1954 I was walking along a corridor at the University of Chicago in company with Leo Strauss, and I taxed him with the strange passage in *Natural Right and History*.[65] He replied, "You must remember, Dr. Kirk, the circumstances of the time when I wrote that paragraph, and the people I was addressing. . . ." At that point were we interrupted; I learnt no more. But this was amusing: Strauss confessing that he himself employed the covert operations of which he accused so many dead writers.

Do you have Peter Stanlis' *Burke and the Natural Law?* If not, I could lend you a copy.

In a confused address at the Heritage Foundation, I am told, recently Jaffa declared, "In all history no one has told more lies than Russell Kirk in so short a space." He's unfair to Ananias.

More another time; best wishes.

Cordially,
Russell

Letter to John O'Sullivan

After O'Sullivan, an English political and journalistic figure, was selected to succeed William F. Buckley Jr. as editor of National Review, *Kirk wrote the following short letter of congratulations.*

August 6, 1988

Mr. John O'Sullivan, Editor
National Review
150 East 35th Street
New York, New York

Dear Mr. O'Sullivan,

As the Ancient of Days who first published the periodical essays of John O'Sullivan, I do bestow my benison upon you in your new august post.[66] Annette and I expect great attainments of you. Although *National Review* may be read by merely one-tenth of one per centum of the population of these United States, it may move mountains. . . .

Annette and I will be in Manhattan on Thursday, September 8— probably staying at the Roger Smith Hotel, and arriving the previous night. Might you be able to lunch with us? If you are engaged then, perhaps we could call on you at your office for a few minutes, and welcome you back to these shores.

Cordially,
Russell Kirk

Letter to George Weigel

Weigel (1951–) is a Catholic theologian and one of America's leading public intellectuals. He currently serves as Distinguished Senior Fellow of the Ethics and Public Policy Center. Weigel is the author or editor of many books, and he has written for many major American opinion journals and newspapers. He was the founding president of the James Madison Foundation, serving in that role from 1986 to 1989. Kirk was on friendly terms with him and considered him a thoughtful voice of lay Roman Catholicism in the late twentieth century.

August 9, 1988

Mr. George Weigel
The James Madison Foundation
733 15th Street, N.W.
Washington, D.C. 20005

Dear Mr. Weigel,

Annette, having read your exchange with Mr. Schindler in the pages of *Communio,* prods me into sending you the enclosed essays of mine that touch upon Locke's influence—grist to your mill, perhaps.[67] All are fairly recent. Do you happen to possess a copy of my fat book *The Roots of American Order,* in which I touch on Locke? If not, pray let me know, and I will dispatch one of the second edition to you, with my compliments. . . .

The best demolisher of the notion that the United States was founded on the abstractions of John Locke, or of any other set of abstractions, is Daniel Boorstin, whose authority few in the field of American history venture to deny nowadays. It was Charles Beard and Vernon Parrington who—along with Leo Strauss, I believe, later—promulgated the illusion that the American signers and framers were doctrinaires who took their politics and their morals out of books.

Our best wishes to you.

Cordially,
Russell Kirk

Letter to H. Keith H. Brodie

Brodie (1939–) is an American psychiatrist, educator, and university administrator. He currently serves as James B. Duke Professor of Psychology and Neuroscience at Duke University, where he is also President Emeritus of the university.

December 9, 1988

Dr. H. Keith H. Brodie
President, Duke University
Durham, North Carolina

Dear President Brodie,

I am grateful for your kind letter of November 20. How surprising to learn that I was selected as this year's recipient of the Distinguished Alumni Award! My wife had told me, recently, that Mr. Elf, my former assistant, had been persuading people to support his nomination of me for that honor; but I had no notion that from among various possible candidates, I should be selected.[68] Your letter of notification astonished me.

Alas, I am unable to accept the award. For I must be in Italy and Germany during May. On receiving your letter, I made inquiry as to whether my speaking-engagements in Europe might be postponed or advanced; but that, I have found, cannot be arranged. I am to speak on T. S. Eliot in Monza, Milan, and Turin; and on American politics in Munich. These are large official celebrations, and I am the principal speaker, so I cannot well withdraw from the speechifying in Italy and Bavaria.

I take it that my presence would be required for presentation of the award; therefore, I suppose, you must pass on to some other candidate—doubtless more deserving of it than I am.

Of many pleasant memories of Duke that occur to my mind from time to time, the studies I undertook there with Charles Sydnor (in Southern history) and Jay Hubbell (in Southern literature) are strongest. Also I think often of the *South Atlantic Quarterly* in the 1940s and 1950s, when several of my early essays were published in that good quarterly—nowadays obsessed, more's the pity, with interminable discussions of "gender and race."

So I do offer you my abject apologies for not being able to accept the Award. Would that it might be otherwise! I am sorry that I cause you and the selection-committee the bother of choosing another alumnus; and sorry, too, that many people were put to the trouble of commending me by letter. My best wishes to you.

Cordially,
Russell Kirk

Letter to Rosemary Virgo

Rosemary Virgo had been a schoolmate of Kirk's during their formative years in Plymouth, Michigan. During the late 1940s, at the time of his postgraduate studies, Kirk had brought "Rosy" to St. Andrews University and shown her around Scotland and portions of Western Europe. For a time it seemed that Kirk might have a future with her, but his innate shyness and youthful hesitancy in matters of the heart led to their parting ways, altogether amicably. In later years the entire Kirk family became friends with Rosy, her husband, Bud, and their daughter, Gracia.

December 15, 1988

Mrs. Richard Virgo

Dear Rosy girl,

You're one of the few who recall the birthday of the venerable Russell Kirk—though Bill McCann does, too. I was at Birmingham, Alabama, for the occasion, and great cakes were served in my honor. Your servant has been speechifying in the District of Columbia, Virginia, Alabama, Louisiana, Pennsylvania, New York, Wisconsin, Illinois, and Michigan. I now settle down for a time, writing hard, with six retainers, one of them Ethiopian. . . .

Kelly's cat Spike is mended, but now has a damaged eye from contending against more aggressive tomcats.[69] Felicia is very happy at Mount St. Mary's now. Andrea loves her school at South Bend, but does not relish the discipline of the family (the school's founder) with whom she dwells; we think of schooling her at home for a term. (We have three qualified teachers dwelling with us now, not counting genuine Doctor Kirk and honorary Dr. Annette Kirk.)

The trouble with writing short stories is that scarcely any magazine remains that will print decent stories. What is your tale about? My head is full of fictional plots, but I can't write them into stories, for I wouldn't be paid. . . .

How goes the struggle over your West Virginian river and the horrid race of developers? Much of Morton Township has been spoilt by the developers of Canadian Lakes, and foreigners who have bought Mecosta property try to obstruct my rustic walks with "No Trespassing" signs. . . .

Great cold has descended upon us here, much to Annette's sorrow. We bought snowshoes last winter, and may be able to employ them now.

The denizens of Piety Hill, who hope to see you before many months are out . . . do wish you and Bud a merry Christmas.

Love,
Russell

Letter to Clyde Wilson

Wilson (1941–) is a longtime American history professor at the University of South Carolina and a paleoconservative essayist for several magazines who is a noted authority on the life and work of the South Carolina statesman John C. Calhoun (1782–1850). He was on friendly terms with Kirk, who had a high opinion of Calhoun for his writings on concurrent majorities in the American body politic. He considered the "Cast Iron Man," along with John Adams, as one of the two most eminent American political writers and described his significance at length in The Conservative Mind. *Kirk sometimes consulted Wilson on points of fact regarding Calhoun.*

February 1, 1989

Professor Clyde Wilson
Department of History
The University of South Carolina
Columbia, South Carolina

Dear Clyde,

Just now I am making the final improvements of my book on the Constitution, meaning to send it off to a publisher very soon. This was originally to be entitled *Edmund Burke and the Constitution of the United States*, the NEH project that you so kindly commended; now I have enlarged the subject to *The Conservative Constitution*, reducing the original subject to a chapter therein, although the wisdom of Burke is referred to in every chapter.

I have an inquiry to make of you: where does the following passage from Calhoun occur? (I have lost my note-card on it, and wish to include the citation in my footnotes.)

"The revolution, as it is called, produced no other changes than those which were necessarily caused by the declaration of independence."[70]

I have quoted that sentence before; it is odd that the source should have slipped out of my memory; but of course you will recognize the passage immediately.

Also, if you think of Framers or Founders clearly influenced by their contemporary Burke, pray let me know. I have set down several in my book, but wish to add others, should you think of some I don't know much about. Did Rutledge, for one, happen to mention Burke once or twice, favorably? I am asking M. E. Bradford, too, to aid me in this. The Framer most clearly and directly under Burke's influence was John Dickinson. . . .

Cordially,
Russell

Letter to Justin Stagl

A longtime sociology professor at the University of Bonn and the University of Salzburg, Austrian-born Justin Stagl (1941–) along with his wife, sociology professor and translator Erika, met Russell Kirk during the 1980s. Like Kirk, Justin Stagl—a visiting scholar at Piety Hill during 1988—is concerned with tradition, culture, beauty, and ordered liberty within the individual and within the commonwealth.

February 14, 1989
Feast of St. Valentine

Professor Dr. Justin Stagl
Schumannstrasse 104
D-5300 Bonn 1
Federal Republic of Germany

Dear Justin,

My tardy thanks to you for your letter of January 4, and your check for the telephone bill. Has the Wilbur Foundation's payment reached you yet? I trust so. Anyway, I shall inquire of Mr. Gary Ricks when, three days from now, Annette and I arrive in Santa Barbara for the annual meeting of the trustees of the Wilbur Foundation.

It is good to have your news. All's well at Piety Hill, where we have much dazzling snow. My book on the Constitution, completed, has been sent off to a publisher. Now I must resume work on my ruminative memoirs; but innumerable lecture-engagements in several states delay me. President Reagan awarded your servant the Presidential Citizens' Medal the day before leaving office.

Our plans for our European expedition are taking shape. I know I am to speak at Salzburg on Tuesday, May 23; this engagement will be sponsored by Prince Vincenz Leichtenstein and the Paneuropa Union people, plus the publishers of *Epoche*. I am to speak at Monza on Friday, May 26; there may be engagements at Milano and Torino, too, about that time.

Thus if I am to speak at Bonn, I suppose the best plan might be for Annette and your servant to fly from the United States directly to Cologne-Bonn, and then to make our way to Salzburg by train. We plan to spend only a fortnight altogether in Europe. It is years since I visited Cologne, and I have never spent any time in Bonn. So I would be very willing to speak at the University and to meet your colleagues and friends; Annette, too, would be delighted. . . .

May 19 definitely would be the best day for me to speak; but if that is impossible, we could shift it back to May 18, and arrive by air on May 17. Is the University still in session on May 19? I suppose so; the American universities in recent years have completed their spring terms ridiculously early.

If the above works out, and you should reserve a hotel room for us in Bonn, pray bear in mind that we prefer *old* inns—provided that a private bathroom is available. I don't know whether any old inns survive in Bonn; probably none in central Cologne. (One did survive near the river, and I stayed in it about 1949; but it had been swept away by the time of my second visit to Cologne.)

More another time; my compliments to Erika.

Cordially,
Russell

Letter to Joseph F. Johnston Jr.

Johnston is a retired attorney and writer. He and his wife, Rhoda, were friends of Kirk and sent him a copy of Ned Conquest's drama Achilles and Company *in early 1989 as a token of their friendship.*

March 19, 1989

Mr. Joseph F. Johnston, Jr.
Alexandria, Virginia 22314

I'm most grateful to you and your wife for the gift of Mr. Conquest's *Achilles and Company,* which I found awaiting me here after returning from much speechifying in Texas and elsewhere. Opening the book at random, I found myself reading the dialogue between Ulysses and Thersites: marveling, I asked myself, "Of what classical work can this be a translation?" I was astounded that I never had heard of such an ancient exchange. And then I discovered that it was all Mr. Conquest's own moral imagination. How successful he is as poet and moral philosopher! Just now I read through his version of *Gawain and the Green Knight;* I had read Lanier's version to my youngest daughter not long ago. Now I shall read her the Conquest version. She knows Tennyson's *Gawain,* too, with the Dore illustrations. Conquest has conquered me, and he shall be my evening reading this week.

Under separate cover, I am posting to you a copy of my little volume *The Wise Men Know What Wicked Things Are Written on the Sky;* I don't believe I sent you one earlier; if I did, you can pass on the earlier copy to some friend.

Annette and I do wish you and Rhoda a goodly Easter.

Cordially,
Russell

Letter to Count Nikolai Tolstoy

A distant cousin of Leo Tolstoy, Count Nikolai Tolstoy (1935–) is a Russian-born British citizen, a prominent figure in UK politics, and a distinguished writer noted for his historical study The Quest for Merlin *(London: Hamish Hamilton, 1985) and the Arthurian novel* The Coming of the King *(London: Guild, 1988). One of the major themes of Tolstoy's nonfiction is the forced repatriation of soldiers and citizens from the Eastern Bloc countries during the months and years after World War II; in many if not most cases, the transferal of these unfortunates into the hands of the Soviets led to imprisonment and death in forced-labor camps.*

March 19, 1989

Count Nikolai Tolstoy
Berkshire OX 13 5HS

Dear Nikolai,

Very good it is to have your recent letter, and to learn that we may contrive to meet again in April. Annette and I will be at Piety Hill from April 1 through 11; on April 1 and 2 we have a Piety Hill seminar on Wilhelm Roepke and a humane economy, but otherwise we have plenty of room to lodge you. (There will be thirty to forty people staying here on April 1 and 2.) Sally Wright was here for two or three days last week, interviewing me for her book about independent folk of humble beginnings.[71]

Annette and I will be in Bavaria, Austria, and northern Italy for a fortnight in the latter part of May, but will have no time, alas, for a British expedition. I am to speak in Monza, Milano, and Torino on T. S. Eliot, and on American politics at an international gathering at Salzburg.

How goes the trial of *Aldington v. Tolstoy?*[72] I mean to send along a contribution to the Defense Fund, once my two sterling accounts in Fife banks are straightened out—which should be quite soon. Ever since my own years as a conscript I have followed closely, and with anguish, the horrors of forced repatriation—in many lands. I suppose that you have seen the new biography of Winston Churchill by Martin Gilbert—Volume VIII, that is.[73] I gather from Henry Regnery's review of the volume—recently sent to me in typescript—that some eyes will be opened to Churchill's complicity in massive deportations. There is Churchill's minute to Eden:

"I cannot see that the Russians are wrong in making 100,000 or 150,000 of these people work their passage. Also we must bear in mind what we promised about leaving Romania's fate to a large extent in Russian hands. I cannot make myself consider that it is wrong for the Russians to take Romanians of any origin they like to work in the Russian coal fields in view of all that has passed."

Eliot always detested Churchill, at all stages of Churchill's progress. What a crew at Yalta!

More another time. We do hope to see you less than a month from now.

Cordially,

Russell

Letter to Jason Karlawish

Karlawish is currently professor of medicine, medical ethics, and health policy at the University of Pennsylvania's Perelman School of Medicine. Early in his medical career, while training in internal medicine and geriatric medicine at the University of Chicago, he wrote to Kirk to share a copy of one of his own early essays, which he believed Kirk would enjoy.

March 20, 1989

Dear Mr. Karlawish,

Thanks for sending me your essay "Telling Truth in Medicine." Very moving it is.[74] I am planning a general *auto de fe* for folk who reproach "sexist language." What a whining, lying age is ours! In one of Ibsen's plays—is it *The Wild Duck?*—a character goes about revealing to people the hard truth about themselves, in his zeal for self-knowledge. They are devastated, and destroy themselves; for we exist through our cherished illusions about ourselves, most of us. It is better, as William Butler Yeats suggests, to put on a mask and become that mask. Ronald Reagan put on the mask of the Western hero, and truly became the Western hero.

All's well at Piety Hill, where we will have a seminar on Wilhelm Roepke next week. I enclose an announcement of the first volume in the Library of Conservative Thought, which I am editing. Another volume (with a lengthy introduction by your servant) comes out this week: W. H. Mallock's *A Critical Examination of Socialism* (1906).

More another time; best wishes.

Cordially,

Russell Kirk

Letter to Robert A. Waters

Waters is a true crime writer and blogger who lives in central Florida. In early 1989, he wrote to praise Kirk for the high worth of his written works.

March 20, 1989

Mr. Robert A. Waters
Ocala, Florida 32675

Dear Mr. Waters,

Let me thank you for your letter of January 15. I hope that Ocala is not utterly changed from the charming place it was when, during the Second World War, I spent a year in the Withlacoochee Land Use Area—that is, Floridian swamps, where we sprayed mustard gas.

I have begun to edit the Library of Conservative Thought, published by Transaction Books; I enclose an announcement of our first volume. Another volume, Mallock's *A Critical Examination of Socialism,* is just now published.

It appears to me that Americans will grow increasingly conservative during the next decade, as the urgent need for restoration becomes obvious to the great majority of people. "Liberalism" already has become a term of opprobrium. But the question remains as to whether conservatively-inclined people possess imagination and resolution sufficient to contend tolerably well with our present discontents and difficulties.

My best wishes to you, with thanks for your kind observations about my books.

Cordially,

Russell Kirk

Letter to Clark Durant

Michigan-born Durant (1949–) was for many years an attorney, an officer at Hillsdale College (where he founded the conservative monthly Imprimis*), and a Republican politician. During the second Reagan administration, he served as chair of the Legal Services Corporation. Durant also cofounded and worked as CEO of Cornerstone Schools, a group of charter and independent schools in Detroit's inner city. In 1990, he sought the Michigan Republican nomination to challenge incumbent U.S. senator Carl Levin, but he lost the nomination to Bill Schuette.*

March 24, 1989

Mr. W. Clark Durant, III
Durant and Durant, P.C.
2300 Penobscot Building
Detroit, Michigan 48226

Dear Clark,

I find in my library a scribbled note saying that Harry Veryser inquires, on your behalf, whether I might write a note endorsing your candidacy. Below, I do so. I note, incidentally, that other candidates are springing up mushroom-like. Paul Henry will be the most formidable rival, I fancy. To win, it will be necessary for you to find time to visit every county in Michigan, meeting the local party leaders and asking for their support; that counts for a great more than billboard or television advertising. It's laborious but not really unpleasant. We would endeavor to organize something in Mecosta County for you: a reception at Piety Hill, perhaps. And, by the way, we have found radio advertising effective, in the form of a brief dialogue between two supporters.

Time was when Michigan sent distinguished men to the United States Senate. Michigan's citizens can do that again, by giving Clark Durant the Republican senatorial nomination and then electing him in November. Mr. Durant has been the courageous Chairman of the federal Legal Services Corporation, and of the Michigan Opportunity Society. I have known him ever since he was a student leader at Tulane University, and I am confident that he would be such a Senator from Michigan as we have not known for many a year.

Russell Kirk
Copy to Harry Veryser

Letter to Cleanth Brooks

In 1989, the distinguished literary scholar Cleanth Brooks agreed to participate in an ISI-sponsored Piety Hill seminar along with his friend Andrew Nelson Lytle. The topic of the weekend seminar was "Literature in an Age of Disorder," and Brooks proposed to speak on T. S. Eliot as a voice in the wilderness of cultural disorder.

May 2, 1989

Dr. Cleanth Brooks
70 Ogden Street
New Haven, Connecticut 06511

Dear Cleanth Brooks,

Your welcome letter of March 30 arrived here nearly a month ago; but I have been wandering over the face of the land, speechifying, and so have not had opportunity to reply until now. I'm home for a fortnight; then my wife and I make our way to Austria and Italy, where I am to speak on a diversity of topics at Salzburg, Monza, Milano, Torino, and Lecce. We'll be back at Mecosta about June 5 or 6.

Probably George Michos has told you about our Piety Hill seminars.[75] For our August gathering to discuss "Literature in an Age of Disorder," we hope that you will give one lecture (on Saturday) and Andrew Lytle another (also on Saturday); I will give an introductory talk on Friday evening and a concluding talk on Sunday. There will be many questions and comments by participants, and probably we will have some of the senior participants offer succinct commentaries on Sunday.

Now when you have time to meditate on the subject, will you let me know the theme and title of your formal lecture? I will endeavor not to overlap, in my remarks, Mr. Lytle's particular subject, or yours.

The Intercollegiate Studies Institute, at Bryn Mawr, will be writing to you about details of your participation, if they've not done so already: they will take care of your air-fares, etc., and supply a modest honorarium. We will have a car meet you at Grand Rapids (Kent County Airport), and transport you back there again whenever you wish. (Possibly you may wish to stay with us until some time Monday, rather than depart on Sunday afternoon.)

The ISI people are delighted and amazed that you have agreed to take part in the seminar. We will have trouble repelling people who will wish to attend: for we can lodge only about thirty people here in the backwoods, and can get into our drawing-room or library only about forty or forty-five.

I enclose another lecture of mine on Eliot—this one blemished with misprints and barbarous sub-headings, the mischief done by Heritage Foundation's youthful editors. Do you mean to attend the Eliot Society gathering at Saint Louis in September? I should like to hear Leonard Unger, who was my host once in Minneapolis, but I don't know yet whether Annette and I can afford the time and money.[76] By the way, a foundation over which I preside is the only foundation to give funding to the Eliot Society! Despite all the attention of TSE, clearly—in this instance and many others—Eliot's influence does not extend to the foundation bureaucracies and the American wealthy.

Annette joins me in best wishes to you. By the way, she has been appointed to the board of the nascent Catholic Museum of the United States, to be situated at Catholic University—the only woman on the board. She plans to spend years building up the Museum.

All's well at Piety Hill, where soon I will be able to canoe the Little Muskegon and the Chippewa; our village very nearly stands on Michigan's watershed.

More another time.

Cordially,
Russell Kirk

Letter to William Campbell

Campbell (1939–) is Professor Emeritus of economics at Louisiana State University and an authority on the work of Austrian economist Wilhelm Roepke. He is a past president of the conservative Philadelphia Society and has been an associate of the Heritage Foundation and the Intercollegiate Studies Institute. A longtime friend of the Kirk family, Campbell advised Kirk in the writing of the latter's textbook Economics: Work and Prosperity *(Pensacola, FL: A Beka Book, 1989).*

May 4, 1989

Professor William Campbell
Louisiana State University

Dear Bill,

I have posted to you a copy of my textbook *Economics: Work and Prosperity.* Alas, your great help is not acknowledged therein: A Beka forgot, and did not send me proof of the acknowledgements page. But this will be remedied in the second printing—which, I hope, will appear fairly soon.

This book is an example of dumbing-up. I wrote it for eighth-graders; but A Beka prescribes it for sections of allegedly talented seniors; and already it is being used for college freshmen (with a different-colored cover, but identical within); what's more, a big business college in Detroit is inclined to make it their prescribed text in economics! Nevertheless, it makes the science of economics possible to apprehend for a student of any age, and breaks with practically all other textbooks in economics by preferring the concrete to the abstract. . . .

More before long; best wishes.

Cordially,
Russell

Letter to William F. Buckley Jr.

Having received a copy of Kirk's substantial memoir published in Gale Re-search's Contemporary Authors Autobiography Series, *Buckley wrote to Kirk on May 22, 1989, to commend his old friend for crafting such an inter-esting piece, noting that Kirk had even taught him a new word: "illation." In response, Kirk wrote the following letter addressing Midge Decter's criticism of a passing statement he had made during a Heritage Foundation lecture: "And not seldom it has seemed as if some eminent Neoconservatives mis-took Tel Aviv for the capital of the United States." Decter and her husband, Norman Podhoretz, reportedly interpreted Kirk's remarks as anti-Semitic. But in a letter to Annette Kirk written several years after this controversy, Decter explained that her remarks to the press about Kirk had to do less with anti-Semitism and more to do with his seeming charge of dual loyalty. "I felt," Decter wrote, "in reading your husband's attack on the neoconservatives—and make no mistake, though humorous, that's what it was, and not for the first time—that my loyalty to my country was being impugned."*

June 6, 1989

Mr. William F. Buckley, Jr.
Editor
National Review

Dear Bill,

Thanks for your recent note, which arrived here while I was speechifying in Munich, Salzburg, Monza, Milano, Torino, and Lecce (distinctly *not* under the patronage of USIA). I do hope that you will favor Gale Research with your succinct autobiography. What huge volumes they produce! . . .

To you I am posting two recent productions of mine, for your amusement. The one is my textbook in economics, *Work and Prosperity,* published by the successful Christian textbook firm of A Beka. . . .

The other book is Mallock's *Critical Examination of Socialism,* with a lengthy introduction by your servant. This is the first edition since 1908; it is the third volume in my series of The Library of Conservative Thought (Transaction Books). Now that you have a prospect of a new book-review editor at *National Review,* perhaps that Great Unknown will be interested [in] even a book edited by Russell Kirk; if you think so, I will have a copy sent to him also.[77] (The one on its way is your personal copy, since it's a book that probably you will wish to keep.) . . .

Have you noticed Midge Decter's silliness in interviews with the *Washington Times* and the *Wall Street Journal*—her recent silliness about Russell Kirk, I mean? Of course anybody who in the slightest degree criticizes any measure of the present government of the secular state of Israel is planning a New Holocaust and is writing a second Protocols of Zion. The Heritage Foundation people tell me that somebody has organized a *sub rosa* campaign to sow dissension among conservative or quasi-conservative groups, and that the *Wall Street Journal* and the *Washington Times* features are the beginning of this. Midge Decter, foolish creature, hoists herself with her own petard, accusing the Bush administration of being composed of Philistines (to be slain by Samson Podhoretz, presumably); but I shall not emulate her, and am declining all interviews on the subject. Are the bloodhounds of the press after you, already, concerning such absurdities?

All's well at Piety Hill. Annette joins me in best wishes. I have six literary interns here this summer. We trust that the transition at *National Review* goes smoothly.[78] . . .

Cordially,
Russell

Letter to Arthur M. Schlesinger Jr.

The conservative Kirk and the liberal Arthur Schlesinger Jr. (1917–2007) were longtime friendly and respectful adversaries on cultural and political matters. Both men deeply admired Orestes Brownson (1803–1876); in the following letter, Kirk commends Schlesinger for his signal role in reviving modern interest in the little-known but influential writer and editor through his first published book, Orestes A. Brownson: A Pilgrim's Progress *(Boston: Little, Brown, 1939).*

as of—P. O. Box 4
Mecosta, Michigan 49332
June 25, 1989

Professor Arthur M. Schlesinger Jr.
Graduate School and University Center
City University of New York
33 West 42nd Street
New York, New York 10036–8099

Dear Arthur,

My tardy thanks to you for your kind letter of 24 April. It arrived here just as I was about to depart for Europe, and only now am I settling down to replying to correspondence that arrived at Piety Hill during my absence.

I am sorry to learn that my romantic notion, expressed in Brother Gilhooley's Brownson anthology to which you contributed the preface, that you might have come upon a dusty volume of Brownson in some decayed bookshop of Cambridge, was mere stuff and nonsense.[79] Be that as it may, you certainly revived our friend Orestes Brownson, and I will emphasize that resurrection in my introduction to the new edition (Transaction Books) of my *Selected Political Essays of Orestes Brownson.*

Charles Brown has got into the fourth chapter of his Niebuhr book.[80] I must resume work on my ruminative memoirs; and then this typewriter [will be put to work] to produce a little book on the meaning of *justice.*

Cordially,
Russell Kirk

Letter to Peter J. Stanlis

Kirk and Stanlis, the latter a longtime professor of English at Rockford College and international visiting scholar, became friends in the early 1950s, after Stanlis read a portion of Kirk's Randolph of Roanoke *and discovered that he and Kirk shared a near-identical interpretation of Edmund Burke's significance. During a friendship that lasted over forty years, the two men exchanged several hundred letters, with Kirk writing the forewords to several of Stanlis's many books.*

August 31, 1989

Dr. Peter Stanlis
Rockford

Dear Peter,

Thanks for your letter of August 27. I look forward to the completion of the final section of your Burke collection; it will be published at quite the right time, the beginning of the Burke bicentenary.[81]

Why don't you send to *National Review* a lengthy letter, or an article, correcting Kesler on natural law? He is childishly ignorant of what he writes about.[82]

William Bennett's present post probably will be the ruin of him, for it is most unlikely that he can devise any means of reducing drug-addiction. We need not dread influences upon Vice-President Quayle: not since Martin Van Buren has a sitting vice-president been elevated to the presidency. The inner circle of Bush advisors most definitely dislike the neoconservatives. . . .

I have just finished writing a formal lecture, "The Rights of Man v. the Bill of Rights," to be delivered to adults at Eckerd College, in

Florida later this month. Now I must prepare a Heritage Lecture on Malcolm Muggeridge. When I receive copies, I will post to you my recent Heritage Lecture on Donald Davidson.

The struggle between the Rockford Institute and Pastor Neuhaus continues, I find.[83] Foundations are inquiring about both sides. Harold O. J. Brown should be a good editor for *Religion and Society*.

More another time; best wishes.

Cordially,
Russell

Letter to Cecilia Kirk

Russell and Annette Kirk's second daughter, Cecilia, was a student at Hillsdale College at the time this letter was written.

September 30, 1989

Miss Cecilia Abigail Kirk
Resident in the Black House
Hillsdale

O my dear Cecilia,

This is your birthday, and you have come of age! I remember that day when you came into this world, seeming not very happy about it, and were welcomed by your beautiful mother and your bookish father. We brought home with you from the hospital a curious and rather frightening animal-doll, an Animal Yacker, one Bernie Bernard, who terrified poor Monica; doubtless he was your familiar. I know that you insist "I've always lived in this house," but really you were born in the old Poorhouse of Mecosta County, near Stanwood.

How I have loved you, my own Cecilia—loved you the more because of our crossgrained ways, your obstinacy, your silences, your strange powers of apprehension; because, when you would sigh, "Nobody can help me!"—why, nevertheless I would help you, and you would burst into laughter. I loved you . . . while I read to you. And

I love you today, when you are so poised and pretty, so full of intelligent curiosity, so ready to be at my side, still so eager to hear my tales. I loved you dearly when you gardened at my side, crying "Me!" and pulling up stones with your tiny fingers. I love you just as dearly now, when you talk with me of ships and shoes and sealing-wax, and whether pigs have wings. I am the only father you ever will have, Cecilia Kirk, and so it is well that I love you, and that you love me.

My secret agents instruct me that during the CCA at Hillsdale, you were most poised and charming, and spoke distinctly and to the point.[84] Would that I might have beheld you, my own Cecilia!

You and I will have only a few more years together, my Cecilia—or, for all we know, only a few more months. In the midst of life we are in death. If, in years to come, you should regret some word you have spoken to me, or some little sin of omission toward your father—why, I tell you now that everything was at once understood and forgiven by your father. At the age of twenty-one years, you have pleased mightily Russell Amos Kirk, who is confident that you never will do any act that would cause him to think less well of you. You are strong of will, active of mind, sound of conscience, my Cecilia. What father could ask more than that of a daughter?

Do you know Yeats' poem "A Prayer for my Daughter"? I read that again tonight, thinking of you, Cecilia. But somewhere else in Yeats' poems is the line I was seeking: "Set a strong ghost to watch over my daughter."[85] Shall I do that? The Wizard of Mecosta might accomplish it. Or shall I be that ghost myself?

Whatever path you may follow in the labyrinth of twenty-first century life—a path on which your mother and your father cannot accompany you—I believe you will move with courage and grace, my dear one. If you marry, you will choose well. You will not be corrupted by evil times. You will not lose faith in transcendent design. You will stand up for the permanent things. And you will not forget how I have cherished you, my Cecilia.

So writes your father, with tears on his cheeks, on the occasion of your twenty-first birthday, Miss Cecilia Kirk. Be of good cheer!

The world is so full of a number of things,
I'm sure that we all should be happy as kings.

So Stevenson; so with Kirk. I pray, my darling, that you may be happy and unafraid in a time of troubles. I send you, this day,

Much love,
Russell Amos Kirk
your father

Letter to James R. Wilburn

The substance of this letter contains Kirk's initial thoughts on writing the short work America's British Culture, *which would appear in 1993.*

November 24, 1989

Dr. James R. Wilburn, Vice-President and Dean
Pepperdine University School of Business and Management
Pepperdine University Plaza
400 Corporate Pointe
Culver City, California 20230

Dear Jim,

With reference to your telephone call about Mr. Salvatori's interest in an address, essay, or pamphlet about the Anglo-Saxon heritage of North America, I think that an important labor to undertake. We are sure to encounter more and more silly demands for study of "nonwestern cultures"; teaching classes in Upper Ippich; repudiation of our inheritance from Britain of the rule of law, a great body of literature, and constitutional government.

Ours is a Christian culture, of course; our religion, then, and in large part our morals, had their origins in Palestine and Italy. But our political institutions, our understanding of law, our commercial and industrial system, our inheritance of humane letters, and much else in our culture, are received for the most part from the old culture of England,

Scotland, and Ireland. It is strange that we have to emphasize this heritage today; once upon a time it was taken for granted.

This renewal of our awareness of our British patrimony might be the subject of an anthology of essays by various hands—and I could suggest the names of scholars and writers competent to the undertaking—but I think it would be more effective if composed by one writer, forcefully. Some power of rhetoric is required for successful completion of the task.

I would be willing to do the writing myself, should you think me capable of it. You will find enclosed my succinct autobiography, as published recently by Gale Research (Contemporary Authors series); also the latest version of my lecture brochure.[86] I believe that about the only thing missing from these publications is my having received the Presidential Citizens' Medal from President Reagan, a few days before he left the White House. Also I enclose my recent Heritage Foundation address on Donald Davidson, as a specimen of my rhetoric.[87]

Cordially,

Russell Kirk

D. Litt. (Sancti Andreae)

Letter to Clyde A. Sluhan

Sluhan, the chairman and chief executive officer of Master Chemical Corporation, was a friend of Kirk who enjoys reading to become a better rounded person. In early December 1989, he wrote to ask Kirk's opinion of a six-volume set of books he was considering for purchase.

December 12, 1989

Mr. Clyde A. Sluhan
Master Chemical Corporation
501 W. Boundary
Perrysburg, Ohio 43351

Dear Clyde,

Thanks for your letter of December 8. I possess the six-volume set of Hume's *History*, concerning which you inquire; and a fine bargain it is. It is the work of David Hume, the Scots philosopher, and it had much influence upon the Americans of the concluding quarter of the eighteenth century. Hume was a Scots Tory, a persuasion reflected in his famous *History of England*. That enraged Thomas Jefferson, who tried—but failed—to arrange for a bowdlerized American edition in which the Tory opinions would be supplanted by Whig opinions. (So much for Jefferson's attachment to freedom of speech and of the press!) This work had more influence in British North America than did any other history of that age. It is written with wit and assurance.

Cordially,

Russell

The 1990s

For conservatives, the first necessity lies beyond politics. It is the regaining of a spiritual and moral object in life, the lack of which is the cause of most of the troubles that afflict mankind nowadays.

from a memorandum to Adam Meyerson, February 1, 1990

Letter to Edwin Feulner

A lifelong conservative spokesman and activist, Feulner (1941–) served for thirty-six years as president of the Heritage Foundation, an influential conservative think tank whose mission (as described on the organization's website) "is to formulate and promote conservative public policies based on the principles of free enterprise, limited government, individual freedom, traditional American values, and a strong national defense." Under Feulner's leadership, Heritage invited Kirk to speak before sizeable audiences at its headquarters in Washington, D.C., on numerous occasions.

January 8, 1990

Dr. Edwin Feulner, President
The Heritage Foundation

Dear Ed,

The denizens of Piety Hill do wish you a most successful Anno Domini 1990.

I have bethought me that it is time to draw up plans for my Heritage Lectures of this new year. Shall we have a new series entitled generally "The Conservative Imagination"? I would emphasize the imaginative power possessed by the conservative mind—a point made strongly by Paul Elmer More in his essay on Disraeli. Below I set down the tentative titles of the four lectures in the intended series.

1. *The Imagination of Edmund Burke.* This year of 1990 is the bicentenary of *Reflections on the Revolution in France,* and I would discuss how Burke's prophetic mind and evocative prose carried the day against radicalism.

315

2. *James Fenimore Cooper and the European Puzzle.* I would discuss (what is rarely undertaken) Cooper's novels set in Europe, and his political teachings therein; and bring in a comparison with recent events in Europe.

3. *The Politics of Joseph Conrad.* The great novelist's analysis of Latin American politics in *Nostromo,* his assault on the anarchists in *Under Western Eyes* and *The Secret Agent,* and his mockery of feminism.

4. *The Reactionary Fables of Jacquetta Hawkes.* An examination of the parable-fiction of the famous English ecologist and anthropologist: her denunciation in parable of social levelling, and her rejection of other modernist errors. (This would be my first lecture about a distinguished conservative woman.)

What say you to the above? If you are pleased, I will commence to work out possible lecture-dates with Betsy Hart.[1]

I note that AEI, doubtless in emulation of Heritage, has commenced a series of cultural or quasi-cultural lectures, under the direction of Dinesh D'Souza. Jeffrey Hart delivered one on Samuel Johnson not long ago.

Possibly you haven't yet seen the autobiography (succinct) of your servant, published a few months ago in the reference volume *Contemporary Authors Autobiography Series.* Anyway, I enclose a copy for you.

Annette and I are mightily grateful for your intercession with Aequus Foundation, resulting in the grant to ACES and carrying on of production of volumes for The Library of Conservative Thought. We have seven volumes published already, and will get out a Transaction Books pamphlet about them soon, I hope. The next to appear will be *Select Political Essays of Orestes Brownson,* and after that Francis Wilson's *The Case for Conservatism*—both with lengthy introductions by your servant; after that, Donald Davidson's *Attack on Leviathan* and two volumes of essays about Burke.

All's well enough at Piety Hill; again, much thanks.

Cordially,

Russell

316

Memorandum to Adam Meyerson

On January 25, 1990, Kirk received a letter from Adam Meyerson, editor of Policy Review, *asking if Kirk would be willing to participate in a major symposium in the magazine's upcoming spring issue. The symposium's respondents were to address a single question posed by Meyerson on the future of conservatism and to list up to ten policy priorities. Kirk responded as follows, writing (uncharacteristically) in memorandum form.*

February 1, 1990

"What should be the most important foreign and domestic policy objectives of the conservative movement in the 1990s?"

1) For conservatives, the first necessity lies beyond politics. It is the regaining of a spiritual and moral object in life, the lack of which is the cause of most of the troubles that afflict mankind nowadays. Without a recognized end in existence, we are flung into what Burke called the "antagonist world of madness, discord, vice, confusion, and unavailing sorrow." For such recovery, the conservative imagination is required; but it scarcely can be pursued as a public policy; rather, the renewal of a moral order must be the work of the insights and the eloquence of individual men and women.

2) In foreign affairs, the policy of the United States should not be the establishment of "democratic capitalism" throughout the world, but instead a salutary neglect of the domestic concerns of other nations. With the collapse of Marxist ideology virtually everywhere (except in Manhattan), and the disintegration of the empire called the Soviet Union, America no longer needs to maintain garrisons in Europe and Asia, nor to buy allies through largesse. We may return, indeed, to the policy outlined by George Washington in his Farewell Address. As Daniel Boorstin puts it, "The Constitution of the United States is not for export."[2] Other countries must be expected to work out their own political and economic patterns, as a general recovery from totalist ideology occurs. We must be sedulous to prevent the perils that a Russian

empire might be succeeded by an American empire; for such domination soon would be execrated universally.

3) In politics, conservatives should labor energetically to resist centralization of power and to restore to state governments and to local agencies, so far as possible, the functions constitutionally assigned to them. To prate of "democracy" but actually to invest decision-making in the hands of administrators at the nation's capital is either hypocrisy or dense ignorance.

4) In economic affairs, the conservative approach is to encourage small-scale and competitive enterprise, and to cease to favor economic concentration and oligopoly. For this, revision of taxation will be required, particularly of inheritance taxes. To rejoice in consolidated economic bigness really is to fulfill the prediction of Marx, who foretold the coming of the day when a huge-scale "capitalism" would have no real defenders.

5) In "social issues," America's most ominous difficulty is the growth of a genuine proletariat in the great cities, a mass of people aimless, usually unemployed, living at public expense, wretchedly schooled and reared, easily attracted to crime and violence; subsisting, as did the old Roman proletariat, by bread and circuses provided from on high. Our cities, with few exceptions, have become more dismal and dangerous than those created by any other civilized people, and that within the past three or four decades. The causes of this unhappy phenomenon have been complex, the remedies must be complex. Johnson's "demonstration cities" and "urban renewal" made matters far worse, in effect being war upon the poor, rather than upon poverty. To healing and restoration, conservative policy-makers should give most urgent attention.

6) Conservatives should not expect overmuch of public policies, especially policies projected by the federal government. Most restoration and improvement must be contrived and effected by individuals and voluntary associations, and in local communities. This is true of schooling especially. A policy of discouraging grandiose and visionary policies, abroad or at home, would be the most prudent of all policies.

Letter to Kevin J. Smant

A historian at the University of Notre Dame (and later at Indiana University), Smant wrote several times to Kirk during 1990 to ask about philosophical correspondences between Kirk and longtime National Review *senior editor James Burnham (1905–1987). At this time, Smant was at work on his study* How Great The Triumph: James Burnham, Anticommunism, and the Conservative Intellectual Movement, *which appeared in 1992 (Lanham, MD: University Press of America). In a February 17, 1990, letter, Smant asked Kirk for his assessment of Burnham's contributions to American conservatism.*

February 25, 1990

Mr. Kevin J. Smant
University of Notre Dame

Dear Mr. Smant
In reply to your letter of February 17, I must confess that I have thought very little about James Burnham, and have not read any one of his books with really close attention. I never have had much of anything to do with New York's intellectual circles; and never having been influenced by Marxism, I am quite outside their climate of opinion. James Burnham was a utilitarian, really, and I suppose I may be classified as a romantic—that is, on the side of Coleridge, Scott, and Southey, in the disputes of the first half of the nineteenth century.

An illustration: long ago Burnham published in *National Review* some account of his travels in Spain. He lamented the backwardness of Spanish cities, with their narrow dark streets, through which it was next to impossible to drive automobiles. How those cities ought to be rebuilt on modern lines, with boulevards! He was wondrously ignorant of the fact that the cities of southern Spain, in particular, were deliberately built with narrow streets and twisting buildings in order to keep off the sun in that clime, so that people might stroll in the cool shade.

Mr. Burnham, in short was a modernist; I am a traditionalist. But I thought him an honest and kindly man.

Cordially,
Russell Kirk

Letter to William Abbott

Abbott is a businessman in Nebraska, specializing in wood-preservative products. In March 1990, he wrote to Kirk to note that the message of Christ and his greatest followers points toward a truly radical (as opposed to traditional) change in one's life and way of living. Abbott asked Kirk for a reading list of what he termed "mystical conservatives."

May 27, 1990

Mr. William Abbott
Columbus, Nebraska

Dear Mr. Abbott,

Thanks for your letter of March 31. I haven't a reading-list for radical conservatives. One needs to remember that Jesus said nothing about war, revolution, slavery, or any other "social question," as we call such now; and Saint Paul enjoined slaves to obey their masters. The order of the soul is distinct from the order of the republic. And Jesus came not to annul the Law, but to fulfill it: both Jesus and Paul carry on the Hebraic legacy. "Be ye perfect," is a radical command in the sense of going to the root of the human condition; but not in the sense of demanding the reconstitution of society.

I enclose a piece of mine that you may not have beheld. My new book *The Conservative Constitution* will be published any day now by Regnery.

More another time; best wishes.

Cordially,
Russell Kirk

Letter to William Bentley Ball

Ball (1916–2000) was a constitutional attorney and Roman Catholic lay-
man nationally known for defending religious doctrine and practice against
inroads by the secularizing state. He is remembered primarily for his role
in arguing for the plaintiff before the U.S. Supreme Court in the case of
Wisconsin v. Yoder *(1972), in which the Court found that Amish children*
could not be compelled to attend school past the eighth grade. That is, the par-
ents' right to freely practice their faith was affirmed to outweigh the state's
interest in educating their children.

August 1, 1990

Mr. William Bentley Ball
Harrisburg, Pennsylvania

Dear Bill,

My tardy thanks to you for the copy of your interesting "Tempting of Robert Bork," which I had seen in *Crisis* even before your note
and copy reached me.[3] I have been very busy trying to finish the writing
of my memoirs, *The Sword of Imagination*, and am perhaps two hundred
letters in arrears in my correspondence. . . .

Herewith I send you a lecture of mine on Original Intent; I don't
think I posted a copy to you earlier.[4] And when the book comes out, I
will send you a copy of *The Conservative Constitution*. I take up in that
book some of the matters you discuss. I disagree with you about describing the Declaration of Independence as a kind of preamble to the
Constitution; that argument plays into the hands of the doctrinaire
egalitarians.

The relationship between the basic positive law of the Constitution and the body of moral thought called the natural law always has
been complex—as we see it, for instance, in the opinions and writings
of Joseph Story. In this century, the justices of the Supreme Court usually have professed Holmes' contempt for natural law—outwardly; but

in practice they have been making decisions on the basis of their own private notion of natural law, or the principles of morality applied to the law. To decide on the basis of "what seems just" is to repair, actually, to natural law—though often natural law misunderstood. School-desegregation decisions, for instance, for the most part were based on a concept of natural law—although rather shallow justification was found in the Reconstruction Amendments.

As you remark, our remedy lies in the appointment of judges with a true knowledge of the natural-law tradition, but possessed of a determination to exercise judicial restraint.

There's much more I'd like to say about your good essay; but a big Piety Hill seminar will occur two days from now, and I must prepare for it. . . .

Annette joins me in best wishes.

Cordially,
Russell

Letter to William F. Buckley Jr.

In late 1990, Buckley stepped down from the day-to-day editing of National Review, *which he had founded in 1955 and served as editor for thirty-five years. Kirk had written for Buckley's magazine for twenty-five years and had known, admired, and verbally sparred with the younger man since before its inception.*

October 15, 1990

Mr. William F. Buckley, Jr.
National Review

Dear Bill,

I take it that the *Review* still will forward your mail, despite your desertion of their premises.

How much you have accomplished by *National Review!* No one else could have made a success of such an undertaking; before you commenced it, I had despaired of the creation of a conservative weekly or fortnightly in this land. The paper arose out of your strong personality; I do hope it may survive your withdrawal. But I fancy you will favor it with your words quite frequently.[5]

As you know, long have I marvelled at how much, or how many things, you contrive to accomplish simultaneously. *National Review* will be your most enduring monument. Some day you must write your memoirs.[6] Mine are written, but I must tighten some of the chapters; you pop up frequently therein.

Have you kept track of how many books of one sort or another you have published? My newest, *The Conservative Constitution,* will appear on October 19, my seventy-second birthday. I think that is my twenty-eighth book—not counting, of course, books edited, contributed to, etc.

On the newest Kirk Brochure, enclosed, you will behold Kirk Paterfamilias and his brood, all of whom send you their best wishes. This is merely a note of appreciation of your work of several decades; more another time.

Cordially,
Russell

Letter to Ronald Jager

A former professor of philosophy at Yale University, Jager (1932–) wrote Eighty Acres: Elegy for a Family Farm *as a memoir of life in northern Michigan's rural Missaukee County during the Great Depression. The book appealed to Kirk's own agrarian leanings and appreciation for well-turned writing.*

October 18, 1990

Mr. Ronald Jager
Washington, New Hampshire

Dear Mr. Jager,
It is good to have your letter of September 30. My copy of *Eighty Acres* has arrived now. How handsomely Beacon Press has produced it!

I expect to arrange to review it somewhere myself, in a national magazine, and to have our youngest daughter, Andrea, aged fifteen, review it for my own quarterly, *The University Bookman*. (The second daughter is a more experienced reviewer, but she is in Scotland, at St. Andrews, this year.)

Doubtless you know Curtis Stadtfeld's book *From the Land and Back*, which celebrates Mecosta County as yours celebrates Missaukee County. At the age of seventeen I first beheld Missaukee County, driving down from the north. My friend and I were collecting county road-maps, and inquired of denizens of Lake City where the county courthouse was situated. They, having ruminated, muttered, "You want the county barns, don't you?" We didn't. No county was more bucolic. Nearly every barn—this was 1936—and nearly every farmhouse was adorned by vast structures of lightning-rods, doubtless testimonials to some brilliant salesman. . . .

Henry Regnery said he would send your typescript to me for a reading, but it never arrived here. As for McBain, various materials used in the little factory at Mecosta, which I bought and turned into my library, had been left over from a builder's construction of a new school at McBain: surplus bricks, tiles, etc.[7]

I will begin reading *Eighty Acres* tonight. (I inherited forty acres of Mecosta pasture, but have had to sell it.) My new book *The Conservative Constitution* (Regnery) should be published tomorrow, my seventy-second birthday. Come to visit us here, if ever you come to Michigan.

Cordially,
Russell Kirk

Letter to Wendell Berry

Kirk deeply admired Wendell Berry (1934–) for his life as an agrarian and for his literary works. In 1990, he invited Berry to speak at a seminar at Piety Hill. Being a working farmer, Berry declined but sent his compliments to Kirk.

October 18, 1990

Mr. Wendell Berry
Port Royal, Kentucky 40058

Dear Mr. Berry,

May you be persuaded to take the principal part in a seminar to be held at my house of Piety Hill, here in the decayed village of Mecosta? We wish to talk about rural America, and hope to learn much from you.

The Intercollegiate Studies Institute, for more than a decade, has been sponsoring what we call the Piety Hill Seminars, with thirty to forty-five people in attendance, lasting for a week-end. Most of the participants are undergraduates or graduate students, from across the country. These have been intelligent, amiable affairs, conducted in my house and my library building. A few months ago we held a seminar in which, for three days, Andrew Lytle and Cleanth Brooks were the principal speakers; more recently, Pierre Coustillas (from France) and I were the principal speakers at a seminar on the political novel—talking especially about Gissing and Conrad.

I may be regarded as a Northern Agrarian—although the last of our family's arable land was disposed of long ago. I have many connections with the Southern Agrarians: for instance, I am soon bringing out, through Transaction Books, a new edition of Donald Davidson's *The Attack on Leviathan*.[8] I enclose a lecture-agent's brochure about myself that may give you some notion of my notions and situation.

The Intercollegiate Studies Institute, with offices at Bryn Mawr, Pennsylvania, would be honored to send you a formal invitation should you be able to join us.[9] . . .

Various people, whose names you may or may not know, are eager to bring you here, having long been your admirers: John Lyon, Michael Aeschliman, the Calvinist agrarians at Mancelona, Michigan, and others. And I am of their number; some years ago, I reviewed one or two of your books.[10]

325

Mecosta, founded by my great-grandfather and his uncle, lies some seventy miles north of Grand Rapids; we would have a car meet your plane at Kent County Airport. Ours is a wooded county on the watershed of Michigan, with little money but good canoeing. We would have handsome lodging and abundant food for you. Do come if you possibly can.

Yours cordially,
Russell Kirk

Letter to Robert L. Bartley

Kirk transitioned swiftly from a strong supporter of George H. W. Bush's presidency to an outspoken critic, largely on the strength of administration's decision to go to war against Iraq in the Gulf War of 1990–91. This put Kirk—along with fellow conservative writers Joseph Sobran and Patrick J. Buchanan—at odds with many men and women of the right, who supported the war.

November 12, 1990

Mr. Robert L. Bartley, Editor
The Wall Street Journal

Dear Sir,

I heartily subscribe to Mr. Arthur Schlesinger Jr.'s article "Iraq, War and the Constitution" in this day's *Journal*. Truly the president of the United States has no constitutional power to make war without the express assent of Congress; and Mr. Schlesinger is right to fear that the executive branch shows a disposition "to drag the republic into war in the Gulf." I rejoice, incidentally, that Mr. Schlesinger now acknowledges, to his credit, that Senator Robert Taft was right in setting himself, in 1950, against President Truman's military action in Korea without congressional approval; and that Mr. Truman and Mr. Schlesinger then were in the wrong on the constitutional question.

Already President Bush and his people are putting into northern Arabia nearly as many men as President Johnson put into South

Vietnam at the height of the war in Indo-China. The Catholic bishops do their duty in protesting against a war for petroleum prices. When, during the French Revolutionary era, the Pitt ministry proposed to fight to secure the navigation of the Scheldt river, Edmund Burke exclaimed, "A war for the Scheldt? A war for a chamberpot!" And later, "The blood of man should be shed but to redeem the blood of man. The rest is vanity; the rest is crime."

Is President Bush emulating President Johnson? A war for Kuwait? A war for an oil-can!

Yours sincerely,
Russell Kirk

Letter to Gloria Whelan

Whelan is an award-winning novelist, short story writer, and poet who lives in Northern Michigan. In October 1990 she received a signed copy of Eliot and His Age *after meeting Kirk at a ghost-storytelling event in Alpena, Michigan. In return, she sent him a copy of one of her short stories, "The Secret Meeting with Mr. Eliot," which had appeared in the* Missouri Review *in 1983.*

November 18, 1990

Mrs. Gloria Whelan
Mancelona, Michigan

Dear Mrs. Whelan,

Very good it is to have your letter of All Saints' Day. All Souls' Eve was a lively time here at Piety Hill: four hundred souls came to be treated, and were tricked in our entrance-hall.[11]

I enclose a fairly recent Eliot piece of mine that may amuse you.[12]

Your Professor Wally is too dreadfully real. I think we would be the better for it if practically all our colleges and universities became even as Nineveh and Tyre, and the owl and bat their revel would keep therein.

You are undoubtedly the best writer of short stories ever to inhabit Michigan! I read several of your stories aloud to Annette, my wife (a generation younger than your servant) and our convalescent third daughter, Felicia. It's sad that next to no place is left in which a good short story can be published, and that university presses now are the refuge of wise and witty fiction. I would write all sorts of short stories, were there expectation of their being published. I am the last master of the uncanny tale, the last leaf on the gallows-tree, Robert Aickman having died in England. Do you have a copy of my *Watchers at the Strait Gate*? If not, pray let me know, and I'll post one to you, inscribed.

I have finished writing my memoirs. Therein is noted a certain similarity between Henry James and the author of *The Conservative Mind*—in character, that is, not in style.[13]

Alas that I have no children left who are young enough to enjoy your children's books! But I mean to track down those books, all the same. . . .

I suspect that you make your way south more frequently than we make our way north. If so, do come to see us and stay with us at Piety Hill. We will lodge you in the Gothick suite, where you will have plenty of room to yourselves, and possibly a wail from the invisible and ancestral Crying Baby. I hope for a word from your husband, too. . . . Piety Hill stands directly on M-20, at the western fringe of Mecosta, a settlement dwarfed by sprawling Mancelona. There is always someone here to answer the telephone or the doors. (We have five buildings.)

How very real your creatures are! They all live in the vicinity of Mecosta.

Cordially,
Russell Kirk

Letter to John Engler

Elected to the state governorship of Michigan in 1990, lifelong Republican John Engler served three terms as the state's chief executive. He was a long-time friend of Kirk, espousing conservative principles during a successful career in state politics.

November 26, 1990

The Honorable John Engler
Senate Majority Leader
Senate of Michigan
Lansing, Michigan

Dear John,

How heartening it has been to read and hear the astonishment expressed over your victory—and to find most of the comment friendly, too! You will become a power in the nation, through your example, as well as in our state of Michigan.

Annette tells me that you have been so kind as to mention that perhaps I could be of assistance to you in the preparation of your inaugural address. You would like to include something about the principle of personal responsibility, I understand. Of course you will be dealing directly yourself with practical measures. About how long do you expect your address to be, and for how long a portion of it should I prepare some suggestions? If you can let me know, I will turn my typewriter soon to this matter. My previous successes in helping public men to prepare formal speeches or lectures have been four:

Senator Goldwater's address at Yale
Senator Goldwater's address at Notre Dame
Cardinal Cooke's address to the Masons of New York
Ambassador Shakespeare's address at the University of Moscow

I believe that Annette has suggested to you that if you should be looking for an able member of your gubernatorial staff, probably Dr. Joseph McNamara, at present a vice-president of Hillsdale College, should be available. He is a doctor of philosophy in English literature, an experienced public relations speaker, and a college administrator. He is honest, clever, and a sound conservative. He is particularly strong on educational standards and policy—and an obdurate opponent [of the]

MEA and NEA. I have known him well for more than a decade, and commend him to you heartily.

Annette joins me in felicitations upon your marriage.[14] We do hope that in such leisure as you may enjoy for the next few years, you will not forget to let us entertain you both at Piety Hill.

Well done!

Cordially,
Russell

Letter to Stephen Cox

A professor of literature, Cox has written extensively on Objectivist writer Ayn Rand (1905–1982) and libertarian novelist and literary critic Isabel M. Paterson (1886–1961), a writer perhaps best remembered for her long-running weekly column "Turns with a Bookworm" in the New York Herald Tribune. *In 2004, Cox published a full-length study,* The Woman and the Dynamo: Isabel Paterson and the Idea of America *(New Brunswick, NJ: Transaction); fourteen years before this accomplishment, he wrote to Kirk to ask about any correspondence that might exist between himself and Paterson.*

November 30, 1990
Mecosta, Michigan

Dr. Stephen Cox
Department of Literature
The University of California, San Diego

Dear Dr. Cox,

For more than two months I have owed you a reply to your letter of September 27. The reason for the delay is that I set my people searching for those letters from Isabel Paterson; but as yet we have not discovered them. We shall continue to keep an eye out for them, and shall write or telephone people who might know where they are. Did Kenneth Shorey, after his 1965 letter send those Paterson letters to Mrs.

Hall?[15] I shall endeavor to inquire of him. It is rather a mystery; little else seems to be missing from the gigantic mass of my papers. The people at the Clarke Historical Library inform me that no Paterson letters are among the papers I have deposited with them.

I don't know whether you have a complete file of IMP's *Herald Tribune* "Turns with a Bookworm." I found in one of my journals a pasted-in copy of that of August 19, 1945; and I enclose a photocopy. I am the sergeant referred to, at some length, in this "Turns."[16] I will see if I can find any entries in my journal to the correspondence with IMP.

If you have any Kirk letters to IMP, I should be grateful for copies thereof, and of course would repay the cost of photostatting, etc.

Should you ever make your way to Michigan, I would be glad to entertain you here and talk about IMP. Meanwhile, you are very welcome to send me questions about our exchange of letters, etc.—not that I have any great stock of knowledge, for we two never met face to face. Below, I offer you some few recollections; and I mean to enclose a copy of a chapter of my memoirs (recently sent off to my literary agent) which will give you the background of the period of my correspondence with IMP.

As William Buckley once wrote, IMP was one of the "intransigents," unwilling to compromise about anything and reluctant to cooperate with anybody. (You might ask Buckley for some memoir of IMP.) Indeed she was thorny. After a lapse of some weeks or months in our correspondence, I mentioned, as a mere civility, that I was sorry not to have replied earlier to her most recent letter. To this, she retorted that I needn't be sorry: she didn't care whether I should write or not. In a later (my last) letter, I happened to mention that we ought not to suppose that most people are persuaded by pure reason. To this she answered angrily that she wouldn't waste her time corresponding with someone who didn't believe in rationality. I did not trouble her thereafter.

The God in the Machine I found a very good book; it influenced me; my copy has vanished. She commended to me Ayn Rand, otherwise unknown to me until many years later. Conceivably I might be able to bring out a new printing of *The God* in a series I edit for Transaction

Books, should Mrs. Hall consent and have a copy to lend; you might be so kind as to inquire of her.

I do wish you success with your writing about IMP.

Cordially,

Russell Kirk

Letter to James McClellan

A longtime law professor and political advisor to several conservative U.S. senators, McClellan (1937–2005) was a well-travelled polymath, conservative traditionalist, and authority on constitutional law. His first book, The Political Principles of Robert A. Taft—*cowritten with his friend Russell Kirk—was published in 1967 (New York: Fleet). By 1990, the book had been out of print for many years; but Kirk contacted Irving Louis Horowitz, president of Transaction Publishers, to discuss its republication.*

December 16, 1990

Dr. James McClellan
Richmond

Dear Jim,

Thanks for your letter of December 2. I enclose Horowitz's letter of December 4, concerning our *Taft*. I think he will publish the book and push it. The thing to do, I believe, is for you to write a fairly lengthy introduction along the lines you suggest in your letter, and for me to add anything I think of, after reading your draft.[17] As for the title change that Dr. Horowitz suggests, that would be all right, I suppose; though perhaps we had best make it *Robert A. Taft: His Politics and Principles*.[18]

Do you know what sort of subvention might be obtained from the Taft Institute? Purchase of copies? Money for advertising? You might inquire on our behalf.

Cecilia Abigail Kirk is in Rome now, happy if bewildered. Like Susannah, she is enchanted with St. Andrews; she has joined half-a-dozen clubs there.[19] She finds that everyone in the town knows, or knows of, her father.

Aye, John Engler, governor-elect of Michigan, is a conservative of the Kirk school, especially in the field of education. He is our friend and neighbor, and gave one of his first public addresses (when standing for the Michigan House) in our drawing-room. . . . I am writing a part of his inaugural address, which will be about the permanent things. He was first representative and then senator from our district. Michigan is supplanting Virginia as the bastion of the conservatives. We should take a Senate seat in 1992—if, indeed, we do not gain it by appointment considerably earlier.

Annette and I expect to make our way to St. Andrews about Easter; you people had best join us.

Cordially,
Russell

Letter to Annette Y. Kirk

The Feast of Saint Valentine
anno Domini 1991

To the most beautiful and loving of wifes,

In March or April we will climb St. Rule's Tower again together; first we climbed it in anno Domini 1962. Forty-three years have speeded by since first I toiled up those stairs.

Soon twenty-seven years will have passed since Annette Courtemanche gave me her promise true; and already three decades have passed since first I gazed upon her.

I have learned to love you better with every passing year, my 'Net. You gave yourself to me out of your goodness; but I have not always been good to you. You have laid up treasure in Heaven by your forgiveness of my surly temper.

So many of our kin and our friends have departed from time and place since you and I were together, Annette, at the Hotel Wellington and at Grove City! The very chapel where we were joined, and St. Michael's Church, and our original house of Piety Hill, have vanished like smoke.

Your parents' little house; our Lake Mecosta cottage; our ancient house of 40 High Street, Pittenweem; our Baldwin House of the Ks; my birthplace at Plymouth—all are ours no longer.[20] Change and decay in all around I see; O Thou who changeth not, abide with us. In the fullness of time, even my books will depart, and my papers.

Yet your Russell you will have with you always, my Persephone. We must have many more happy times together here below, my darling one, that those occasions of joy, where time and the timeless intersect, will be with us in eternity.

There are tears in my eyes just now, O Best Beloved, and I needn't tell you that words are tools that break in the hand. But I do love you, love you, love you; and will to the end of time and beyond.

Much love,
Russell

Letter to Anne Husted Burleigh

Author of the political biography John Adams *(New Rochelle, NY: Arlington House, 1969) and the spiritual memoir* Journey up the River: A Midwesterner's Spiritual Pilgrimage *(San Francisco: Ignatius Press, 1994), Burleigh is a frequent contributor of essays and reviews to* Crisis, Modern Age, *and other periodicals. In 1991, Kirk and publisher Irving Louis Horowitz considered her life of Adams for inclusion in the Library of Conservative Thought. Although Burleigh initially chose not to make the editorial changes Horowitz urged, eventually she revised the work, which Transaction Books published in 2009.*

June 20, 1991

Mrs. Anne Husted Burleigh
Cincinnati, Ohio 45244

Dear Anne,

I enclose a copy of a letter—received two days past, when Annette and I returned from Europe—from Irving Louis Horowitz, the able and sometimes sardonic publisher of Transaction Books and the Library of Conservative Thought. You will perceive that he is tempted to publish your *John Adams*, but would like some improvements. Horowitz's advice usually is very sound. Do you think you might find time to make such revisions and additions as he suggests? There would be no hurry, so far as the Library of Conservative Thought is concerned. The matter of superlative adjectives is easily remedied, of course. One always can improve a book by rewriting it; it is a question of finding the time for such a labor.

Sherwood Sugden, this month, is bringing out a new edition of my *Beyond the Dreams of Avarice* (1956), and early next year Regnery will publish a considerably-revised third edition of my *Roots of American Order*. Such revisions require much close work, of course, but I have found the chore worthwhile because it makes available to the rising generation studies which otherwise they might never have encountered.

At your leisure, do let me know your decision. Best wishes.

Cordially,

Russell

Letter to William F. Buckley Jr.

When Buckley began to prepare his manuscript "Why I Am a Catholic" (eventually published, in 1997 [New York: Doubleday], under the title Nearer My God: An Autobiography of Faith*) he approached nine respected Roman Catholic friends to ask their responses to nineteen key questions. Kirk replied at moderate length to each of Buckley's questions, providing key insights into his own Christian beliefs.*

March 10, 1992

Mecosta, Michigan

Mr. William F. Buckley, Jr.
National Review
150 East 35th Street
New York, New York 10016

Dear Bill,

You will find enclosed my response to your nineteen enquiries, in nineteen pages, for *Why I Am a Catholic*. I hope this document may serve your turn. Best wishes for your new book.

Annette and I are immensely busy running the Buchanan campaign in Michigan; we will know not long after you receive this letter whether we succeed in getting a higher percentage of the Republican vote in Michigan than he has received anywhere else. We travel about with his entourage most days, and have appeared together on various television programs and before several cheering youthful crowds. It is rather like the days of 1964. You should be with us. Shall we gather at The Breakers?

You now have among your henchmen the equivalent of Gore Vidal, I find: William Bennett, describing Buchanan as a Fascist. A man in a rural county of Michigan who had planned to put on a big affair for Mr. Buchanan called Annette and cancelled the program, having learned from Mr. Buckley's magazine that Mr. Buchanan was an anti-Semite. Annette informed him that Mr. Buckley had since denied meaning that, but the deserter from our cause refused to believe the retraction. "He wrote it right in the magazine." A considerable proportion of the Americans who take an active part in party politics, you will have noticed, are rather unpleasant eccentrics rejected elsewhere in society, but welcomed to party because they can supply a little money and a tolerable amount of volunteer work. Annette has sent several such packing.

I note that the *New York Times* is beginning to review my books again—I know not why. My next book out will be *The Politics of Prudence;* then *America's British Culture*. By the end of this year, some twenty-two or twenty-three volumes of my *Library of Conservative Thought* should be in print, published by Transaction.

Annette and I hope you are in tolerable health. The *Washington Post* now describes me as "the aging gray eminence of conservatism," but I am in better shape than I was a decade ago.

Su seguro servidor,

Russell

RESPONSES TO THE QUESTIONNAIRE ON RELIGION, MARCH 2, 1992, SENT BY MR. WILLIAM F. BUCKLEY, JR.

1. "Do you consider that the advent of the person of Jesus Christ is established beyond reasonable doubt?"

Reply: Nothing in the history of the ancient world is better established than the life of Jesus of Nazareth. We have four separate accounts by four witnesses, contemporaries; also the Epistles of Saint Paul, a brief account by the Jewish historian Josephus, and various mentions by Greek and Roman writers of Jesus and his followers. By contrast, of Socrates we have accounts by only two ancient writers, Plato and Xenophon, who knew him; and of some of the great men included in Plutarch's *Lives of the Noble Greeks and Romans,* we have inherited next to no account except Plutarch's own. It has been pointed out that it would be no more absurd to maintain that Napoleon Buonaparte was a figure merely of myth than to argue that a real Jesus never walked the earth. We even have the Shroud of Turin, almost certainly Jesus' burial-garment, with its scientifically-inexplicable image (like a photographic positive) on the linen. Nobody challenges the existence and the deeds of Augustus or of Herod, Jesus' contemporaries of his early years; why try to maintain that the Carpenter of Nazareth was a figment of the imagination, and that the Christian religion, which swept across the world, had no founder at all?

2. "In your judgment, is the evidence in the gospels that he committed miracles convincing?"

Reply: For Jesus' "Great Works" we have chiefly, of course, the Synoptic Gospels and certain traditions recorded in Eusebius' *History* and lesser gospels of the early centuries. Astounding wonders appear to have been worked. That nobody works such wonders near the end of the twentieth century of the Christian era is no reason for disbelief: by definition, miracles are rare exceptions to the ordinary operation of the laws of nature. See C. S. Lewis' little book *Miracles.* If the Word became flesh a second time, presumably such miracles as the Great Works would be beheld again. It is said that faith works miracles, and that miracles are worked in order to rouse up faith. Were miracles worked in medieval times at the shrine of St. Thomas Becket in Canterbury cathedral, or at the shrine of the bones of St. Andrew in St. Andrews cathedral, Scotland? And if so, why did those miracles cease to occur well before the coming of the Reformation? Is it perfect faith that conjures up the miracle? Why is it that no miracles have been recorded at the splendid shrine of the most wondrous of all relics, the Shroud of Turin, but a good many are said to have come to pass at the shrine of the girl-saint Bernadette Soubirou? Are miracles, like beauty, in the eye of the beholder? I do not doubt that Jesus worked his miracles; yet how long the results thereof endured, and whether what the witnesses beheld was physically "real," we have no means of knowing. O for a revelation!

3. "In your opinion, is Christ's resurrection critical to your faith? Critical to Christianity? If so, why?"

Reply: The Resurrection lacking, what we call Christianity would be a mere congeries of moral exhortations, at best; and exhortations founded upon no more authority than the occasional utterances of an obscure man whose hints of divinity and half-veiled claims of power to judge the quick and the dead might be regarded as the manifestations of delusions of grandeur. Many false prophets are gone forth into the world. It is no wonder that the Pharisees regarded with suspicion—nay, horror—the Nazarene who advised them not to resist evil. But the Resurrection in the flesh—which some now hint was bound up with nuclear disintegration and reintegration, our solid flesh being known now to consist of innumerable electrical particles, held in coherence by means of which we know nothing—proved that indeed Jesus the Son had transcended matter and was divine. Without that Resurrection, which prefigures our own resurrection and life everlasting, one might as well turn again to the gods of the Greeks, or to Epictetus, Marcus Aurelius, and Seneca. The Resurrection is critical both to my personal faith and to the whole elaborate edifice called Christianity. It is now more rationally possible to believe in the Resurrection than it was in Saint Paul's time: although he had perceived the risen Christ, much to his bewilderment, he could offer no explanation of how such a thing might be in this world of substantial things.

4. "How much importance do you attach to the 'uninventability' of Christ? (It was C. S. Lewis's contention that the life and in particular the preachings of Christ could not have issued from somebody merely human.)"

Reply: "He speaks as one having authority." Of this the Pharisees accused Jesus. Indeed, only a madman or a divine being could so have spoken. Anyone desiring imposture on a grand scale, or endeavoring to create a powerful (and deceptive) myth, would have told a neater tale, with the Gospels perfectly consistent one with another, and any implausibilities deleted, or perhaps otherwise shored up with greater detail. The claim to be the truth, the way and the life; to be the only channel through which a soul might pass to the Father; to confer the keys to heaven and hell; to open the gate to Paradise for the repentant thief—these and other passages, and especially the Sermon on the Mount, are too startling to have been invented—and soon to have been widely believed—by a mystagogue. The doctrine of the resurrection of the flesh and of the life everlasting was far more than any Orphic cult ever had suggested, and scarcely could have been accepted by Disciples and Apostles except for an overwhelming impression of wondrous knowledge and truth that those who had known Jesus of Nazareth had received from his presence and his words, and had communicated in turn to their auditors. Paul of Tarsus, and Peter the Fisherman, possessed intellects that would have detected imposture or fantasy.

5. "Was there one feature of the Catholic Church, distinguishing it from other Christian sects, that in particular drew you toward the Church? If so which was it? Or them?"

Reply: What I found in the Church was Authority. Catholicism is governed by Authority; Protestants, by private judgment. I had become painfully aware of the insufficiency of Private Judgment in the twentieth century—every man creating his own morals. In my search, over the years, for a sound apprehension of the human condition, I came at last to recognize in the Roman Church the elements of Truth, as sustained by two thousand years of continuity; by the wealth of wisdom in the Church's pronouncements; by the lives and words of Saint Augustine of Hippo and Saint Gregory the Great, particularly, among the Church Fathers; by Acton's observation, if you will, that no institution purely human could have survived, over the centuries, so many blunders.

I was not "converted" to the Church, but made my way into it through what Newman calls *illation*—fragments of truth collecting in my mind through personal experience, conversations, knowledge of exemplars, and much reading and meditating. (I was not baptized in any church until 1964, when I attained the age of forty-five years.) Mine was the god of the philosophers, Pascal notwithstanding (though I read Pascal, too), rather than the god of Abraham, Isaac, and Jacob. Father Hugh O'Neill, S.J., at the University of Detroit, who gave me some instruction during 1953–54, replied in answer to an inquiry of mine that most people seeking knowledge of church doctrines came to him out of some psychological distress or want. It was not so with me: rather, I still was seeking the source of wisdom.

6. "Was there one feature, or more, of the Catholic Church that kept you from joining it sooner than you did? If so, please say which, and a) explain why they antagonized you; and b) how you overcame that antagonism, if indeed you did."

Reply: Although nothing in doctrine or dogma in any way repelled me, I was not attracted by the rite of confession—not that in my unchurched years I was much given to committing deadly sins, mine being the sins of omission, chiefly. (One thinks of a line from an Edwardian comedy: "I'm afraid I was a very *good* young man; but I'm not sorry; for that has enabled me to be a very wicked old one.") Shy and self-sufficient, I resented being expected to open my smug heart to anybody. My wife remarks that I do not let anyone into my secret garden.

My attitude toward confession has not much improved since my baptism in the Church, although requirements for frequency of confession have diminished since then. But much more repugnant than the old sort of confession in some antique carven confessional is the latter-day notion—popular with "advanced" priests, especially those who rejoice in what they call the Jesus-centered liturgy (actually the priest-centered liturgy)—of the public or open or collective confession—reducing the sacrament to absurdity and hypocrisy.

I recognize now that confession fulfills a most important psychological function, as did the ritual ablutions of the ancient Greeks in some sacred river, washing away the haunting consciousness of grim guilt. But I refrain from confessing the outrageous sin of wandering thoughts at mass; that failing of mine is incurable.

7. "Looking back, is it your impression that you coasted in toward Catholicism? That the inevitability of your conversion became manifest, and you simply let matters take their course?"

Reply: Quite. Many people took it for granted that I was a practicing Catholic during the late 'Forties, the 'Fifties, and the early 'Sixties, because my writing appeared frequently in religious journals of a Catholic character on either side of the Atlantic in those years—*America, Commonweal, The Voice of St. Jude, Catholic World, The Dublin Review, The Month* (that magazine's most frequent American contributor), others. Also I contributed to Anglican, Methodist, and evangelical magazines. Yet although much interested in church history, theology, and religious aspects of humane letters, I felt no strong urge during those years to enter any communion. Like my Massachusetts ancestors of the seventeenth century, I remained an Independent, and content enough to linger on the Stoa, the porch of Christianity. Besides, the nearest church to my ancestral house at Mecosta was several miles distant; I was unmarried, and did not drive an automobile, and no public transportation existed in Mecosta County. Upon such accidents, great things in our lives may depend.

8. "Or was the ride bumpy? Were there periods during which you wondered, Yes or No to convert? What were the principal obstacles to your conversion, outside of anything touching on Catholic Christian teaching? For instance, a) family resistance; b) friends' resistance; c) pride in the religion you were leaving; or pride in the non-religious character of your outlook?"

Reply: The ride was untroubled. It sufficed me to reflect that great and good men, over the centuries—I thought of Samuel Johnson in particular—had examined Christian orthodoxy and found it good. Who was I to dissent from their judgments? Sir Thomas Browne, too, was among my favorite apologists; and C. S. Lewis; and Chesterton; and Father Martin D'Arcy.

At no time did I wonder whether I ought to resist my virtually effortless progress toward Popery.

The principal obstacle to my submission was my invincible indolence.

My affectionate kith and kin offered no resistance, although my father was a Mason, so was an uncle, and so my grandfather on the distaff had been. The family, or families, had fallen away from any recognizable form of Christianity generations before. I had no communion to depart from; nor had I any pride in any non-religious outlook, being favorably disposed toward the "higher religions" on the assumptions of Chateaubriand's book *The Genius of Christianity*.

9. "Would you be disappointed?—outraged?—defiant?—if the Church were to a) authorize non-celibate orders; b) withdraw its disapproval of birth control measures that don't require the use of abortifacients? C) authorize divorce and remarriage?"

Reply: I would not be disappointed, outraged, or defiant at such changes, although I would think them misguided. I set down below my reasons.

The marriage of members of the clergy was not forbidden in the early centuries of the Western Church, and is common to the present day in the Eastern Church. It is desirable that ecclesiastics should not marry—for one reason, they are better able, if celibate, to devote their lives to their pastoral duties—but already the twentieth-century Church receives as priests married Anglican priests who have come over to Rome. If not enough celibates can be found for the Church to carry on its mission nowadays, doubtless it will be found unnecessary to require celibacy for all of them.

The rhythm method of birth-control already being approved by the Church, it might be no very radical step to tolerate the use of contraceptives—not that I advocate aught of the sort.

Ease of Church annulment of marriages being notoriously loose nowadays, limited indulgence of divorce and remarriage would not be astounding—although I would not readily approve of it.

10. "In your opinion is the sex code of the Church integral to Christian practice, properly taught?"

Reply: Most certainly. Lechery is the most pervasive of the Seven Deadly Sins, in our time and our American land: the concupiscence of the flesh. Pornographic publications almost everywhere available; licentious television programs, films, and videos; prescribed "sex education" curricula of a secular-humanist character; the corrupted manners of the rising generation; the decay of the authority of parents—all these and other phenomena break down the norms of sexual conduct that have been imparted by Christian teaching for two millennia. Among the consequences of this decadence are hideous venereal diseases that spread across oceans, the damaging of the institution of the family, the creation of a proletariat of children conceived out of wedlock, the perversion of human beings' gift of procreation, and a sated sexual boredom and weariness that come from erotic excess.

A good many Catholic clergy and laypeople—parents especially—have been reluctant to take a stand on such matters, fearing lest they be thought "Puritanical" or "Jansenical." Such timidity is misguided. The rising generation needs to be instructed once more in the nature of the Seven Cardinal Virtues and the Seven Deadly Sins. Now and again one encounters young Catholic communicants who are quite unaware that the Church reproaches "premarital sex," for sound reasons.

11. "Would you favor a general return to the Latin Mass?"

Reply: Emphatically. Much was lost when the mass in the vernacular tongues triumphed. When first I encountered this unhappy innovation, I was aboard a German liner, crossing the Atlantic: my wife and I could not comprehend a German mass, and neither could any of the other passengers, it appeared. Unfamiliar forms of worship bring with them incertitude and doubt. The Latin mass, universal, made it possible for communicants of all nations to worship readily in common. All Catholics acquired some familiarity with the mother-tongue of the

Western Church—a knowledge that would serve them elsewhere than at church, too. The employment of Latin reminded Catholics of the antiquity and roots of the Church, inspiring veneration. For Africans, with their hundreds of different tongues and distinct dialects, the Latin mass provided a common patrimony. It softened linguistic and national rivalries—as between Flemings and Walloons, for instance, or Czechs and Slovaks. In America, it reminded people that Christianity is much more, really, than a religion of ephemeral sociability. What was good enough for the Western Fathers is good enough for me.

12. "Do you see in the new mass, departures from the Tridentine mass that are upsetting to you theologically?"

Reply: Yes, more's the pity. Here are some instances: The Holy Ghost has been transformed into the Holy Spirit. "Ghost" implies the supernatural; and modernists are alarmed by that; all they will tolerate is a vague Spirit, a *Zeitgeist*, the Spirit of the Age or the Spirit of Lake Success, etc.—a harmless and perhaps blameless sentiment, but silly.

"He descended into Hell" generally has been deleted from the Creed, in most churches. Advanced thinkers know that Hell doesn't exist, or that it's merely "mental torment"—which, as Stephen Leacock puts it, "nobody minds." An antidote to this silliness, by the way, is Robert Frost's poem "The Black Cottage," in which a minister had thought to please "our liberal youth" by omitting "Descended into Hades"—but changes his mind, learning that "Truths will come round again."

The woman who lost a *denarius* now is said to have lost a dime—which makes it appear that she must have been a frantic booby. But changes of that sort are trivial, by the side of such significant alterations as the reduction of " . . . and my soul shall be healed" to "I shall be healed"—in the flesh, one takes it. If the soul's existence is now dubious, why fret about unseen healing?

13. "Is it your opinion that the low quality of the English translations used in most masses is incomprehensible? Or is it a faithful reflection of the low cultural level of those who a) did the translations; and b) approved of them? Or do you believe that the John-Jane-Gyp prose

is a conscious effort by intellectuals some of whom, for all we know, are closet belletrists, to seek out a populist vernacular?"

Reply: When "born in a manger" becomes "born in a feed box" [and] appears in the liturgy or even merely in the Confraternity of Christian Doctrine classes, obviously translations or renderings, in large part, are being appropriated by persons quite humorless who do not well understand the rich English language. This is not to condemn all twentieth-century translations: Ronald Knox's has some high merits, and much of the Jerusalem Bible is worthy. But the "Priest's Bible" is truly execrable. Occasionally a new translation will make certain verses clearer: for instance, "Now we are looking into the riddle of a mirror" elucidates the more moving phrase perceiving "in a glass, darkly." But in general the Douay and King James versions do more to rouse the moral imagination. I do not find the inferior translations incomprehensible; rather, they are dully simplistic. Aye, their translators appear to be democratists and neoterists, self-righteously reducing solemn mysteries and noble language to the lowest common denominator.

14. "In your judgment, did the discontinuation of the distinctive Catholic rules on fasting and abstinence demoralize many Catholics? Or were these reforms overdue? Or, if you prefer, exactly due at the time they were promulgated?"

Reply: Whether or not Catholics were thus demoralized, certainly those requirements' abolition or radical modification diminished the distinctions between Protestants and Catholics, to the disadvantage of the latter. Far from being overdue, in our present era of decadence the better policy would have been to ask for stricter manifestation of adherence to Christian doctrines of atonement and resistance to the lures of the world, the flesh, and the devil. No horrid suffering resulted from abstaining from beef or pork on Fridays, nor any malnutrition. Abstinence during Lent produced the joys of Carnivale. In memory of Him who was crucified, such tokens of gratitude are very little to ask.

Behind this sweeping away of ancient observances lay the American Catholics' yearning to be "just like everybody else"—in this instance, to emulate Protestants in indifference to tradition and custom.

The same folk object to having their children wear uniform dress in Catholic schools, because "The Protestants don't have to do it." This is bound up with the silly persisting inferiority-complex notion that Catholics are second-rate Christians who must endeavor strenuously to become indistinguishable from Baptists, Methodists, and Presbyterians.

15. "If Pascal was right, that anyone who is looking for God will find him, does the opposite tend to be true? Or do you usually accept the notion that Grace will find its mark, quite irrespective of whether there is any complementary spiritual energy in that mark?"

Reply: I have known not a few men and women, brands for the burning, who have been depraved since their youth—indeed seemingly since infancy, in some cases. In Adam's fall we sinned all, as my ancestors' New England Speller put it. Some are made vessels for honor, others for dishonor. Grace will not enter into the souls of those who strenuously resist it and persist in attachment to the Seven Deadly Sins; some effort is required on the part of those who feel, if ever so faintly, a yearning to be healed. It may suffice to murmur, with Augustine, "O make me pure, O Lord—but not quite yet." But the eyes will not be opened to those muttering to themselves, "Evil, be thou my good." Stefan Andres tells us that "We are God's Utopia," and like Pelagius hopes for salvation, through grace in death, from the hideousness of our sins. But our instinct for justice, hereafter if not here, tells us that although Heaven might be deleted from Christian doctrine, surely Hell must remain, "built by primal Love," as Dante instructs us. I shed no tears of compassion over the punishment of the graceless depraved.

Your soul deserves the place to which it came
If having entered Hell, you feel no flame.

16. "If you had/have a child or a friend who has lost his faith, would you do more than merely pray that he will recover his faith?"

Reply: Prayer is made efficacious by works. But few persons—few adults, anyway, their egos and defensive mechanisms having been fully developed—are satisfactorily moved to a change of convictions or conduct by direct confrontation and dialectic by an officious well-wisher.

And sometimes the alleged "loss of faith" is trivial and ephemeral. My step-mother once announced abruptly, and with indications of distress, that she had lost her faith. We had not known previously that she had possessed any such, ever. We were tempted to ask her if it might have tumbled under the bed.

Chesterton instructs us that all life is an allegory, and that we can understand it only in parable. With children, I have found—and I have cheered a good many besides my own four—that the best means for restoring faith in a transcendent order is parable. Especially helpful in this have been MacDonald's *The Princess and Curdy*, Collodi's *Pinocchio*, Ruskin's *The King of the Golden River*, and Andersen's tale *The Snow Queen*. For adults—although one doesn't often read to *them* aloud—Lewis' most useful fable or parable, I think, is *The Great Divorce*. And much may be learned from pondering on what may seem an improbable choice, Conrad's *Victory*.

17. "In the book *Difficulties*, Arnold Lunn propounded to Ronald Knox difficulties he had as a non-Catholic with certain Catholic dogma and practices. He was especially resistant to the notion that God, postulated as omniscient, must know what will be the outcome of any overture to God—in behalf of the sick, of the endangered, or for that matter, the weather. Do you believe that free will is excluded by omniscience? Or do you believe that the apparent incongruity is nothing more than a comment on the limitations of human perception? Or does the subject trouble you?"

Reply: Much in heaven and earth must remain undisclosed by Horatio's philosophy or anybody else's philosophy. The Church recognizes the existence of mysteries. Milton's angels may debate eternally the questions of "free will, fixed fate, foreknowledge absolute," but I heed Alexander Pope's admonition "presume not God to scan." Perhaps the disciples of the Great Ox too greatly emphasize the Thomistic doctrine that Reason may discover so much—right reason, that is. It will not do to think of the Author of Our Being as a kind of computer, perpetually geometrizing (according to Spinoza) and answering pray-inquiries the answers to which are already set down, pre-computed, in

His awareness. That way lies human madness; for our ways, like Job's, are not His ways. We must assume that God very rarely suspends His own laws of nature; we cannot count upon private miracles in our private favor. Pursued far enough, Lunn's misgivings may lure us into the solipsistic prison-house of Mark Twain's *The Mysterious Stranger*.

18. "Are you troubled, as Lunn was, by a Bible that is at once accepted as divinely inspired, and yet is in so many respects inexplicable in the light of Christ's teachings? (E.g. the God-ordained destruction of entire towns, including women and children; that kind of thing.)"

Reply: Here Lunn risks falling into Marcionism, the second-century heresy that Yahweh (Jehovah) was the Demiurge, malignly afflicting the human race; and that Christ only was true God. (I am a member of a League against Marcionism.) The Old Testament is a record of the gradually-dawning apprehension of a beneficent but stern Supreme Being; to Him Judah and Israel attributed all the great successes or failures of their earthly experiences. But as the centuries pass and the prophets perceive more—or, to speak more orthodoxly, more Light is given unto them—by the time of the last of the major prophets, Isaiah II, God is known as the beneficent Creator who loves all mankind. Vengeance is His alone, but he does not direct man's inhumanity to man.

Much of the Bible is symbol and myth. (Myth is not *per se* falsehood.) Are we to take literally the parable of the Unjust Steward, so defrauding our employers? Nay, not so. Why then carpet-bomb Iraq and justify it by certain ferocities attributed by the Hebrew peoples to their early apprehension of a Divine Being? The sacred history called the Old Testament ought not to be read as if it merely chronicled certain events of long ago, their significance to be taken literally.

19. "When you joined the Church, did you anticipate that there would be moments when you would question your faith? If so, and/or if such moments arise, could you advise me what you do to fight for the retention of your faith?"

Reply: Being congenitally skeptical, I did anticipate moments when I might question my faith. "I believe, O Lord; help Thou my unbelief." My palliative is to remind myself of the words of Newman on Authority: "Conscience is an authority; the Bible is an authority; such is Antiquity; such are the words of the wise, such are hereditary lessons; such are ethical truths; such are hereditary memories, such are legal saws and state maxims; such are proverbs; such are sentiments, presages, and prepossessions." One hears, too, the echo of a voice from the expiring classical culture: "Believe what all men, everywhere, always have believed." In my erring reason's spite, can the words of reassurance uttered over the centuries by great and good men, prophets and sages and seers and doctors of the schools, be relied upon? Why, yes: it is not I who am omniscient.

(I have answered every question above at some tolerable length, though insufficiently: a mere affirmation or a mere negation would be of small avail, except in a mere poll of opinions; and even in such a mere poll of *doxa*, the meanings and motives of those persons who should submit the brief responses would differ much.—R. K.)

Letter to Thomas A. Braccio

Braccio was a longtime teacher from Upstate New York who wrote a letter to the editors of the Catholic magazine Crisis *inquiring about similarities between John F. Kennedy's famous "Ask not . . ." quotation to a passage from Orestes Brownson's works.* Crisis *forwarded Braccio's letter to Kirk, who responded as follows.*

August 16, 1992
Mecosta, Michigan

Mr. Thomas A. Braccio
Bainbridge, New York

Dear Mr. Braccio
    I have found in the labyrinth of my files a letter from you to the editors of *Crisis* (and forwarded from that office to me) dated January

14, 1991. In it you inquire about a sentence from Orestes Brownson's commencement address at Dartmouth College. It appears to me that your letter never has been answered—although possibly one of my assistants replied but did not make a copy of his letter to you. At any rate, I do reply now.

Although Brownson several times expressed the sentiment also expressed by President Kennedy in his inaugural address, I believe the clearest instances are to be found in [his] oration to the Gamma Sigma Society of Dartmouth College during commencement exercises on July 26, 1843. I have in mind particularly his concluding sentences: "Ask not what your age wants, but what it needs; not what it will reward, but what, without which, it cannot be saved; and that go and do; do it well; do it thoroughly; and find your reward in the consciousness of having done your duty, and above all in the reflection, that you have been accounted worthy to suffer somewhat for mankind."

Now during his successful campaign for the presidency and at the time of his inauguration, President Kennedy's most notable speechwriter was Professor Arthur Schlesinger Jr. Mr. Schlesinger's first book was about Orestes Brownson, and he has written about Brownson later, too. Brownson's Dartmouth address has been quoted by Schlesinger in his writings. In short, I infer that the phrases "Ask not what your country can do for you, but what you can do for your country" in the Kennedy address, Mr. Schlesinger borrowed directly from the commencement address of 1843, so well known to him. I doubt whether Kennedy himself had read anything by Brownson.

Cordially,
Russell Kirk

Letter to Hirotsugu Aida

Hiro Aida (1951–) is chief editorial writer at Tokyo's Kyodo News *and the author of numerous books. An admirer of Kirk, he visited Mecosta with his family in 1992. Shortly after that visit, he received the following letter from Kirk.*

December 28, 1992

Mr. Hiro Aida
Tamashi, Tokyo
Japan

Dear Mr. Aida,

How kind of you to send me the copy of *Ugetsu Monogatari*'s un-canny tales![21] I mean to read them during a trip to Detroit a few days from now. I have been fighting my way so far through the introduction by the American editor, which is somewhat verbose and overly stud-ded with footnotes, after the pedantic fashion of American graduate schools. But I can see that the tales themselves will compensate, and more than compensate for their editor's pedantry.

I am asking Transaction Publishers to send you a complimentary copy of my newest book, *America's British Culture*, published this pres-ent week. This is a counterblow to the silly but baneful "Multiculture" movement in the United States. Another book of mine, *The Politics of Prudence*, will be published soon.

I enclose a clipping about the question of whether the Ameri-can Air Force at one time meant to drop a nuclear bomb on Kyoto. A close friend of mine who had been an intelligence officer of the Royal Air Force (and who, although his mother was Japanese, had access to British, American, and (during the occupation) Japanese secret docu-ments, told me about 1948 that Kyoto had been scheduled for destruc-tion. I reproached the American government for thinking of such a thing, in the first edition of *The Conservative Mind*, or perhaps in the first edition of *Program for Conservatives*. (I must check on this.) If Henry Stimson prevented this, I now think much better of him than I once did.[22]

If I don't forget, I will enclose, too, an examination of Fukuyama's books by John Lukacs, that admirable historian.

Annette and our daughters and I do hope that someday Clan Aida will come again to our haunted house. Never have we had more

351

pleasant visitors. All's well here, except that dentists must set to work upon me once more.

Cordially,

Russell Kirk

Letter to Richard M. Nixon

Former First Lady Patricia Nixon died on June 22, 1993, after fifty-three years of marriage to the former president. Kirk, who had visited Richard Nixon in the White House on two occasions, wrote the following words of condolence to his old friend.

June 28, 1993

The Honorable Richard Nixon

Dear Mr. Nixon,

Not long after we were married, in 1964, Annette and I happened to dine with Father Martin D'Arcy, S.J., historian and Christian apologist. Annette earnestly inquired of that wise man what is meant by the words "In Heaven is no marriage or giving in marriage." Does this signify that beyond the jaws of death, husband and wife will be forever parted?

Father D'Arcy replied that Heaven is a state of being in which all the good occurrences and things of one's temporal life are eternally present, whenever the soul desires them; and present not merely in recollection, but in all their fullness. Thus the sacrament of marriage makes husband and wife one flesh beyond time. On the other hand, Hell is a state of being in which all the evil of one's earthly existence, inescapably[, is also eternally present].[23] I have been much moved by Martin D'Arcy's insights.

And so will it be with you and Pat. We human beings are meant for eternity. Beyond time and space, as we conceive those things in our feeble reason, you will know Pat always—and not in memory merely.

Her courage and loyalty through the course of your many tribulations will not be extinguished. *Amor dure.*

Cordially,
Russell Kirk

I enclose a piece of mine that you may not have seen—not a new essay—that suggests, among other things, certain similarities in the upbringing and early experiences of Richard Nixon and Russell Kirk.[24]

Letter to Andrea Kirk

The youngest of Russell and Annette Kirk's four daughters, Andrea was called "the Fire-Baby" by her father because she was conceived shortly before the Ash Wednesday Fire of 1975. As Kirk noted in his memoir, Andrea "turned out to be the merriest of the Kirk daughters, the most affectionate and creative" (432).

August 15, 1993

O dear daughter Andrea,

Presumably this is my last communication to you before you return to Piety Hill in all your youthful vigor.

I, on the other hand, am in all my aged decrepitude, and will be grateful for your aid and comfort as Literary Apprentice and Chief Gardener. I am indeed in decayed health; perhaps I may obtain good counsel at the Mayo Clinic—although I'd prefer the Mustard Clinic—but also it seems possible, *entre nous*, that my seventy-fifth year, supposing me to survive at least until October 19, may be my last year. I write this not to alarm you, but to prepare you. But how fortunate you, Andrea, and I are! If this is to be my final year here below, you and I will be together for it, writing and gardening and walking and reading and talking together, and you the most affectionate of daughters.

One of our principal tasks will be to finish converting the basement to a suite of offices, with many books and some files. The children's library must be transferred to Fay's cabin—where we can have bookshelves built—and part of it must be given to the Hillsdale College Library, together with other books of mine. You will be of much help in this selection. Then we must complete the season's gardening, including a little more grass-planting. . . . Also we shall do historical reading (including historical fiction) together, with much discussion; and we will initiate you into the art of being your father's literary successor here. How perceptive, by the way, you are about Thoreau! We will read Scott, Hawthorne, and Stevenson, the three great writers who influenced me most in my youth.

Together, the Wizard and the Fire-Baby will endeavor to insure that the Safe House of Piety Hill survives the distresses of our time and stands for the permanence and the pleasure of future generations of our family. So be of good cheer, Andrea Seton Kirk, your father's darling, and forget me not.

Much love,
Russell Amos Kirk
your father

Letter to Sally Cook

A longtime friend of the Kirks, artist Sally Cook presented the family with a whimsical oil painting depicting Russell Kirk seated in his library surrounded by cats.

October 21, 1993

Mrs. Sally Cook

Dear Sally,

We are about to hang the huge symbolic picture. The dozen cats are especially appreciated. We were catless for some months—nay, about three years—here; but now Andrea has supplied the deficiency, over her mother's protest, by bringing me an "indoor" cat for the library. Andrea is now a shepherdess—really and truly—on a farm between Mecosta and Remus, where there are cats to spare.

The painting is much admired, and we are grateful for it. What a labor you undertook!

This is a month of celebration of Kirk's Work and Kirk himself.[25] The next affair, a few days from now, will occur in Washington, from which city we have just returned: *Crisis* magazine and the Brownson Society will present me with an award, and I must present them with a short address. All these things are some compensation, I suppose, for now being three quarters of a century aged.

I enclose a copy of one of my more recent lectures. We often think of you, and hope that we may contrive to meet again.

Cordially,

Russell

Letter to Fred Douglas Young

A teacher at the Westminster Schools in Atlanta, Georgia, Fred Douglas Young wrote to Kirk in late 1993 while conducting research for a book he was writing on Richard Weaver. (This work was published in 1995 as Richard Weaver, 1910–1963: A Life of the Mind *[Columbia: University of Missouri Press].) At the time the following letter was written, Kirk's health was declining seriously; and within two months Kirk would be advised by his doctor to set his affairs in order.*

December 8, 1993

Mr. Fred Douglas Young
The Westminster Schools
Atlanta, Georgia

Dear Mr. Young,

It is pleasant to receive your letter of yesterday(!), to which I reply with a promptitude fairly unusual in your servant. I am confined to an upper floor of my house of Piety Hill, for a whole month, by illness; and this imprisonment may have been providentially ordained to compel me to make inroads upon my mountainous arrears of correspondence.

I enclose a lecture of mine about Donald Davidson; it is included in my recent book *The Politics of Prudence* (Intercollegiate Studies Institute). There will be a section on Richard Weaver in my lengthy memoirs, *The Sword of Imagination,* to be published by Eerdmans next autumn. I will have that section photocopied and sent to you tomorrow.

Richard Weaver distinctly *was* an original thinker, and not part of an alleged "conservative movement." He had only the slightest of acquaintance with William F. Buckley; and he never met James Burnham, I believe. His intellectual connections were with the Southern Agrarians, rather, although he had few personal relationships with them; most of them were a generation older than Weaver. He was brought to the attention of other conservatives chiefly by me—for instance, by my review in *Sewanee Review* of his *Ethics of Rhetoric* and Nisbet's *Quest for Community.*

When the University of Chicago Press published his *Ideas Have Consequences* (1948), I purchased a copy, found the book original and important, and featured copies of it in The Red Cedar Bookshop, East Lansing, Michigan, a shop I then owned. Not long later I invited Weaver to come to Michigan State to lecture to the George Ade Society, a discussion group that I had organized. I saw him in Chicago from time to time after that, and once he came to visit me at Mecosta, which he found more rustic and remote than Weaverville.

Of conservative writers in the 'Forties and 'Fifties, only Weaver discussed the relationship of Scholastic thought to our present discontents. I found both his first book and his later ones the work of an original and perhaps somewhat crotchety mind.

Such conservative writers as admired him had next to no personal acquaintance with him—Willmoore Kendall, for instance—nor did he attend any conferences in their company. He did participate in a Chicago conference that resulted in publication of the volume *A Nation of States* (a conference about federalism). James Jackson Kilpatrick, Father Francis Canavan, and I also participated, and like Weaver were invited as conservatives; so far as I know, he went to no other gatherings of the sort; at that conference, he shyly said next to nothing—not that I was garrulous.

At the University of Chicago, his acquaintance was confined pretty much to three friends: Canon Bernard Iddings Bell, then chaplain to Episcopalian students there; Edwin "Pongo" McClellan, now professor of Japanese literature at Yale, whom I had brought over from St. Andrews (a young man with an Ulsterman father and a Japanese mother); and Carl B. Cone, Burke's biographer, with whom Weaver breakfasted daily at International House.[26] (Weaver was not very well acquainted with Burke studies.)

Weaver felt a deep antipathy toward the varieties of Utilitarianism. Once he debated on Chicago radio Dr. Aaron Director, the University of Chicago economist, often called "conservative"; he found Director astoundingly arrogant and wrongheaded. Weaver had an agrarian's suspicion of great industrial and commercial corporations, and of financial speculation.

In short, Weaver I found to possess the greatest originality of mind to be encountered among conservative writers of that period. For that matter, he was the first of such writers, *Ideas Have Consequences* being published in 1948. My *Randolph of Roanoke* did not appear until 1951; my *Conservative Mind*, until 1953; Nisbet's *Quest for Community* in 1953; Francis Wilson's *Case for Conservatism* in 1951 or 1952.

Did you obtain earlier copies of my correspondence with Weaver? If not, you can get photocopies from the Clarke Historical Library, Central Michigan University, Mount Pleasant, Michigan. Let me know before you write, though, so that I can authorize the librarian there to produce copies for you.

Cordially,
Russell Kirk

Letter to Henry Regnery

Writing just a few months before his death, Kirk commends his old friend and publisher after reading his recently published study Creative Chicago: From The Chap-book to the University *(Evanston, IL: Chicago Historical Bookworks, 1993). At the time of this writing, Kirk was in poor health and mostly housebound, and the autumnal tone of his letter—itself pep-*

pered with strikethroughs and typographical errors—foreshadows his coming departure.

January 15, 1994

Mr. Henry Regnery
2960 Lake Shore Drive
Chicago, Illinois 60657

Dear Henry,

I have finished reading your *Creative Chicago,* and am much instructed thereby. How much of the old literary culture will survive this age of ours is uncertain; but I have my misgivings. In Chicago, as in every large American city, the crust of culture is thin and various ideological follies are eating away at it. The literature that I took to be the interest of everybody, when I was a little boy beside the railroad yards outside Detroit (much less cultured than Chicago), is now confined to a few; and the mad folk tenured at universities [remove it] from curricula. My daughter Cecilia asks me, "Dad, how do you know all these things?" There is much she hasn't read; nevertheless, she is a shining intellectual light among her contemporaries.

We wish to review *Creative Chicago* in the *University Bookman.* Would you, or Chicago Historical Bookworks, be so kind as to send a review-copy to—

Dr. Louis Filler
The Belfry
P. O. Box No. 1
Ovid, Michigan 48866.

He will enjoy your book and knows a great deal about its contents. Have you ever met him? When a small boy in St. Petersburg, he fled in 1918, taking the last train to freedom. He is now at least eighty-five years old, but turns out new books, and new editions of his older books, annually; he has a youngish wife and two small children. They dwell in a huge picturesque church, its various levels converted into house and library. Many thousands of books, some highly valuable, are stacked everywhere; I don't know how he finds anything in that confusion. America is his religion.

ISI had done a good job of selling my *Politics of Prudence*, despite having had no means of distributing it until after it was published and reviewed. I enclose a recent Heritage Lecture of mine that you may not have seen before.

I type this missive in my new study, formerly our chief guest-room, splendidly paneled in woods taken chiefly from demolished churches, and some of it from the former elevators of the Hotel Stevens, now the Conrad Hilton, Chicago. (The work was done by our John Mulcahy, formerly a building-inspector in Harlem; Annette brought him and his family to Mecosta.) I'll not return to my library down Franklin Street until spring. I see almost no traffic on M-20 outside my huge northern window. Out of the southern window I behold my five acres of large trees planted by myself, chiefly in 1963; they are heavily snow-covered, a pleasant sight. The temperature here is far below zero, and on the few occasions when I must leave the house I swathe myself in an anorak. I continue enfeebled, though ambulatory at a slow pace; my days of hill-walking and canoeing are ended, more's the pity. Had I never smoked cigars and consumed much chocolate, I might be vigorous still.

Annette is writing to you about your astounding gift. What a help! Now she can turn Feminist and leave me to my fate: no one ever gave her ten thousand dollars before. Henry Salvatori will be making me a grant of twenty-five thousand dollars to write what he calls a "monograph" on seven heroes of the Revolutionary period—what I call "conservative revolutionaries": it is mostly his idea. So we will be tolerably well off for a time. Next I must beg some money from foundations to carry on publication of *The University Bookman*, for which *National Review* no longer pays the bills. . . .

I now have ten whole days in which to try to come abreast of my arrears in correspondence; nobody is scheduled to visit us during this period. More another time. You will hear separately from Annette. Compliments to Eleanor.

Cordially,

Russell

Letter to James J. Novak

Severely weakened by congenital heart failure, Kirk dictated to Annette the following letter to James Novak—brother of the conservative Catholic writer Michael Novak—a little over a month before his own death. Novak was interested in learning if Kirk had ever written at any length on V. L. Parrington, a progressive historian best known for his influential three-volume study, Main Currents in American Thought *(New York: Harcourt, Brace, 1927).*

March 23, 1994

Mr. James J. Novak
Southbridge Towers
299 Pearl Street, Apt. 4H
New York, NY 10038

Dear Mr. Novak,

I am very pleased to have your letter of March 10th. I recall earlier meetings; one at an I. S. I. summer school, and other occasions. Having returned home after the affair at the Dearborn Inn, I collapsed physically. For three months I have been confined to my house, and to the second floor thereof, amidst the great snows of Mecosta. Some recuperation has commenced although I do not expect to travel anywhere.

I read Parrington during my freshman year in college, 1936. I most admired his scholarship but found myself in opposition to many of his views. Much earlier, at the age of eight, I obtained a copy of H. G. Wells' *An Outline of History,* and while fascinated by Wells' writings, I suspected him of being wrongheaded. So it was with Parrington. I admired the breadth of his learning and found his style felicitous. Some years later—about 1948—while writing *The Conservative Mind,*

I came to understand that Parrington stood in the tradition of Ralph Waldo Emerson but I in that of Nathaniel Hawthorne.

Sidney Gair, agent for Henry Holt and Company, asked me to write a conservative answer to Parrington—about 1940—and I purchased many books with a view toward doing that, but never found the time for the project. Recently I obtained a copy of a letter, previously unknown to me, by Donald Davidson to his New York publishers who had asked him to write an answer to Parrington. He recommended to them that I do so instead, that about 1952.

I have, however, no knowledge of writing about Parrington nor have I ever had the opportunity to study the influence of Trilling and Adorno in pulling down the old culture. I do hope you will persevere in your examination of that project.

Probably we will not be able to meet again at any public gathering, but I hope that Annette and I may be able someday to entertain you here at my house of Piety Hill in the wild of backwoods Michigan.

Cordially,
Russell Kirk
by Annette Y. Kirk

Acknowledgments

It is a great honor to publish a selection of Russell Kirk's letters; and such an undertaking would not be possible without the encouragement and generosity of Annette Y. Kirk, president of the Russell Kirk Center for Cultural Renewal and executor of her late husband's literary estate. As research for this volume commenced, she made available to me the images that grace the jacket and frontispiece of this volume along with the archives of Kirk's correspondence, going so far as to seek out private letters that had never been read by anyone outside her immediate family—and in two cases, letters that had never been read by anyone other than herself. This was an act of faith on her part, and it enabled me to make a fair, interesting, and revealing selection of her husband's letters. Thank you for making this possible, Annette.

I am grateful to James Piereson for a substantial grant that was most helpful in funding the travel and research essential to this project.

Generous fellowships from the Marguerite Eyer Wilbur Foundation also enabled me to complete this work in a timely manner, and I am grateful to have received them.

Thanks are rightly due to Carol A. Leadenham, assistant archivist for reference at the Hoover Institution Archives in Stanford, California. She provided essential help in locating and providing several key letters from Kirk to B. E. Hutchinson and other notable figures.

I benefited greatly from the advice and generous help of Bradley J. Birzer, author of the magisterial *Russell Kirk*: *American Conservative* (University Press of Kentucky, 2015). Professor Birzer discussed this project with me and shared his own Kirk-specific research during the early stages of my work, and I am thankful for the benefit of his expertise and labors.

In addition, welcome encouragement and suggestions were proffered by historian George H. Nash; Bruce Frohen, professor of law at Ohio Northern University School of Law; and Gleaves Whitney, director of the Hauenstein Center for Presidential Studies at Grand Valley State University. I am honored to call these gentlemen my friends.

To the supportive staff at the University Press of Kentucky who agreed to publish *Imaginative Conservatism* and then patiently worked with me through the editorial production process, many thanks!

Finally, I am deeply grateful for the encouragement and support of my wife, Lista, who patiently endured my being away from home while conducting research trips for the sake of this book and who accommodated the many hours her husband spent at home preparing this work for publication.

Notes

The 1940s

1. John Abbot Clark (1903–1965) was an associate professor of English at Michigan State who exercised a strong influence on Kirk. In *The Sword of Imagination*, Kirk described Clark as "a tall, lanky, humorous, melancholy man who had played football for the University of Missouri long before, and at Michigan State taught literary criticism and the history of criticism. . . . John Clark, who had read everything, had actually been published (a rarity at MSC then) in such periodicals as *Commonweal* and *The South Atlantic Quarterly*" (*The Sword of Imagination: Memoirs of a Half-Century of Literary Conflict* [Grand Rapids, MI: Eerdmans, 1995], 37). The two men, so similar in interests, became close friends and fellow members of the George Ade Society in East Lansing during the late 1940s.

2. Called "the dean of scholars in American and Southern literature" by Rayburn S. Moore, Jay B. Hubbell (1885–1979) was a longtime English professor at Duke University and the founder of the quarterly *American Literature*. He is perhaps best known for his acclaimed study *The South in American Literature: 1607–1900* (Durham, NC: Duke University Press, 1954). Kirk greatly respected him, considering Hubbell a true southern gentleman: gracious and learned. For his part, Hubbell thought highly of the precocious Kirk and expected the younger man to return to Duke after receiving his master's degree, in 1941, to pursue a doctorate. The onset of World War II, however, put an end to Kirk's short-term plans for further graduate study at Duke.

3. Kirk refers to the structure known today as The Inn at Teardrops, located on West King Street in Hillsborough, as the town became known in the late 1960s. Built in the mid-eighteenth century, the restored, impressively appointed building has served over the years as an inn, a hotel, a private residence, and (today) a bed-and-breakfast.

4. Republican presidential candidate Wendell Willkie (1892–1944) decisively lost the 1940 election to "the Country Squire," incumbent President Franklin Roosevelt. Kirk held a strong dislike for Roosevelt, whom he considered a high-toned demagogue and promoter of class envy.

5. This was William Marion Gibson (1904–1951), associate professor of political science at Duke during Kirk's year on campus and author of *Aliens and the Law: Some Legal Aspects of the National Treatment of Aliens in the United States* (Chapel Hill: University of North Carolina Press, 1941).

6. Rudolf Hess (1894–1987) was Adolf Hitler's deputy as leader of the Nazi Party in Germany. On May 10, 1941, he created an international stir when—without Hitler's knowledge—he flew to Great Britain and parachuted into Scotland as part of an ill-considered scheme to negotiate peace between the warring countries. Captured and treated as a prisoner of war, Hess was tried at Nuremberg after the war, convicted of war crimes, and spent the rest of his life in Spandau Prison, in western Berlin.

7. Kirk's friend and former instructor at Michigan State College, John Abbot Clark, had published *The College Book of Essays* in 1939 (New York: Holt). This work was a selection of exemplary essays spanning the centuries, from Plato to James Thurber.

8. In a letter to Kirk in mid-May, McCann had mentioned the plight of a mutual friend, an instructor at Michigan State, whose department superiors had forced him to reverse a failing grade he had given a student, despite the student having clearly earned a failing mark.

9. As undergraduates at Michigan State, Kirk and his friends poked gentle fun at the very name of this East Lansing institution, referring to it in conversation as "The People's Church—formerly God's."

10. Field Marshal Sir Claude Auchinleck (1884–1981) was a British military commander during World War II, seeing active duty in India, the Middle East, and North Africa.

11. Kirk refers to John Moore-Brabazon, Lord Brabazon of Tara (1884–1964) an English aviation pioneer and Conservative Party politician, whom Prime Minister Winston Churchill appointed to serve as minister of aircraft production in May 1941. He was forced to resign the following year, after declaring his hope that the German and Soviet armies—then engaged in the Battle of Stalingrad—would destroy each other. (With the Soviet Union an ally of Great Britain against the Axis at the time, Brabazon's remark was considered harmful to the war effort.) On May 28, 1942, he delivered the thirtieth Wilbur Wright Lecture, which Kirk references, in London.

12. The Women's Army Auxiliary Corps, a branch of the U.S. Army, was established in 1942. During World War II, members of the WAAC served

as switchboard operators, mechanics, bakers, postal clerks, drivers, stenographers, and clerk-typists.

13. Kirk referred to his mother as Mama; he called his maternal grandmother, Eva Johnson Pierce (1871–1953), Mom.

14. Kirk's father, Russell Andrew Kirk (1897–1981), had suffered a heart attack, which impaired his ability to work. He took months to mend and eventually retired from his longtime job with the Pere Marquette Railway.

15. Albert Jay Nock, *Memoirs of a Superfluous Man* (New York: Harper & Brothers, 1943), 276.

16. Ibid., 95.

17. Ibid., 249.

18. Pietro Badoglio (1871–1956) was an Italian general during both world wars. During World War II, he led Italian forces to victory in Abyssinia; but he resigned from the General Staff after the botched invasion of Greece in 1940. Three years later, with the Allies advancing on Rome, Badoglio joined with others in the Italian government in issuing a vote of no confidence in Benito Mussolini's government, leading to the surrender of Italy and the alignment of that nation with the Allies. In October 1943, Badoglio and the Kingdom of Italy declared war on Germany. Badoglio served as prime minister for another nine months, until Ivanoe Bonomi replaced him in mid-1944.

19. Leon Henderson (1895–1986) served as the administrator of the Office of Price Administration from 1941 to 1942, during the third Roosevelt administration. Controversial and widely unpopular, he was replaced in late 1942 and entered the private sector in a business career and was an occasional commentator on world affairs.

20. A scenic resort area of rolling hills and lakes in south-central Michigan, roughly fifty miles from his boyhood home in Plymouth.

21. Although remembered primarily as a poet, writer, and librarian of Congress, Archibald MacLeish (1892–1982) was also a key political figure in Democratic politics during Franklin Roosevelt's wartime administration. During World War II, he assisted in developing a branch of the Office of Strategic Services, the precursor to the Central Intelligence Agency. MacLeish also directed the U.S. War Department's Office of Facts and Figures and served as the assistant director of the Office of War Information, jobs heavily involved in developing and disseminating wartime propaganda.

22. Kirk refers to A. J. M. Smith's *Book of Canadian Poetry: A Critical and Historical Anthology* (Chicago: University of Chicago Press, 1943). Smith (1902–1980) gained fame as a member of the modernist "Montreal

Group" of Canadian poets but became a naturalized American citizen during his twenties. He became a professor at Michigan State College in 1936 (the same year Kirk entered MSC as a freshman) and served there until retiring in 1972.

23. Adrian "Red" Smith successfully negotiated the purchase of the ten-thousand-volume personal library of Justice Howard Wiest (1864–1945); and he and Kirk opened the Red Cedar Book Shop in East Lansing in 1946. They employed Kirk's sister Carolyn to serve as the store's sales clerk. The shop operated for roughly two years before closing its doors.

24. Percy Jones General Hospital, now closed, was located in Battle Creek, Michigan.

25. *Tomorrow* magazine (1941–1962) was devoted largely to works of psychic phenomenon, fantasy, and science fiction. In 1950, Christopher Isherwood's three-page rave review of *The Martian Chronicles* launched Kirk's friend Ray Bradbury into the limelight as a major writer.

26. A friend of both Kirk and McCann for many years, Dorson (1916–1981) was a distinguished folklore specialist who taught at Michigan State for many years, beginning in 1944.

27. Rosemary Virgo (née Ray) was a friend Kirk had known from his school days in Plymouth, Michigan. She traveled with Kirk to Britain for postgraduate studies and wanderings to interesting places; and for a time, it seems, Kirk believed he and "Rosy" might have a future together. While she drew back from developing a closer relationship with Kirk, she maintained a strong lifelong friendship with both Russell and his wife, Annette.

28. Sir D'Arcy Wentworth Thompson (1860–1948) was a Scottish mathematician and biologist who served as chair of natural history at the University of St. Andrews for over thirty years. He is best known for his authoritative zoological study *On Growth and Form* (Cambridge: Cambridge University Press, 1917).

29. The Tennessee Valley Authority (TVA) was a massive rural electrification program undertaken during the 1930s as one of President Franklin Roosevelt's programs designed to put people to work and alleviate poverty during the Great Depression. With a series of dams in the Tennessee River Valley and other floodplains throughout the American South, inexpensive electricity was brought to the homes of millions of people.

30. Kirk wrote affectionately and at length on John "Jack" W. Williams, professor of history at the University of St. Andrews (1929–1955), who oversaw the development of the work that eventually appeared as the first edition of *The Conservative Mind* (Chicago: Henry Regnery, 1953).

The 1950s

1. 873 Mill Street was the home of his late grandfather, Frank Pierce, in Plymouth's North End, where Kirk had spent most of his formative years.

2. Referencing Mecosta, Kirk means specifically the wooden frame house there called Piety Hill, which his great-grandfather built in the 1880s.

3. A native Scot, Thomson was one of Kirk's friends during his years studying at the University of St. Andrews. She attained a medical degree and practiced overseas and in a small town in the Highlands, where she resides to this day.

4. Lancaster was a renowned English cartoonist, whose early works were collected in such volumes as *Drayneflete Revealed* (London: John Murray, 1949) and *Façades and Faces* (London: John Murray, 1950).

5. Kirk means F. J. Shirley's *Richard Hooker and Contemporary Political Ideas* (London: Society for Promoting Christian Knowledge, 1949).

6. "Skyberia" was rejected by the *American Mercury* but accepted by *Queen's Quarterly,* where it appeared in the summer issue in 1952. The story was later published in Kirk's collection *The Surly Sullen Bell* (New York: Fleet, 1962).

7. This was Kirk's doctoral thesis, published as *The Conservative Mind*: *From Burke to Santayana* (Chicago: Henry Regnery, 1953).

8. Robert Maynard Hutchins (1899–1977) served as president and, later, during the mid-twentieth century, chancellor of the University of Chicago.

9. This was a private joke, its details now lost.

10. Henry Regnery had floated the idea of the need for a conservative quarterly. The prospect of such an undertaking was entirely in line with Kirk's own desire to found and edit a periodical in the tradition of the influential *North American Review* (1815–1940) or T. S. Eliot's *Criterion* (1922–1939).

11. John Henry Newman's essay "The Tamworth Reading Room," which originally appeared as seven letters written to the *Times* of London in February 1841, contains the following statement, which articulates a central belief of Kirk's: "The heart is commonly reached, not through the reason, but through the imagination, by means of direct impressions, by the testimony of facts and events, by history, by description. Persons influence us, voices melt us, looks subdue us, deeds inflame us. Many a man will live and die upon a dogma: no man will be a martyr for a conclusion."

The gist of Peel's "Address on the Establishment of a Library and Reading-Room" in the borough of Tamworth, Staffordshire, on January 19, 1841, is that secular literature and institutions stimulate reason, which holds the key to human fulfillment. Reason alone, Peel implied, points the way to

God—a stance that offended Newman, one of the foremost Christian writers of the nineteenth century.

12. It is known that Alexander III, King of Scotland, visited the laird of Yester Castle, Sir Hugo de Giffard on May 24, 1278. According to legend, on an earlier occasion the king rode to Yester and encountered Sir Hugo—a reputed warlock and necromancer—emerging from the subterranean Goblin Ha' (or Hobgoblin Ha,' which can still be seen today), dressed in a sorcerer's garb: an encounter immortalized in Sir Walter Scott's poem *Marmion* (1808). Alexander asked Sir Hugo to foretell the outcome of a coming battle with Haakon IV, King of Norway, whose troopships were standing off the Firth of Clyde. While declining to answer this request, the wizard told the king that if, at midnight, he would go to a specific spot some four miles away and sound his trumpet, he would behold an "elf": the ghostly semblance of his worst enemy, who could tell him the battle's outcome. At midnight, Alexander did as instructed and was confronted by the wraith of the King of England, Edward I, who in later years became Scotland's worst enemy. After a short, bloody struggle, Alexander struck down the "King of Elfland," who declared that Haakon would be overcome. Shortly thereafter, Scotland's army drove off the Norwegians after an inconclusive battle, and Haakon's successor later negotiated the Treaty of Perth with Alexander.

13. In this paragraph, Kirk shows early evidence of what became a lifelong penchant for using somewhat archaic sentence structures ("Many an adventure had I") and little-used but highly descriptive words (such as "ogival," "douce," "bogle," and "syne"), often Scottish in origin.

14. James Burnett, Lord Monboddo (1714–1799) was a Scottish philosopher and judge who is remembered today as one of the founders of modern comparative historical linguistics and—in the eyes of some scholars—a developer of early concepts of evolution.

15. Kirk explains his remark about "roofs coming off" in the final paragraph of this letter.

16. Hermann Schnitzler (1905–1976) was a distinguished German art historian whom Regnery had met as a young man. Schnitzler exercised a profound formative influence on Regnery, introducing him to the best in Western art and music. In Regnery's words, Schnitzler "helped me appreciate what the human spirit is capable of achieving as well as to give direction and purpose to my life."

17. Knopf eventually wrote to Kirk indicating that he would publish his work if Kirk were willing to cut the manuscript's length in half. Kirk was indignant at this demand, retrieved his manuscript from Knopf, and sent it to Regnery, who published it in May 1953 as *The Conservative Mind: From Burke to Santayana*. (In his memoir *The Sword of Imagination: Memoirs of a Half-*

Century of Literary Conflict [Grand Rapids, MI: Eerdmans, 1995], 148), Kirk claimed that "for years Knopf would resent bitterly Kirk's having taken back the typescript from him.")

18. Regnery never published Quennell's *Spring in Sicily*, nor did he discuss the matter with representatives from the UK publisher, Weidenfeld & Nicolson

19. Eliot and Kirk had discussed the possible need to make slight revisions to the final chapter of *The Conservative Mind* to place less emphasis upon George Santayana, whom Eliot had known and did not consider a conservative figure. (Thus, the Faber & Faber edition, published in 1954, appeared simply as *The Conservative Mind*, without the subtitle affixed to the American edition: "From Burke to Santayana.")

20. D. J. B. Hawkins reviewed the Faber edition of *The Conservative Mind* for *Month* 12 (October 1954): 237–39; and P. N. N. Synnott assessed it for the *Dublin Review*, no. 467 (First Quarter 1955): 98–101. The *Fortnightly Review* did not review the book, while an unsigned critique of the American edition, written by Denis William Brogan, appeared in the *Times Literary Supplement*, July 3, 1953, 427. Eliot lamented this last-mentioned development, telling Kirk that it seemed unlikely the TLS would be willing to review Faber & Faber's edition after having already treated the earlier edition.

21. Hollis's favorable review of *The Conservative Mind* had recently appeared in the Catholic *Tablet* 202 (August 22, 1953): 174–75.

22. It was nearly twenty years before *Eliot and His Age* appeared, published by Random House in February 1972 (though with a 1971 copyright date).

23. Kirk refers here to a work he presumably began but for which no manuscript exists.

24. Robert A. Nisbet, *The Quest for Community* (New York: Oxford University Press,1953). This work is often grouped among the remarkable clutch of conservative books published in the early 1950s, along with William F. Buckley Jr.'s *God and Man at Yale* (Chicago: Henry Regnery, 1951), Whittaker Chambers's *Witness* (Chicago: Henry Regnery, 1952), and Kirk's *The Conservative Mind* (Chicago: Henry Regnery, 1953).

25. Reinhold Niebuhr, *Christian Realism and Political Problems* (New York: Charles Scribner's Sons, 1953). Kirk was not, in fact, given the opportunity to review this book, though he maintained a lifelong respect for Niebuhr's thought. One of his final published writings was a laudatory review of Charles C. Brown's *Niebuhr and His Age: Reinhold Niebuhr's Prophetic Role in the Twentieth Century* (Philadelphia: Trinity Press International, 1992) and *A Reinhold Niebuhr Reader* (Philadelphia: Trinity Press International, 1992), edited by Brown. This review appeared a few months after Kirk's death, in *Modern Age* 37 (Fall 1994): 73–75.

26. Despite Kirk's reservations about the quality of his review, Eliot was impressed by its perceptiveness and wrote to Kirk in appreciation, saying that he found it surprising that a reviewer could apprehend so much of a play's essence after viewing only one performance and without a text at hand.

27. Bonamy Dobrée's review, "*The Confidential Clerk,* by T. S. Eliot," appeared in the *Sewanee Review* 62 (Winter 1954): 117–31.

28. F. A. Harper (1905–1973) was an American economist of the Austrian School who helped found the Foundation for Economic Education in 1946.

29. Frank Chodorov (1887–1966), an influential libertarian writer and editor, founded ISI in 1953. William F. Buckley Jr. (1925–2008) served, for a short time, as the organization's first president.

30. Kirk sent as an enclosure a copy of his essay "The Ethics of Censorship," which had recently appeared in *Shenandoah* 5 (Spring 1954): 3–17.

31. Victor Cousin (1792–1867), French philosopher whose theories, derived from the eighteenth-century school of common-sense realism, influenced French educational theory.

32. Kirk met Patricia Owtram, a British poet and (eventually) television producer with the BBC, during his years at St. Andrews University. They maintained a relationship for a short time, though eventually they parted amicably because of the distance between them.

33. Leo Wolman (1890–1961) was an American economist, government official, university professor, and supporter of Jewish rights in Israel. His political positions were staunchly opposed to President Franklin Roosevelt's New Deal policies and the expanding rights and activities of labor unions. Suggested by Wolman, Kirk's "The Debacle of the Fabians" appeared in the June 28, 1954, issue of the *Freeman,* a monthly journal then edited by Frank Chodorov.

34. Journalist and essayist Garet Garrett (1878–1954) was a libertarian journalist and essayist whose work stressed the need for the United States to remain true to its founding principles as a republic of limited government, avoiding adventurism overseas. His best-known work, *The People's Pottage* (Boston: Americanist Library, 1953), is a collection of three long, prescient essays. Regnery published Garrett's *The American Story* in 1955.

35. Chodorov, who was associated with the original *Freeman* (1920–1924), edited by Albert Jay Nock as well as that magazine's later incarnation during the 1950s, became editor of *The Freeman* in 1954.

36. At this time, Cyprus was in the early stages of an anti-British program of violence by Greek Cypriot nationalists. Acts of violence grew in intensity throughout 1955.

37. Kirk's assessment of *The Heresy of Democracy* by Lord Percy of Newcastle appeared in the fifth number of the new conservative periodical *National Review* 1 (December 11, 1955): 29–30.

38. Robert Maynard Hutchins (1899–1977) served for many years as president, and later chancellor, of the University of Chicago. According to Robert Morse Wooster, Hutchins was "a man who combined political liberalism with traditional views on education." He was affronted that Kirk's study *Academic Freedom* contained a substantial section on his removal of W. T. Couch as director of the University of Chicago Press in November 1950. A friend whom Kirk much admired, Couch had been released after the publication of Morton Grodzins's *America Betrayed: Politics and the Japanese Evacuation* (1949), a well-documented history of America's internment of Japanese Americans during World War II. University colleagues of Hutchins had complained to him, and Couch was eventually terminated for being "in open conflict with the senior officers of the administration" over the matter.

39. Kirk had sent Eliot a copy of the Regnery edition of *A Program of Conservatives* (1954), hoping Eliot would convince Faber & Faber to publish a UK edition. The editorial board at Faber eventually declined to publish the work, with Eliot writing Kirk to deliver the disappointing news.

40. Eliot declined the invitation to contribute to *Collier's Encyclopedia*, to which Kirk contributed fairly regularly during the 1950s.

41. Kirk's essay "The American Intellectual: A Conservative View" appeared in the Autumn 1955 issue of the *Pacific Spectator* and was reprinted in his essay collection *Beyond the Dreams of Avarice* (Chicago: Henry Regnery, 1956).

42. This remark about Buckley is written in response to Buckley's harsh review of Kirk's *Academic Freedom*, which appeared in the July issue of the *Freeman*. In a portion of *Academic Freedom*, Kirk had taken issue with a point Buckley made in *God and Man at Yale* (Chicago: Henry Regnery, 1951): that professorial viewpoints antithetical to Christian dogma do not constitute protected speech and should be duly considered by administrators and alumni when determining whether to retain university employees.

43. W. C. Mullendore (1892–1983) was chairman of the Southern California Edison Company and a longtime, outspoken supporter of conservative causes.

44. At the time this letter was written, Kirk and Henry Regnery had succeeded, after much effort, in lining up several financial backers to fund their long-discussed new quarterly, the "Conservative Review." But someone—and Kirk was convinced it was Meyer and Chodorov—sent to each of those same backers copies of the July 1955 issue of the *Freeman*, containing Meyer's sustained attack on Kirk, titled "Collectivism Rebaptized," presumably in an

effort to diminish Kirk and steer funding away from the *Conservative Review* and toward Buckley's soon-to-be-launched periodical, *National Review*.

45. Arthur M. Schlesinger Jr., "The New Conservatism: Politics of Nostalgia," *Reporter* 12 (June 16, 1955): 9–12; Peter Viereck, "The Rootless 'Roots': Defects in the New Conservatism," *Antioch Review* 15 (June 1955): 217–29.

46. Kirk was optimistic. The "Conservative Review" did not commence publication until the autumn of 1957, under the name *Modern Age*.

47. Contrary to Kirk's wishes, Buckley listed Kirk as an editor on *National Review*'s inaugural masthead. Kirk immediately protested, and Buckley removed his name but retained his services as a regular contributor for the next twenty-five years.

48. After resigning from the University of Chicago in 1951, Hutchins became president of the newly established Ford Foundation. In this position, he steered millions of dollars into causes and foundations that interested him. The Fund for the Republic, for example, was founded with a $15 million grant from the Ford Foundation in 1952, with Hutchins serving as president and noted progressive W. H. Ferry as vice president. In Wooster's words, "Hutchins and Ferry thought they would use the Fund for the Republic to fight McCarthyism, but in hindsight the fund's chief function was to place a 'kick me' sign on the foundation's front door and invite conservatives to comply."

49. In 1955, the Fund for the Republic published a work called *Bibliography on the Communist Problem in the United States*, edited by Charles Corker, with a foreword by Clinton Rossiter. This annotated work lists roughly five thousand books and shorter publications on communism and leftism in America.

50. The Congress of Industrial Organizations (CIO) was an alliance of industrial labor unions in the United States and Canada that flourished from 1935 until 1955. At that time, the CIO joined the American Federation of Labor to form the AFL-CIO.

51. Kirk refers to the CIO's Political Action Committee (CIO PAC), which provided financial backing to CIO-endorsed political candidates and supported pro-labor legislation. and the National Education Association (NEA), the nation's most powerful teachers' union.

52. Kirk refers to the introductions he wrote to Regnery's Gateway editions of Orestes Brownson's *Selected Essays* and Friedrich Gentz's *The French and American Revolutions Compared*, both published in 1955.

53. The ellipses here are Kirk's own.

54. Kenneth W. Colegrove (1886–1975) spent ten years of his long and varied academic career as a professor of history at C. W. Post College. The proposed Institute of Politics, which Colegrove was to head, never came into being.

55. Wilhelmsen's article "History, Toynbee, and the Modern Mind: Betrayal of the West" appeared in the inaugural number of *Modern Age,* the summer issue of 1957. Davidson's initial contribution to the periodical, "General Jackson," appeared in *Modern Age* 2, no. 4 (Fall 1958), an issue devoted entirely to American southern culture.

56. David Lindsay, 28th Earl of Crawford and 11th Earl of Balcarres (1900–1975), was a longtime friend of Kirk. He and his wife, Mary, frequently entertained Kirk at their sixteenth-century manor, Balcarres House, during his stays in Scotland.

57. Cairns (1904–1985) was an American author, literary scholar, and attorney who served in several key positions within the National Gallery of Art from 1943 to 1965. During the 1950s, he entertained the idea of establishing a post-graduate academic-research college in the United States similar in scope and prestige to Oxford's All Souls College. In this regard, Cairns was responsible for the creation of the Center for Hellenistic Studies in Washington, DC, in 1961.

58. As Kirk noted in his memoir *The Sword of Imagination,* Eliot replied, in February 1957, that he examined several of O'Connor's short stories when he had last been in New York "and was quite horrified by those I read. She has certainly an uncanny talent of high order but my nerves are just not strong enough to take much of a disturbance" (182). With wry irony, Eliot added later in the same letter, "I do not like being terrified. Apart from the general aversion to prose fiction which I share with Paul Valéry, I like pleasant, sunny comedies such as I write myself."

59. Perhaps a reference to *Hamlet,* Act I, Scene 5, in which the prince complains that "time is out of joint." Kirk believed that for the most part, movies and "movie people" tended to cheapen and degrade noble things for the entertainment of the masses, just as Hamlet lamented the "cursed spite" that he had lived to see evil times.

60. This line from one of Kirk's favorite poems, Samuel Johnson's "The Vanity of Human Wishes," properly reads, "A petty fortress, and a dubious hand."

61. Molnar's article, often reprinted, appeared in *Modern Age* 2 (Winter 1957–1958): 33–39.

62. A few years after Kirk wrote this letter, Molnar indeed published *The Decline of the Intellectual* (Cleveland, OH: World, 1961) and *The Future of Education* (New York: Fleet, 1961), the latter containing a foreword by Kirk.

63. In 1958, University of Chicago chancellor Lawrence Kimpton held up publication of the *Chicago Review*'s year-end issue because it contained lengthy excerpts from the writings of Jack Kerouac and William Burroughs's *The Naked Lunch,* which some readers deemed inappropriate, if not obscene.

64. Cousins (1915–1990) was the longtime editor of the *Saturday Review,* the successor to the *Saturday Review of Literature,* which Henry Seidel Canby had launched in 1924.

65. Having retrieved this article from the *Saturday Review,* Kirk published it in the January 4, 1960, issue of *Christianity Today.*

66. Coincidentally, the editorship of *Modern Age* passed from Kirk to former Yale University Press editor Eugene Davidson (1903–2002), mentioned in another context three paragraphs earlier.

67. Gerrit E. Van Wissink served as business manager of *Modern Age* during its early years. In that role, he performed numerous editorial responsibilities, given that the magazine's working staff otherwise consisted of only Kirk, Collier, and Regnery.

68. With Kirk's knowledge, and, indeed, encouragement, W. T. Couch (editor in chief at *Collier's Encyclopedia* and former director of the University of Chicago Press) contacted Regnery to commend du Berrier as a writer of integrity and skill whose recently spiked article on Vietnam would be a most worthwhile contribution to *Modern Age.*

69. This article by Hilaire du Berrier (1905–2002) was never published in *Modern Age,* though a fair taste of the writer's outlook on the growing crisis in Vietnam may be found in his "Report from Saigon," which was published in the September 1958 issue of the *American Mercury.* Born in North Dakota, du Berrier was a colorful character: a barnstorming pilot, smuggler, and all-around daredevil who worked for a time as a double-agent during the Spanish Civil War and as a journalist in Vietnam.

70. Cates (1924–2006) was a Paris-born American biographer best known for his lives of George Sand, Friedrich Nietzsche, and André Malraux. His article "Integration in Algeria," though accepted for publication by Kirk, was never published in *Modern Age.*

71. The Bookmailer was a small New York–based publisher and mail-order distribution house run by former CIA agent Lyle H. Munson, who published short general-interest books along with anti-Communist works.

72. Kirk's review-article on Roger A. Freeman's books *School Needs in the Decade Ahead* (Washington, DC: Institute for Social Science Research, 1958) and *Federal Aid to Education: Boon or Bane?* (Washington, DC: American Enterprise Association, 1955) indeed appeared in the Fall 1959 issue of *Modern Age.*

The 1960s

1. Separately, Kirk and Cheney visited Ireland at the same time in early 1960 but were unable to meet during their travels abroad.

2. This book, containing Kirk's essay "The Inhumane Businessman," was published in 1965 as *The Intemperate Professor and Other Cultural Splenetics*, by the Louisiana State University Press (Baton Rouge).

3. Kirk had published a piece titled "The Mont Pelerin Society" in the October 21, 1961, issue of *National Review*, in his regular column, "From the Academy." In this article, Kirk took the society to task for its evolution into a forum characterized at times by a marked hostility toward the Christian faith as a source of guidance in one's views of money, wealth, and markets. In response, Mont Pelerin Society members Aaron Director, Milton Friedman, and George J. Stigler cosigned a letter published in *National Review* on December 1, 1961. In it, they politely took Kirk to task for presenting "no doubt inadvertently, a misleading picture" of the society.

4. Kirk's friend Wilhelm Roepke (1899–1966) played an influential role in the economic recovery of Central Europe during the years of reconstruction after World War II. A founding member of the Mont Pelerin Society, he served as the society's president from 1961 to 1962 but quarreled recurrently with Hayek. In 1962, he stepped down from the presidency and ended his association with the society.

5. Kirk reviewed *Freedom and Serfdom: An Anthology of Western Thought*, edited by Albert Hunold (London: Springer, 1961) in the March 13, 1962, issue of *National Review*.

6. In early January 1962, Kirk attended a two-day meeting in Palm Beach, Florida, with Buckley, Jay Gordon Hall, and several others for a strategy session with Senator Barry Goldwater. This meeting was held during the early stages of the Goldwater-for-president movement, though Kirk would later write that the meeting "cannot be said to have accomplished much." He recorded this impression in *The Sword of Imagination: Memoirs of a Half-Century of Literary Conflict* (Grand Rapids, MI: Eerdmans, 1995), 257.

7. *The Surly Sullen Bell: Ten Stories and Sketches, Uncanny or Uncomfortable, with a Note on the Ghostly Tale* (New York: Fleet, 1962).

8. The strange story of the miser "Jingo Cracky" formed a considerable portion of Kirk's ghost story "Fate's Purse," which appeared in the *Magazine of Fantasy and Science Fiction* in 1979.

9. Kirk was the ghostwriter of two speeches on Goldwater's behalf: one delivered to the student body at the University of Notre Dame on February 6, 1962, the other delivered to the student body at Yale University on April 18, 1962.

10. A successful Michigan businessman, political figure, and philanthropist, Bentley (1918–1969) established the Alvin M. Bentley Foundation in 1961 to promote academic excellence in the State of Michigan.

11. Kirk likely sent Pournelle a copy of a speech he had written on Goldwater's behalf and which the Arizona senator had delivered at the University of Notre Dame on February 6, 1962. In this speech, which touches on themes central to the writer's thinking, Kirk wrote,

> Man was made to know God, and enjoy Him forever. Man is not a thing, but an immortal essence. And freedom, ordered liberty, is man's birthright; for without true freedom, man could not choose between good and evil; he could not become fully human; he would remain, at best, childish. There exists a natural order for man, with natural rights. Worldly powers and dominations are not morally entitled to treat man as a pawn in a social Chess-game: the masters of the state have no right to deal with human beings as if they were animals—no right to manipulate and alter and liquidate human persons."

12. Kirk, "The Mood of Conservatism," *Commonweal* 78 (June 7, 1963): 297–300. This essay was reprinted in Kirk's *Confessions of a Bohemian Tory* (New York: Fleet, 1963).

13. The following year, 1964, Pournelle completed his doctoral dissertation, titled "The American Political Continuum: An Examination of the Validity of the Left-Right Model as an Instrument for Studying Contemporary American Political 'Isms,'" at the University of Washington.

14. For roughly eight years, the subject of individualism had been a minor point of contention between Kirk and his friend William F. Buckley Jr. In *Academic Freedom* (Chicago: Henry Regnery, 1955) Kirk had taken Buckley to task for championing the mutually contradictory doctrines of the Christian faith (with its emphasis upon community) and individualism (with its emphasis on the autonomous self) in *God and Man at Yale* (Chicago: Henry Regnery, 1951). "I personally agree that the first of these is a good thing, and I think that Mr. Buckley knows what he means by it," wrote Kirk. "I do not agree that 'individualism' is a good thing, and I do not think that Mr. Buckley knows what he means by it."

15. Kirk refers to the Foundation for Economic Education, a libertarian economic think tank headquartered in Irvington-upon-Hudson, New York, and publishers of the long-running libertarian magazine the *Freeman* (1950–2016).

16. "Immanest" is a neologism coined by Kirk, and it refers to people who seek to "immanentize the eschaton," in Richard M. Weaver's phrase. That is,

an "immanest sectarian" is someone who seeks (through positive legislation and legal coercion) to bring into being the perfection of humankind, which requires in fact an inner, spiritual change that properly belongs to God alone.

17. Russell Kirk, *Randolph of Roanoke: A Study in Conservative Thought* (Chicago: University of Chicago Press, 1951).

18. Russell Kirk, *Confessions of a Bohemian Tory: Episodes and Reflections of a Vagrant Career* (New York: Fleet, 1963).

19. "The Death of Theatre" was written, but there exists no evidence that the book was ever published.

20. The presidential hopes of Senator Barry Goldwater (R-AZ) were at their highest in mid- to late 1963. But the assassination of President John F. Kennedy in November of that year effectively ended Goldwater's chances, with the American electorate rallying around the slain president's successor, Lyndon B. Johnson, to finish his work.

21. In his memoir *The Sword of Imagination,* Kirk describes at length his first encounter with Annette Courtemanche at a conservative-themed conference held at New York's Wellington Hotel in February 1960. At the time, she was a junior at Molloy Catholic College for Women and was on the conference agenda to speak on Kirk's *The American Cause.* Shortly after the conference, Kirk described the seminar in his *National Review* column, mentioning Annette as "surely the most beautiful champion of conservative doctrines ever found" (8 [March 12, 1960]: 171).

22. Russell and Annette were married later in 1964, at Our Lady of the Skies, Idlewild Airport's Catholic Chapel, New York.

23. Kirk refers here to Annette along with her older brother, Regis, and her younger sister, Marie.

24. Kirk refers to Henry James's short story "The Real Right Thing," originally published in 1899 and republished in *The Novels and Stories of Henry James*, vol. 17 (London: Macmillan, 1921).

25. Mickie Teetor and her husband, Charles (Chuck), lived in Manhattan and had been Kirk's friends since the mid-1950s. During visits to New York for *National Review* editorial meetings—and later, for visits with Annette's family on Long Island—he was a houseguest at the Teetors' downtown apartment.

26. There is a story behind Kirk's use of the term "ritualistic kisses." In October 1963, he had taken an extended trip to Europe and North Africa along with his friend Thomas Molnar. In *The Sword of Imagination* Kirk recalls: "When Annette greeted him in Long Island on his return from foreign parts, he kissed her hand, after the Austrian fashion. She was mildly embarrassed: 'What is this ritual?' Not long later, Kirk sent her a copy of

Jessie Weston's book *From Ritual to Romance,* which augmented her suspicions about Russell's attentions and intentions—as if there could have been any reasonable doubt" (288–89).

27. Despite Kirk's assurance of its imminent publication, this book did not appear for several years, and then under a new title: *Enemies of the Permanent Things* (New Rochelle, NY: Arlington House, 1969).

28. Russell Kirk, *A Creature of the Twilight: His Memorials* (New York: Fleet, 1966).

29. Best known as a big-band leader and superb clarinetist during the 1930s and '40s, Shaw (1910–2004) was also a writer of some renown after his retirement from music in 1954. His short-lived intent to promote the filming of *Old House of Fear* (New York: Fleet, 1961) never came to fruition.

30. As Kirk noted in *The Sword of Imagination,* "The popular prejudice against Goldwater on the trigger-happy issue was so powerful as to outweigh prejudices in his favor on some other issues. Cheskin predicted the margin by which Goldwater would lose; as matters turned out, Goldwater on November 7 would do a little better, although not much, than Cheskin had estimated. Once elected, Lyndon Johnson would become far more trigger-happy in Vietnam than ever Goldwater would have thought of being" (301).

31. The lengthy article Kirk wrote for Shapiro appeared in the *New York Times Magazine* on August 7, 1966, under the title "New Direction in the U.S.: Right?"

32. Publication of "Balgrummo's Hell" was delayed until July 1967, when it appeared in the *Magazine of Fantasy and Science Fiction.* It was later reprinted in the collection *The Princess of All Lands* (Sauk City, WI: Arkham House, 1979).

33. In the months before the birth of their first daughter, the Kirks learned that Annette's attending physician would not accept cash payment for his services; he preferred to be paid with food that could be given to the poor of Mecosta County. To compensate him, the Kirks obtained two yaks from a Western agency that sold such animals. Arriving in Mecosta County, the yaks flourished on a bison ranch near the Kirks' home. After the birth of Monica Kirk in 1967, the animals were given to the doctor who had delivered her.

34. The play *Dandelion Wine,* based on Bradbury's beloved novel, enjoyed a short run at the Lincoln Center's Forum Theatre in April 1967. Christopher Votos starred as the story's central character, Douglas Spaulding.

35. The first of Russell and Annette Kirk's four daughters, Monica Rachel, was born July 23, 1967.

36. Kirk refers, first, to *The Political Principles of Robert A. Taft* (New York: Fleet, 1967), a work he cowrote with his friend James McClellan. "The

Recovery of Norms" became the lengthy opening section of Kirk's *Enemies of the Permanent Things*.

37. Kirk touches on this strange episode in his chapter on Bradbury in *Enemies of the Permanent Things*, 120.

38. A week before the writing of this letter, the Nigerian Civil War erupted. The two-and-a-half-year war was caused by tribal, ethnic, economic, and religious tensions between the Igbo people of the small breakaway Republic of Biafra and the Hausa, Fulani, and Yoruba people of Nigeria.

39. Kirk wrote this letter while the Six-Day War (June 5–10, 1967) was in progress. Israel defeated the combined forces of Egypt, Syria, and Jordan.

40. In a letter to Kirk on August 9, Regnery had expressed a view of Eric Voegelin's thought as profound and of great importance, but burdened by the thinker's turgid writing style. He suggested the need for a book by a Voegelin authority who could render Voegelin's ideas with clarity, thereby creating an important and perhaps influential book.

41. Kirk refers to *The Pope and the Council* (London: Rivingtons, 1870), a work cowritten by Johann Joseph Ignaz von Doellinger and Johannes Huber under the joint pseudonym "Janus." This work argued against the doctrine of papal infallibility, which was dogmatically defined at the First Vatican Council in 1869–70. John Courtney Murray (1904–1967) was an American Jesuit priest and theologian. He was especially known for his writings that focus on the relationship between the democratic modern state and the limits of religious freedom. Regnery never had the opportunity to follow through on Kirk's suggestion, for Murray died two days after this letter was written.

42. Avon Publications, a paperback firm, published the fourth revised edition of *The Conservative Mind* in 1968.

43. "What Killed the Civil Rights Movement?" appeared in the inaugural issue of *Phalanx* (Fall 1967) and was later reprinted in *Willmoore Kendall Contra Mundum*, ed. Nellie Kendall (New Rochelle, NY: Arlington House, 1971).

44. Bishirjian (1942–) is an American academic who studied under Gerhart Niemeyer and Eric Voegelin at the University of Notre Dame. He has published many professional essays and reviews in the field of political theory and is the author of *The Conservative Rebellion* (South Bend, IN: St. Augustine's Press, 2015). Currently Bishirjian is president and professor of government at Yorktown University. Beginning in autumn, 1968 he studied for a year with Oakeshott at the London School of Economics and worked on his doctoral dissertation on Thomas Carlyle and nineteenth-century gnosticism.

45. Northrop Frye, "The Knowledge of Good and Evil," in *The Morality of Scholarship*, ed. Max Black (Ithaca, NY: Cornell University Press, 1967), 3.

46. The full sentence from Burke's *Reflections on the Revolution in France*, 12th ed. (London: Macmillan, 1890), reads: "We know that *we* have made no discoveries, and we think that no discoveries are to be made, in morality,— nor many in the great principles of government, nor in the ideas of liberty, which were understood long before we were born altogether as well as they will be after the grave has heaped its mould upon our presumption, and the silent tomb shall have imposed its law on our pert loquacity" (83).

47. In his memoir *The Sword of Imagination*, Kirk attributes "the ineptitude of the Goldwater organization" to the effective takeover of the senator's campaign by a clique of politically tone-deaf handlers led by William Baroody, who marginalized Kirk, Buckley, Jay Gordon Hall, and other conservative spokesmen who had been among Goldwater's early circle of supporters and speakers on behalf of the senator's candidacy.

48. Fiery segregationist and American Independent Party candidate George C. Wallace (1919–1998) in fact carried five southern states and tallied forty-six electoral votes. Democrat Hubert H. Humphrey (1911–1978) carried thirteen, and Republican Richard M. Nixon (1913–1994) won thirty-two states, crushing Humphrey in electoral votes (301–191) but edging him by only 1 percent of the popular vote.

49. Salinas (1926–2014) was a politician, writer, and historian whose work specializes in the history of Bolivian independence as well as relations between Bolivia and Chile.

50. A longtime California political figure, Finch (1925–1995) served as Nixon's secretary of health, education, and welfare (1969–1970) and counselor to the president (1970–1972).

51. This was published as *Eliot and His Age: T. S. Eliot's Moral Imagination in the Twentieth Century* (New York: Random House, 1971).

52. Kirk refers here to a small house he owned at 40 High Street in Pittenweem, Fife. He and Annette stayed at this house during their periodic visits to Scotland, renting it to trusted friends and acquaintances between times.

53. Married for over fifty years, John and Joanne Emmons were longtime friends of Russell and Annette Kirk. Over time, Joanne was elected to a succession of positions in public office, eventually becoming a state senator, representing a sizeable swath of Michigan's central Lower Peninsula.

54. As a guest of the Lorimers, Kirk spent many pleasant days at Kellie Castle, north of Pittenweem, from the time of his postgraduate studies at St. Andrews until Hew and Mary Lorimer sold the castle to the National Trust for Scotland in 1970.

55. Within a short time, Kirk indeed sold 40 High Street, to meet the expenses of a growing family.

56. Monica is Hew and Mary Lorimer's daughter.

57. Kirk here refers to Hew and Mary Lorimer's eldest son and daughter-in-law.

58. The National Trust of Scotland opened the estate to the public as a shrine to the artwork of Lorimer and his family: Hew's father, Sir Robert Lorimer, was a renowned architect who designed the Scottish National War Memorial. Hew's wife, Mary Wylie McLeod, was a painter of note.

59. Kirk, "Nixon after Six Months: Six Appraisals," *New York Times Magazine*, July 20, 1969, 5.

60. Kirk, "Wilson: Abstraction, Principle, and the Antagonist World," *Confluence* 5 (Autumn 1956): 204–15.

The 1970s

1. The United States Information Agency (USIA) was a federal agency that existed from 1953 until 1999. It was primarily a publishing and broadcasting apparatus designed to present pro-Western, pro–free market news and information to readers and listeners in the Soviet Union and other Communist-ruled nations. The essay Kirk references is a portion of "The World of Ray Bradbury," which had appeared in *Enemies of the Permanent Things* (New Rochelle, NY: Arlington House, 1969).

2. Eliot's ashes are interred beneath an oval memorial stone in the Parish Church of St. Michael in East Coker, Somersetshire. The stone is inscribed with lines from the poet's "East Coker": "In my beginning is my end" and "In my end is my beginning." Visitors are enjoined to "Pray for the repose of the soul of Thomas Stearns Eliot, Poet."

3. St. Michael's Catholic Church on the outskirts of Remus, Michigan—a few miles east of Mecosta—was the parish church Russell, Annette, and their children attended. The earthly remains of Annette's parents (Regis and Mary Courtemanche), the Kirks' hobo-butler Clinton Wallace, and Kirk himself are interred in the church cemetery.

4. Henry Lorimer (1939–2011) was the son of Kirk's friend Hew Lorimer (1907–1993), the renowned Scottish sculptor. Despite Kirk's misgivings, Henry served successfully in the world of commerce, working for thirty years at a brewery, then as the Scottish director of wine merchants Justerini and Brooks.

5. As quoted in Kirk's memoir, *The Sword of Imagination: Memoirs of a Half-Century of Literary Conflict* (Grand Rapids, MI: Eerdmans, 1995): "'Heaven is a state,' D'Arcy told Annette, 'in which all the good things of your life are present to you whenever you desire them'—not in memory merely, not somehow re-enacted, but present, beyond the barriers of time, in all their

fullness. Thus husband and wife would experience in eternity, when they should will it, what they had experienced within mundane time, linear time; and human creatures, resurrected, will have perfected bodies.

"But Hell, Father D'Arcy continued, is a state of being in which all the evil one has done is eternally present—and there is no escape from it. So it is that human creatures make their own destiny, their own Heaven and their own Hell" (341).

6. A two-day symposium on Voegelin's thought was held at the University of Notre Dame, April 29–30, 1971. Participants at the symposia and lectures included such esteemed academicians as Walter Berns, Stephen Tonsor, Dante Germino, and Gerhart Niemeyer, among others, with the final speaker being Voegelin himself.

7. *The Southern Review* n.s. 7, no. 1 (1971) was a special Henry James issue. Pride of place among its articles was given to Voegelin's essay "*The Turn of the Screw*," which appears on pages 9–48.

8. Voegelin, "On Hegel—A Study in Sorcery," *Studium Generale* 24 (1971): 335–68; republished in *The Collected Works of Eric Voegelin;* vol. 12, *Published Essays, 1966–1985,* ed. Ellis Sandoz (Baton Rouge: Louisiana State University Press, 1990).

9. Kirk refers to *A History of Political Theory* (New York: Holt, 1937) by George Holland Sabine of Cornell University. This authoritative work traces the history of political theory from the era of Plato to the age of Hitler and Mussolini.

10. In a speech before midwestern news executives on July 6, 1971, Nixon said, in part, "I think of what happened to Greece and to Rome and, as you see, what is left—only the pillars. What has happened, of course, is that great civilizations of the past, as they have become wealthy, as they have lost their will to live, to improve, they then have become subject to the decadence which eventually destroys a civilization." He added, "The United States is now reaching that period. I am convinced, however, that we have the vitality, I believe we have the courage, I believe we have the strength out through this heartland and across this Nation that will see to it that America not only is rich and strong, but that it is healthy in terms of moral strength and spiritual strength." Kirk was to gently remind a discouraged Nixon of the essence of these remarks in a meeting in the White House in 1972. (The transcript of this speech is available online at the *American Presidency Project:* "Remarks to Midwestern News Media Executives Attending a Briefing on Domestic Policy in Kansas City, Missouri," July 6, 1971, http://www.presidency.ucsb.edu/ws/?pid=3069.

11. Innergellie is a handsome country house located outside Kilrenny, Fife.

12. Robert Sencourt, *T. S. Eliot: A Memoir* (New York: Dodd, Mead, 1971), 59.

13. Lady Ottoline Morrell (1873–1938) was a noted English aristocrat, society hostess, and patron of distinguished artists and writers. She conducted a salon for the members of the Bloomsbury Group at her country house; Garsington Manor; provided early financial sponsoring for T. S. Eliot's periodical the *Criterion* for several years; and befriended the likes of W. B. Yeats, Duncan Grant, and Siegfried Sassoon, among many others.

14. As a gift appropriate for someone living in Michigan, with its long cold season, Margret Christie had woven a pastel-colored lap robe for Annette's sister, who lives a short distance from Mecosta.

15. Schiff was the publisher at New York's Fleet Publishing, which printed Kirk's *Old House of Fear* and *A Creature of the Twilight* during the 1960s.

16. At this time, Collier was shopping the yet-unpublished *Roots of American Order* among several publishers. Kirk hoped that Random House, with which he had enjoyed cordial relations during its handling of *Eliot and His Age*, would be interested in his new book. Eventually Random House passed on the opportunity, and Open Court published the work in 1974.

17. *Eliot and His Age* would be published in early February 1972 to largely favorable reviews.

18. According to Kirk's memoir *The Sword of Imagination*, Stephen Shadegg (Goldwater's campaign manager for Arizona) was also present at this gathering.

19. Kirk, "Conservatives and Fantastics," *America* 106 (February 17, 1962): 643–45.

20. Kirk, "Conformity and Legislative Committees," *Confluence* 3 (December 1953): 342–53. Though not mentioning McCarthy by name, Kirk made it quite clear who he had in mind in this critique of the conformist mind. At one point he writes, "Loyalty cannot be forced, any more than love. The patriotism which is the product of fear or of self-interest is truly the last refuge of the scoundrel. We may prosecute for perjury one man who swears fidelity to the state, and then breaks his oath; but positive law cannot create loyalty" (342). The young Henry Kissinger edited *Confluence* at Harvard University, where he was working toward his PhD in political science at the time.

21. Kirk refers to the Foundation for Economic Education (FEE), a libertarian economic think-tank and longtime publisher of the *Freeman*.

22. Kirk, "The Debacle of the Fabians," *Freeman* 4 (June 28, 1954): 695–98. Kirk inserted the blank underscore in this sentence as a placeholder because he could not remember the surname of the *Freeman*'s managing editor in 1954, Florence Norton.

23. John Cardinal Newman, *Newman's "Apologia Pro Vita Sua": The Two Versions of 1864 and 1865* (Oxford: Oxford University Press, 1913), 333.

24. T. S. Eliot, introduction to Pascal's *Pensees* (New York: E. P. Dutton, 1958), xi.

25. The reviews in question were written by liberal friends of Kirk: Charles Lam Markmann's review appeared in the *Nation*, March 27, 1972, 409–11, while William C. McCann's was printed in the *Progressive* 36 (April 1972): 48–50.

26. Chaimowicz contributed the essay "Die Wiederentdeckung Burkes" (roughly "The Rediscovery of Burke") to the anthology *Rekonstruktion des Konservatismus*, edited by Gerd-Klaus Kaltenbrunner (Freiburg: Rombach, 1972), 389–407.

27. Muggeridge, review of *Eliot and His Age, Esquire*, November 1972, 79.

28. The Kirks' efforts came to naught when the U.S. Supreme Court's landmark *Roe v. Wade* decision effectively overturned any remaining abortion restrictions in all fifty states.

29. T. S. Eliot, *Notes towards the Definition of Culture* (New York: Harcourt, Brace, 1949).

30. Gantkowski (1903–1989) was a Polish-born filmmaker who fled the Soviet occupation of his homeland and lived for most of his life in exile in the United States, working as an instructor at Pepperdine University. Best known for the bittersweet wartime documentary *Kraj Mojej Matki*, translated as *Land of My Mother* (1943), he knew and respected Kirk and continually urged him to write *The Roots of American Order*, hoping an American producer would do a film adaptation of the book. Annette Kirk has stated that Kirk wrote *The Roots of American Order* primarily because of Gantkowski's persistence in urging him to do it.

Jameson Campaigne Jr. (1940–) has worked in conservative politics and publishing for his entire adult life. Having helped found the Philadelphia Society and worked for the Henry Regnery Company during the 1960s, he joined Open Court Publishing Company as manager of its scholarly book division in 1973. Three years later, he formed his own publishing company, Green Hill Publishers (now Jameson Books).

31. To Kirk's disappointment, Ford selected former New York governor Nelson Rockefeller (1908–1979) as his vice president. To Kirk and other conservatives, Rockefeller represented the sort of thoughtless, rudderless, country-clubbish politician who is at home in the liberal wing of either of America's two major political parties.

32. Republican Richard Lugar had served as mayor of Indianapolis since 1968. He ran unsuccessfully against incumbent Senator Birch Bayh in 1974

but won a senate seat in his next outing against another incumbent Democrat, Vance Hartke, in 1976.

33. Kirk had arranged for a set of galleys to be sent to Richardson in the hope that he would write a blurb for the back cover. Richardson was impressed with *The Roots of American Order* and commended the volume as "enormously impressive both in the scope of its learning and in the cogency of its exposition."

34. Other contributors of blurbs included Gerhart Niemeyer, George Carey, Malcolm Muggeridge, John Chamberlain, Robert Speaight, and several others.

35. During the Ford administration, Richardson served as the U.S. ambassador to the Court of St. James.

36. Rockefeller endured a largely contentious confirmation process and was confirmed as Ford's vice president on December 10, 1974.

37. In the story, the appearance and life story of the protagonist, Frank Sarsfield, was based on the Kirks' "burglar-butler," Clinton Wallace.

38. W. Clement Stone (1902–2002) was a self-made millionaire in the Horatio Alger mode, a philanthropist, and an advocate of positive thinking, which he termed "Positive Mental Attitude."

39. Forrest D. Hartmann served as the attorney for Arkham House, while Roderic Meng was the publisher's longtime operations manager.

40. The collection *The Scallion Stone* was published in 1980 by the small but highly respected Whispers Press (Chapel Hill, NC), with an introduction by Kirk.

41. This project never came to fruition.

42. Boardman's authoritative study, *Between Heaven and Charing Cross: The Life of Francis Thompson*, appeared in 1988 (New Haven: Yale University Press).

43. Boardman had heard, indirectly, of a small, vocal movement of "Pentecostal Catholics" living and working in Ann Arbor, Michigan, primarily among the student body of the University of Michigan. This was the Word of God community, which flourished during the 1970s and emphasized a blend of Roman Catholicism and such Charismatic gifts as speaking in tongues.

44. *The Letters of Wyndham Lewis*, ed. W. K. Rose (Norfolk, CT: New Directions, 1963).

45. Actually, the two pieces Kirk mentions are basically one and the same. His death notice of Lewis, published in *National Review* in 1957, was revised slightly and published in *Confessions of a Bohemian Tory* in 1963.

46. Stone was the author of a two-part study: "The Ideas of Wyndham Lewis," *American Review* 1 (October 1933): 578–99; and "The Ideas of Wyndham Lewis, Part II," *American Review* 2 (November 1933): 82–96.

47. A scholar who has written much on Lewis, Wagner is perhaps best known for *Wyndham Lewis: A Portrait of the Artist as the Enemy* (New Haven: Yale University Press, 1957).

48. In an earlier letter, Leander informed Kirk that recently, while rummaging through a storage closet in his house, he had discovered a case of thirty-two first-edition copies of his *Humanism and Naturalism*. He sent them to Kirk, asking that the copies be distributed to those persons and institutions that would most clearly value them.

49. Kirk's review of Ayer's *Part of My Life: The Memoirs of a Philosopher* appeared in the June 11, 1978, issue of the *Birmingham News*.

50. A frequent contributor to LewRockwell.com, Franke is the longtime director of Liberty Press, the book-publishing arm of Liberty Fund. Despite his mildly sarcastic remarks on Franke's entreaty, Kirk was quite pleased with the quality of the third revised edition of *John Randolph of Roanoke* that Liberty Press published in 1978.

51. Regnery took Kirk's advice and made this suggested change.

52. The story Kirk wrote and submitted, "Watchers at the Strait Gate," appeared in *New Terrors*, edited by Ramsey Campbell in 1980 (London: Pan Books) and was reprinted in Kirk's own collection *Watchers at the Strait Gate* in 1984 (Sauk City, WI: Arkham House).

53. Kirk has confused two stories he wrote within a few weeks of each other. "Lex Talionis" actually appeared not in a collection by McCauley but in *Whispers II*, edited by Stuart Schiff in 1979 (New York: Doubleday). McCauley published Kirk's "The Peculiar Demesne" in his *Dark Forces: New Stories of Suspense and Supernatural* Horror in 1980 (New York: Viking). Both stories were reprinted in Kirk's *Watchers at the Strait Gate*.

54. "The Companion" is one of Campbell's outstanding early horror stories.

55. Kirk's short story "The Peculiar Demesne," featuring the intriguing protagonist Manfred Arcane, was published alongside fiction by Joyce Carol Oates, Richard Matheson, Ray Bradbury, Stephen King, Theodore Sturgeon, and several others in 1980 in the award-winning anthology *Dark Forces*. Four years later, it was published as "The Peculiar Demesne of Archvicar Gerontion" in Kirk's own collection, *Watchers at the Strait Gate*.

56. Before publication in 1979, Kirk and St. Martin's Press agreed on the title for this, the author's final novel: *Lord of the Hollow Dark*.

57. Good to his word, Kirk produced the additional stories that rounded out his second collection, *The Princess of All Lands*, published by Arkham House in 1979.

58. Williams (1925–1985) was a British professor of English, journalist, and cultural critic best known for his study *Trousered Apes* (London: Churchill Press, 1971), which examines the destructive effects of nihilistic modern literature and theater on Western culture. A frequent visiting professor at colleges and universities in the United States, he, like Kirk, sometimes served as a visiting professor at Hillsdale College.

59. A mutual friend of Kirk and Hoffman, as well as a fellow Burke scholar, Gaetano ("Tom") Vincitorio (1921–2007) was a longtime professor of history at St. John's University in New York City who specialized in modern European history.

60. Nothing came of this publishing endeavor.

61. Leonard Gilhooley, ed., *No Divided Allegiance: Essays in Brownson's Thought* (New York: Fordham University Press, 1980). Kirk's contribution to this volume is titled "Orestes Brownson and T. S. Eliot" (163–74).

62. Kirk reviewed Stassinopoulos's book *After Reason* in the June 10, 1979, issue of the *Birmingham News,* whose book-review editor was Kenneth Shorey, a former Kirk assistant.

63. While Kirk was a champion of the free-market economy, he detested the word "capitalism," with its origins in the literature of Karl Marx.

64. *Democracy and Leadership* was originally published in 1924, in London by Constable & Co.

65. Neither Farrell's letter nor a response from Kirk are extant in the archives at the Russell Kirk Center in Mecosta. In a review published in *Western Political Quarterly* in 1954, Kirk wrote,

> Babbitt himself was surprised at the fierce animosity his books provoked among naturalists and men of the Left; they seem to have recognized in him and in More their most intelligent and courageous opponents. This hatred, hardened into dogmas of negation, lingers on. In a recent number of *Confluence,* Mr. James T. Farrell denounced Babbitt as the arch-priest of 'traditionalism'; but it was apparent to anyone familiar with Babbitt's work that Mr. Farrell simply did not know what Babbitt actually believed.

66. In his study *The Demon of the Absolute* (1928), More, Babbitt's friend and another proponent of literary humanism, famously described Dos Passos's novel *Manhattan Transfer* as "an explosion in a cesspool"—an assessment derided by enemies of the New Humanism and embraced by literary traditionalists.

67. Both the *Nation* and he *Progressive* had favorably reviewed Kirk's *Eliot and His Age*, perhaps in part because the reviewers—Charles Lam Markmann and William C. McCann—were on cordial terms with Kirk, with McCann being a politically liberal friend of Kirk since the latter's days as an undergraduate at Michigan State.

68. American historian Barbara W. Tuchman (1912–1989) was long associated with the leftist *New Statesman* magazine and best known for her work *The Guns of August* (1962).

69. Nearly seven months after this letter was written, *The Princess of All Lands* and *Lord of the Hollow Dark* were reviewed glowingly by Thomas Howard, in the May 30, 1980, issue of *National Review*.

70. Frank Meyer was the first book-review editor at *National Review;* and while he and Kirk disagreed about much, Meyer respected Kirk, made sure his books were reviewed, and sent him books to review for the magazine.

The 1980s

1. Kirk refers to Joseph Sobran's "No-Fault Media Bias," a lengthy review of a new edition of Friedrich von Hayek's *The Constitution of Liberty*, which contains as an appendix the author's essay "Why I Am Not a Conservative." Kirk and Hayek had clashed in a public debate on this very matter at a meeting of the Mont Pelerin Society in 1957; and in the years that followed, the two men had kept a respectful distance each from the other.

2. Devin Adair Garrity (1905–1981) was founder of the conservative Devin-Adair Publishing Company, which brought out Kirk's *The Intelligent Woman's Guide to Conservatism* in 1957.

3. *Edmund Burke and His World,* by Alice P. Miller (New York: Devin-Adair, 1979).

4. In his reply to this letter, Buckley explained that he had recently overheard Kirk remark about his high telephone bills and that he had sent Kirk a telephone card simply as a kind gesture to ease that expense. There was no ill intent, Buckley concluded, adding crisply, "Visit not your crotchets upon me."

5. Known as the Father of the Hydrogen Bomb and a vociferous proponent of the Strategic Defense Initiative (which Senator Edward Kennedy and others derisively called "Star Wars"), Edward Teller (1908–2003) appeared on Buckley's program *Firing Line* on several occasions to discuss U.S. foreign policy. Here, Kirk refers to the installment of that program titled "Is SALT II a Disaster?" (aired September 6, 1979), in which Teller declared the SALT II arms-control treaty an instrument of political wishful thinking that should not be ratified by the U.S. Congress.

6. NBC produced *The Martian Chronicles* as a three-part miniseries, which aired in January 1980. Starring Rock Hudson, Bernadette Peters, Roddy McDowell, and Darren McGavin, the adaptation was considered a failure, lacking in the wonder and imagination of Bradbury's novel. Bradbury himself considered it boring, despite its having been written by a close friend and accomplished screenwriter, Richard Matheson.

7. Kreeft's *Love Is Stronger than Death* was indeed a finalist for the 1980 National Book Award for Religion/Inspiration (Hardcover), which was won by *The Gnostic Gospels* by Elaine Pagels. Interestingly, the 1980 award for Religion/Inspiration (Paperback) was won by *A Severe Mercy*, a spiritual memoir by Kreeft's good friend Sheldon Vanauken, a writer Kirk greatly respected.

8. Six years (not two years) earlier, Kirk had attacked the National Book Awards in one of his "To the Point" newspaper columns. He cited the curious, recent case of the NBA judging committee initially declaring Anthony Kerrigan's translation of Migel de Unamuno's *Tragic Sense of Life* an award winner but then rescinding this decision a few days later in favor of another book by the same publisher, a translation of Paul Valéry's *Monsieur Teste*. Kirk speculated that his friend Kerrigan was cheated out of the award for political reasons by both the NBA and the publisher. Kirk wrote, "Perhaps the moral of all these shenanigans is that intelligent people ought to make their own judgments about books because one can't trust those awarders of literary prizes—or trust many publishers of books, either." See his column "Deliver Us from Literary Juries," *Prescott (AZ) Courier*, May 28, 1974, 4.

9. Kirk makes this specific reference in numerous letters he wrote after arriving at Malibu. He refers to a massive rain-induced landslide that closed a portion of the Pacific Coast Highway in April 1979. Crews of workmen labored for three months to remove rocks and miscellaneous debris from the road and shore up the land above the highway to avoid future landslides.

10. Despite Kirk's dislike for the anthology, *Dark Forces*, edited by Kirby McCauley, won the World Fantasy award for best collection/anthology in 1981. It contains a short novel by Stephen King as well as stories by the likes of Robert Aickman, Ramsey Campbell (both of whom Kirk admired), Isaac Bashevis Singer, Robert Bloch, Joyce Carol Oates, Richard Matheson, and Theodore Sturgeon, among others. Kirk's contribution was "The Peculiar Demesne," reprinted as "The Peculiar Demesne of Archvicar Gerontion" in his own collection *Watchers at the Strait Gate* (Sauk City, WI: Arkham House, 1984).

11. Kirk treated this very theme in his ghostly tale "An Encounter by Mortstone Pond," published in *Watchers at the Strait Gate*.

12. During her college years, Mary Stallings Coleman (1914–2001) was twice voted Miss University of Maryland, long before her nine-year career on

the Michigan Supreme Court. Although Reagan had a high regard for Kirk, he chose Sandra Day O'Connor (1930–) as the first female justice of the U.S. Supreme Court, in 1981.

13. As editor of *The Portable Conservative Reader,* Kirk had hoped to include Buckley's 1967 essay "The End of the Latin Mass," which appears in Buckley's collection *The Jeweler's Eye* (New York: Putnam, 1968).

14. Fadge is the mean-spirited editor of a London paper, the *Current,* in George Gissing's 1891 novel. As editor, Fadge specializes in a journalism of jaded flippancy, especially in the paper's book-review section.

15. These lectures were collected in *Reclaiming a Patrimony* (Washington, DC: Heritage Foundation, 1982).

16. Kirk, "Decadenza e rinnovamento della religion in l'America di Reagan," *I problemi di Ulisse* 16, no. 94 (1983): 143–49.

17. Kirk, *Redeeming the Time,* ed. Jeffrey O. Nelson (Wilmington, DE: Intercollegiate Studies Institute, 1996).

18. Kirk refers to the first edition of *Russell Kirk: A Bibliography* (Mt. Pleasant, MI: Clarke Historical Library, 1981) which was prepared by his longtime friend and archivist Charles C. Brown. To this edition, Regnery contributed a lengthy biographical and critical essay, titled "Russell Kirk: An Appraisal."

19. Founder of the foundation that bears her name, Marguerite Eyer Wilbur (1889–1982) was a respected historian and member of the California and Southern California Historical Societies.

20. Barzun, "William James, Author," *The American Scholar* 52 (Winter 1982–83): 41–48.

21. Kirk refers to the commission's landmark report *A Nation at Risk* (Washington, DC: National Commission on Excellence in Education, 1983).

22. Kirk included three stories from his long-out-of-print collection *The Surly Sullen Bell: Ten Stories and Sketches, Uncanny or Uncomfortable, with a Note on the Ghostly Tale* (New York: Fleet, 1962), in *Watchers at the Strait Gate*: "Uncle Isaiah," "The Surly Sullen Bell," and "What Shadows We Pursue."

23. Karl's sister Walburga (1958–) visited Mecosta and other destinations within the United States in 1982, learning the craft of a serious journalist and consulting Kirk often in this quest. In his memoir *The Sword of Imagination,* Kirk would later describe his guest as "the first Archduchess ever to set foot on Mecostan soil" (211).

24. Ludwikowski, *Main Currents of Polish Political Thought, 1815–1890* (Warsaw: Polish Scientific Publishers, 1982).

25. Kirk, "Libertarians: Chirping Sectaries," reprinted in *Redeeming the Time.*

26. Kirk refers here to an event that transpired at the annual meeting of the Mont Pélerin Society in 1957, when he debated extemporaneously with Hayek after the latter read his paper entitled "Why I Am Not a Conservative." This event is briefly described in Kirk's *The Sword of Imagination* and in Henry Regnery's *Memoirs of a Dissident Publisher* (New York: Harcourt Brace Jovanovich, 1979).

27. Meyer, "Collectivism Rebaptized," *Freeman* 5 (July 1955): 559–62, republished in Meyer's *In Defense of Freedom, and Related Essays* (Indianapolis: Liberty Fund, 1996), 3–13; Meyer, "Conservatism and Individualism," *American Mercury* 67 (July 1953): 140–42.

Kirk is possibly referencing the article "As Frank Chodorov Sees It," *Freeman* 6 (April 1956): 18–21. In this editorial comment, Chodorov scoffs at Kirk for referring to John Stuart Mill's thought as "outdated" in his article "'Mill's *On Liberty* Reconsidered" in the January 4, 1956, issue of *National Review* (23–24).

Kirk may be referring to Rothbard's largely favorable review of Henry Hazlitt's *The Free Man's Library* (Princeton, NJ: D. Van Nostrand, 1956), which provides a listing (with commentary) of 550 books essential to the thinking libertarian. Writing under the pseudonym "Jonathan Randolph" in *Faith and Freedom* 8 (September 1956): 30–31, Rothbard dismisses the inclusion of Kirk's *The Conservative Mind* as being among 130 or so books listed by Hazlitt that he (Rothbard) considers "statist" and "either outright leftish, or so weak that they serve no clear libertarian purpose."

28. Benjamin's father was Jeffrey Hart, longtime professor of English at Dartmouth College and senior editor at *National Review*.

29. van den Haag, "Libertarian Ideology," *National Review* 31 (June 8, 1979): 725–39. In this article, van den Haag warned against conservatives allying themselves with libertarians: "Libertarians are antinomians, i.e., opposed to law and traditional institutions. . . . Libertarianism is opposed to all conservative traditions, to tradition itself."

30. Kirk stated his objections to the bombings of Hiroshima and Nagasaki in the pages of *Prospects for Conservatives*, not *The Conservative Mind*.

31. Lindy Ellingwood served as one of Kirk's editorial assistants during the mid-1980s.

32. Kirk's essay "Prescription, Authority, and Ordered Freedom" had appeared in an anthology of conservative writings edited by Meyer titled *What Is Conservatism?* in 1964 (New York: Holt). Relations between the two men had been prickly since the mid-1950s, when Meyer published a small number of articles depicting Kirk as an apostle of collectivism.

33. Kirk wrote the foreword to Peter J. Stanlis's influential book *Edmund Burke and the Natural Law*, published by the University of Michigan Press in

1958. The two men, deep admirers of Burke, had met in the early 1950s, and they remained lifelong friends.

34. A scholar of the culture and literature of the American South, Havard (1923–) is Professor Emeritus and former chairman of the political science department at Vanderbilt University.

35. Regnery Gateway published Kirk's *The Wise Men Know What Wicked Things Are Written on the Sky* in 1986. This selection of Kirk's Heritage Foundation lectures is one of the author's undeservedly least-known books.

36. Conservative Senator John P. East (1931–1986) was a former Marine, college professor, and writer of note. Regnery Publishing, not the University of Illinois Press, published the book Kirk mentions, East's *The American Conservative Movement: The Philosophical Founders*, in 1987.

37. Regnery had recently told Kirk that his publishing company would be shifting its offices from Chicago to Washington, D.C., during 1986.

38. Kirk's book was eventually published by Regnery Gateway as *The Conservative Constitution* (1990).

39. Buckley had reimbursed the Kirks for the expenses they incurred while attending a celebration of *National Review*'s thirtieth anniversary of publication on December 5, 1985, in New York.

40. *The Temptation of Wilfred Malachey* (*Goblin Tales*) (New York: Workman, 1985).

41. A longtime friend of Kirk, Filler (1911–1998) was an eclectic scholar whose politics and personal philosophy leaned toward populism and classical liberalism.

42. In 1987, Regnery indeed published Wolfe's *Right Minds: A Sourcebook of American Conservative Thought*. Buckley contributed a foreword to this work.

43. Buckley and his wife, Pat, wintered annually in Gstaad, Switzerland. There Buckley skied and wrote his Blackford Oakes spy novels.

44. Kirk is referring to Regnery's wife, Eleanor (1909–2001), and son Alfred S. Regnery (1942–), an attorney and figure in the world of conservative publishing.

45. A fixture within the world of conservative journalism and publishing, Vigilante was for a time the articles editor at *National Review*.

46. Kirk's "Lost Souls: A Meditation" appeared in the December 31, 1987, issue of *National Review*, 30–31.

47. The seven contenders included Michael Dukakis, Jesse Jackson, Joe Biden, Richard Gephardt, Paul Simon, Al Gore, and Gary Hart.

48. A meeting of the campaign directors for Senator Robert Dole, Rev. Pat Robertson, Congressman Jack Kemp, and Bush was indeed held in

Lansing in 1988; and Bush secured Michigan's Republican delegates by winning the state county caucuses that year.

49. Four years later, Kirk served as state chairman of Republican Patrick J. Buchanan's insurgent (and unsuccessful) candidacy to unseat Bush.

50. In the most storied sea battle of the American Revolution, John Paul Jones's USS *Bonhomme Richard* battled HMS *Serapis* in the North Sea. In the early going, Jones's ship was badly damaged. The British commander called on the Americans to surrender, and Jones famously responded, "Sir, I have not yet begun to fight." The Americans fought with renewed vigor and forced the surrender of the *Serapis*, which they boarded shortly before their own ship sank.

51. Kirk refers to the French philosopher Gabriel Marcel (1889–1973), who had several of his books translated and published by the Henry Regnery Company during the 1950s and '60s. Kirk's quotation is from *Men against Humanity* (London: Harvill, 1952), in which Marcel warns against "the same phantasm, the same 'crowned ghost' which I have been so incessantly denouncing: I mean the idea of a 'meaning of history,' a 'direction of historical progress' as constituting the criterion in the name of which certain human beings are to be preserved or even set on high for admiration and others thrust aside, which is to say, eliminated" (184).

52. Kirk was fascinated by the windswept Isle of Eigg in the Hebrides, with its legends and violent history, and he used it as the model for the Isle of Carnglass in his successful "Gothick novel," *Old House of Fear.*

53. A Wilbur Fellow who lived at Piety Hill in 1988, Ann Findlay is Gavin Scott-Moncrieff's niece. Alan Scott-Moncrieff is one of George's sons from his second marriage; he is Gavin's half-brother.

54. A large island resort on the eastern end of Michigan's Upper Peninsula, Drummond Island is a quiet, largely undeveloped retreat for sportsmen, religious groups, nature lovers, and vacationers. In early 1988, the Kirks attended a retreat for Catholic clergy and laity on the island and spoke at length with Cardinal Bernard Francis Law (1931–), who was at the time Archbishop of Boston. Other attendees included Michael Novak, George Weigel, and Richard John Neuhaus.

55. John Cardinal Newman, *Newman's "Apologia Pro Vita Sua": The Two Versions of 1864 and 1865* (Oxford: Oxford University Press, 1913), 495.

56. "Grim Irony" is a poem Lecuru wrote after attending a recent ISI seminar on Burke and after reading Kirk's essay "Lost Souls: A Meditation," which had appeared in the December 31, 1987, issue of *National Review.*

57. In a review of a paperback edition of *The Roots of American Order* published in *The Detroit News* on December 22, 1982, McDonald concluded: "Long and complex as the story is, in Kirk's telling it is easy enough to follow.

Narrative and analysis are skillfully combined, and though the work is not flawless, the errors are few and usually insignificant. While it cannot be said that the book is 'indispensable' to an understanding of the current crisis of Western Civilization, it is certainly among the most lucid expositions of the Western tradition that one is likely to find."

58. This edition appeared in 1991, a Regnery publication, with an epilogue by Frank Shakespeare (1925–), a longtime American diplomat and media executive.

59. McDonald's second published book, *We the People: The Economic Origins of the Constitution* (Chicago: University of Chicago Press, 1957), is the premiere scholarly rebuttal to Charles A. Beard's influential *An Economic Interpretation of the Constitution of the United States* (New York: Macmillan, 1913). Beard's Progressive view held that the Framers of the Constitution designed the document solely to protect their own status and economic holdings. McDonald countered that while economic motivation was certainly a factor, there were many other clearly discernable cultural and political factors at work in their decision making.

60. Don Lipsett (1930–1995) was a conservative activist and founder of the Philadelphia Society.

61. See the lectures "A Dispassionate Assessment of Libertarians," reprinted in Kirk's *The Politics of Prudence* (Bryn Mawr, PA: Intercollegiate Studies Institute, 1993), and "Libertarians: Chirping Sectaries," reprinted in *Redeeming the Time* (Wilmington, DE: Intercollegiate Studies Institute, 1996).

62. Kirk here quotes the concluding lines of Henry Wadsworth Longfellow's poem "The Children's Hour."

63. Kirk, *A Dispassionate Assessment of Libertarians* (Washington, DC: Heritage Foundation, 1988).

64. This was published in 1979 as part of a series of textbook evaluation reports commissioned by America's Future, a conservative organization "dedicated to the preservation of our free enterprise system and our constitutional form of government."

65. In *Natural Right and History* (Chicago: University of Chicago Press, 1953), Strauss argued that Locke—whose social-contract theory Straussians claimed as a formative philosophy of the U.S. Constitution—was himself greatly influenced by the thought of Thomas Hobbes. However, traditionalist historians hold with Kirk, that "Americans of the Republic's formative years did not take their politics from closet philosophers, nor yet from philosophers who dabbled in practical politics, after Locke's fashion. Historical experience, practical considerations, religious convictions, established political

usage: these were the foundations of the Constitution of the United States." See Kirk's essay "John Locke and the Social Contract" in his *Rights and Duties: Reflections on Our Conservative Constitution*, ed. Mitchell Muncy (Dallas, TX: Spence, 1997), 95–109.

66. In 1970, Kirk's *University Bookman* published O'Sullivan's article "Universities and the State in Britain: A New Proposal," the first piece of writing for which O'Sullivan was paid an honorarium.

67. An exchange of responses had appeared in the Roman Catholic periodical *Communio*, edited by David Schindler, in opposition to an article Schindler had published in 1987 titled "Is America Bourgeois?"

68. Randolph Scott Elf was a Wilbur Fellow and served as Kirk's assistant during the mid-1980s. He is currently a practicing attorney.

69. The unfortunate cat belonged to Kelly Kelice, at the time a recent Hillsdale College graduate who lived and studied with the Kirks for three years.

70. From Calhoun's short treatise *A Discourse on the Constitution and Government of the United States*, originally published in 1851. See Calhoun, *A Disquisition on Government and a Discourse on the Constitution and Government of the United States* (Charleston, SC: Walker & James, 1851), 189.

71. A friend of the Kirk family and an admirer of the works of Leo Tolstoy and C. S. Lewis, Wright (1951–) published "Nikolai Tolstoy: Writing in the Tolstoy Tradition" in *Chronicles: A Magazine of American Culture 13* (April 1989): 53–56. Her book about "independent folk of humble beginnings" was written but never published.

72. In a pamphlet published in 1987, Tolstoy accused Lord Aldington (1914–2000) of having handed over thousands of Cossack and Yugoslav prisoners to the Soviets at the end of World War II, leading to their execution by Soviet authorities. Claiming that Aldington effectively signed the death sentence of these prisoners through "a combination of duplicity and brutality without parallel in British history," Tolstoy was sued by Aldington for libel. In 1989 the High Court awarded the plaintiff £1.5 million, in a decision Tolstoy unsuccessfully appealed.

73. *Winston S. Churchill:* vol. 8, *Never Despair, 1945–1965* (Boston: Houghton Mifflin, 1988).

74. See Karlawish, "Truth Telling in Medicine," *Persona* 1 (1990): 30–37.

75. Michos studied under Kirk as a Weaver Fellow in 1989 and then pursued his master's degree at Yale University, where he lived for a time in Brooks's home. "The example these men have shown me," he wrote in 1991, "is that any worthwhile social philosophy must look beyond questions of sheer quantity, with their attendant emphasis on the means of production, and inquire instead into the quality of life we desire for ourselves."

76. Unger (1916–2006) was a longtime professor of English at the University of Minnesota and a prolific scholar of Eliot's works. He is perhaps best known for his short but authoritative and widely translated work *T. S. Eliot* (1961), published by the University of Minnesota Press.

77. At around this time, *National Review*'s literary editor, Chilton Williamson Jr., left the magazine and was replaced by Brad Miner.

78. The year 1989 was indeed one of transition at *National Review*: in addition to Chilton Williamson resigning as literary editor, longtime publisher William A. Rusher stepped down and was replaced by Wick Allison, and Buckley assumed the role of editor in chief, hiring John O'Sullivan as editor, to run the journal's day-to-day operations.

79. Leonard Gilhooley, ed., *No Divided Allegiance: Essays in Brownson's Thought* (New York: Fordham University Press, 1980).

80. Kirk's longtime friend and archivist Charles C. Brown wrote *Niebuhr and His Age: Reinhold Niebuhr's Prophetic Role and Legacy* (Harrisburg, PA: Trinity Press International, 1992), to which Schlesinger contributed the introduction.

81. Kirk may be referring to Stanlis's long-delayed collection *The Best of Burke: Selected Writings and Speeches of Edmund Burke*, which appeared in 1999, the bicentennial of Burke's death (Washington, DC: Regnery Publishing).

82. A professor of government / political science at Claremont McKenna College and Claremont Graduate University, Kesler (1956–) had published a lengthy review of *The Rebirth of Classical Political Rationalism: An Introduction to the Thought of Leo Strauss*, edited by Thomas L. Pangle in the August 18, 1989, issue of *National Review*. Kesler claimed (in part) that America's Burkean paleocons find modern democracy unsatisfactory compared to the aristocratic manners of the Old South and reject "calculation in favor of a romantic appreciation of passion, the grandeur of the past, personal and national idiosyncrasy." To Kirk and Stanlis, this was a caricature of traditionalist conservatism.

83. Richard Neuhaus (1936–2009) was a Canadian-born American cleric and writer who rose to prominence first as a Vietnam-era antiwar activist and later as a prominent voice of neoconservatism. He was for many years a Lutheran minister, and he became a Roman Catholic priest during the last years of his life. In 1984, he established the Center for Religion and Society under the auspices of the Rockford Institute, publisher of the paleoconservative monthly journal *Chronicles: A Magazine of American Culture*. In 1989, Neuhaus and the center were evicted from the institute's offices in New York during an internal power struggle.

84. The Center for Constructive Alternatives (CCA) at Hillsdale College, according to its official description, "sponsors one of the largest college

lecture series in America. CCA seminars are held four times a year on wide-ranging topics."

85. Kirk is remembering imperfectly the opening words of Yeats's poem "A Prayer for My Son," which begins: "Bid a strong ghost stand at the head / That my Michael may sleep sound."

86. "Russell Kirk," in *Contemporary Authors Autobiography Series*, vol. 9 of 30, ed. Mark Zadrozny (Detroit, MI: Gale, 1989), 89–105.

87. Kirk, *The Attack on Leviathan: Donald Davidson and the South's Conservatism* (Washington, D.C.: Heritage Foundation, 1989), reprinted in Kirk's *Politics of Prudence.*

The 1990s

1. Director of lectures at the Heritage Foundation during the era of George H. W. Bush's presidency, Betsy Hart later served Heritage as senior writer for development.

2. Here Kirk interpolates something that appeared in Boorstin's *The Genius of American Politics* (Chicago: University of Chicago Press, 1953), in which the author wrote, "We must refuse to try to export our commodity. We must refuse to become crusaders for conservatism, in order to conserve the institutions and the genius which have made America greater" (189).

3. Ball, "The Tempting of Robert Bork: What's a Constitution without Natural Law?" *Crisis* 8 (June 1, 1990): 28. Ball criticized Judge Bork for excluding natural law as a source of principles in constitutional adjudication.

4. Kirk, *The "Original Intent" Controversy* (Washington, DC: Heritage Foundation, 1987). Kirk concluded this lecture with the words, "The original intent of the Framers of the Constitution was to give the American people a Republic of elevated views and hopes. They desired to establish an independent judiciary; they did not mean to create a new form of government, unknown to Plato or Aristotle; that might be termed an *archonocracy*—a national domination of judges. As John Randolph of Roanoke observed, with reference to tendencies of the federal courts in his own time, 'I can never forget that the Book of Judges is followed by the Book of Kings.'"

5. After his retirement in 1990, Buckley continued to serve *National Review* as editor at large and éminence grise, contributing commentary and shaping the editorial direction of the periodical until 2004. He died four years later.

6. Ten years after Kirk's death, Buckley published his well-received *Miles Gone By: A Literary Autobiography* (Washington, DC: Regnery Publishing, 2004).

7. McBain is a small town in Missaukee County and figures in Jager's book.

8. Originally published by the University of North Carolina Press, *The Attack on Leviathan* made a strong impression on Kirk when, as an undergraduate at Michigan State in 1938, he discovered it. In 1991, Transaction republished the book as *Regionalism and Nationalism in the United States: The Attack on Leviathan,* with an introduction by Kirk titled "Donald Davidson and the South's Conservatism."

9. Founded in 1953, the Intercollegiate Studies Institute was headquartered in Bryn Mawr for many years. Since 1996, ISI's offices have been located in Wilmington, Delaware.

10. Kirk reviewed Berry's *The Unsettling of America: Culture and Agriculture* in the June 4, 1978, issue of the *Birmingham (AL) News*.

11. Halloween was a holiday close to Kirk's heart, as it brought out his boyish sense of fun. The Kirk family, the Wilbur Fellows, and all other guests at Piety Hill participated in transforming the Kirk home into a haunted house that children for miles around thrilled to visit.

12. It is likely that Kirk sent Whelan a photocopy of his essay "*Cats, Eliot, and the Dance of Life,*" *Renascence: Essays on Values in Literature* 40, no. 3 (1988): 197–203.

13. James's literature is a favorite of Whelan, as she noted in her letter to Kirk, who privately found James's work boring to the point of being soporific.

14. In December 1990, Engler wed Michelle De Munbrun, an attorney, who as First Lady chaired the Michigan Community Service Commission. Under her leadership, the commission achieved national recognition for its success in expanding volunteer opportunities in the State of Michigan.

15. Shorey served as an assistant to Kirk during the early 1960s. At one time, he prepared to cowrite a biography of Kirk with Peter Ruber, an author and an editor for Arkham House. This project never developed. Muriel Hall was Paterson's literary executor.

16. Paterson wrote,

> We have a report from one in a great desert camp of his
> recent reading for pleasure, which includes "Greek Revival
> Architecture in America," "Memoirs of a Superfluous Man,"
> and Osbert Sitwell's "Left Hand, Right Hand." The high
> standard is gratifying and there is an economic note added quite
> casually. "Our real world dominance comes from American
> energy—the force which made it possible for most of the rest of

the world to fight this war. If we propose to exchange this for Spartan overlordship, we shall soon find ourselves without either economic energy or military supremacy." The sergeant hails from Detroit.

From Paterson's "Turns with a Bookworm," in *New York Herald-Tribune*'s Weekly Book Review, August 19, 1945, quoted in *Russell Kirk: American Conservative*, by Bradley J. Birzer (Lexington: University Press of Kentucky, 2015), 76.

17. In his December 2 letter to Kirk, McClellan loosely outlined how to address two areas of Taft's life with which one reviewer had found fault within the original *Political Principles of Robert A. Taft*. These areas were Taft's failure to criticize the excesses of his fellow Republican senator Joseph McCarthy during the early 1950s, and Taft's so-called isolationism from 1939 (when he entered the U.S. Senate) until America's entry into World War II in late 1941.

18. Transaction eventually published the book under its original title, in 2010.

19. Susannah is McClellan's daughter, who attended St. Andrews University at the same time as the Kirks' second daughter, Cecilia.

20. The "Baldwin House of the *K*'s" was a house Kirk bought for his elderly father and stepmother in Baldwin, Michigan. There were large decorative letter *K*'s under the eaves of the house, thus its name.

21. *Ugetsu Monogatari* (translated as "Tales of Moonlight and Rain" or "Tales of a Clouded Moon") is a collection of Japanese and Chinese supernatural tales by Ueda Akinari (1734–1809). It has been translated into English several times, beginning in 1938.

22. Stimson (1867–1950) was an attorney and lifelong Republican political figure who held high office in the presidential administrations of William Howard Taft, Calvin Coolidge, Herbert Hoover, and Franklin Delano Roosevelt. During World War II, as Roosevelt's secretary of war, he directed the development of atomic weaponry for use against the Axis. Unlike many conservatives, Kirk openly believed that the atomic bombing of Hiroshima and Nagasaki were acts of unconscionable barbarism that brought shame to the United States.

23. Kirk inadvertently did not complete this sentence. The bracketed phrasing follows closely his other, similar quotations of Martin D'Arcy.

24. Possibly Kirk sent Nixon a copy of his autobiographical essay "Reflections of a Gothic Mind," which appears as the introductory portion of the collection *Confessions of a Bohemian Tory* (Chicago: Henry Regnery, 1963). One

paragraph that may have suggested "certain similarities in the upbringing and experiences" of Nixon and Kirk runs as follows:

> In the 1920s, the old Tom Sawyer sort of life still persisted,
> little altered, among American boys in places like Plymouth.
> But I shared none of Huckleberry Finn's rebellion against things
> established. I felt a strong suspicion of change, and a longing
> for continuity. To lie with my father beneath an oak on the
> hill above the mill-pond . . . or to walk with my grandfather
> in search of fossils and arrowheads upon the terminal moraine
> four miles north of the town—in such occupations even when
> I was too young to criticize my own prejudices, I felt a deep
> satisfaction, having joined past and present.

25. Earlier in the month, on October 1 and 2, Kirk was honored at a two-day celebration of the fortieth anniversary of the appearance of *The Conservative Mind,* at the Dearborn Inn in Dearborn, Michigan. Present at this event were hundreds of guests representing the great and small within the world of conservative letters and politics, including William A. Rusher, Peter J. Stanlis, M. Stanton Evans, Lee Edwards, and Michigan governor John Engler, among many others. In his memoir *The Sword of Imagination: The Memoirs of a Half-Century of Literary* Conflict (Grand Rapids, MI: Eerdmans, 1995), Kirk recorded that the month's activities left him "cheerfully worn out"—so much so that his doctor prescribed a month's bed-rest to recover (468).

26. Carl B. Cone (1916–1995) was the author of the two-volume *Burke and the Nature of Politics* (Lexington: University of Kentucky Press, 1957, 1964).

Bibliography of Kirk's Works

Randolph of Roanoke: A Study in Conservative Thought. Chicago: University of Chicago Press, 1951. Enlarged and published as *John Randolph of Roanoke: A Study in American Politics.* Chicago: Henry Regnery, 1964. Third edition, Indianapolis, IN: Liberty Fund, 1997.

The Conservative Mind: From Burke to Santayana. Chicago: Henry Regnery, 1953. Third revised edition, published as *The Conservative Mind: From Burke to Eliot*, 1960. Seventh revised edition, 1986.

St. Andrews. London: Batsford, 1954.

A Program for Conservatives. Chicago: Henry Regnery, 1954. Abridged and published as *Prospects for Conservatives*, 1956. Revised edition, 1989.

Academic Freedom: An Essay in Definition. Chicago: Henry Regnery, 1955.

Beyond the Dreams of Avarice: Essays of a Social Critic. Chicago: Henry Regnery, 1956.

The Intelligent Woman's Guide to Conservatism. New York: Devin-Adair, 1957.

The American Cause. Chicago: Henry Regnery, 1957. Second edition with an introduction by John Dos Passos, 1966. Revised edition with an introduction by Gleaves Whitney. Wilmington, DE: ISI Books, 2002.

Old House of Fear. New York: Fleet, 1961.

The Surly Sullen Bell: Ten Stories and Sketches, Uncanny or Uncomfortable, with a Note on the Ghostly Tale. New York: Fleet, 1962.

Confessions of a Bohemian Tory: Episodes and Reflections of a Vagrant Career. New York: Fleet, 1963.

The Intemperate Professor and Other Cultural Splenetics. Baton Rouge: Louisiana State University Press, 1965. Revised edition, Peru, IL: Sherwood Sugden, 1988.

A Creature of the Twilight: His Memorials. New York: Fleet, 1966.

Edmund Burke: A Genius Reconsidered. New Rochelle, NY: Arlington House, 1967. Revised edition, Peru, IL: Sherwood Sugden, 1985. Second revised edition, 1988.

With James McClellan. *The Political Principles of Robert A. Taft.* New York: Fleet, 1967.

Enemies of the Permanent Things: Observations of Abnormity in Literature and Politics. New Rochelle, NY: Arlington House, 1969. Revised edition, Peru, IL: Sherwood Sugden, 1984.

Eliot and His Age: T. S. Eliot's Moral Imagination in the Twentieth Century. New York: Random House, 1971. Revised edition, Peru, IL: Sugden, 1984.

The Roots of American Order. La Salle, IL: Open Court, 1974. Second edition, Malibu, CA: Pepperdine University Press, 1980. Fourth edition, Wilmington, DE: Intercollegiate Studies Institute, 2003.

Decadence and Renewal in the Higher Learning. South Bend, IN: Gateway, 1978.

Lord of the Hollow Dark. New York: St. Martin's, 1979.

The Princess of All Lands, Sauk City, WI: Arkham House, 1979.

Editor. *The Portable Conservative Reader.* New York: Viking, 1982.

Reclaiming a Patrimony: A Collection of Lectures, Washington, DC: Heritage Foundation, 1982.

Watchers at the Strait Gate: Mystical Tales. Sauk City, WI: Arkham House, 1984.

The Wise Men Know What Wicked Things Are Written on the Sky. Washington, DC: Regnery, 1987.

Economics: Work and Prosperity. Pensacola, FL: A Beka Book, 1989.

The Conservative Constitution. Washington, DC: Regnery, 1990. Revised and expanded as *Rights and Duties: Reflections on Our Conservative Constitution.* Edited by Mitchell S. Muncy. Dallas, TX: Spence, 1997.

America's British Culture. New Brunswick, NJ: Transaction, 1993.

The Politics of Prudence. Bryn Mawr, PA: Intercollegiate Studies Institute, 1993.

The Sword of Imagination: Memoirs of a Half-Century of Literary Conflict. Grand Rapids, MI: Eerdmans, 1995.

Redeeming the Time. Edited by Jeffrey O. Nelson. Wilmington, DE: Intercollegiate Studies Institute, 1996.

Off the Sand Road. Volume 1 of *Ghost Stories.* Edited with an introduction by John Pelan. Ashcroft, BC: Ash-Tree Press, 2002.

What Shadows We Pursue. Volume 2 of *Ghost Stories.* Edited with an introduction by John Pelan. Ashcroft, BC: Ash-Tree Press, 2003.

Ancestral Shadows: An Anthology of Ghostly Tales. Edited with an introduction by Vigen Guroian. Grand Rapids, MI: Eerdmans, 2004.

The Essential Russell Kirk: Selected Essays. Edited with an introduction by George A. Panichas. Wilmington, DE: ISI Books, 2007.

Index

Index